The Readers' Advisory Guide
to Genre Fiction

ALA READERS' ADVISORY SERIES

The Readers' Advisory Guide to Genre Fiction

Second Edition

Joyce G. Saricks

American Library Association

Chicago   2009

Joyce G. Saricks worked as coordinator of the Literature and Audio Services Department at the Downers Grove Public Library from 1983 to 2004. In addition to authoring *Readers' Advisory Service in the Public Library* (3rd ed., ALA, 2005), she has written numerous articles on readers' advisory, presented workshops on that topic for public libraries and library systems, and spoken at state, regional, and national library conferences. In 1989 she won the Public Library Association's Allie Beth Martin Award, and in 2000 she was named Librarian of the Year by the Romance Writers of America. Currently she serves as read-alike coordinator (and author) for EBSCO's NoveList and columnist and audio reviewer for Booklist. She also teaches readers' advisory at Dominican University's School of Library and Information Science (Illinois).

The paper used in this publication meets the minimum requirements of American National Standard for Information Sciences—Permanence of Paper for Printed Library Materials, ANSI Z39.48-1992. ∞

Library of Congress Cataloging-in-Publication Data
Saricks, Joyce G.
    The readers' advisory guide to genre fiction / Joyce G. Saricks. — 2nd ed.
        p. cm. — (ALA readers' advisory series)
    Includes bibliographical references and index.
    ISBN 978-0-8389-0989-8 (alk. paper)
    1. Fiction in libraries—United States. 2. Readers' advisory services—United States.
    3. Reading interests—United States. 4. Fiction genres. 5. Fiction—Bibliography.
    I. Title.
    Z711.5.S27 2009
    025.5'4—dc22   2008051029

ISBN-13: 978-0-8389-0989-8

Printed in the United States of America
13   12   11   10   09   5   4   3   2   1

For Chris, who has always enjoyed a good story as much as I do

CONTENTS

FIGURES

ACKNOWLEDGMENTS

Revising this book has brought both pain and joy: pain at losing older titles I still remember with pleasure, because there are newer titles that make the same point and may be more familiar to readers, and joy as I've looked through notes that cover the books I've read over the last eight years and discovered so many new treasures to share. While I have attempted to highlight the most up-to-date authors and trends, I hope that we won't forget the older titles that still have the power to enchant, titles that should stay in our hearts—and libraries—as long as we share books.

I've long argued that readers' advisory is collaborative, and that is never clearer than when one is writing a book! We can never read enough—and certainly never remember enough of what we do read. That's what friends, patrons, and fellow librarians are for—they fill in the gaps in our knowledge and our memory.

Once again I have been fortunate in finding good friends to act as readers, willing to devote time and energy to reading drafts of all the genre chapters and offering their suggestions. Fellow readers' advisory librarians Sue O'Brien (Downers Grove Public Library, Illinois), Lynne Welch (Herrick Public Library, Wellington, Ohio), Georgine Olson (North Star Borough Public Library, Fairbanks, Alaska), and Becky Spratford (Berwyn Public Library, Illinois) argued for and against authors and sometimes ideas. Their comments about the genres and authors they know and love were especially useful. Thanks also to Bonnie Reid and the Reference Department of the Downers Grove Public Library for their nonfiction suggestions. Katherine Johnson, adult editorial lead of EBSCO's NoveList, offered invaluable comments from the perspectives of editor and reader. My aunt and friend Marty Charles once again read everything; to my mind, this was the perfect punishment for the person probably most responsible for my life spent reading, from the adventures of Nancy Drew and Cherry Ames to Gail Bowen and Christopher Buckley.

My thanks also to Duncan Smith for his encouragement and comments. He remains an inspiration, and I am fortunate to count him as a friend.

As the best of friends do, Neal Wyatt not only signed me up for the American Library Association's Reading List award committee (thus compelling me to read the most recent genre fiction), but she has also forced me to keep my eye on the big picture and create a book that will lead readers' advisors beyond these pages to the world of readers. If I have succeeded in that, it is to her credit. Her comments, always, are thoughtful, instructive, and invaluable.

I am fortunate in family too. My parents encouraged me to read everything, and they collected a vast personal library in a town too small for a public library. And finally, heartfelt thanks to my husband Chris, who more and more has become the other half of my brain as we age together. Small wonder after more than forty years of love and friendship.

1

UNDERSTANDING THE APPEAL
OF GENRE FICTION

This is not a book written by a genre specialist but by a generalist, albeit one who enjoys genre fiction, reads widely, and has worked for more than thirty years with genre readers and librarians. This is not intended as a definitive study but as a guide, created to help others who find themselves as I did, at a loss helping readers at my library. This book has been developed to help librarians become familiar with fiction genres, especially those we do not personally read by choice. It is designed to be a springboard for further study—and certainly a training tool.

When we first created a separate Readers' Advisory Department at the Downers Grove Public Library (Illinois) in 1983, we knew we had to learn about popular fiction quickly. We developed a list of authors, grouped by genres, and used that to familiarize ourselves with the authors and genres our readers already knew and loved. As we read and talked with readers, we learned that there were factors that influenced their choices of one author over another, especially when they were trying to find similar authors or read-alikes—new authors who wrote just like an author they loved. We talked with these readers, and we listened to both the way they described books and their responses to vocabulary we developed to try to help them. We learned early on that the subject of the book was not the most important factor. Readers were not looking for any book with spies; they wanted one that moved with the same fast pacing that Robert Ludlum employed. Or one that delved into motivations and psyches as John le Carré's books do. And, most important, they were pleased to find someone to talk with about what they enjoyed, especially because this someone might be able to find them more authors that would satisfy them.

As we progressed, we realized that although the genres differed widely, the way we learned about them did not. When we thought about what we knew about genres in which we did read, how we worked with readers, and how we approached helping them further, we saw that we could use the same techniques with genres with which we were less familiar. We also recognized what we call appeal elements. Pacing, characterization, story line, frame (physical setting and atmosphere), tone and mood, and style and language played important roles in what readers enjoyed about one book over another and helped us recognize others we might suggest. We explored these appeal elements in more depth as we started doing genre studies.

Every book we read and every conversation we had seemed (and, frankly, still does seem) to raise more questions than it answered. What is the audience for a book like Dan Simmons's *The Terror*?[1] Is it for Horror readers who might appreciate the mounting fear from the unexplained threat? Or for Historical Fiction readers who might relate to the details of life and explorations in the 1840s? Would a fan of Literary Fiction also appreciate the layered story with its provocative look at voyages of discovery on physical, emotional, and intellectual levels? What about the Adventure fan? How might I describe the book differently to readers to let them know that there are elements in this book that might appeal to them?

Many of the questions we encountered were—and still are—simply unanswerable. But we talked with readers and among ourselves; we practiced describing books and listened when others talked about books they had enjoyed; and we learned what works—and what does not. Some books seem to sell themselves. Other, equally wonderful books are almost impossible to describe in a way that makes them sound inviting.

Learning to suggest, rather than recommend, was another major breakthrough. *Recommend* is a word fraught with unintended meaning and emotion. Recommending places us in the role of expert saying, "Take this book; it is good for you." Suggesting, on the other hand, makes us partners with readers in exploring the various directions they might want to pursue. Simply altering our vocabulary took some of the pressure off us—and readers—as we shared books.

We learned early on that we could never read enough or remember enough of what we did read. We needed a framework to help us remember. The appeal elements seemed to do that—magically. Thinking about books in terms of their appeal, rather than their subject or plot, meant that we remembered more. And what we remembered was what we needed to offer the book to readers. In the readers' advisory interview, it is appeal—comments about pacing or frame—that readers respond to, not just plot summaries.

It is from this background and experience working with readers that this book evolved. Our goal as librarians has always been at least twofold: to help readers discover titles they are currently in the mood to read, and to expand their reading beyond strict genre boundaries to other books that have the same elements they appreciate.

This second edition builds on the first and expands the role of appeal as a way to see beyond the confines of a particular genre. While knowledge of a genre's conventions is vital in understanding its appeal to readers, the ability to see beyond the boundaries makes us an even more valuable resource and guide for readers. As genres continue to blend and overlap, thinking along strict genre lines has become increasingly difficult. Authors known for writing in one genre have experimented in another or have imported elements from another genre that then push the boundaries of their familiar genre. Genre borders blur and readers follow authors and appeal elements that please them.

In the eight years since I wrote the first edition of this book, genre fiction has changed dramatically. Authors like John Grisham and Dennis Lehane, whom we happily boxed into Legal Thrillers and Mysteries respectively, have broken free, perhaps never to return to their former genres. The influence of the paranormal has infiltrated every genre. Just as the genres have evolved, so has our thinking about them and how we share them with readers. As I continue to read genre fiction and teach genres and readers' advisory techniques, I have realized that appeal lies at the root of our understanding of genre fiction. No matter how the genres change, an understanding of appeal is invaluable not only at the micro level—studying individual genres—but at the macro level as well, as we connect genres to each other and study groups of genres. That revelation has inspired the revision of this work and offers what I hope is a new and broader way for readers' advisors to consider appeal and genre, a way that makes it easier to see links between one book a reader enjoys and another.

This revised edition organizes genres into four genre appeal groups: Adrenaline Genres, Emotions Genres, Intellect Genres, and Landscape Genres. While this edition continues to examine individual genres, these larger groupings illustrate how appeal works across genre lines. For example, readers who appreciate fast-paced books don't honestly care whether we call these Suspense, Thrillers, or Adventure. They want the page-turning pace that drives these genres. Grouping these together as Adrenaline genres, along with Romantic Suspense which shares that characteristic, helps us understand that we can often offer titles from any of these to readers who talk about their desire for a book that pulls them into the story quickly and keeps them turning pages until the very end.

Adrenaline Genres—Adventure, Romantic Suspense, Suspense, Thrillers—all appeal to readers who appreciate intricately detailed stories told at a pace that moves almost more quickly than they can turn pages. Pacing is the most important element; it engages readers from the first and offers multiple plot twists that keep them on the edge of their chairs.

Emotions Genres include Gentle Reads, Horror, Romance, and Women's Lives and Relationships. Although they may seem the most disparate, all appeal primarily to the emotions of their readers. In each genre, the author creates a particular, evocative mood. It is enhanced by language and pacing to create a strong emotional pull—be it the satisfaction found in Romances and novels of Women's Lives and Relationships, the terror of Horror, or the comfortable feeling engendered by Gentle Reads.

The Intellect Genres—Literary Fiction, Mysteries, Psychological Suspense, and Science Fiction—present puzzles that engage the mind. They may delve deeply into social and ethical issues, as is often the case in Literary Fiction and Science Fiction, explore the workings of a disturbed mind in Psychological Suspense, or present a more straightforward "whodunit." Like Agatha Christie's detective Hercule Poirot, fans enjoy using their little grey cells to work out the solution. These are often the titles for readers who appreciate meaty books that inspire thoughtful consideration and rumination.

Finally, the Landscape Genres—Fantasy, Historical Fiction, and Westerns—focus on an intricately described background, real or imaginary. The goal of these is to take us there—to create worlds and set readers in them. Both frame (the background details) and mood become essential in establishing these authentic, believable worlds.

Crossover, of course, exists within the groups and beyond them. A fast-paced book cataloged as Mystery might very well appeal to Adrenaline fans, and fans of Horror and Psychological Suspense readily recognize the links between those genres. The possibilities are endless. This expanded framework provides a way to see the appeal of larger groups and an introduction to the potential for crossover, within fiction and beyond to nonfiction works as well. Each separate genre chapter pursues these crossover links, with authors that might lead a reader into a genre because of similarities to a familiar genre, as well as authors that might lead a fan of one genre into others.

The advantage to this approach is that it provides a broader perspective. We are no longer limited to a single genre, but we see how a group of genres share an appeal, and that takes us more easily beyond genre boundaries. We recognize these obvious links and that leads us to connections with genres in other groups. Now, when faced by the reader who only reads Mysteries or Romance, we listen to their descriptions of the books they enjoy, and we can more quickly see links to other genres and authors.

As in the first edition, each separate genre chapter includes strategies to expand our knowledge of the genre and to work with readers, even if we know very little about that particular genre. Everything in this book builds on the premise that to learn about fiction and to satisfy readers, we need to be open to a range of possibilities. Most readers appreciate the conversation and the process more than a quick answer. The readers' advisory interview is a conversation about books. We are not expected to know all the answers; readers want us to listen and help them explore.

This book is meant to be provocative. You will disagree with some of my statements and certainly with the choice of some of the authors I have included. Genres are not static; writers are not confined to certain genres or types of books; readers take from books what strikes them, whether or not it goes counter to common knowledge of a book and expert opinion. Again, this book is not meant to be definitive but rather suggestive of possibilities. Your questions, and the answers you discover through your own explorations, will lead you to a deeper understanding of authors, genres, and why readers enjoy them.

WHAT THIS BOOK IS NOT

This book is not a comprehensive study of any genre. Each chapter provides an introduction to the genre and considers why fans love it. Examples are meant to be indicative of the genre's appeal to readers. Readers interested in pursuing their study of genres beyond this book will find a wealth of book and web resources, free and fee, as well as useful blogs and electronic discussion lists devoted to individual genres. For the most up-to-date list of available resources, post a query on Fiction_L, the readers' advisory electronic discussion list (www.webrary.org/rs/flmenu.html).

This book is not meant to be prescriptive. My goal has been to create a framework that makes understanding the appeal of genre fiction easier. My experience in providing readers' advisory and training staff indicates that it is important to have such a framework so that we can see how to go beyond it. When we discover an author or hear a patron describe a title or author, we can use the mental framework to see how that author or book might fit in a genre or to see that it does not fit exactly, that it has elements of this genre and that, and that it might appeal to this kind of reader or that one.

One false impression that this kind of book might give is that all authors can be classified, or slotted, within a specific genre. This is not a genre classification guide. It is important to guard against the temptation of overclassifying when we think in terms of genres. Not every author fits into a genre, not every book by an author fits in the same genre, and not all readers see an author (or a genre) in the same way. Rather than to create boxes to contain authors so that we can examine them, this book aims to break down the walls of classification so we can see beyond genre borders to the way readers really read and writers write. It is hoped that the conception of the large genre groups will also help alleviate that tendency.

WHAT THIS BOOK COVERS

This book is an introduction to fiction genres, but what is a genre? In *Readers' Advisory Service in the Public Library,* genre is defined as "any sizable group of fiction authors and/or specific titles that have similar characteristics and appeal; these are books written to a particular, specific pattern." Genres, then, are not limited to the traditional Mysteries, Romances, and so forth, but the idea can be expanded to include any larger group fiction that shares characteristics and appeal elements.

The following genres are examined in individual chapters: Adventure, Fantasy, Gentle Reads, Historical Fiction, Horror, Literary Fiction, Mysteries, Psychological Suspense, Romance, Romantic Suspense, Science Fiction, Suspense, Thrillers, Westerns, and Women's Lives and Relationships. The omission of two popular "genres" may raise some questions: although Multicultural and Inspirational authors are mentioned in the chapters, these groups are not considered on their own. By my definition they are not individual genres; rather, the books understood to constitute each really cut across genres. For example, among Multicultural authors there are writers who fall into all the genres included. That they are African American or Hispanic does not mean that they write a unique type of book. Their Mysteries are far more similar to other Mysteries than they are to Romances or Science Fiction by other Multicultural authors. It is not possible to group their writing and identify characteristics shared by Multicultural authors; their writing does not constitute an individual, separate genre. In the same way, Inspirational authors write across genres. That their stories contain religious elements is not enough to declare them a separate genre. Inspirational Romances are part of the Romance genre, and their link to Inspirational Mysteries or any other Inspirational titles is that they both share a religious flavor.

In the tradition of the genre it explores, each chapter follows the same pattern, discussing each topic described below.

1. *Definition of the Genre.* Although these working definitions may be familiar, they are based on how readers perceive the genre: what they expect to find in these books, how they would define it if they were asked. In some cases, there is discussion of what this genre is not—how it differs from related genres.

2. *Characteristics and Appeal.* Anyone familiar with my previous book, *Readers' Advisory Service in the Public Library,* will not be surprised to see that these characteristics are based on six elements of appeal found in books: pacing, characterization, story line, frame and setting, tone and mood, and language and style. The appeal of genres seems to fall out naturally in these six basic categories. Each chapter lists the characteristics of the genre, based on these appeal elements, followed by a descriptive narrative with examples.

3. *Key Authors.* Key authors are those whose names are familiar to genre fans. These are authors to recognize and perhaps to read, as they represent the range of the genre. Only in the Mystery genre have I also included appeal-based subgenres as well as key authors. Over the last eight years, changes in other genres have made these subgenre distinctions less useful, and they have been eliminated in this edition.

4. *What We Know about Fans.* This section covers what fans of each genre expect to find in that genre. There are also strategies, readers' advisory tips that are specific to the genre discussed but also often more general ideas that can be applied across the board in understanding genres and working with readers.

While fans are familiar with their favorite genres, we librarians often are not. One of the greatest obstacles to our reading a wide range of genres is the fear that there is nothing in the unfamiliar genre that we will enjoy. To help counteract that, each genre chapter includes a list of authors who write in that genre, and these authors are linked to other genres with which they share appeal elements. The pattern of this list is the same in every chapter; only the name of the genre and, of course, the suggested authors change. For example, Adventure fans might be more willing to sample a Science Fiction novel if they knew it also included a large dose of the Adventure elements they enjoy. Thus, in the Adventure category of this list in the Science Fiction chapter, I have suggested Science Fiction authors for fans of Adventure to try. Although the list is designed for librarians to expand their reading interests and gain familiarity with genres they do not regularly read, it can also be used to tempt fans of one genre to experiment with another.

5. *The Readers' Advisory Interview.* When we ask them to describe books they enjoy, what do readers say they like about an author or genre? And how do we get from that response to book suggestions? These questions are explored in this section of each chapter. I also provide suggestions of how to talk about the genre and genre titles, even those we have not read, because, obviously, we will never read everything that might appeal to readers or that they might ask us about.

Sure Bets, those titles that appeal consistently to a wide range of readers, from fans of the particular genre to others, are included in this section of each chapter. As we explore each genre, we need to identify and collect Sure Bets. These are valuable because mentioning them allows us to let fans know that we have read something in the genre and that we understand its appeal. A list of Sure Bets in a genre, or across genres, also becomes a lifesaver when our minds go blank and we cannot remember anything, not even the book we are currently reading.

6. *Expanding Readers' Horizons with Whole Collection Readers' Advisory.* Just as there are authors that can lead fans of one genre into another, there are authors that take readers beyond the genres they frequently read. This list and accompanying explanatory paragraphs are included in every chapter. It is designed to help readers of each genre chapter find authors to their liking in another genre or nonfiction.

7. *Trends.* Genres are never static. This section identifies some current trends, popular authors, and directions in each genre.

Additionally, an appendix offers the Five-Book Challenge, a list of five authors and titles that represent the appeal of each genre. This list, along with the authors and titles mentioned in each chapter, is included to help librarians expand their knowledge.

HOW TO GET THE MOST FROM THIS BOOK

Individual Training

This book was envisioned as a guide for an individual to explore fiction genres. Although you may want to read quickly through to gain an overview of the genres covered, I would encourage you to take time with a genre. Read the chapter, explore the authors and titles, and talk with fans and staff about what they enjoy. Use your newfound knowledge to add that genre to displays, create an annotated booklist, suggest titles to fans, and attract others to the genre.

Staff Training

This book was also designed as a tool to train both new and experienced staff, as both an initial training document and a genre refresher. Even if staff members are familiar with a genre, the description, authors, and titles included act as a reminder of aspects they might have forgotten and of links among authors and genres. It opens us up to the way we need to think about books and readers to do the best readers' advisory.

Genre Study

Although this book is really the result of a number of genre studies, with each section "Characteristics and the Genre's Appeal" reflecting the kind of list one would expect to be developed from such a study, it could certainly also be the starting point for your own genre study. Remember, however, that it is not meant to be prescriptive. You will make additional discoveries as you read and talk about a genre among your staff and with fans at your library. What your readers read will not necessarily parallel what users of my library enjoy. Genre study is about making connections, within a genre and beyond. Tips for "Studying a Genre" as well as guidelines for setting up a genre study group are discussed in some detail in *Readers' Advisory Service in the Public Library*. Use those guidelines to embark on your own genre study.

HOW TO KEEP UP WITH CHANGES IN A GENRE

Studying a genre and reading it extensively provide us with an understanding of its appeal at a certain point in time. Even if we could explore these genres, one after another, how can we possibly keep up with new developments and new authors when we have gone on to another genre? With new books published every year and authors continually pushing the boundaries of the genres in which they write, the prospect of staying current seems beyond even the most compulsive librarian!

Because we can never read as much as fans of a genre, it is important to develop ways to keep up on developments, trends, and new authors. Reading reviews is probably the easiest, most efficient technique. Library reviewing journals are generally good about reviewing genre fiction. Both *Booklist* and *Library Journal* consistently highlight genre titles. *Booklist* also provides regularly scheduled genre overviews, devoting much of an issue to articles relating to a particular genre and read-alikes for popular authors, as well as booklists. *Library Journal* offers regular columns on readers' advisory and on genres such as Romance, in addition to their fiction reviews. *Publishers Weekly* also covers genre fiction in the fiction reviews and publishes genre overviews regularly throughout the year. Blogs related to the genres and covering the publishing industry in general can also be helpful, as are electronic discussion lists devoted to individual genres.

Fans of the genre, if they are comfortable talking with staff, are an excellent source of information on developments in the genre. Soliciting their comments, as well as observing trends in reserves, can provide us with extensive information.

Consistently including a selection of genres in our broad reading of fiction certainly helps. However, it is important to remember that we cannot read everything, and we can never read as much as fans of a genre. It is better to cultivate genre fans among patrons and other staff members, to identify useful journals, and to set up a manageable plan for keeping up on genre trends.

BEYOND THIS GUIDE

Frankly, genre classification is antithetical to readers' advisory work, where we focus on what a reader wants to read and cross genres with abandon as we make suggestions. So why devote years of reading and writing to create and then revise a book that defines genres and identifies themes and authors? Because understanding fiction is the backbone of our work, and understanding genre conventions and the authors that exemplify them is what allows us to move readers from one to another, to be the knowledgeable resources that readers expect and deserve.

Our task as readers' advisors, librarians who work with readers, is to show that we value all fiction genres and nonfiction subjects and their fans. We demonstrate this by becoming familiar with the genres and by making our collections accessible to readers, by acquiring reference sources that allow us to serve readers better, and by talking with readers, indicating that we understand what they are looking for when they ask for reading suggestions and helping them find what they seek.

As readers ourselves, we know how important it is to be able to have books to suit our mood. Our patrons are readers too, and their needs are no different from ours. Sometimes we want a page-turner, a book that keeps us so engrossed that we race through to the end. Sometimes we prefer a book that pulls us in, and we want to savor every word. Sometimes we seek a book that makes us think about the world in a new way, and at other times we simply want a book we can read without thinking at all. Just as there is a reader for every book, according to Ranganathan, there is a book for every mood and need.[2] We help readers find the books they are in the mood to read.

To serve readers better, we have an obligation to read and talk about what we read. We must also make readers comfortable so that they feel safe asking for suggestions and assistance. This book offers ways to let readers know we value their questions.

Readers' advisors have a corner on the market of all the best things in the world. We have a collection of books at our fingertips, and we know how to find just what we want. We understand, too, that popular fiction and nonfiction meet a variety of needs that range from pure escapism to paradigms by which we make life's important decisions. We know we can find passion, suspense, adventure, intrigue, mystery, provocative issues, and intellectual stimulation in the pages of the books we read. In turn we are privileged to share the world of story with our readers. Stories that feed our spirits, our emotions, and our intellects. Stories that help us understand our own predicament and that of others, that teach us tolerance, amuse us, and inspire us. Sharing these stories becomes both our goal and our pleasure.

NOTES

1. Dan Simmons, *The Terror: A Novel* (New York: Little, Brown, 2007).
2. S. R. Ranganathan, *The Five Laws of Library Science* (1931; reprint, New York: Asia, 1963).

Part 1

Adrenaline Genres

2

ADVENTURE

All of us have come across readers who are fans of the Indiana Jones and James Bond movies. They like the action and the fast-paced story; the characters amuse them, and they follow the exploits of the hero from movie to movie. They can hardly wait for the next one! Or they are great fans of all those war movies—the ones that focus on the action, featuring the hero who leads his band of men to outwit and escape enemy forces, despite the odds against them. Both types allow viewers to become armchair warriors who experience danger and overcome obstacles in exotic locales. And when they have seen all the movies, many come to us looking for books that offer this same appeal. This is when we turn to the Adventure genre: old-fashioned action stories with broad appeal.

From those movies and books it is just a short jump to Dan Brown's *The Da Vinci Code* and similar novels involving quests for more literary and artistic treasures and riddles.[1] The Adventure genre is experiencing a true renaissance, as readers and viewers are clamoring for these action-packed tales of missions and treasure hunts, filled with danger and suspense, intriguing details, formidable obstacles, and characters we love—and love to hate.

A DEFINITION

In his classic discussion of genre fiction, *Adventure, Mystery, and Romance: Formula Stories as Art and Popular Culture*, John G. Cawelti defines Adventure fiction as the story "of the hero—individual or group—overcoming obstacles and dangers and accomplishing some important and moral mission."[2] He also alludes to the archetypical nature of this story pattern, which can be traced back to ancient myths and epics. The traditional Adventure hero passes through an array of frightening perils to reach some goal, as in such classics as *The Odyssey* and *Beowulf.* Thus, novels in the Adventure genre are action-packed, feature a hero on a mission, and are often set in exotic locales during times of war or peace. With the popularity of Dan Brown's *The Da Vinci Code* and the myriad titles that followed in its wake, the genre gained new energy and popularity. Heroes on missions, whether involving physical or more intellectual pursuits and puzzles, struggle to decipher the codes that lead to treasure and sometimes, to save the world.

Thus, the prototypical Adventure story features a hero on a mission, and he must face a range of obstacles along the way. The reader gets a firsthand look at the exotic locale in which the story is set. The reader participates in suspenseful derring-do, joining the hero as he extricates himself from multiple dangers along the way and overcomes the physical dangers to complete his mission successfully. Figure 2.1 summarizes the characteristics of Adventure novels.

Figure 2.1   *Characteristics of Adventure*

---

1. Pacing is generally brisk, as the hero escapes from one dangerous episode to the next. Adventure novels often take place within a short time span, and time/date stamps at the head of chapters often drive the pace.

2. The story line focuses on action, usually a mission, and the obstacles and dangers met along the way. Physical adventure and danger are paramount, as the hero is placed in life-and-death situations from which he must rescue himself and others. There is generally a happy ending, with the hero safe and order restored.

3. There is always an identifiable hero, a character whom readers like and to whom they relate. Through ingenuity and skill, he accomplishes his desperate mission.

4. Detailed settings are important. These stories are set "elsewhere," and this foreignness underlines the sense of danger and obstacles to be overcome. Maps often accompany these novels. Worlds of art, antiques, antiquities, and books also provide intriguing backgrounds.

5. In response to the life-threatening situations, the mood of many Adventure novels is dark, menacing, foreboding. In some, humor lightens the tone.

6. Colorful language and jargon (often military) fill these tales, and this conversational language invites the reader to participate in the hero's exploits.

CHARACTERISTICS AND THE GENRE'S APPEAL

Pacing

Here, as in all Adrenaline genres, brisk pacing drives the story, and all else is secondary to the sense of forward motion. The action moves the story along at a breakneck speed, with the hero and his crew escaping from one dangerous situation to the next. Even the longer Historical Adventure novels seem to move quickly. The urgency of the mission requires a page-turning pace. Time/date stamps at the head of chapters emphasize the idea that every minute counts, and this is a mission that must be accomplished within a limited time frame. This fact telescopes and intensifies the action. In Matthew Reilly's series starring Australian commando Jack West and his oddly assorted crew, for example, the team whips around the world, working against the clock to battle the bad guys and save the world from destruction. The action leaves the reader breathless. (7 *Deadly Wonders* starts the series.)[3]

Story Line

Action distinguishes this genre, and the story line emphasizes this orientation. In Adventure the plot usually concentrates on a desperate mission. It is always physically dangerous to those involved and usually has serious—life-and-death—ramifications. There is generally one overwhelming obstacle that must be overcome, although there are often lesser difficulties along the way. In *Garden of Beasts,* Jeffery Deaver takes readers to 1936 Berlin for an intricately plotted, fast-paced Historical Adventure.[4] Captured by federal agents, German American hit man Paul Schumann is given a choice: spend his life in jail or go to Germany and assassinate one of Hitler's top advisers. Since the latter choice would also give him a new lease on life, including $10,000 to start over, he joins the American Olympic team as a reporter. Once in Berlin he is almost immediately under suspicion from German police, both local and national, and they dog his tracks, always only a step or two behind him as he sets up his kill. The complex and provocative story line, which covers just two days once he's in Berlin, is filled with unexpected twists and revelations. It compels readers to keep turning pages swiftly, despite the wealth of historical detail. Readers follow his meticulous preparations, and even though dramatic action does not fill every page, the intensity builds and keeps us enthralled. The story moves quickly, from one danger to the next, as we feel—and see, as the time is revealed at each chapter heading—the clock ticking, reinforcing the Suspense elements inherent in the Adventure genre.

Story lines may be contemporary or historical, involving civilians or military personnel. Although violence seems a fixture in much genre fiction today, especially in the Adrenaline genres, there is a range in Adventure fiction, from the graphic violence and high body count in popular authors like Steve Berry, James Rollins, and Matthew Reilly to cartoon violence of Clive Cussler's novels and the less descriptive violence and the suggestion of violence in some of the more literary Adventure stories, such as Kate Mosse's *Labyrinth*.[5]

Other features of the Adventure story line include survival amid the elements, with physical, human, and animal dangers; escape from perilous situations; and the nature of these wide-ranging missions—from military operations to quests for treasure—covered by the genre. Remember, too, that despite the danger and obstacles, the hero is successful. Others may be lost along the way, but the hero almost always prevails and survives—often to embark on further adventures in later books. Conclusions may not be the typical happy ending of the Romance genre, but they are certainly satisfactory; the mission is carried out, and among the survivors are those we as readers care most about.

Characterization

The nature of the hero is another hallmark of the Adventure genre. (Although inroads have been made by women, as will be seen below, this remains a male-dominated genre.) He is a strong, honorable man, committed to his assigned mission. Both physical and intellectual skills are required: the hero must act to accomplish his mission, but he must also be able to figure out the puzzles along the way. As do hard-boiled detectives (covered in chapter 11, "Mysteries"), the Adventure hero operates under a strong moral code, although it may be one of his own devising. Whether or not these heroes are the appointed leaders of their groups, they are the ones who display the ingenuity and skill that accomplish the mission and save the team from disaster. The hero's natural leadership ability, combined with intuitive skill at interpreting dangers and discovering solutions, sets him apart from the others on his team.

Although characters may be stereotypes, and secondary characters are more often either good or bad rather than fully developed, the hero and his plight capture the imagination and sympathy of the audience.

Having said this, I must add that some authors do shade their characters, making them grayer and adding the depth of characterization that some readers seek. For example, in Paul Sussman's series featuring detective Yusuf Khalifa of the Luxor police, both Khalifa and his Israeli counterpart are portrayed sympathetically, with the characterizations offering insights into contemporary Middle East issues, and fully realized characters inhabit both the contemporary and historical story lines. (Try *The Last Secret of the Temple* to sample the series.)[6] The Adventure genre frequently inspires series characters, so that even if the hero is not as fully developed as in Literary Fiction, fans follow his exploits and the changes in his life from book to book and thus gain a sense of knowing the character.

On the other hand, the villains are almost always drawn in extremes and are very evil. Ian Fleming and his followers specialize in cardboard (but always fascinating) villains to pit against hero James Bond. The antagonist is as likely to be a group (Germans or Japanese against the American or British military, for example) or a physical obstacle, as an individual. For example, in Paul Garrison's *Sea Hunter*, the ocean is as dangerous as any villain and as serious (albeit impartial) a foe as the most obsessed megalomaniac.[7]

Adventure is often called Male Romance because it focuses on male characters, ensures a happy ending, and features a community of men. In fact, these are the closest equivalent to novels of Women's Lives and Relationships, with their close-knit groups of men starring in stories written primarily by and for men. (However, there are likely many more female readers of Adventure than there are male readers of novels of Women's Lives and Relationships.) This community is most visible in Adventure with military story lines. Here men are seen almost exclusively on the battlefield or in preparation for battle, always involved in military activities. Because it is not standard military practice, there is seldom one man operating alone. Usually there is a group of men, although one emerges as the leader (not necessarily because of rank) when the difficult situation arises. In other Adventures the hero almost always has a group to assist him, and it traditionally comprises men. From the military novels of Bernard Cornwell and W. E. B. Griffin (not to mention the friendship of Maturin and Aubrey in Patrick O'Brian's long-running historical naval Adventure series) to Jack Higgins's ongoing tales of male colleagues pursuing missions and Ian Caldwell and Dustin Thomason's college friends in *The Rule of Four*, sorting out a puzzle, male bonding and male friendship play an important role.[8]

Until recently Adventure was singularly devoid of female protagonists or, in fact, of interesting women characters in any role. These were communities of men, and the women, if they appeared, were clearly secondary. Exceptions were often single titles, such as Ken Follett's *Jackdaws*.[9] Dedicated to England's female spies during World War II, this Adventure follows Felicity "Flick" Clairet and the crew she recruits to cripple German telephone service in France just before D-day. Bristling with danger at every turn, the story line dramatizes the courage and skill of this mostly female team, bent on achieving their goal at any cost, and that cost is high. The popularity of more literary adventures, puzzles, and treasure hunts that do not require an exclusively male cast has allowed an increase in the number of female protagonists. Kate Mosse, for example, places women in danger and in charge in her Adventure novels featuring contemporary and historical plotlines (*Labyrinth*). Also meeting these criteria are Jennifer Lee Carrell's *Interred with Their Bones*, an action-packed story of scholar Rosalind Howard's perilous search for a lost Shakespearean play and Katherine Neville's *The Fire*, a sequel to the popular Sure Bet *The Eight*, which features further dangerous undertakings involving the chess set once owned by Charlemagne.[10] For now, the Adventure genre remains primarily a man's world, but perhaps not for long.

Frame/Setting

Physical setting plays an important role in Adventure stories. Heroes must go on a mission to another place, often exotic or unknown and certainly mysterious. This must then be described in physical and cultural terms, sometimes in more than one time period. For example Steve Berry often devises tales with time lines past and present. Readers learn history—details of the last resting place of Alexander the Great or of the famous Amber Room, dismantled and captured as Nazi treasure—while following a present-day story that might also span the globe.

Historical settings have wide appeal. Authors such as Cornwell and O'Brian appeal to readers who appreciate both the military and historical detail these novelists emphasize in creating their characters and settings as well as just good Adventure stories. O'Brian's series of almost twenty novels, beginning with *Master and Commander*, is set during the Napoleonic Wars and features Jack Aubrey, an officer in the British navy, and his unorthodox friend, intelligence officer Dr. Stephen Maturin.[11] O'Brian's novels are all part of an ongoing story, each an episode linked to those before and after. Details of ships, the lives of sailors, and the politics and reality of war aboard ship fill these historically set tales.

Cornwell has several Adventure series set in the past: the Richard Sharpe series, set primarily in the Napoleonic Wars (*Sharpe's Tiger* comes first chronologically); the Starbuck Chronicles (*Rebel* is the first), set in the U.S. Civil War; the Grail Quest series starring Thomas of Hookton and set in fourteenth-century England and Europe (*The Archer's Tale* starts the series); and the Saxon Stories (starting with *The Last Kingdom*), set in ninth-century Britain.[12] These feature series characters, and each book leads up to and describes, in detail, a particular battle. Historical notes at the end of each book add an informative and authoritative touch, setting the books firmly in the period they describe.

To support the frame of their stories, authors often include maps or detailed plans of ships. Extensive historical notes, as at the end of each of Cornwell's titles, relate the known historical facts of the fictionalized events and are more and more frequently found in other books with historical settings.

The addition of novels like *The Da Vinci Code* to the genre has highlighted another type of frame, long employed by Adventure novelists including H. Rider Haggard and Robert Lewis Stevenson: the treasure quest. While some stories are straightforward treasure hunts, many are couched in elaborate frames involving secret societies, historical personages and their secrets, and lost treasures and their provenance. Danger is not lessened in these tales that feature elaborately detailed background frames, but the details do tend to dominate the story, whether Hawke's pirate treasure map in Ted Bell's series (*Hawke* is the first), a lost Shakespeare play in Carrell's *Interred with Their Bones,* or the tantalizing intellectual puzzles and clues from art, history, and ancient manuscripts in Brown's books.[13] Code breaking is often an integral element, sometimes involving computers, science, art, or text. These authors blend fascinating bits of information on art, science, religion, and more into provocative puzzles that readers enjoy trying to solve from the safety of their own armchairs as they follow Adventure heroes on their quests.

Tone/Mood

It's no wonder that the tone of Adventure novels is often dark and moody, reflecting the dangers the heroes face. In Cornwell's popular Saxon Stories, for example, the dark tone reflects the violent times—ninth-century England during the Viking invasions. Others present a lighter touch or tongue-in-cheek humor to soften the danger—and the body count.

Michael Chabon's swashbuckling spoof of the Adventure genre, *Gentlemen of the Road,* introduces two paladins in search of adventure and gold around the Black and Caspian Seas in the tenth century.[14] Employed to escort a prince home to his rightful inheritance, they discover early on that all is not what it seems. These confidence men-of-the-road stumble from one danger to the next, while the reader remains confident that all will be well in the end.

Style/Language

As do all genres, Adventure exhibits a range of styles, including the poetic, elegant prose of Caldwell and Thomason's *Rule of Four* and Jon Fasman's *The Geographer's Library,* and, at the other end of the spectrum, authors like Cussler and James Rollins, whose more prosaic, conversational prose creates a different mood and attracts a different audience.[15] Here, too, the tongue-in-cheek humor and exaggerated characters and peril simply add to fans' enjoyment. These are not dangers that touch us closely. In Historical Adventures, the ornate style of Arturo Pérez-Reverte's Captain Alatriste series with its nod to flowery seventeenth-century Adventure prose contrasts with the spare prose of Cornwell in his multiple series, especially those set in more ancient times. Suffice it to say that here, as elsewhere, there are stylistic differences. However, we should not be surprised to hear a fan laud Cussler for his "well-written" stories, even if we know this comment is counter to literary taste. Any writer whom a reader enjoys writes well, no matter what the style. It is a question of personal definition and a subject best avoided in the readers' advisory interview.

Colorful language, rich in the jargon of the milieu, fills Adventure novels. Even in a classic such as Stevenson's *Treasure Island,* literary style is not the draw, but the patois of the pirates holds the audience.[16] Authors relying on military backgrounds provide language and idioms appropriate to the setting, while the antiquarian puzzle Adventures may include literary references as well as more elegant prose.

These are frequently novels of excess, with many featuring characters who are more extreme, plots that are more far-fetched, and locales that are exotic and potentially more dangerous. Many also present situations that may be ludicrously violent and dangerous. Over-the-top is the key to many Adventure novels. It comes as no surprise then that soldier-of-fortune tales, epitomized by Richard Marcinko's Rogue Warrior series, fit in this genre. (*Rogue Warrior II: Red Cell* is the first novel in this series.)[17]

Because their extensive military skills are not needed by their own countries, these mercenaries, including a team of Navy SEALs, use their skills and experience to battle a range of villains from terrorists to the Russian mob and neo-Nazis. The series features fast-acting, hard-talking mercenaries, as well as cartoon villains and heroes, exotic locales, and out-of-the-ordinary plotlines. Marcinko's books, however, include more violence than most in this genre. The language is also harder, not only in terms of the professional jargon (luckily, he provides a glossary as well as an index!), but also in the amount of profanity. His books are not for every reader, yet we have fans of both sexes who are not put off by the violence and strong language and who clearly appreciate the missions on which the hero and his men are engaged.

In contrast, other Adventure novels with a military background are firmly grounded in fact and often center around real historical events and characters. William Dietrich writes a series of Adventure novels that feature Napoleon Bonaparte. His hero, American Ethan Gage (a protégé of Ben Franklin), finds himself in Egypt with Napoleon's troops in the first (*Napoleon's Pyramids*), and events there (real and fictional) set up the series, which focuses on a mysterious medallion that he acquires.[18]

Adventure stories focused more on treasure hunting and puzzles with their details of rare books and antiquities fall somewhere in between. The story lines are generally not as over-the-top as Cussler's and Marcinko's. While they may include real historical personages and events, their focus is the puzzle laid out before them, a puzzle the hero must solve to reach the treasure, whatever that is. Dan Brown popularized this particular story line with a wide range of readers but it has been familiar to Adventure fans for centuries.

KEY AUTHORS

For most readers, one name says it all when it comes to Adventure: Clive Cussler. Since his first book in 1976 (*Raise the Titanic*), Cussler, or really his hero Dirk Pitt, has set the standard for the Adventure genre.[19] Pitt is the typical Adventure hero: the independent protagonist who, in early novels at least, was not necessarily the highest ranking among his community of men, but he is certainly the one turned to when disaster strikes and the one who manages to regroup the men and achieve the mission. He is resourceful and inventive in the way he brings about a solution to whatever problems he faces. He does not necessarily resort to violence, and, especially in earlier titles, he is often without the expensive gadgetry that accompanies his later escapades. With the most innocuous and prosaic tools, just a little string and wax perhaps, Pitt can fix or rig almost anything. Although Adventure—the mission to be accomplished and the obstacles met along the way—is the focus of each Pitt novel, there is also usually a measure of suspense and often a treasure to be found. Cussler's books also feature humor, not only in the outrageous antics of Pitt and his friends, but in other characters and situations as well as in the dialogue. Because there is little or no sex and seldom extended and graphic violence, these are often titles requested by and suggested to younger readers, who appreciate the action elements. Women seldom play a critical role in Cussler's books; his series typifies the prototypical man's world. In the midst of all the action, Cussler does highlight important ecological issues. To get a sense of Cussler's style, try *Sahara,* a classic example of his action-filled writing.[20] In his inimitable style, Pitt investigates an epidemic in the Sahara and a mysterious influx of organisms endangering coastal waters off the African coast, and he learns of the fate a missing 1930s aviatrix and a secret concerning Lincoln's assassination. All in a day's (or perhaps two or three days') work.

Fans of Military Adventure praise W. E. B. Griffin (fondly called Web by his myriad fans). His novels have taken millions of readers back through the rigors of World War II and beyond with the U.S. Marines. His Adventure series include The Brotherhood of War (Korean War), The Corps (World War II), Men at War (OSS agents in World War II), and Presidential Agents (post–September 11 adventures starring a Homeland Security agent).[21] These are blockbuster Adventure novels, featuring the fast pace, sense of immediacy, and danger that the genre requires, as well as the series characters that fans appreciate and learn to know intimately. Readers wanting to sample his newer series should read *By Order of the President,* first in the Presidential Agents series.[22] Carlos Castillo, Delta Force Major, West Point graduate, and veteran of Desert Storm, now serves the president and investigates unusual situations around the world. Here, a Boeing 727 has been hijacked in Angola, and Charlie's mission is to discover who's responsible and why. Military jargon and technology and locales around the world provide the perfect backdrop for Griffin's work.

With numerous Historical Adventure series, Bernard Cornwell is an excellent suggestion for readers looking for rigorously researched historical backgrounds. His elaborately described battle scenes give readers a "you are there" sense. He ends each novel with notes detailing the historical sources and events he drew upon for the story. Depending on a reader's interest in a particular time period or battle, any of his titles makes a good suggestion. Overall, *Sharpe's Rifles,* a classic title of the Napoleonic Wars, remains among his most popular.[23] In January 1809 the newly minted Lieutenant Sharpe must rally his disgruntled troops and stay alive as they are drawn into an aristocratic Spanish officer's dangerous mission.

It is hard to believe that there are any readers who have not read Dan Brown's *The Da Vinci Code* or *Angels and Demons,* but he is certainly an author to know.[24] Another of his titles, *Deception Point,* also makes a good suggestion for fans of Cussler's over-the-top action-packed stories.[25] For the time being, at least, Brown stands as the author to whom many readers compare other authors, so librarians need to know him and recognize his skill at blending tantalizing bits of information on art, science, and religion in his compulsively readable and conspiracy-filled Adventures.

Newer Adventure authors James Rollins and Matthew Reilly should also be familiar to librarians and readers. Rollins's entertaining, suspenseful Adventure novels feature exotic locales and plots that are frequently over-the-top and sometimes employ supernatural elements. Recent novels feature the Sigma Force, an elite American special operations team. Headed by Gray Pierce, the group must solve baffling puzzles that range from the scientific to the arcane, and the fate of the world is often at stake. Fast (and violent) action, series characters, and challenging conundrums (which make them a possible suggestion for Brown readers) characterize these books. Start with *Map of Bones.*[26]

Matthew Reilly offers video-game Adventure for his many fans. Series character Shane Schofield, a Marine Corps captain, appears in several early titles and an international team of commandos (plus two children and a scientist) make up his most recent team of heroes. Chases, treasure, and dangers that might come from humans, animals, or environment drive these nonstop action stories. As stated earlier, *7 Deadly Wonders* starts his recent series.

WHAT WE KNOW ABOUT FANS

Readers of Adventure are a diverse lot who may also read in a number of related genres. There are, however, several general characteristics that describe these fans. First, Adventure readers expect the general template of characteristics mentioned earlier in the chapter: a hero on a mission; detailed, exotic settings; danger, with action, whether frequent or following a suspenseful buildup; and the ultimate success of the mission with the hero safe. Cinematic is a term often applied to Adventure story lines, and it is one readers may also employ as they describe books they enjoy. These are stories made for the big screen, with larger-than-life heroes on seemingly impossible missions, often striving for the ultimate goal of making the world safe, if not actually saving it through their efforts. As in Romance and Suspense, readers expect a happy ending.

Some readers revel in the exaggerations of characters and story line, which they find most frequently in nonmilitary Adventure. They appreciate the over-the-top humor. The comments about these authors focus on the character of the villain, the foreignness of the setting, and the details of the gadgetry.

Fans not only read Adventure for the vicarious danger/escape motif, but they also read many of the authors for the details of the times, weaponry, or the additional obscure facts they provide. Clive Cussler fans praise the curious details of treasure hunting, for example, a technique to raise the Titanic (before its popularity skyrocketed with the blockbuster movie). Readers of Cornwell and O'Brian prize their characters, stories, and the details of life in another time and place. Fans of Dan Brown appreciate the puzzles, along with the background knowledge demanded by the treasure hunt. Military fiction readers devour the details of battle as well as the preparations and forays to discover the special information the missions involve.

And as in all genres, fans read for the formula that pulls them in—the characters they can relate to and the stories that enthrall them. These are mythic heroes, off to face their dragons, in whatever form, in order to accomplish their missions. They only lack the beautiful princess as reward.

If you are not a reader of Adventure, start with the key authors discussed above. Those are among the most popular authors, the ones your readers most likely refer to when they talk about Adventure they have read and loved. Figure 2.2 shows some additional authors, whose Adventure novels may remind you of genres you already read and enjoy.

THE READERS' ADVISORY INTERVIEW

Adventure is one of the genres for which, if you cannot elicit useful information about books readers have enjoyed, you can often successfully ask about movies. Potential fans may find the movies easier to recall

---

Figure 2.2 *An Introduction to the Adventure Genre*

Adventure Writers to Try, If You Enjoy . . .

Adrenaline:	Ted Bell
	Matthew Reilly
	James Rollins
Fantasy:	Wilbur Smith (River God series)[27]
Gentle:	Dorothy Gilman
	Anthony Horowitz
	Robert Lewis Stevenson
Historical Fiction:	Patrick O'Brian
History:	Bernard Cornwell
	Mark Frost
Horror:	Gary Jennings
Humor:	George MacDonald Fraser
	Arturo Pérez-Reverte (Captain Alatriste series)[28]
Inspirational:	Tim F. LaHaye and Greg Dinallo (Babylon Rising series)[29]
Literary:	Michael Chabon
	Arturo Pérez-Reverte
Mystery:	Dan Brown
	Kate Mosse
Natural History:	Jack B. Du Brul
Romance:	Dorothy Dunnett
Saga:	Wilbur A. Smith (Courtney family)[30]
Travel:	H. Rider Haggard
	James Rollins
True Adventure:	David Poyer
	Jeff Rovin
Westerns:	Robert Lewis Taylor

---

than books, and because many classic Adventure movies were based on books—*Von Ryan's Express, The Bridge on the River Kwai,* and *The Guns of Navarone,* to name a few—it is often easy to convince those who have enjoyed the movie to try these or similar books. Check out the American Film Institute's lists ("100 Cheers" and "100 Thrills" both list a number of films that please Adventure fans).[31]

This is also a genre in which we can discover a great deal about books we have not personally read, just by looking for a few signs as we work with patrons. Maps, whether of a large area or with details of a specific terrain, often indicate that there are Adventure elements in the story. Not that maps or detailed drawings are lacking in other genres, but in Historical Adventure novels especially, they often give a clue to the story line. A map of the United States, for example, suggests a journey and surely adventures along the way. On the other hand, the detailed drawings of nineteenth-century ships in Patrick O'Brian's Military Adventures also validate the accuracy of the detail to be included in the novel. And as they do in the Thriller genre, covers of Adventure novels may also indicate their theme.

When suggesting titles, do not forget the classics. In fact, occasionally a reader will ask for more books like those he enjoyed in his youth: the great Adventure tales of Robert Lewis Stevenson, Alexandre Dumas, C. S. Forester (the Hornblower series), and Rafael Sabatini. More recent classic Adventure writers include Dorothy Dunnett, with two series in renaissance Europe; and Nevil Shute, whose quiet and mild-mannered protagonists often make unlikely heroes in tales set primarily in the 1930s through 1950s.

One last point in the readers' advisory interview. Many unthinkingly consider this a genre read only by men. Those of us who work with readers know this is not true, especially if we expand the genre to include those involving puzzles and treasure hunts like *The Da Vinci Code*. Although the audience may once have included more men than women, there is much in this genre that appeals to readers of both sexes: action, exotic locales, and happy endings among the most important.

Sure Bets

When all else fails—our minds are blank and we can come up with no suggestions for readers—try describing these Sure Bets. Wilbur A. Smith's series of novels of ancient Egypt, beginning with *River God*, provide exciting adventure, political machinations, random and ritual violence, and the lives of the fictional characters close to the throne of the pharaoh.[32] Extensive details frame these stories, from clothing, customs, manners, and mores to crucial information about the times (1780 BC) when Egypt was politically divided. Later titles in the series also include magical and more fantastical elements.

Spanish author Arturo Pérez-Reverte works as a Sure Bet in my library. Readers enjoy the elegant prose, the intricate, often literary puzzles, the intriguing characters, and the layered stories with their fascinating treasure quests. *The Flanders Panel* makes a good starting place.[33] His description of the medieval painting that forms the crux of the story is so vivid that I had to pull both hard- and softcover copies to prove to a patron, who had read and appreciated the book, that the painting was not on the cover. Fans of old-fashioned Historical Adventure will also appreciate his series starring Captain Alatriste, a seventeenth-century Spanish swordsman who is equally skilled battling with blades or wits (*Captain Alatriste* is the first).[34] For Adventure from literary to swashbuckling and crossover with Mysteries and Thrillers, Pérez-Reverte has broad appeal.

For readers waiting for another blockbuster from Dan Brown, suggest Steve Berry. His most recent novels feature antiquarian book dealer and ex-intelligence officer Cotton Malone, always on dangerous missions to discover treasure—the secrets of the Knights Templar, the fate of Alexandrian library, or what lies buried with Alexander the Great. Berry employs fascinating historical details, exotic locales, and danger at every turn to satisfy his fans' love of the intellectual puzzle and the fast-paced story. Almost any title works as a Sure Bet, but *The Templar Legacy*, first in the Malone series, is a good title to offer.[35]

Some authors have written timeless Adventure novels that remain popular long after their deaths. Louis L'Amour's *The Walking Drum*, set in twelfth-century Western Europe and the Middle East, is one with which I have had success.[36] It is the story of a young man who desires revenge for the death of his mother and the destruction of his estate by a neighboring lord. He also seeks his father, a corsair whom he believes is held captive in Turkey. There is action in almost every chapter; either there is an actual fight or battle scene, or we follow the intense buildup to such a scene in the next chapter. The action drives the pacing, pushing us as readers to read faster and faster. L'Amour is an unexpected find for fans of this genre, as he is a writer who appeals to a wide range of readers across several genres, even though he is best known as a writer of Westerns.

Dorothy Dunnett's two excellent Adventure series with detailed historical settings also make good suggestions. These long, captivating novels of adventure, intrigue, and romance, freely laced with literary quotations and allusions, offer pleasant diversion for a wide range of readers. The first series features Francis Crawford of Lymond, the second son of a sixteenth-century Scots family. This picaresque hero amuses himself with intrigue in the courts of France, the Middle East, Russia, and England and eventually finds his place and his love in six elegant, witty, erudite, adventure-packed novels, beginning with *The Game of Kings*.[37] The second series, set in fifteenth-century Netherlands and Europe, features Nicholas (Niccolo) vander Poele, merchant, banker, and adventurer. The first of the series is *Niccolo Rising*.[38] These intricately plotted Adventures explore Renaissance culture, business, and politics across Europe and as far afield as Africa and Iceland, as Nicholas travels for business and, sometimes, revenge.

EXPANDING READERS' HORIZONS WITH WHOLE COLLECTION READERS' ADVISORY

Since the fast-paced action of the Adventure genre is a feature of many genres, there are many directions to send fans. Although adventure may not be the key element, any Fantasy novel involving a quest certainly requires a great deal of action, not to mention exotic locales and possibly military encounters. Suggest Raymond E. Feist, Robin Hobb, Robert Jordan, or Terry Goodkind to Adventure readers ready for something different, or offer Scott Lynch's series beginning with *The Lies of Locke Lamora*.[39] It follows the career of a thief and con man who moves from one dangerous escapade to the next. In Science Fiction, military tales make excellent suggestions for Adventure fans, as do novels of exploration and discovery.

Historical Fiction offers numerous possibilities in almost all historical periods. Fans should sample a range from Henryk Sienkiewicz's *With Fire and Sword*, first of a massive trilogy set in seventeenth-century Eastern Europe; to the Romantic Historical Adventure novels of Sara Donati (*Into the Wilderness*) and Diana Gabaldon (*Outlander*), which include history, romance, intrigue, and adventure in eighteenth-century England and America; to the more serious and character-centered *Hannibal* by Ross Leckie, which tells of the Carthaginian general's attack on Rome, as well as the personality of the man who engineered it.[40] Tim Willocks's awardwinning *The Religion*, first in his Tannhauser series, is also a good bet for fans of Historical Adventure, Military Adventure, and swashbuckling tales.[41]

Although many titles in the Romance genre offer adventure in exotic settings, suggesting this genre to Adventure fans raises other questions. How will readers react to a suggestion to move from a genre that, for the most part, excludes women to one that focuses on women? Readers willing to take this chance will find action-filled plots in the Historical Romances of Loretta Chase and Mary Jo Putney, as well as in Elizabeth Lowell's contemporary treasure-hunting Romances.

In Romantic Suspense we are confronted with the same basic issue as in Romance: The protagonists are women. Still, writers such as Sandra

Brown and Catherine Coulter add strong action and adventure elements to their novels of Romantic Suspense, and Suzanne Brockmann's series featuring Navy SEALs provide heroes and adventure.

The other Adrenaline genres, Thrillers and Suspense, offer a number of directions for Adventure fans to pursue. Fans of the exploits of James Bond or Dirk Pitt may also enjoy Tom Clancy's Jack Ryan stories or Patrick Robinson's submarine Techno-Thrillers, in which the technical detail, exotic locales, and increasingly fantastic plots usually compensate for the more conventional characters. Michael Crichton's action-filled, fast-paced, Scientific Thrillers may also satisfy Adventure fans, as might Ridley Pearson's Suspense series featuring Idaho sheriff Walt Fleming.[42] Don't forget true-life Adventure, such as Sebastian Junger's *The Perfect Storm* or Jon Krakauer's *Into Thin Air,* as well as biographies and histories of historical and contemporary adventurers.[43]

Swashbuckling tales are not as common today, but they do exist. Try the Fantasy Sword and Sorcery novels by Steven Brust and George MacDonald Fraser's Flashman series or Westerns by Louis L'Amour.[44]

Figure 2.3 offers additional authors to take readers beyond the Adventure genre.

TRENDS

The popularity of this genre has grown enormously over the past decade, as the boundaries have expanded to include the treasure-hunting missions of Dan Brown and others who have imitated his formula. These new titles have also expanded the role of women, and Adventure novels now sport more and more convincing heroines.

The graphic novel format also expands the genre's reach, as adventure themes play important roles in many, and these often lead to films, which create an even wider audience for the genre. Alan Moore's *The League of Extraordinary Gentlemen* is a good starting place and another Adventure novel made into a movie.[45] In addition, maps and illustrations figure prominently even in nongraphic adventure novels. Check out Matthew Reilly's *The 6 Sacred Stones* for a wealth of maps and other drawings.[46] Even here the paranormal is beginning to play an important role, and that will likely continue. Certainly this genre shares the same genre-crossing tendencies that all others seem to have adopted, spilling over into the other Adrenaline genres as well as Fantasy, Historical Fiction, and Science Fiction, to name just a few directions.

Figure 2.3 *Expanding Readers' Horizons*

Authors to Take Readers beyond the Adventure Genre

Adrenaline:	Michael Crichton
	Ridley Pearson
	Patrick Robinson
Fantasy:	Raymond E. Feist
	Robert Jordan
	Scott Lynch
Gentle Reads:	Dorothy Gilman
Historical Fiction:	Steven Pressfield
	Henryk Sienkiewicz
	Tim Willocks
History:	Robert Kurson (*Shadow Divers*)[47]
Literary:	Isabel Allende (*Zorro*)[48]
Romance:	Elizabeth Lowell
	Mary Jo Putney
Romantic Suspense:	Suzanne Brockmann
	Sandra Brown
	Catherine Coulter
Science Fiction:	Jack McDevitt
	Larry Niven
	John Ringo
	David Weber
Travel:	Thor Heyerdahl
	Marco Polo
True Adventure:	Tony Horwitz
	Sebastian Junger
	Jon Krakauer
	Tom Wolfe (*The Right Stuff*)[49]
Western:	Louis L'Amour
Women's Lives:	Isabella L. Bird

Novels in the Adventure genre appeal to our wanderlust and to our desire to test our limits and explore the boundaries of our universe. Adventure takes us from the confines of our ordinary lives to traverse the known world and beyond. With a select group of companions, we embark on our quest, facing danger and privation, and always succeed in the end, despite the rigors of the trip. Adventure novels are stories of action, heroes, villains, danger, and survival—not to mention ultimate success. They appeal to a deep-seated desire to participate in a quest and to attain the grail. Small wonder that they remain so popular and blend so well with other currently popular genres—Thrillers, Science Fiction, Fantasy, Romance, Romantic Suspense, Suspense, Westerns, and many nonfiction Travel, Biography, History, and True Adventure tales. In Chabon's Historical Adventure romp, *Gentlemen of the Road*, the narrator observes, "There was no hope for an empire that had lost the will to prosecute the grand and awful business of adventure."[50] Readers can relax in the knowledge that novelists have not neglected their responsibility.

Notes

1. Dan Brown, *The Da Vinci Code: A Novel* (New York: Doubleday, 2003).
2. John G. Cawelti, *Adventure, Mystery, and Romance: Formula Stories as Art and Popular Culture* (Chicago: University of Chicago Press, 1976), 39.
3. Matthew Reilly, *7 Deadly Wonders: A Novel* (New York: Simon and Schuster, 2006).
4. Jeffery Deaver, *Garden of Beasts, A Novel of Berlin 1936* (New York: Simon and Schuster, 2004).
5. Kate Mosse, *Labyrinth* (New York: G. P. Putnam's Sons, 2006).
6. Paul Sussman, *The Last Secret of the Temple* (New York: Atlantic Monthly Press, 2005).
7. Paul Garrison, *Sea Hunter* (New York: HarperCollins, 2003).
8. Ian Caldwell and Dustin Thomason, *The Rule of Four* (New York: Dial, 2004).
9. Ken Follett, *Jackdaws* (New York: Dutton, 2001).
10. Jennifer Lee Carrell, *Interred with Their Bones: A Novel* (New York: Dutton, 2007); Katherine Neville, *The Fire: A Novel* (New York: Ballantine, 2008); Neville, *The Eight* (New York: Ballantine, 1989).
11. Patrick O'Brian, *Master and Commander* (Philadelphia: Lippincott, 1969).
12. Bernard Cornwell, *Sharpe's Tiger* (New York: HarperPaperbacks, 1997); Cornwell, *Rebel* (New York: HarperCollins, 1993); Cornwell, *The Archer's Tale* (New York: HarperCollins, 2001); Cornwell, *The Last Kingdom* (New York: HarperCollins, 2005).
13. Ted Bell, *Hawke: A Novel* (New York: Atria, 2003).
14. Michael Chabon, *Gentlemen of the Road: A Tale of Adventure* (New York: Del Rey, 2007).
15. Jon Fasman, *The Geographer's Library* (New York: Penguin, 2005).
16. Robert Lewis Stevenson, *Treasure Island* (Oxford: Oxford University Press, 2007).
17. Richard Marcinko, *Rogue Warrior II: Red Cell* (New York: Pocket Books, 1994).
18. William Dietrich, *Napoleon's Pyramids* (New York: HarperCollins, 2007).
19. Clive Cussler, *Raise the Titanic* (New York: Viking, 1976).

20. Cussler, *Sahara* (New York: Simon and Schuster, 1992).

21. W. E. B. Griffin, Brotherhood of War series, beginning with *The Lieutenants* (New York: Jove, 1982); Griffin, The Corps series, beginning with *Semper Fi* (New York: Jove, 1986); Griffin, Men at War series, beginning with *The Last Heroes* (New York: Jove, 1985).

22. Griffin, *By Order of the President* (New York: G. P. Putnam's Sons, 2004).

23. Cornwell, *Sharpe's Rifles* (New York: Viking, 1988).

24. Brown, *Angels and Demons* (New York: Pocket Books, 2000).

25. Brown, *Deception Point* (New York: Pocket Books, 2001).

26. James Rollins, *Map of Bones* (New York: Morrow, 2005).

27. Wilbur A. Smith, River God series, beginning with *River God* (New York: St. Martin's, 1994).

28. Arturo Pérez-Reverte, Captain Alatriste series, beginning with *Captain Alatriste,* trans. Margaret Sayers Peden (New York: G. P. Putnam's Sons, 2005).

29. Tim F. LaHaye and Greg Dinallo, Babylon Rising series, beginning with *Babylon Rising* (New York: Bantam, 2003).

30. Smith, Courtney family series, beginning with *Birds of Prey* (New York: St. Martin's, 1997).

31. American Film Institute, "100 Cheers," http://en.wikipedia.org/wiki/AFI%27s_100 _Years..._100_Cheers; American Film Institute, "100 Thrills," http://en.wikipedia.org/ wiki/AFI%27s_100_Years..._100_Thrills.

32. See series citation above.

33. Pérez-Reverte, *The Flanders Panel,* trans. Margaret Jull Costa (New York: Harcourt Brace, 1990).

34. Pérez-Reverte cited above.

35. Steve Berry, *The Templar Legacy* (New York: Ballantine, 2006).

36. Louis L'Amour, *The Walking Drum* (New York: Bantam, 1984).

37. Dorothy Dunnett, *The Game of Kings* (New York: Putnam, 1961).

38. Dunnett, *Niccolo Rising* (New York: Knopf, 1986).

39. Scott Lynch, *The Lies of Locke Lamora* (New York: Bantam, 2006).

40. Henryk Sienkiewicz, *With Fire and Sword* (1884; in modern translation by W. S. Kuniczak, 1st ed., Fort Washington, PA: Copernicus Society of America; New York: Hippocrene Books, 1991); Sara Donati, *Into the Wilderness* (New York: Bantam, 1998); Diana Gabaldon, *Outlander* (New York: Delacorte, 1991); Ross Leckie, *Hannibal* (Washington, DC: Regnery, 1996).

41. Tim Willocks, *The Religion* (New York: Farrar, Straus, and Giroux, 2007).

42. Ridley Pearson, Walt Fleming series, beginning with *Killer Weekend* (New York: G. P. Putnam's Sons, 2007).

43. Sebastian Junger, *The Perfect Storm: A True Story of Men against the Sea* (New York: Norton, 1997); Jon Krakauer, *Into Thin Air: A Personal Account of the Mount Everest Disaster* (New York: Villard, 1997).

44. George MacDonald Fraser, Flashman series, beginning with *Flashman: From the Flashman Papers, 1839–1842* (New York: World, 1969).

45. Alan Moore and Kevin O'Neill, *The League of Extraordinary Gentlemen* (La Jolla, CA: America's Best Comics, 2000).

46. Reilly, *The 6 Sacred Stones* (New York: Simon and Schuster, 2007).

47. Robert Kurson, *Shadow Divers: The True Adventure of Two Americans Who Risked Everything to Solve One of the Last Mysteries of World War II* (New York: Random House, 2004).

48. Isabel Allende, *Zorro: A Novel* (New York: HarperCollins, 2005).

49. Tom Wolfe, *The Right Stuff* (New York: Farrar, Straus, and Giroux, 1979).

50. Chabon, *Gentlemen of the Road,* 176.

3

ROMANTIC SUSPENSE

Before the line "It was a dark and stormy night" became a cliché, it was the phrase (and the introductory sentence of Edward Bulwer-Lytton's *Paul Clifford*)[1] that epitomized the Gothic novel, the forerunner of the Romantic Suspense genre. In these prototypes, the final scene often did take place on a dark and stormy night, with the innocent young heroine on the battlements of the isolated, crumbling castle, forced to choose between the two men who have promised safety and, ultimately, happiness. Tension has built throughout the story, and it is only in this last, fateful encounter that she can distinguish between the two, one the hero and the other the villain. Although the trappings have changed, the essence of that story remains in today's novels of Romantic Suspense. The threatened heroine is placed in jeopardy, and even though she now may save herself rather than relying on a hero to rescue her, she is still faced with a dilemma concerning the hero. Either she must choose between two men, one who turns out to be good and the other bad, or she must reconcile her feelings toward the traditional bad-boy hero and learn to trust him, appropriating a theme from the Romance genre.

A DEFINITION

Romantic Suspense is a genre with roots in both the Romance and Suspense genres. Elements from Mystery, Espionage Thrillers, and especially Suspense combine with Romance to create a story that does not fit comfortably in any of the genres it draws from. The best examples blend Romance and Suspense so completely that it is only possible to consider them as their own genre.

This genre has changed dramatically in the last thirty years. Traditionally, Romantic Suspense was a Romance with an element of danger introduced. Classic authors—Phyllis Whitney, Victoria Holt, and Barbara Michaels—rarely included actual violence, just the underlying suggestion that violence was possible or that it had occurred sometime in the past. The language was gentle, the romantic interest asexual, and any true violence offstage. In the 1980s, popular Romance writers such as Nora Roberts and Sandra Brown began writing romances with edgy Suspense, explicit sex, strong language, and graphic violence. This style transformed the genre. These Romance authors brought many of their readers with them, and this hot new version of Suspense attracted others to make this a very popular and viable genre today, one read by men and women.

This genre is a curious hybrid, and while the best evenly blend Suspense with Romance, the books do not necessarily appeal to fans of both those genres. The powerful romantic entanglement, usually involving explicit sex, may not please Suspense fans, just as the more violent and suspenseful episodes may offend some readers of Romances. In addition, these books are not to be confused with the softer Suspense of Mary Higgins Clark, because the violence occurs on stage and the romantic interest is too pervasive for Clark fans. See figure 3.1 for a summary of the genre's characteristics.

CHARACTERISTICS AND THE GENRE'S APPEAL

Pacing

As in all the Adrenaline genres, pacing here is crucial. Although a sense of uneasiness underlies the whole story, the action often starts at the first page and builds to the confrontation at the end. For example, the pacing in Karen Robards's *Obsession* pulls the reader in from the first paragraph.[2] The heroine, Katherine Lawrence, is bound in the kitchen of her townhouse, relentlessly questioned about the location of a safe she knows nothing about. Rescued and taken to the hospital, she awakens, unable to trust either her memory or those who claim they are there to help. On the run throughout the novel—even though she doesn't know why until late—Katherine both fears and desires to discover the truth. Robards's skill at doling out the clues and information a bit at a time demands that readers turn pages quickly to uncover the reason for Katherine's danger.

Figure 3.1 *Characteristics of Romantic Suspense*

---

1. Pacing is fast. The action often starts on the first page, sometimes in a prologue, and continues relentlessly at a breakneck speed, driven by the danger to the heroine and frequent plot twists.

2. The story is told from the threatened heroine's point of view. Heroines are increasingly resourceful and independent, and their survival usually depends on their own skill, with minimal help from the hero.

3. Edgy tales of Suspense combine with sensuously explicit Romance in these blended stories. Story lines may include graphic details, reflecting the harder-edged end of the Suspense genre and the more sensual end of the Romance genre.

4. A sense of uneasiness prevails even in quieter moments and affects the tone of these novels.

5. The language shares similarities with Romances, as smart dialogue and witty repartee, along with sensual descriptions, characterize the style. Strong language and explicit sexual descriptions are also common.

6. Intriguing, detailed backgrounds and exotic settings often frame these stories.

As in many titles in both the Suspense and Romance genres, there is enough action to move the story quickly. For the most part, these stories are not densely written. Identification with the protagonist and her plight, the desire to unravel the mystery behind events, as well as the building suspense, make these page-turners.

Characterization

Point of view is key to the appeal of Romantic Suspense. Although readers appreciate the suspenseful and romantic story line, they also demand the reassurance that the heroine has survived. The story needs to be told from, filtered through, her point of view. If it is not, fans may consider the story suspenseful but will also recognize that something is missing. And even though other points of view are often represented—including the hero's and, as in all good Suspense stories, the villain's—the heroine remains the central character. It is for her story, because they identify and sympathize with her, that readers flock to novels of Romantic Suspense.

In Lisa Jackson's *Shiver*, Abby Chastain, a young woman photographer from New Orleans, is haunted by her mother's death, even after twenty years.[3] When a police detective comes to tell her that her ex-husband has been murdered, she's drawn back into those memories—and the gaps in those memories—of her mother's death at a nearby psychiatric hospital. This is her story, even though we also have the murderer's thoughts and actions, as well as the point of view of the policeman who becomes romantically involved with Abby. The point of view of the threatened heroine dominates the story.

Just as the nature of the heroine has changed in today's Romantic Suspense, so has that of the hero. In bygone years there were usually two men vying for her affection—one truly the hero and the other the villain—but not until the end could she, and the reader, distinguish between the two. In today's version, the heroine is more independent, but there is always a man to whom she is attracted. Now, rather than choosing between two men, she must often come to terms with the true nature of the man she has come to love, despite her concerns about him. The hero may even appear as a villain, and he certainly seems untrustworthy in some way. In the end, however, he always exhibits the traits of a true hero.

Story Line

The most dramatic changes in the genre over the past few years have been in the increase in explicit sex and violence and the addition of strong language. In the hands of classic writers Daphne du Maurier, Mary Stewart, Holt, and Whitney, these were books one could hand "safely" to any reader concerned about that content. Today, the genre is dominated by Romance writers who have turned to Suspense writing, and, interestingly, it is their contribution that has altered the genre's tone from softer- to harder-edged. Although these authors—Brown, Robards, Iris Johansen—made their names and reputations writing Romances, they have added so much suspense to their novels, as well as violence and strong language, that they are no longer considered Romance writers by fans of that genre. Yet the romantic language, tone, and situations in their novels play too important a role for them to be considered writers of straightforward Suspense. In fact, many have drawn their Romance fans with them to this reimagined Romantic Suspense genre, and although the readers may not find the Romances they expect in current titles by their favorites, author loyalty and strong romantic elements have encouraged them to stay fans.

Today Nora Roberts writes Romantic Suspense almost exclusively, sometimes with substantial paranormal elements. In *High Noon* Savannah provides the steamy backdrop for the sexy, suspenseful yet heartwarming story of single mom/police lieutenant/hostage negotiator Phoebe MacNamara, who has been rescuing people since she was a young girl and saved her mother and brother from a brutal attacker.[4] Now she's being stalked by a psychopathic killer. Is this someone related to one of her failed hostage negotiations or an ex-cop with a grudge? Duncan Swift, bartender/ex-cabdriver/entrepreneur/lottery winner provides the love interest, and Phoebe's and Duncan's extended families furnish a host of quirky characters and humor. Roberts establishes a vital romantic relationship, and the romantic elements remain as intense and important as the suspense.

Although it is the heroine's story, the hero—or in many cases hero and villain—must also be carefully portrayed for the romantic elements to come together. Even with the increase in explicit violence, sex, and language, the romantic tone and relationship remain crucial to the story. If that strong romantic relationship is missing, the book probably fits in the Suspense genre instead.

In Suspense we usually can distinguish the hero from the villain; although we have the villain's point of view, he is usually a shadowy figure, not necessarily identified by the author or protagonist. This is often not the case in Romantic Suspense. Here, we have reason to suspect the motives of both men, hero and villain, and not until the end do we—and our heroine—discover which is really which. In Sandra Brown's *Chill Factor* Lilly Martin, ex-wife of police chief Dutch Burton, finds herself stranded in their mountain cabin in a snowstorm.[5] Also caught by the storm is writer Ben Tierney, whom Lilly rescues. However, Lilly becomes increasingly concerned that he might be the serial murderer responsible for five missing women in the area, and when Burton realizes the two are trapped together, the tension ratchets up several notches. The claustrophobic tone also elevates the tension, as Lilly wonders whether there is more danger from the storm or her cabin mate.

In other Romantic Suspense novels, the heroine has difficulty accepting that the male character could be a hero, even though we as readers know him to be one. Jayne Ann Krentz typically portrays bad-boy heroes who must overcome that image in order to win the heroine's trust and love. The hero is a man with a shady past, not the stock straight-arrow hero, and the heroine must uncover his virtues as their relationship develops. Traditional Romantic Suspense and especially Gothics, with their brooding heroes, seemingly set apart from the heroine and her needs, also reflect this characterization.

Until recently Romantic Suspense novels rarely featured series characters. The accidents and dangers that assailed the heroine were often so dramatic that few sane readers would expect to find her in the same situation again. Occasionally secondary characters reappeared in subsequent titles, or main characters from one novel appeared as secondary characters later. As they do in other genres, series now feature prominently in Romantic Suspense. Elizabeth Peters, Iris Johansen, and Catherine Coulter, to name just a few, feature series characters in their novels, described below. The heroine's profession allows her to be placed in jeopardy in more than just a single adventure.

Tone/Mood

In addition, a particular tone pervades titles within the Romantic Suspense genre. There is always a sense of uneasiness, even in quieter moments within the story. We as readers sense that not all is as it seems, that danger still awaits our heroine, and often even before she sees the actual danger, we have sensed it. As in much Suspense, we are kept on the edge of our chairs waiting for danger to intrude. From the sense of menace and foreboding in titles such as *Chill Factor,* described above, to the physical danger of Robards's *Obsession* or titles in J. D. Robb's Eve Dallas series, this feeling of edginess and uneasiness, a direct link to the genre's roots in Suspense, intensifies the descriptions and actions in these novels, and novels without this feeling do not satisfy fans of the genre in the same way.

Style/Language

Expletives and graphic descriptions of both sex and violence raise red flags for many readers, especially fans of traditional Romantic Suspense, which only suggested such imprecations and explicit images. These words and images are becoming more and more a part of popular culture—in books, movies, television, and music—and they are inescapable in most novels of Romantic Suspense. Interestingly, many readers hardly notice this change, as they read so quickly that they pass right over passages that might otherwise offend or disturb.

Like Romances, novels of Romantic Suspense display a language rich in adjectives and descriptions. Elizabeth Lowell's books, filled with lush prose, exemplify this. Fans will also find the witty repartee they prize in Romances, as hero and heroine spar frequently. Smart dialogue, characteristic of both Romance and Suspense, also propels the stories.

Frame/Setting

Although most Romantic Suspense novels feature contemporary settings, several authors also add rich historical details. Amanda Quick adds such details to the historically set titles in her Arcane Society series,[6] and Historical Romance authors have long added elements of suspense and intrigue to their novels. Stephanie Laurens, Dorothy Garlock, and Brenda Joyce, for example, consistently balance passion and danger to make their recent novels Romantic Suspense, rather than Romance.

Other authors employ frames in the way that many Mystery, Thriller, and Romance authors do, as fascinating detailed backgrounds. Elizabeth Lowell is known for her elaborate frames, often featuring jewels (Donovan Family series, beginning with *Amber Beach*); rare textiles, paintings, and manuscripts (Rarities Unlimited series, beginning with *Moving Target*); and genealogy, the Mexican drug trade, money laundering, and art forgery (St. Kilda Consulting series, beginning with *Always Time to Die*).[7] While fans certainly appreciate these intriguing details, they only provide the backdrop for the primary focus on Romantic Suspense.

Iris Johansen has long explored another frame: the paranormal. Psychics and psychic powers play increasingly important roles in her novels—both in the Eve Duncan series and in her stand-alone titles. They feature the relentless pacing, the moody tone, the heroine who must navigate her way out of danger and discover the hero, as well as the added element of paranormal powers in the form of ghosts and highly developed mental powers. Jayne Anne Krentz (also writing under her pseudonym Amanda Quick) employs similar elements, especially in the Arcane Society series, as do Kay Hooper, Lisa Jackson, Roberts, and Coulter in their series.

KEY AUTHORS

Nora Roberts remains one of the most popular writers today, and it is likely that her success in helping the genre evolve has tempted other Romance writers to join her in writing Romantic Suspense. In her stand-alone titles (usually published in hardcover), Roberts portrays strong women in difficult situations, explicit violence, and strong sexual themes; her heroines are supported by caring family, lovers, and friends, who may also be put in danger but who ultimately help to resolve the problem. In addition, Roberts has written a number of paperback Romantic Suspense series that add paranormal elements to this basic framework. Several recent trilogies—The Circle, The Sign of the Seven, In the Garden, The Key, and Three Sisters Island—have focused on the paranormal and battles between good and evil, making them interesting suggestions for Fantasy and Horror fans as well as for Romance and Romantic Suspense readers.[8]

As J. D. Robb, Roberts continues to write the adventures of futuristic New York City police detective Eve Dallas and her super-rich husband Roarke. Dallas fights for justice in a gritty world where danger always threatens, a sure draw for Suspense fans. The steamy relationship between the couple provides the requisite Romance elements to ensure her readership. *Naked in Death* is the first in this long-running series.[9]

Suzanne Brockmann has brought a fresh voice to the genre with her Troubleshooters series, starring an elite group of Navy SEALs. Her first military Romances were the Tall, Dark, and Dangerous series, later expanded into the Team Sixteen adventures.[10] These nontraditional Romantic Suspense novels often star men—and in her breakthrough *All through the Night* she offers a gay romance—but Romance and Suspense vie for equal prominence in all. *Unsung Hero,* first of her Navy SEAL Team Sixteen series, sets up the requisite Suspense and Romance in an edgy, layered story with intriguing, multi-dimensional characters, fast pacing, snappy dialogue, multiple points of view, and more than a touch of humor.[11]

Dee Henderson writes critically acclaimed Christian Fiction Romantic Suspense that features the standard elements along with religious underpinnings to the story and the characters' moral stature. Although the Romance may not be as steamy, the Suspense elements are certainly gritty, and her compelling characters and story line make her an attractive alternative for readers looking for a somewhat gentler story. *Before I Wake* is a recent title.[12]

Don't forget the masters of traditional Romantic Suspense: Daphne du Maurier, Mary Stewart, Victoria Holt, and Phyllis A. Whitney. They represent a style that has practically disappeared from the publishing scene, much to the disappointment of some fans. Many readers enjoy reading, and rereading, the classic authors, although others find the situations and characterizations dated.

WHAT WE KNOW ABOUT FANS

Many fans of this genre grew up with the classic stories of Stewart, Whitney, and Holt. Now, they see changes in their genre that may send them to other types of books. Other readers may have been Romance readers who have followed their favorite authors as their writing has changed. Still others may generally read Suspense but have been attracted to Romantic Suspense by popular authors whose names they recognize from the best-seller lists.

In all cases, readers expect and demand that the story be told from the threatened heroine's point of view. The story may be narrated first-person or it may be told in third person, but it is crucial that the reader be allowed to follow the heroine, her plight, and her point of view throughout the story. Otherwise, readers lose that emotional link with the heroine and the danger she confronts.

Many readers choose Romantic Suspense for the exotic settings in which these stories often take place. The atmosphere, intensified by the isolation or foreign setting, heightens the suspense. The heroine must be isolated, either physically or emotionally, from those who might help her extricate herself from the dangerous situation into which she has fallen. Elizabeth Lowell/Ann Maxwell writes of East Asia, Australia and the western United States; Elizabeth Adler sets her novels, characterized by more than a touch of the rich and famous, primarily in European resorts and vacation locales; and Roberts often chooses the hot and sultry southern states. Wherever they set their stories, these authors can be counted on to provide the details that create an excellent sense of place.

Although some authors use that traditional Gothic trapping, the crumbling castle (Elizabeth Peters's Vicky Bliss adventure *Borrower of the Night* is a good example), others simply isolate their heroines in more or less familiar places, which can prove as frightening as the exotic.[13] Roberts does this in *Blue Smoke,* where arson investigator Reena Hale finds danger very close to home. Emotional isolation, keeping the heroine away from family and friends who might support her, remains a crucial element, but one easier to develop in more traditional stories, since heroines were more easily manipulated.[14] Now with heroines taking an active role in their own futures, authors seek other ways to isolate them. Cherry Adair's *On Thin Ice* places heroine Lily Munroe in the grueling Iditarod.[15] Even though special agent Derek Wright is there to protect her, he can't do it without her assistance and knowledge, and she's far too independent to admit she's in danger. Although carefully watched, she is isolated—often physically and certainly emotionally—from her traditional support group.

Readers of Romantic Suspense expect a satisfactory resolution to their stories. As fans are drawn from both Suspense and Romance genres, not to mention Mystery, this should not seem unusual. These stories are end-oriented; readers know what will happen at the novel's conclusion. (The loose ends will, of course, be tied up and the heroine safe.) Fans seek a romantically written novel of a woman placed in a dangerous situation. No matter which type of Romantic Suspense or author they choose, they expect to feel the heroine's plight, and they anticipate experiencing a range of emotions from that tingle of menace to outright fear. They read to discover just how the author will save the heroine—or allow her to save herself.

As in every genre, it is important to become familiar with Romantic Suspense writers popular with our patrons. In addition to the representative authors described above, those on the list in figure 3.2 provide an introduction for librarians—and other readers—who generally read in another genre.

THE READERS' ADVISORY INTERVIEW

If a reader actually requests this genre, she may mean the classic authors such as Phyllis Whitney and Victoria Holt. (Readers of today's Romantic Suspense are more likely to request specific authors—Nora Roberts or Tami Hoag—than the genre.) Although there are few recent examples of this style, it is always good to keep a list of names to offer, while continuing to watch reviews for new authors. The annotated booklist for Traditional Romantic Suspense at my library is still popular, even though it hasn't been updated for a decade because there simply are not enough new authors to include.

One of the advantages of a library, however, is that we can keep popular titles, even if they are not recent, and make them available to readers. We keep the lists of Traditional Romantic Suspense authors, because we know the books will still be in our collection or available through inter-library loan. Our job is not to convince fans of this type of Romantic Suspense that they must accept and read newer authors—although we should keep an eye out for new titles in this classic mode. (Elizabeth Adler often works for these readers, since she tells a gentler story and the language and themes seem closer to the old-fashioned stories.) We continue to put Stewart, du Maurier, Holt, and others on our displays, and fans discover or rediscover these authors and read their books.

Figure 3.2 *An Introduction to the Romantic Suspense Genre*

Romantic Suspense Writers to Try, If You Enjoy . . .

Adrenaline:	Suzanne Brockmann
	Sandra Brown
	Tami Hoag
	Anne Stuart
Fantasy:	Nora Roberts (Circle Trilogy)[16]
Gay/Lesbian:	Suzanne Brockmann
Gentle Reads:	Debbie Macomber (Cedar Cove series)[17]
Horror:	Barbara Michaels
	Kay Hooper
Humor:	Mary Kay Andrews
	Elizabeth Peters (Vicky Bliss series)[18]
Inspirational:	Hannah Alexander
	Kristine Heitzmann
	Dee Henderson
Multicultural:	Beverly Jenkins (*Deadly Sexy*)[19]
Mysteries:	Beverly Barton
	Iris Johansen (Eve Duncan series)[20]
Romance:	Virginia Kantra
	Elizabeth Lowell
	Nora Roberts
Saga:	Stephanie Laurens
Science Fiction:	Susan Grant
	Linnea Sinclair
True Crime:	Iris Johansen (Eve Duncan series)
Westerns:	Elizabeth Lowell (*Fire and Rain*)[21]
Women's Lives:	Elizabeth Adler

Because fans of the new Romantic Suspense are more likely to request authors by name, we must verify first whether they seek those authors' Romances or Romantic Suspense titles. If they talk about a title, we can usually tell. Simply asking if it was suspenseful also achieves the desired result. Some of these authors now write Romantic Suspense exclusively, while others continue to write straight Romances. With the former group, we need to keep their Romance titles, cataloging them and adding to our collections when the author's newfound success prompts the reprinting of all her titles. Coulter continues to add to her historical Brides series in paperback, while publishing contemporary Romantic Suspense in hardcover (her FBI series).[22] Coulter is another author who has brought her Romance fans with her and attracted new fans by adding the element of danger to her books. This popularity in one genre is clearly a straightforward way to offer crossover into the other. We should watch for authors who write in more than one genre, as that helps us understand better what readers say they enjoy about one type of book and opens the door to the other.

Remember, too, that these authors may be published only in paperback and that they, too, may write in more than one genre. Award-winning author Anne Stuart writes Contemporary and Historical Romances as well as Contemporary Romantic Suspense, and all are characterized by dangerous heroes, humor (with witty repartee between hero and heroine), and steamy sexual scenes. Try *Black Ice* with its unassuming translator/heroine trying to make a little extra money and finding herself in real danger among illegal arms dealers in a French country estate.[23]

Sure Bets

Depending on what our readers are seeking, there are a number of Romantic Suspense authors who make Sure Bets. Du Maurier, Stewart, Holt, and Whitney have retained many of their loyal readers—and gained new fans—with their classic stories of women in jeopardy. Newer fans flock to Roberts, Hoag, Coulter, Robards, and Brown, all of whom attract readers by their presence on the best-seller lists, and these can certainly be successfully suggested to readers who do not mind more sex and violence.

Elizabeth Lowell's Romantic Suspense titles clearly depend on the romantic relationship as well as the Adventure and edgy Suspense elements. Romance readers will find that frisson of sexual tension that epitomizes Romances and the stereotypical first kiss, which, as in Romances, awakens passions that have lain dormant in these characters. Fans from the Suspense camp will appreciate the fast-paced action and building tension that leads to the story's resolution. In addition, the fascinating frames add another dimension to her stories. In *Always Time to Die*, the first in the St. Kilda Consulting series, genealogist Caroline May discovers unexpected ancestors in a prominent New Mexico politician's lineage—and finds her own life in danger.[24] Many of Lowell's titles make excellent Sure Bets.

Iris Johansen's Eve Duncan stories (*The Face of Deception* starts the series) are increasingly hard-edged, although they are still sought by fans who remember her historical novels of Adventure and Romance.[25] These more recent novels feature a forensic sculptor who lost her own child—who was abducted and murdered—and now seeks to identify the bones of other lost children. Stalking, graphic violence, building suspense, and an undercurrent of romance as well as the paranormal characterize these page-turners.

EXPANDING READERS' HORIZONS WITH WHOLE COLLECTION READERS' ADVISORY

Whom else might readers of Romantic Suspense enjoy? Fans of the traditional end of the genre might explore Cozy Mysteries with more adventure than puzzle. Try authors such as Elizabeth Peters and Kerry Greenwood's Phryne Fisher series, set in Australia between the first and second world wars. The more romantic Thrillers of Gayle Lynds may also appeal, but few new titles of this type are currently being published. Mary Higgins Clark's Suspense novels may have enough of a romantic tone to satisfy these readers, and they will appreciate the lack of graphic descriptions and strong language.

The reader who mentions best-selling authors such as Roberts and Brown is looking for the newer version of the genre. They may also enjoy titles of harder-edged Suspense, if they feature strong heroines, such as T. Jefferson Parker's *L.A. Outlaws*, featuring the exploits of Allison Murrieta.[26] They may also find some of the Medical Thrillers by authors such as Robin Cook and Tess Gerritsen (described in chapter 5, "Thrillers") satisfying, as these also often feature strong women in dangerous situations from which they must extricate themselves. See figure 3.3 for suggestions of links to other genres.

TRENDS

While most novels in this genre used to be single titles, now more and more are parts of series. Having the same heroine placed in jeopardy in every book demands a profession that lends itself to multiple dangerous cases. Thus, Coulter has created her FBI series, Johansen has a forensic sculptor who becomes involved in cases, and Dee Henderson's heroines may be on the police force.

Figure 3.3 *Expanding Readers' Horizons*

Authors to Take Readers beyond the Romantic Suspense Genre

Adrenaline:	Tess Gerritsen
	Gayle Lynds
Fantasy:	Laurell K. Hamilton (Meredith Gentry series)[27]
Historical Fiction:	Lauren K. Willig
Horror:	Kelley Armstrong
Mystery:	Kerry Greenwood
Romance:	Christine Feehan
Science Fiction:	David Weber
Westerns:	Kate Bridges

Crossover dominates the Romantic Suspense genre as it does most others. In addition to the expected overlap with the Romance and Suspense genres, there are increasing elements of the Mystery and Thriller genres in order to accommodate those more dangerous and investigative professions necessary to sustain a series character.

Paranormal elements have long been popular in this genre with its roots in Gothic Romances, but that trend has become even more pronounced. Popular Romance writers Kay Hooper, Roberts, Krentz/Quick, Johansen, and Lisa Jackson have all become known for the effective use of paranormal elements in their novels.

Fans of the traditional Romantic Suspense have likely seen the death of that type of novel, for the time being at least. As Gothics and Paranormal Romantic Suspense become more popular, they also tend to reflect the more modern values of today's Romantic Suspense, with graphic language and descriptive sex and violence.

Historical Romantic Suspense seems to be on the rise, as authors such as Quick have moved from Historical Romance to Romantic Suspense. Strong elements of suspense and danger blend with historical details and Romance in these novels.

Although many of us regret the demise of traditional Romantic Suspense, readers have certainly managed to adjust to the genre's new image, and there are probably more novels of Romantic Suspense on the best-seller lists than ever before. Readers, primarily women, remain true to this genre that reflects the importance of strong female characters caught in dangerous situations who rescue themselves as well as those they love. Seemingly as long as the genre continues to emphasize interesting and intense romantic relationships, the increasing level of explicit violence does not deter fans.

Notes

1. Edward Bulwer-Lytton, *Paul Clifford* (London: George Routledge and Sons, 1948).
2. Karen Robards, *Obsession* (New York: G. P. Putnam's Sons, 2007).
3. Lisa Jackson, *Shiver* (New York: Kensington, 2006).
4. Nora Roberts, *High Noon* (New York: G. P. Putnam's Sons, 2007).
5. Sandra Brown, *Chill Factor* (New York: Simon and Schuster, 2005).
6. Amanda Quick, Arcane Society series, beginning with *Second Sight* (New York: G. P. Putnam's Sons, 2006).
7. Elizabeth Lowell, *Amber Beach* (New York: Avon, 1997); Lowell, *Moving Target* (New York: Morrow, 2001); Lowell, *Always Time to Die* (New York: Morrow, 2005).
8. Roberts, The Circle trilogy, beginning with *Morrigan's Cross* (New York: Jove, 2006); Roberts, Sign of the Seven trilogy, beginning with *Blood Brothers* (New York: Jove, 2007); Roberts, In the Garden trilogy, beginning with *Blue Dahlia* (New York: Jove, 2004); Roberts, Key trilogy, beginning with *Key of Light* (New York: Jove, 2003); Roberts, Three Sisters Island trilogy, beginning with *Dance upon the Air* (New York: Jove, 2001).
9. J. D. Robb, *Naked in Death* (New York: Berkley, 1995).
10. Suzanne Brockmann, Team Sixteen series, beginning with *Unsung Hero* (New York: Ivy, 2000).
11. Brockmann, *All through the Night: A Troubleshooter Christmas* (New York: Ballantine, 2007); Brockmann cited above.
12. Dee Henderson, *Before I Wake* (Carol Stream, IL: Tyndale House, 2006).
13. Elizabeth Peters, *Borrower of the Night* (New York: Dodd, Mead, 1973).
14. Roberts, *Blue Smoke* (New York: G. P. Putnam's Sons, 2005).
15. Cherry Adair, *On Thin Ice* (New York: Ballantine, 2004).
16. Roberts cited above.
17. Debbie Macomber, Cedar Cove series, beginning with *16 Lighthouse Road* (Don Mills, ON: Mira, 2001).
18. Peters cited above.
19. Beverly Jenkins, *Deadly Sexy* (New York: Avon, 2007).
20. Iris Johansen, Eve Duncan series, beginning with *The Face of Deception* (New York: Bantam, 1998).
21. Lowell, *Fire and Rain* (New York: Silhouette, 1990).
22. Catherine Coulter, Brides series, beginning with *The Sherbrooke Bride* (New York: Jove, 1992); Coulter, FBI series, beginning with *The Cove* (New York: Jove, 1996).
23. Anne Stuart, *Black Ice* (Don Mills, ON: Mira, 2005).
24. Lowell cited above.
25. Johansen cited above.
26. T. Jefferson Parker, *L.A. Outlaws: A Novel* (New York: Dutton, 2008).
27. Laurell K. Hamilton, Meredith Gentry series, beginning with *A Kiss of Shadows* (New York: Ballantine, 2000).

4

SUSPENSE

Suspense is a genre that suffers from an ambiguous name. The term *suspenseful* is easily understood, and we use it to describe myriad titles and a number of genres. However, publishers, reviewers, readers, and librarians are never quite certain what is meant when a book is labeled "Suspense" or when books in that genre are sought. Yet when readers come to librarians looking for fast-paced books that they do not want to put down, often it is Suspense fiction we put in their hands. Just as Suspense movies draw a crowd of captivated viewers, their book counterparts encourage the burning of the midnight oil simply to see the book to its satisfactory conclusion. Like other books and films that fall within the Adrenaline genres, Suspense demands a page-turning pace that draws readers in from the first page and keeps them reading to the final twist.

A DEFINITION

Suspense is an important element in many fiction genres, and any number of books in other genres might be called suspenseful. However, the key to identifying books that fit within the strict confines of this genre is that suspense is the focus of the book. In Suspense novels, all else—Mystery, Espionage, Romance, Adventure—is secondary to this building of tension and uneasiness. As Andrew Klavan wrote in his article "The Uses of Suspense," "Suspense is not about the things that are happening; it's about the things that might happen, that threaten to happen."[1]

Titles that fit within the strict confines of the Suspense genre feature a story in which tension builds. We know that something is going to happen; there is danger lurking, as yet perhaps unseen. A sense of menace permeates the book from early on. (In fact, many authors use a prologue to reveal the dangerous situation, then go back and tell the story up to that point, with the reader kept on the edge of his chair, understanding all along what will happen soon and anxiously anticipating the danger awaiting the protagonist.) We know that the protagonist is in peril; and even though we readers know much of what is going on and sometimes even who is responsible, we feel the protagonist's plight and anticipate his discoveries as he seeks the sinister cause of this deadly threat. Although we readers are really a step ahead of the protagonist, we are still kept on edge. Like the protagonist, we want to find out what will happen next and why. We eagerly anticipate the twist with which the best authors end their stories. Apprehension—this building of tension—forces readers to read quickly to find out how the plot will be resolved.

Part of the difficulty in defining this genre is that suspense plays a key role in many genres. Thrillers, Mystery, Romantic Suspense, Horror, Adventure, and even Romance rely on suspenseful situations to intensify their stories. Yet in each of these, the central focus is on something other than suspense. Mysteries, for example, create a puzzle and it is important to offer clues while withholding vital information from the reader. In Suspense the reader needs to know almost everything and certainly more than the protagonist. In both Mystery and Suspense, there is a puzzle, but in a Mystery, the reader's (and detective's) goal is to get into the puzzle, to discover its workings, in order to solve it. In Suspense the protagonist must get out of a puzzle, generally a confusing set of sinister circumstances, to escape and survive. In a Mystery, something has happened, and we want to find out "whodunit." In Suspense, something is going to happen; there is a sense of menace, lurking danger, and we are held in delicious anticipation as we try to discover what, why, and when.

The pattern of Suspense novels, as discussed in detail below, often parallels the pattern of Horror novels, with danger entering the sphere of someone's normal life. In Suspense, however, the danger comes from human agents, while in Horror the danger usually contains an element of the supernatural. Additionally, in Horror the protagonist does not always survive, while in Suspense the survival of the hero or heroine is generally guaranteed.

Other Adrenaline novels also feature the fast-paced chase sequences that appear frequently in the Suspense genre, but the distinguishing feature of these chases in Suspense novels is that the protagonist often does not know who is chasing him or her—or why. Along with the protagonist we must sort out the history of events that has led to this particular situation. In Adventure and Thrillers, on the other hand, the chase is part of the action emphasis of the story line and serves to move the plot. In Romantic Suspense, suspense must share top billing with the romantic elements; thus, it does not dominate the story as completely.

Traditional Romances often add a measure of suspense to move the plot along quickly. Suspense introduces an element of danger and apprehension to enliven the plot. In these and all other suspenseful novels, however, the suspense is secondary, a device for creating a more compelling story. In books that fall within the Suspense genre, the building of tension is one of the keys to the book's success and readers' appreciation.

Suspense novels generate a sense of menace from the first pages, and pacing increases as we come closer and closer to the danger. Since readers are often privy to the thoughts of both hero and villain and know more than the protagonists, they are kept at the edge of their chairs, anticipating every danger and turning pages to reach the satisfactory conclusion. All of these characteristics are vital in the creation of Suspense, but the most important, and the key to the appeal of the genre, is the point of view from which the story is told and the way it draws the reader into the story. The reader knows of whom and what to be frightened, even though the protagonist does not. The reader is kept on edge, always anticipating the danger to come. Even if the hero thinks he is safe, the reader knows he is not. In Suspense, the author draws the reader into the protagonist's story and emotions. We feel and see the danger; we see it build but are powerless to act, to do anything but keep on reading. See figure 4.1 for a list of characteristics.

CHARACTERISTICS AND THE GENRE'S APPEAL

Pacing

Suspense novels exhibit a characteristic pacing. In most cases the action takes place within a narrow time frame, often only a matter of days. There may be flashbacks to previous events to fill in details, but the actual story moves quickly within a limited time frame. Some books are even laid out in sections, day by day, or even with specific times throughout the day. In Jeffery Deaver's *The Sleeping Doll*, time/date/place stamps at the start of each chapter orient readers, while the cat-and-mouse chases move the pace at a frantic speed.[2] Along with short chapters and alternating points of view, Deaver also employs cliffhanger chapter endings, often reversing expectations, to drive the pace in this complex tale of a California Bureau

Figure 4.1 *Characteristics of Suspense*

1. The action usually takes place within a narrow time frame, often in only a few days, and the reader is made aware of the danger to the protagonist early on.

2. A dark, menacing atmosphere is essential and underscores the danger to the protagonist. As the story unfolds, tension grows, and the reader, because he knows the danger, feels this uneasiness and uncertainty even before the protagonist senses anything is amiss.

3. In the genre's distinctive style, the action begins early, often in a prologue or first chapter that sets up the danger and leaves readers anticipating the final confrontation. Then the plotline skips back in time and builds to that point, with suspense mounting and pacing increasing on every page.

4. The reader empathizes with the protagonist and his peril. However, the reader often follows the antagonist's thoughts and actions, too, and thus knows more than the protagonist.

5. Stories follow a similar pattern, with unexpected danger from an unknown source intruding into the protagonist's normal life. The resolution is brought about through a confrontation between the hero or heroine and the villain, and the protagonist survives.

6. While some authors create elaborate backgrounds and establish a strong sense of place, with others the tension and building suspense are more important than setting. Softer-edged Suspense tends to focus more on descriptions of characters, while hard-edged Suspense features gritty depictions of crime scenes.

of Investigation interrogator and body-language expert on the trail of a Pied Piper–like escaped serial murderer. There's danger at every turn, and the plot twists contribute to the fast pace, despite the wealth of investigative details.

The telescoping of events and relationships into exceptionally short time frames intensifies the action and sense of danger. This strategy tends to make Suspense books compelling reads. The books grip the reader; the complex and action-filled plots force us to keep reading; we cannot put the book down, and when we must, the story stays with us, drawing us back to finish the book.

As is clear in Deaver's books and many more, Suspense is also engendered by the action—that cat-and-mouse game and ultimately the chase.

In most cases, the tension builds early and never lets up. Especially in the harder-edged novels which generally star police or other law enforcement figures, the pacing seems relentless, with fewer breaks, building inexorably to the final confrontation between hero and villain. Once the scene is set, we are seldom allowed to return to normalcy until all is resolved; the tension and the knowledge that the situation is so dangerous sustain the mood. As in the Suspense movies that keep us on the edge of our seats until the last scene, there is a sense of continuous movement, of action, and the reader is engrossed in the plot and the building suspense. Twist follows twist and layers of suspense unfold and force the reader quickly through the book.

As in other Adrenaline genres, short chapters (just three or four pages) often propel the pace as well. James Patterson and Harlan Coben are masters of this style, and as the tension builds, readers find themselves unable to resist reading just one more chapter, then another—until they find themselves at the end of the book.

Tone/Mood

Suspense is also characterized by a special atmosphere, an uneasiness that is essential. The author often uses setting to create a heightened sense of danger, through an isolated physical setting or, more simply and frequently, just through mood. In Suspense much of the action takes place at night or on rainy or cloudy days. There are not many cheery, sunny days in Suspense novels, and even the sunshine often takes on ominous overtones. This is often the case in Greg Iles's hard-edged Suspense novels. Set in the South, they feature dangerous villains and gory murders. The sunshine and daylight there offer no safety; instead, the murky heat and humidity underscore the menacing tone and the nightmare situation. On the other hand, John Sandford's titles featuring Minneapolis detective Lucas Davenport usually take place in the winter. The frigid, desolate landscape and the inhospitable climate can be just as effective in establishing the dangerous tone of the story.

Authors mix these elements to underscore the danger to the protagonist, and the sinister atmosphere thus created is crucial to the readers' impression of the story. Sometimes there is a nightmare quality to this frame, with the hero caught up in a situation he cannot understand and pursued although he does not know why or by whom. Alfred Hitchcock mastered this technique in his movies, with the sense of menace lurking just below the serene surface. However it is used, this menacing atmosphere is crucial to the readers' impression of the story.

Style/Language

In this genre, the action generally starts early in the book. Suspense novels typically do not rely on the longer setup of events found in related genres, such as Mystery or even Political/Espionage Thrillers. The story unfolds quickly in the first few pages. In his recent stand-alone Suspense novel, *Blue Heaven,* C. J. Box opens the novel with two children on the run.[3] They've witnessed a murder in the woods, and now they know neither whom to trust nor where to run. Box fills in details later, but this opening scene hooks readers, drawing them into the children's plight.

In fact, many authors use a prologue to introduce the villain and set up the atmosphere of danger and uncertainty before the story itself even begins. In *I Heard That Song Before,* Mary Higgins Clark uses a prologue to raise our suspicions of her heroine's husband.[4] In a scene set twenty-two years earlier, young Kathryn Lansing, the landscaper's daughter, accompanies her father to watch the festivities at a large estate where he works. She overhears a cryptic conversation—and the next day, a young woman who had attended the party is missing. Peter, the son of the house, was cleared of blame, and he and Kathryn meet again much later and marry. Now when a body is found on the estate, suspicion again points to Peter. This early scene primes us to suspect him, and as Clark fills in the story with details, past and present, the tension continues to build.

Another stylistic technique involves a roller-coaster style that builds the feeling of dreaded anticipation. Clark typifies this style, and each chapter starts afresh, usually from a different character's point of view, so the chapters begin with suspense at low ebb and build to climax, a mini-cliffhanger. Then the new chapter, from another character's point of view, drops the reader down to that initial level again. This flow keeps us reading; we want to know what will happen, but we also get some respite from potentially dangerous situations. However, we read quickly to return to the story line that was left hanging at the end of the previous chapter.

Characterization

Many Suspense novels feature a unique point of view. In the best, readers know the thoughts of both main characters, the hero and the villain, and thus more than the protagonist knows. This technique heightens the feeling of uncertainty and builds tension, because we know the danger the character is walking into before he or she does. In *The Torment of Others,* a hard-edged Suspense novel featuring series characters Tony Hill and Carol Jordan, Val McDermid even puts the prologue in the killer's point of view and then alternates throughout between the killer and series characters.[5] Although we identify with the protagonist, we also recognize the danger and are drawn more completely into the story, hoping the villain is not successful in his sinister plans.

This link between reader and protagonist is a powerful tool. If the reader does not feel it, the story may be suspenseful, but it will not be as successful. The degree to which the reader is pulled in is important: In the best stories we feel every threat to the protagonist and the shock of every revelation, whether we want to or not. The mood created by this device can be very intense, even chilling, and this is exactly what readers expect.

Like the protagonist we often cannot tell exactly who the villain is until it is almost too late. We may not be surprised by the identity of the villain, because we have been following his "voice" since the beginning— sometimes in separate chapters, sometimes alerted by a different typeface. Although discovering who the villain is remains important, of even more interest is why the protagonist is in jeopardy. We have more clues than the protagonist, so it is often possible for us to guess the villain's identity. Why the deadly danger exists is often the more difficult question.

Protagonists are often ordinary people whose lives are suddenly invaded by someone very dangerous, and they often do not know why. This creates a nightmare quality. Harlan Coben excels at removing his characters from normal worlds. Within the first few pages, Coben's characters find themselves wrenched from their safe lives and caught up in very dangerous situations. Coben disarms readers as well as his characters; like them, we no longer know whom to trust or what to believe. In *No Second Chance,* a pediatric reconstructive surgeon's life is forever altered when he is shot.[6] He awakens twelve days later to find his wife shot and killed and his baby kidnapped. Why? By whom? Although the story extends over a longer time span than many Suspense novels, the pacing never flags, as the hero, along with the reader, peels away the layers of the complicated plot to discover answers.

In many harder-edged Suspense novels, the protagonist is more likely a law enforcement officer, rather than an "everyman." If the hero is a law enforcement professional whose role is to stop the violent antagonist before more people are hurt or killed, he may not actually be in physical danger himself until the very end. However, throughout the novel he is engaged in an intricately developed cat-and-mouse game with the villain. His life and the life of the person he is trying to protect are both in danger.

Damaged characters are also popular in many Suspense novels. Thomas Harris's chilling *Hannibal* practically forces us to sympathize with this notorious villain by offering even more dangerous antagonists.[7] Chelsea Cain's visceral and disturbing debut novel *Heartsick* follows an escaped serial murderer.[8] One protagonist is a police detective who had formerly captured infamous serial murderer Gretchen Lowell, but she held him captive and tortured him before her eventual arrest. Even now, years later, he remains in her thrall. Haunted heroes and villains add another level to our relationship with the characters in Suspense novels.

Story Line

In genre fiction the story line generally follows a prescribed formula and Suspense is no exception. Readers of Suspense recognize the pattern immediately. A nightmare intrudes into the hero or heroine's normal life. He or she works out how to overcome this threat. The ending brings the confrontation between good and evil, and the protagonist always survives, although bodies may be strewn along the way, and even characters we care about may die.

This pattern sets up the inevitable chase scene, usually at the end of the novel, but sometimes at intervals throughout. The protagonist and villain have been skirting each other, but in the end there is always a classic chase, with the protagonist in real physical jeopardy, and a showdown. All previous action and atmosphere generate the tension that leads to this confrontation. The buildup to this final scene drives the pace of the novel.

Fans of Lee Child will certainly find this pattern familiar. Child's hero, Jack Reacher, comes into town, like a paladin of old, uncovers the dangerous situation, investigates, and eventually finds himself face to face with his opponent. Child develops complex plots rich in detail, but despite the complexity, the story moves inexorably to this concluding scene. There may be dangerous confrontations along the way, and each adds another layer to the ultimate peril we know awaits us. Although his books don't have as much page-turning action as some others, the intensity never flags, holding readers captivated as it builds. Even though we know Reacher will be successful and survive, we're engrossed as the details of his plan unfold.

Bad Luck and Trouble is a good example of this technique.[9] When Reacher realizes that someone is killing off old military colleagues, he calls in those remaining from the elite group to investigate. The complexity increases as the plot careers along to that final showdown.

This confrontation between hero and villain is important to the success of a Suspense novel. The more closely matched the two, the more tension is created. The match does not have to be exact. There may be a physically strong antagonist pitted against a weaker but more intelligent protagonist, as in Mary Higgins Clark's books. The woman may not be a physical match for the male threatening her, but she escapes because she outwits the villain. In harder-edged Suspense, the protagonist is often a law enforcement officer who acts for the beleaguered victim. Although the dynamic may be different, the necessity of this confrontation and of its outcome remains the same.

The basic plot structure may be similar across the genre, but there are still enough twists and unpredictability in the best of Suspense to keep us guessing as well. The pattern may follow an expected course, and the reader may know a great deal about the danger, but the twists keep us turning pages. Keeping the reader guessing about the outcome is particularly difficult in the numerous series this genre seems to inspire. An excellent example is James Hall's Thorn series. The reclusive Thorn's home base is a shack on Key West, but the suspenseful investigations that attract his talents lead him farther afield. In *Magic City* he's in Miami to care for girlfriend Alexandra Rafferty's father, who has Alzheimer's.[10] The father's 1964 black-and-white photo provides the link to a murder, drives Thorn's investigation, and puts everyone in danger. Each novel features an evocative, menacing atmosphere; an intelligent, inventive protagonist; and relentless pacing.

Frame/Setting

Settings for Suspense novels are almost always contemporary. Although suspense may be an element in books with historical settings, novels within the genre are set almost exclusively in the present day. The reason for this likely relates to both the necessity for immediacy in the stories and the pacing. Creating an effective historical setting takes time away from the suspense, and such a setting may seem too foreign, too alien for the reader identification necessary to make these such compelling reading.

In some genres, the background details are of prime importance. In Suspense, the strenuous pace doesn't allow for as much development of the background. However, many authors still manage to provide the details readers appreciate. Hall, in the title mentioned above, includes extensive details of Miami politics, especially events back in the 1960s, and of the craft of photography. David Hewson's Nic Costa series, set in contemporary Rome, takes advantage of the art, history, church history, and archaeology of the region. The danger of adding all these details is that they might slow the plot. In the best stories, they never do.

In Suspense, the details we get as readers more likely describe the characters or the police and investigative procedures. In the softer-edged end of the Suspense genre, we learn more physically about the protagonist, usually a woman, and her lifestyle. At the hard-edged end, readers find countless details of both the crimes and police procedures, in part because the protagonist is usually a law enforcement officer.

Violence forms a necessary backdrop to these life-and-death tales. At the softer end, there are stalking and threats; the harder-edged novels are grittier throughout and the violence is frequent and graphic. Sexual violence or other sexual situations, along with stronger language, play an important role. We see the underside of life, a much bleaker portrayal of the world than the more romantic view of the softer-edged novels. Crimes and criminals are more sordid at this end of the genre. Descriptions are also much more graphic; we see the bodies, rendered in intimate and gruesome detail, and the victims are often described during and after the killings. Characters are involved in intimately depicted life-and-death situations, well beyond the stalking and threats of the softer-edged titles, and the language used underlines the deadly nature of the situation portrayed. On the other hand, many readers who abhor violence in novels have commented on how totally absorbed they have become in several of these harder-edged novels. I find myself agreeing with these readers who acknowledge the frequent and graphic violence in James Patterson and others—but who cannot stop turning the pages because the story is so engrossing and compelling.

Let me add, however, that there are not necessarily multiple and frequent graphically violent scenes in these books, although the impact of the scenes may leave the reader with that impression. The harder edge comes not only from violent episodes, but also from the reader's and the protagonist's perceptions that the situation and the villain are out of control. Even everyday activities become more sinister, when they become a part of this deadly game between hero and villain.

KEY AUTHORS

This genre offers a wealth of popular, best-selling authors, most of whom write the more violent, harder-edged Suspense. Must-know names on that end of the genre include Harlan Coben, Lee Child, Jeffery Deaver, James Patterson, and John Sandford. At the softer end of the genre, Mary Higgins Clark stands almost alone.

Coben began his career as a Mystery writer with a popular series featuring a sports agent. However, his first stand-alone Suspense title, *Tell No One*, jump-started his career.[11] In that title, a man suddenly receives a message from his wife, killed eight years earlier. Is she still alive? His search uncovers old secrets and puts his own life in danger. Intricately twisted and terrifying but believable plots, frantic pacing, sympathetic protagonists pitted against evil villains, and a menacing tone keep readers burning the midnight oil with every new Coben title.

With his Jack Reacher series, starring a character who lives disconnected from the grid but, like a medieval knight errant, arrives to save the day, Child has set a high standard for the Suspense hero. Like the heroes of Westerns, Reacher is a wanderer and a vigilante who meets danger and brings justice wherever he goes. Child's moral dramas feature fine writing, fast pacing, a menacing atmosphere (leavened by his dry wit), and intricately layered plots. *The Killing Floor* starts the series.[12]

Best known for his long-running series starring quadriplegic criminalist Lincoln Rhyme and Amelia Sachs, Deaver writes series Suspense novels and stand-alones that pit his characters against the ticking clock. The frenetic pacing drives his character-rich stories and makes them almost impossible to put down. Investigative and often violent, these tales also possess a nightmare quality, intensified by the telescoped time frame. *The Bone Collector* (also a movie starring Denzel Washington) is the first Rhyme novel.[13]

James Patterson's is one of the most recognizable names in the genre, possibly in all genre fiction. Initially famous for his ongoing series starring psychiatrist and Washington, DC, policeman, then FBI agent, Alex Cross (beginning with *Along Came a Spider*), Patterson continues to write blockbuster Suspense novels alone and with coauthors.[14] His second series, the Women's Murder Club, stars four female San Francisco professionals—a judge, a newspaperwoman, a coroner, and a policewoman—who become involved in dangerous cases.[15] Fans flock to his fast-paced novels (where no chapter is longer than four pages), filled with appealing protagonists, depraved villains, twisted plots, and heart-stopping tension.

John Sandford stands out as a solid practitioner of the Suspense genre. His most popular series, nearly twenty books all with *Prey* in the title, feature Minneapolis detective Lucas Davenport (*Rules of Prey* is the first).[16] In addition, he has several nonseries Suspense titles, a Davenport spin-off series starring Minneapolis detective Virgil Flowers, and the Kidd novels, featuring a criminal and computer whiz protagonist.[17] Sandford's Prey books in particular are popular with readers and critics alike. They offer a consistently high degree of suspense, and, of course, the concomitant satisfactions of an ongoing character whom readers know and to whom they relate. His melancholy hero must conquer his own self-doubts in each adventure, as he uses his sharp deductive skills to fight corruption (within both the police and criminal worlds) and to nab serial killers before they can kill again. Elegant writing, strong characterizations, and fast-paced suspense characterize his series and nonseries titles.

While these authors above all write hard-edged, violent Suspense, Mary Higgins Clark has honed the softer-edged end of the spectrum to an art form, and her enormous popularity makes her the most recognized name in the genre. Her stories feature women in danger, but not the weak, clingy heroines of the Gothics, an eighteenth- and nineteenth-century predecessor of Romantic Suspense. And although some readers may consider her writing generically "Mysteries," Clark clearly falls within the Suspense genre, with puzzles to be escaped, not solved. These stories do not focus on who, as do Mysteries, but why. Clark's heroines are smart career women, not passive victims. They play an active role in extricating themselves from dangerous situations. Clark also keeps her novels up to date by centering the plots around timely topics: health care and beauty issues, post-traumatic stress disorder, and serial killers. Although they are women of substance (and the books often contain rich-and-famous elements), these heroines are always down to earth and nice; certainly they come across as very appealing to Clark's fans. In contrast to the harder-edged Suspense, these novels exhibit a more romantic worldview, in the sense that we see less violence and more details of the characters' ordinary lives. However, these are not to be confused with Romantic Suspense, covered in depth in chapter 3, in which Romance genre characteristics play a more important role and a romantic relationship involving the heroine is a necessity. There may be relationships, but romantic interests are very low on the scale of what is important in these novels. Stalking and threats of violence play important roles in Clark's novels, and they help establish the menacing atmosphere that drives the pacing and the action. And while her formula seems simple enough—classy heroine threatened by an unknown danger from which she must save herself—other authors tend to add more sex or violence. No one matches Clark for topical and genteel tales of danger and suspense. Old-fashioned story telling and topical subjects set her books apart.

WHAT WE KNOW ABOUT FANS

Fans of the Suspense genre often read a wide range of suspenseful books. What they primarily seek are fast-paced books in which they identify with the protagonist and share his or her rocky ride to the satisfactory resolution of the story. They read Suspense to find the elements described below.

First, readers choose Suspense because of the pacing of these books. They expect to be hooked in the first few pages and pulled quickly into the story and the fate of its protagonist. If the story does not grab them immediately or pull them in totally, they do not consider it a good, or typical, representative of the genre. They also expect the story and the growing apprehension to pull them along. The story must be engrossing and capture their interest; they read with breathless anticipation, turning the pages quickly to find out how the story will be resolved.

Readers expect to follow the point of view of the protagonist but also to know what is happening with the antagonist as well. They anticipate having some inkling of what will happen, and they derive pleasure and satisfaction from knowing more than the protagonist. However, they also expect a final twist at the end, a twist consistent with the plot, but one that catches them off guard and underlines the fact that even they have not foreseen all of the author's stratagems.

Closely related is the fact that the reader knows that the protagonist will survive. Whether this book is a part of a series or not, readers understand that the hero or heroine will not be one of the victims. Even if the ending is not always precisely upbeat, there is resolution and the hero is among those left alive.

Readers know that the plot is leading up to a confrontation between good and evil, the heart of many genre books. In this genre, because we know more than the protagonist, we feel the evil looming sooner, and the intensity that leads to the final confrontation drives the pace and holds us spellbound, reading as quickly as we can, anticipating the twists along the way but never quite certain how all will work out in the end.

Finally, readers may seek particular themes in the Suspense titles they read. They may want novels about serial killers or ones that feature

---

Figure 4.2 *An Introduction to the Suspense Genre*

Suspense Writers to Try, If You Enjoy . . .

Adrenaline:	Jeff Abbott
	Jeffery Deaver
	James Grippando
Gentle:	Mary Higgins Clark
Historical Fiction:	Matthew Pearl
Horror:	Greg Iles
	John Saul (*Perfect Nightmare*)[18]
Humor:	Dean R. Koontz (Odd Thomas series)[19]
Inspirational:	Ted Dekker
Literary:	Laurie R. King
Multicultural:	James Patterson (Alex Cross)
Mystery:	David Hewson
	John Sandford
Psychological Suspense:	Chelsea Cain
	Laurie R. King
	Dean R. Koontz
Romantic Suspense:	Lisa Gardner
True Crime:	Sarah Lovett

---

a forensic pathologist, rather than a detective. Reference resources can be useful in identifying these. Remember, too, that patrons asking for these themes may also enjoy suspenseful titles in other genres.

Readers (and librarians) who are fans of other genres but are interested in exploring the Suspense genre might sample titles from the list in figure 4.2. These are Suspense authors and titles that share similarities with books in other genres with which readers might be familiar.

THE READERS' ADVISORY INTERVIEW

Probably the most important factor to consider in working with readers is the amount of violence they will tolerate in the Suspense novels they seek, since many fans have strong feelings on this topic. Some prefer the softer-edged Suspense, typified by Clark's writing, while others accept more violence. It is important to have a mental list of authors in mind to suggest, to help us establish an acceptable level, just as it is vital to suggest a range of authors and let readers choose.

Note that it may be more difficult to offer the harder-edged Suspense titles to patrons, simply because it is awkward to inquire whether they like a lot of violence in the books they read. Formulating a question so as not to offend on some level is not an easy task. We might ask, "Do you mind a book that has vivid descriptions of violence?" *Mind* seems to be a key word, replacing *like* or *enjoy* in putting a different slant on the issue. When I know, and certainly if a patron inquires, I will try to indicate the level of violence or strong language. On the other hand, violence in books, television, and movies has become more ingrained in our popular culture. Unless readers comment on wanting something "like Mary Higgins Clark writes," it is unlikely they will notice more violent scenes unless the descriptions are extreme.

If I have someone who wants to read Suspense, I ask the reader to name an author he or she has enjoyed or is in the mood to read. If the reader mentions Clark, verify the appeal characteristics: "You like normal, ordinary people put in jeopardy; the body and violence offstage, but a real sense of danger as the villain stalks the hero or heroine." Readers of Clark may also enjoy Amateur Detective Mysteries, if there are a female protagonist, enough Suspense, and not too much violence (perhaps Susan Wittig Albert, Diane Mott Davidson, daughter Carol Higgins Clark, or Gillian Roberts), and Romantic Suspense (Iris Johansen or Karen Robards), if there is not too much romance or violence.

If the reader mentions John Sandford or another writer of harder-edged Suspense, verify the desire for details of the crime, perhaps more violently presented, and the relentless pacing. These readers may also like nonfiction true crime books, because they appreciate details of the crime and characters involved, and they are not interested in figuring out the identity of the murderer. They may also read hard-edged crime novels, such as those by Andrew Vachss, Elmore Leonard, and Ken Bruen, as these portray strong protagonists caught up in dangerous situations. In these, however, the bleak atmosphere may be the link to the Suspense genre, rather than a similar plotline and the building of suspense that characterize books that fall more strictly within the genre.

Remember also if comments from the reader during any readers' advisory interview lead you to suspect Suspense may be a good suggestion, describe examples from the range of the genre and give the reader choices. Readers who talk generally about fast-paced books or page-turners often appreciate Suspense. We need to remember that our role is not to slot titles into specific genre places but to see how they might appeal to a range of readers. Most readers do not choose books solely by genre classification. They enjoy certain elements in books and seek to find those characteristics in others. Suspense titles make good crossover reading for fans of other genres (see figure 4.2), and Suspense readers often find books that appeal to them in other, related genres, as indicated in figure 4.3 later in this chapter.

As in all genres, there is a range of what readers read and do not read, and we cannot always understand or anticipate their reactions. It is not uncommon to hear readers state they will not read any books in which children are placed in jeopardy, but Clark is one of their favorite authors. Because Clark has frequently employed the child-in-jeopardy theme, especially in her earlier books, it is clear that there is something in the way she handles the subject that is not offensive to the reader. We need to remember also that books affect us in different ways at different times, and we should be open to what patrons say they are seeking in the books they read. It is useful, too, to remind readers that if something offends them in a title, they should simply close the book and return it. There are many more possibilities that might please them, and they should certainly not spend time with a book that doesn't satisfy them.

Unlike some other genres, in Suspense the setting is usually less important to readers. If patrons request particular locations or settings, reference resources often lead us to suggestions. Generally, however, fans are seeking a particular feel generated in fast-paced books that spiral to a satisfying conclusion.

Just as we can often recognize Thrillers by the book jackets, we can often identify Suspense from the titles. Jeff Abbott's one-word titles—*Panic* and *Fear*—are certainly indicative of what awaits the reader.[20] Lisa Gardner's *Hide, Gone,* and *Alone* are equally effective.[21] Jackets can be revealing too. Currently red and black indicate Suspense in publishing circles, so, in an interview with a reader, we can make an educated guess from the cover alone.

Sure Bets

Suspense is a very popular genre at my library, and in addition to those authors who appear regularly on the best-seller lists (especially Child, Clark, Deaver, Coben, Patterson, and Sandford), we frequently have reserve queues for many Suspense authors. One of my Sure Bet authors remains Thomas Perry. His Jane Whitefield series, starring a part Native American guide who creates new identities for people on the run, worked for a wide range of readers, and his recent stand-alone titles are equally effective. Part of his appeal, and what makes him a good Sure Bet, is that he crosses genre boundaries, adding Thriller, Mystery, Crime, and sometimes Romance elements to many of his stories. Fast-paced, violent, and compulsively readable, Perry's elegant Suspense novels offer the action, building tension, and layers of story that fans appreciate. His recent *Nightlife* features a shape-shifting female serial murderer, a Portland homicide detective, and a Los Angeles private investigator caught up in a deadly chase.[22]

Although he has left his popular Lou Boldt/Daphne Matthews series set against the moody Seattle climate, Ridley Pearson has begun a new series set in Sun Valley, Idaho. *Killer Weekend,* the first, is a classic Suspense novel.[23] It takes place literally over a weekend; we know the villain early on and follow him and the thoughtful hero; the cleverly constructed plot offers unexpected twists; and the suspense builds throughout the novel with dangers looming ever nearer as the hero sorts out the plot threads. There's also the menacing atmosphere to contend with—a strong sense of foreboding and attacking animals as well as violence in the natural landscape. Give it to fans of Michael McGarrity's or William Kent Krueger's Mysteries where landscape plays an important role.

T. Jefferson Parker is another author of Sure Bets for Suspense fans. *Storm Runners* features a sublime first sentence, which sets up the story and reader anticipation.[24] In this edgy novel, which also includes fascinating details of water and weather issues in the Los Angeles area, someone is after the protagonists (ex-LA detective Matt Stromsoe and television weatherwoman Frankie Hatfield). Despite the wealth of investigative and weather details, the story spins along, with the sense of foreboding building in the edgy atmosphere.

EXPANDING READERS' HORIZONS WITH WHOLE COLLECTION READERS' ADVISORY

Faced with Suspense readers who have read everything by their favorite authors or are interested in ranging farther afield, we have a variety of directions to pursue, because so many genres rely on elements of Suspense to move the plot.

Other Adrenaline genres provide numerous possibilities. Adventure offers stories of missions fraught with danger, and suspense builds along with the danger as the participants reach their goal. Try Steve Berry's stand-alone titles as well as his series featuring ex-CIA operative and rare book collector Cotton Malone, or any book by Matthew Reilly and James Rollins. In Thrillers, tension builds as the story races to the denouement. In addition, there is often a chase, and the protagonist is involved in ferreting out "why?" rather than "who?" Titles by John Case and David Baldacci make good suggestions. Of course, Romantic Suspense depends on the Suspense element in equal measure with Romance. Catherine Coulter, J. D. Robb, and Iris Johansen all offer titles that Suspense fans might enjoy, if they don't mind the additional romantic elements.

Fantasy quests make good suggestions for Suspense readers, as they share much of the same adventure appeal. Raymond E. Feist (his Riftwar series) and Robert Jordan (Wheel of Time series) offer the mix of adventure and intrigue that create suspense.[25] Other titles, John Connolly's *Book of Lost Things* for example, exhibit a nightmare tone that might also appeal to Suspense fans.[26] In Science Fiction, on the other hand, the suspense may be part of the unknown and unexpected intervening in the story. Frank Herbert's *Dune* and its sequels certainly build to suspenseful episodes that move the story, as do titles many by Catherine Asaro.[27]

Mystery provides perhaps the greatest scope for crossover across the spectrum of the genre. As I mentioned above, Amateur Detective Mysteries (Diane Mott Davidson, Kerry Greenwood, Elizabeth Peters) are good suggestions for readers who prefer less violent Suspense, and Private Investigator and Police Detective Mysteries (Laura Lippman, Sara Paretsky, George Pelecanos) often work for readers at the harder-edged end of the spectrum. Edna Buchanan's Cold Case Squad series even offers a suspenseful prologue, along with building suspense throughout.[28]

Although Psychological Suspense generally lacks the faster pace of the Suspense genre, it creates a similar chill. This is not necessarily the crossover genre for readers of Clark and the softer end of the genre, as there is generally a very dark cast to the books and often violence. Carol Goodman's novels might work for Clark fans, with their plucky heroines and secrets from the past, while Peter Abrahams's chilling and often violent novels make a good suggestion for readers of harder-edged Suspense.

From the nonfiction collection, Suspense fans might also enjoy True Crime (Ann Rule) and True Adventure (Sebastian Junger) books. They usually know the outcome from the beginning, but they do in Suspense novels as well. They read to see how things will be worked out, not to know that they are, and the same intensity of a suspenseful story will carry many readers through. See figure 4.3 for the names of other authors to suggest.

Figure 4.3   *Expanding Readers' Horizons*

Authors to Take Readers beyond the Suspense Genre

Adrenaline:	David Baldacci
	Steve Berry
	John Case
	Matthew Reilly
	John Rollins
Fantasy:	John Connolly (*Book of Lost Things*)
	Raymond E. Feist
	Robert Jordan
Historical Fiction:	Matthew Pearl
History:	Erik Larson
Horror:	Dean R. Koontz
Mystery:	Edna Buchanan
	Diane Mott Davidson
	Kerry Greenwood
	Laura Lippman
	George Pelecanos
Natural History:	Richard Preston (*The Hot Zone*)[29]
Psychological Suspense:	Peter Abrahams
	Carol Goodman
	Jeffry Lindsay
Romantic Suspense:	Linda Howard
	Iris Johansen
	Elizabeth Lowell
	J. D. Robb
Science Fiction:	Catherine Asaro
	Frank Herbert

TRENDS

Serial murder remains a popular theme in Suspense novels. New forensic details and computer technology help investigators track murderers, but not too quickly—not before more killings occur—of course. Both the investigators and the murderers have become more skilled, and the details of both their methods add another layer to the suspense.

The popularity of serial murderers goes hand in hand with the heightened level of violence and violent descriptions (not to mention strong language and explicit sexual scenes) in this genre and others. Villains are more mad and dangerous, protagonists more damaged, the stakes higher and the collateral damage more graphically described. Suspense novels are simply grittier now. For the most part, novels in this genre are not for the faint of heart. Or stomach.

In Suspense too, technology plays a greater and greater role. Forensics, used by criminals and criminalists alike, up the ante on crime solving, and forensic details fill books and movies. Computers are also used more frequently by good guys and bad. Jeffery Deaver's *The Broken Window*, with its complex tale of identity theft, is a good example of the ripped-from-the-headlines feel that technology can give to Suspense tales.[30]

Although the Suspense genre may be hard to define precisely, there is no question that it has a broad appeal for a wide range of readers who look for stories of characters placed in jeopardy who must work their way out of a bad situation. Readers who enjoy page-turners, those fast-paced, tension-filled stories that generally end with issues satisfactorily resolved, often choose Suspense. However, in the real world of readers and librarians, whether a novel truly falls within the confines of the Suspense genre or not is not the issue. If we have explored this genre and others, we have a good idea of the range of books that might appeal to readers who enjoy both Suspense and suspenseful stories.

Notes

1. Andrew Klavan, "The Uses of Suspense," in *The Writer's Handbook*, ed. Sylvia K. Burack (Boston: Writer, 1996), 213.
2. Jeffery Deaver, *The Sleeping Doll* (New York: Simon and Schuster, 2007).

3. C. J. Box, *Blue Heaven* (New York: St. Martin's Minotaur, 2008).
4. Mary Higgins Clark, *I Heard That Song Before* (New York: Simon and Schuster, 2007).
5. Val McDermid, *The Torment of Others* (New York: St. Martin's Minotaur, 2005).
6. Harlan Coben, *No Second Chance* (New York: Dutton, 2003).
7. Thomas Harris, *Hannibal* (New York: Delacorte, 1999).
8. Chelsea Cain, *Heartsick* (New York: St. Martin's Minotaur, 2007).
9. Lee Child, *Bad Luck and Trouble* (New York: Delacorte, 2007).
10. James Hall, *Magic City* (New York: St. Martin's Minotaur, 2007).
11. Coben, *Tell No One* (New York: Delacorte, 2001).
12. Child, *The Killing Floor* (New York: G. P. Putnam's Sons, 1997).
13. Deaver, *The Bone Collector* (New York: Viking, 1997).
14. James Patterson, *Along Came a Spider: A Novel* (Boston: Little, Brown, 1993).
15. Patterson, The Women's Murder Club series, beginning with *1st to Die* (Boston: Little, Brown, 2001).
16. John Sandford, *Rules of Prey* (New York: G. P. Putnam's Sons, 1989).
17. Sandford, Flowers series, beginning with *Dark of the Moon* (New York: G. P. Putnam's Sons, 2007); Kidd series, beginning with *The Fool's Run* (New York: Holt, 1989).
18. John Saul, *Perfect Nightmare: A Novel* (New York: Ballantine, 2005).
19. Dean R. Koontz, Odd Thomas series, beginning with *Odd Thomas* (New York: Bantam, 2003).
20. Jeff Abbott, *Panic* (New York: Dutton, 2005); Abbott, *Fear* (New York: Dutton, 2006).
21. Lisa Gardner, *Hide* (New York: Bantam, 2007); Gardner, *Gone* (New York: Bantam, 2006); Gardner, *Alone* (New York: Bantam, 2005).
22. Thomas Perry, *Nightlife* (New York: Ballantine, 2007).
23. Ridley Pearson, *Killer Weekend* (New York: G. P. Putnam's Sons, 2007).
24. T. Jefferson Parker, *Storm Runners* (New York: Morrow, 2007).
25. Raymond E. Feist, Riftwar Saga series, beginning with *Magician* (Garden City, NY: Doubleday, 1992); Robert Jordan, Wheel of Time series, beginning with *The Eye of the World* (New York: Tom Doherty, 1990).
26. John Connolly, *The Book of Lost Things* (New York: Atria, 2006).
27. Frank Herbert, *Dune* (Philadelphia: Chilton Books, 1965).
28. Edna Buchanan, Cold Case Squad series, beginning with *Cold Case Squad* (New York: Simon and Schuster, 2004).
29. Richard Preston, *The Hot Zone* (New York: Random House, 1994).
30. Deaver, *The Broken Window: A Lincoln Rhyme Novel* (New York: Simon and Schuster, 2008).

5

THRILLERS

For many readers and librarians, the genre classification Thriller is synonymous with the Espionage stories so popular in the 1970s and 1980s. Many types of books share similar characteristics and fit under the Thriller umbrella, however, as they combine fast-paced action and adventure with traditional heroes and an abundance of technical details. For example, Robert Ludlum, John Grisham, and Michael Crichton are linked for fans by their pacing, as well as the nature of their heroes and the obstacles they face, even though their stories focus on disparate subjects. This chapter will explore a wide range of Thrillers—Political/Espionage, Legal, Medical/Scientific, Corporate/Financial, and Crime/Caper. Each type offers an insider's look into a field of expertise or profession and addresses the perennial question posed by titles in the genre and among Adrenaline titles in general: Whom can the hero trust?

A DEFINITION

The size and diversity of the Thriller genre make it difficult to define in a straightforward fashion. Basically this genre focuses on a particular profession—espionage, medicine, or the law, for example—and tells an action-packed story that reveals the intricacies of that profession and the potential dangers faced by those involved in it. The details supplied, their authenticity and their scope, are key to reader satisfaction. Although important to a good story, the character of the hero is generally secondary to the action and detail. Readers can easily distinguish the good from the bad among these stereotypical characters.

The Thriller genre shares elements with the Adventure, Suspense, and Mystery genres. As an Adrenaline genre, Thrillers demand the breakneck pacing that drives Adventure, Romantic Suspense, and Suspense novels. Thrillers also require an element of suspense, but it is not the focus of the book. Readers of Thrillers follow the action step-by-step, and, in the best, participate intellectually and emotionally in the unraveling of the plot complications. Here, however, the physical, emotional, and mental dangers faced by the hero are not ubiquitous and constant; they are simply a part of the picture. Intrigue and the solving of a puzzle, appeals borrowed from the Mystery genre, figure prominently as well. All these elements add layers to titles in this genre, but the distinguishing feature in a Thriller is the frame of the story, the details of the profession, and the way in which the hero uses his skill and knowledge within that profession to extricate himself from a dangerous situation. For example, in a Legal Thriller, it is the hero's knowledge of the law that allows him to succeed and escape the dangerous situation in which he finds himself, and it is the presentation of these often arcane details from the legal profession—an insider's insights—that enthrall readers.

What, then, is a Thriller? It is a gripping, plot-centered story, set in the detailed framework of a particular profession, which places heroes or heroines in dangerous situations from which they must extricate themselves. These books are a cinematic blend of adventure, intrigue, and suspense. Although characters may not be in life-and-death situations, they always face danger of some kind, certainly from a conspiracy if not a physical antagonist. Twists of plot play a major role and keep the reader guessing, not necessarily about the outcome, but about exactly how the triumph will be effected. And although justice is the end result, the means of achieving this may not always be strictly by the letter of the law. These are satisfying reads, with the good guys—usually the underdogs—victorious and the bad guys punished, although the victory never comes without cost and pain. The general characteristics in figure 5.1 amplify this bare-bones definition.

CHARACTERISTICS AND THE GENRE'S APPEAL

Pacing

As is the case with all Adrenaline genres, pacing drives these books, and readers are hooked in the first pages, compelled to read as quickly as possible through the convoluted stories to the very end and the satisfactory denouement. Nonfans may wonder how one can possibly allege that an

---

Figure 5.1 *Characteristics of Thrillers*

---

1. Thrillers move at a rapid pace, driven by the danger or threat of danger faced by the protagonist. Although some are densely written and the action may be more cerebral than physical, their building intensity makes them compelling page-turners.

2. Extensive details and technical language related to each occupation are vital, and they are woven into the story in a way that does not detract from the pacing. They offer the reader an insider's view of that profession.

3. These cinematic stories center on the plot and the action generated by the intricately involved narrative. There is often a political focus with either national or international ramifications, and hot topics from the news are frequently explored. Conspiracies thrive here. Protagonists face frightening perils, physical and emotional, and violence or the threat of violence propels the story line.

4. Protagonists are usually strong, sympathetic characters, whether heroes or antiheroes. Secondary characters are less well developed and may even be caricatures. Protagonists often operate alone, as they can never be certain, in their worlds of betrayal and deception, whom they can trust.

5. The tone of Thrillers is often dark, and gritty details contribute to this mood. Spoofs may produce a lighter but still menacing tone.

6. The language of Thrillers reflects the jargon of each profession. Styles range from elegantly literary to more informal and conversational.

850-page book, full of carefully researched details about military hardware, for example, is fast-paced. The answer seems to be that the books are compelling reads; they pull the reader in with the sympathetic portrayal of the hero and his plight, and the action as well as the detail keeps the reader turning the pages, since readers understand that key plot elements can depend on these intricacies and details. The more cerebral Thrillers of a literary stylist such as John le Carré or Alan Furst seem just as compelling as the action-packed dramas by Gayle Lynds, because the reader is drawn into the hero's moral dilemmas, as well as into interpreting the shades of gray that pervade his story. *Engrossing* is a term often applied to this genre, and the books are often what readers want when they request page-turners. These gripping stories hook readers early on and keep them satisfied as the intricately twisted plot unfolds. We keep reading to find out what will happen next. These books have the feel of fast pacing, even though they may not actually read quickly.

Frame/Setting

As will be underscored throughout this chapter, the details and the jargon of each profession are vital. These must be profuse and accurate. Readers anticipate being immersed in the legal or medical professions, for example, and they expect their lawyers and doctors to sound just like the ones they know—or see on television. In fact, if the details are good enough, it does not matter for some readers how exciting, or even plausible, the plot or how realistic the characterizations. Although some readers may skim the technical details in Tom Clancy's Techno-Thrillers, for example, the most fervent fans of this type see these as the core of the book.

These books also provide an insider's view of the profession. Readers of Legal Thrillers expect to explore the fine points of law and courtroom procedures, while fans of Medical and Scientific Thrillers relish details about the operations of the hospital or research lab, medical procedures, and the nature of the disease or virus that precipitates the action. Readers expect these details to be presented in an understandable fashion, rather than as dry, and perhaps overwhelmingly incomprehensible, facts.

This is not to say that the view of the profession is always positive. In fact, Thrillers often point up the problems—and certainly the dangers—associated with it. In Legal Thrillers, for example, the legal profession does not necessarily come off well. These are books that are enjoyed by lawyers as well as by those who claim to dislike lawyers and the legal profession. Our insider's perspective allows us to see that the corruption and greed the lawyer fights are as often within the profession as without. The protagonist is the white knight, strong enough to wage a battle against the corruption wherever he encounters it. This story line opens up endless variations on questions of moral and social issues, and no venue—from the White House to the boardroom—is safe from the investigative talents of our knight on his quest.

Historical settings also make a popular frame, primarily in the Political Thrillers, with tales of spies in times past. Topicality is important for many Thrillers, but currently World War II backgrounds are especially popular. Alan Furst's dark dramas of espionage in the 1930s and 1940s set the standard. Atmosphere dominates in these moody tales featuring world-weary spies involved in complicated conspiracies, and they sometimes end badly for the protagonist. *The World at Night* offers the claustrophobic feel of wartime Paris.[1] Anne Perry writes a dark, moody World War I Thriller series, beginning with *No Graves as Yet,* and several authors have stand-alone titles worth exploring, particularly Joseph Kanon (*The Good German*) and Mark Frost (*The Second Objective*).[2] In Linda Fairstein's series featuring sex crimes prosecutor Alexandra Cooper, historical details of New York City locations and buildings add another layer to the complex stories of modern-day crimes. Fans of Thrillers with historical settings demand rich and accurate backgrounds, as do Historical Fiction readers, who may also enjoy these novels.

Story Line

Story lines in Thrillers tend to be complicated, with frequent plot twists that surprise protagonist and reader alike. Power is often at the heart of the action: The antagonist plots to gain power for his own ends, and the hero is out to stop him or her. There is violence or the threat of violence, and a sense of constant movement, which increases the pace of the story. The emphasis of the story line is on action and conflict, namely the prevention of the power-hungry villain from gaining control. Ultimately, the hero triumphs over evil and survives—although there may be a price to pay.

Thrillers cover a broad spectrum—law, politics, crime, medicine, business and finance—but the story lines share several characteristics. First, these stories are cinematic, and many books have become the basis of television shows and movies. Colorful details, black/white/gray characters, intricately woven stories, and provocative issues lend themselves to the small and large screen. One need only consider the success of movie versions of Elmore Leonard's criminal romps (*Get Shorty,* for example), Tom Clancy and John le Carré's political dramas (*The Hunt for Red October* and other Jack Ryan tales and *The Spy Who Came in from the Cold, The Tailor of Panama,* and more) to understand their appeal.[3] Movies have been made from the books of most major Thriller writers—David Baldacci, Grisham, Scott Turow, and Robin Cook, to name a few.

Thriller plotlines are provocative, introducing a wide range of social and moral issues, and examining them in the story line. From the international (Israeli/Palestinian relations and their geopolitical tie-ins in Daniel Silva's fine series starring art restorer/spy Gabriel Allon) to the more personal (John Rain's efforts to leave his job and reputation as a contract killer in Barry Eisler's introspective series), these books raise a wealth of issues.

Legal Thrillers address abuses of the law and often pit a David against the Goliaths of corrupt lawyers, legal firms, and justices; Medical and Scientific Thrillers fight the dangers of Big Medicine as well as mad scientists; Political Thrillers pit terrorists, spies, and governments against each other, both currently and historically; Financial Thrillers attack big business, big government, and megalomaniacs controlling influential power blocs; and Crime Thrillers uncover abuses within police departments as well as in organized crime and the criminal underworld.

Hot topics from the news always find their way into intriguing Thriller plots. This is where we learn the dangers of the latest virus (medical and computer) and meet conspiracy, corruption, and nefarious machinations of every sort. Authors of Medical Thrillers, especially, skillfully manipulate the plot and characterizations to play on our worst fears. Assassinations and conspiracies flourish in these pages, as do financial schemes that could take down a government and throw the world into chaos.

The topicality of subjects, that ripped-from-the-headlines immediacy, may cause some Thrillers to date more quickly. Still, those that transcend the specific event described remain classics in the genre. A good example is Frederick Forsyth's masterpiece, *The Day of the Jackal,* written in 1971.[4] Vivid details of the Jackal's preparations for his attempt to assassinate de Gaulle dominate the story and linger in the reader's mind. These step-by-step preparations and the concomitant details—the breaking down and transporting of his weapon across borders, the elements of his disguise— keep us reading, as we simultaneously follow the race to catch him. The wealth of details makes the story very real and all the more frightening, and even though it is tied to a specific event, it feels timeless and universal, as if it could happen again tomorrow.

Thriller fans cherish convoluted plots—the more intricate the better— and these twists are a hallmark of the genre. Nothing is ever as it seems in a Thriller, and one never knows whom to trust. Readers of Thrillers expect the unexpected, the out-of-the-ordinary, and situations that change frequently and in unanticipated directions. These are layered puzzles, and for many readers, the more complex and intricate the puzzle and the more elegant the execution of the solution, the more satisfying the story. *Labyrinthine* describes these plots; double crosses are essential, and a final twist near the end often completes the story—and surprises the reader.

Betrayals, secrets, conspiracies, and revenge make up many story lines. David Baldacci's complex Political Thrillers provide an excellent example. They often feature multiple, interwoven story lines; complex plot twists; and investigations on several levels. Try his Camel Club series to sample his style. In the first, *The Camel Club*, a group of misfits and conspiracy theorists, living mostly off the grid in Washington, DC, witness a murder and are threatened by a dangerous cabal propagating a conspiracy that threatens the fate of the world.[5]

Violence and the threat of violence figure prominently in this genre. High body counts seem to be the norm in almost all publishing currently, and Thrillers tend to drive up those numbers. This may be troubling for readers unfamiliar with the genre, but for most fans the page-turning pace at which they read means that the violence sometimes goes practically unnoticed, unless it is unusually descriptive. Violence remains an integral part of the stories in this genre, and they are probably not our first suggestion for a reader who prefers Gentle Reads and others that feature less graphic and dangerous story lines. On the other hand, the violence plays an important role in underlining the dangerousness of the situations. Calculated violence and even torture run through Daniel Silva's critically acclaimed Political Thrillers starring Mossad agent and art restorer Gabriel Allon. These thoughtful tales of the struggles between Israelis and Palestinians demand this authenticity.

Characterization

As do most Adventure heroes and private investigators in the Mystery genre, Thriller protagonists often seem to operate under their own personal moral codes, which may be at odds with the law or common practice. Any reader of the genre also recognizes that these heroes are faced with a serious dilemma: Whom among the characters who surround them—and often appeal to them for assistance—can they really trust? This dilemma creates moral questions and drives the plot, often even turning the hero away from the police or anyone in authority as a possible betrayer and forcing him to use his own skills and knowledge to overcome all obstacles in his way.

Heroes may be male or female. Unlike the Adventure genre, which is dominated by men, Thrillers, Legal and Medical especially, often feature strong female protagonists. More important than gender is the fact that the reader relates to the hero and his or her plight. Our involvement with these characters draws us to these stories and keeps us reading to discover the fate of the characters we have embraced. Sometimes there is a cast of characters, as in Lisa Scottoline's series featuring an all-female legal firm in Philadelphia. Each novel stars one of these lawyers, and we learn of their careers, their pasts, their relationships with others in the firm, and their dreams. *Everywhere That Mary Went* is the first in this long-running series.[6] In Silva's Political Thriller series, we discover Allon's tragic past as the series progresses, and, as in some Mysteries, his personal story can be as much of a draw as his professional activities. In *The Kill Artist*, the first entry, Silva introduces us to his complex, haunted hero and gives us a glimpse into his past and motivations as he must stalk another kill artist, a professional assassin almost as skilled as he.[7]

Although we expect likeable and sympathetic protagonists, albeit often flawed and very human, this genre also offers another twist—Crime Thrillers that star dangerously flawed and even amoral heroes. As criminals or part of the underworld, they are not always characters with whom we can comfortably sympathize. This switch creates a different kind of book. Unlike our reaction to most heroes and heroines in genre fiction, we may find that we do not always like these flawed characters. In fact, they may surprise us with their amorality and casual acceptance of illegal activities. Lawrence Block's compilation of noir short stories, *Hit Man*, and its sequels feature the day-to-day activities of the title character, as he completes assignments and deals with the everyday annoyances of his life.[8] The "hero's" chilling amorality creates an extraordinarily disturbing and compulsively readable collection.

On the other hand, many of these protagonists have a genuine allure. Who can resist the wacko creations of Carl Hiaasen and Laurence Shames or Elmore Leonard's appealing low-life characters? Authors at both ends of the spectrum from noir to comic offer a range of irresistible bad guys. From Donald Westlake's hapless Dortmunder gang, which has bungled more operations than anyone deserves, to Mario Puzo's sinister Mafia family, protagonists run the gamut.

Secondary characters and villains fare less well, except in Crime Thrillers, where the villain is frequently the protagonist. Often characterizations are black and white, with the hero portrayed as very good and the antagonist very bad. Readers generally have no doubt which are the good guys and which the bad, although, as will be seen below, in some (especially in Political Thrillers) there are more shades of gray among the characterizations, and the threats to the hero may come from inside his organization or profession as well as from without. Terrorists thrive in this genre, usually as secondary characters, whose mission and politics are threats that must be sought out and disarmed. Occasionally authors will play with this convention; characters who appear to be terrorists are actually the protagonists, deep under cover. Then the dilemma of whom to trust becomes even murkier, as the "good guys" suspect these heroes and their motives, but these terrorist/heroes know that danger lurks for them in both camps. Recently, Frederick Forsyth in *The Afghan* and Alex Berenson in *The Faithful Spy* have spun this twist to critical acclaim.[9]

Series characters figure prominently across the Thriller genre as well as every other. In fact, only a few best-selling Thriller writers— John Grisham, Ken Follett, Forsyth, Joseph Finder, Joseph Kanon, Brad Meltzer—have yet to create series characters! Many write series and stand-alone novels, often alternating between the two to keep series fresh but also to explore new directions. Series characters ensure sales, as readers follow their adventures from title to title. Among popular series today are Legal Thrillers by Fairstein (Alexandra Cooper) and John T. Lescroart (San Francisco lawyer Dismas Hardy and San Francisco Police Department's Abe Glitzky); Stephen J. Cannell's Police Thrillers (Shane Scully of Los Angeles Police Department); Barry Eisler's Crime Thrillers (assassin John Rain); Medical/Crime Thrillers by Karin Slaughter (Dr. Sara Linton and police chief Jeffrey Tolliver); Medical Thrillers by Robin Cook (Jack Stapleton and Laurie Montgomery); Political Thrillers by Nelson DeMille (John Carey), Vince Flynn (Mitch Rapp), Kyle Mills (Mark Beamon), and Daniel Silva (Gabriel Allon). While the pacing, details, and story line may dominate, fans also read to discover more about the series characters, both the secrets of their past and their future as it unfolds in the current episode.

Tone/Mood

With violence and danger dominating the genre, it is small wonder that the tone of most Thrillers is dark. Even though the resolution is usually satisfactory, with the good guys triumphing over evil, the tone is often bleaker than might be expected in books with this positive outcome. As mentioned above, these victories are often not without cost, and no satisfactory ending is completely without loss. Gritty details and the building of suspense and danger add to this ominous mood. Political Thrillers, with their spy heroes, can be especially bleak, reflecting the sense of alienation and paranoia that plagues these agents. All of the novels by classic Espionage writer John le Carré exemplify this tone, as do those of Furst and Joseph Kanon. The best in the genre also capture that claustrophobic mood and loneliness, the paranoia of the amateur who has not yet learned whom to trust and of the jaded professional who knows he can trust no one. For the most part, this is a world of one man or woman, operating alone, and with only a government bureau, not a family, as backup. These are not bright and happy books, and even though these characters are successful on their missions—and they have saved the free world once again—the mood is generally uncompromisingly bleak. Le Carré provides the classic examples of this melancholy tone. No one can read *The Spy Who Came in from the Cold*, for example, without a deep sense of tragedy created by betrayal and double cross.[10]

Crime Thrillers, too, are often edgier and darker. In Chuck Hogan's *Prince of Thieves*, for example, antihero Doug dreams of breaking away from his life of crime, but his addiction to the high it produces drives this sympathetic character to a tragic end in this layered, provocative, noir drama.[11]

As always, there are exceptions. Newsman Jim Lehrer writes a series that features the one-eyed lieutenant governor of Oklahoma, a crusader against corruption on a slightly less global and dangerous level. Lehrer demonstrates that not all Thrillers have to be serious—although these clearly find a different audience or an audience that reads them for different reasons. The series opens with *Kick the Can* and throughout reflects both the characteristics of the Thriller genre and Lehrer's love of small-town life and people in Oklahoma and Kansas.[12] As do a number of Thriller writers, Cannell leavens his Police Thrillers featuring Los Angeles police detective Shane Scully with humor (often black) and smart remarks. This contrasts sharply with the dangers and tough issues Scully faces, intensifying their effect.

Capers make up the lighter side of Crime Thrillers. These are the stories of Hiaasen, Shames, Leonard, and Westlake. They are peopled by characters who delight readers with their outrageous disregard for law and practically all other conventions. Marne Davis Kellogg's charming series starring Katherine Day (Kick) Keswick offers the female perspective on this theme. Cat burglar Kick is a classy lady of a certain age, size, and style. She is skilled at creating fake jewels (which often reside among the treasures of the rich and famous while the real gems rest safe in Kick's personal vaults), and she lives a life of leisure among the upper crust, enjoying the pleasures of good food and wine while planning her next heist. Comedy—she marries an ex-Scotland Yard detective who has quirks of his own—and endless name- and label-dropping frame this engaging series. *Brilliant* is the first.[13]

Hiaasen, with his over-the-top skewering of life in south Florida, typifies Crime/Capers. His enormous popularity has inspired imitators, and the south Florida scene is well covered by him, along with Leonard,

Shames, and Tim Dorsey. The typical Hiaasen Crime/Caper Thriller features murder and black humor, over-the-top secondary characters and situations, an antihero protagonist, corruption promulgated by those in authority, and labyrinthine plots. His venal and often loopy characters seem destined to turn south Florida simultaneously into an environmental disaster and a madhouse. Try *Native Tongue* to sample his work.[14] Here, eco-terrorists threaten a sleazy Disney-style theme park.

Style/Language

Certainly the distinctive jargon of each profession figures prominently in all these novels. We learn the patois of spies and terrorists, the cant of thieves, and the specialized language of medicine and science.

The language must also fit the story and its characters. Some authors develop distinctive cadences that immediately tell readers—or listeners to these novels on audio—much about the story and characters. Leonard is a good example. His distinctive dialogue identifies his cast of characters and sets the stage for the black humor and details in his urban crime dramas.

Some authors employ language and style to add a regional flavor to their Thrillers. Greg Iles's southern idioms and speech patterns underline the sense of place in the deep South. William Lashner's Legal Thrillers employ smart dialogue that reveals much about the tough and cynical character of his second-rate lawyer Victor Carl and his background from the streets of Philadelphia.

For some authors literary style is important too, and Thrillers range from elegantly written literary novels to informal and conversational glimpses into another world, depending on the authors and the stories they tell. Since these are Thrillers and pacing is crucial, the best never let details impede the pacing. They skillfully interweave detailed layers of information with the story and characters.

Like stories in the Suspense genre, these novels sometimes provide a prologue that sets up the action. P. T. Deutermann's *The Cat Dancers* opens with a dramatic scene with a man dangling from a rope in the rugged North Carolina mountains, as he tries to get a picture of a cougar, thought to have vanished from that area.[15] Our curiosity piqued, we read frantically, following Lt. Cam Richter of the county sheriff's office as he investigates to discover the secret of these cat dancer/photographers. Nelson DeMille's *Night Fall* opens with a couple on the beach watching jets taking off from JFK airport in New York.[16] Did something strike TWA flight 800 before it exploded? Their story gets pulled back into the investigation of a possible terrorist plot that ends on the eve of September 11, 2001. Readers feel an extraordinary sense of anticipation because they know what happens next, and the possibility that these events are connected drives the pacing and the story line.

KEY AUTHORS

In such a big and popular genre, there are many names that could be brought forward as "key." Dozens appear consistently on the best-seller lists, and even more remain popular in our libraries. A handful of best-selling and acclaimed authors—David Baldacci, Tess Gerritsen, Lisa Scottoline, and Daniel Silva—are good examples to illustrate the range of the genre.

Baldacci continues to cover a lot of Thriller territory with his diverse plots. Big business (*Total Control*), financial manipulations (the lottery in *The Winner*), abuse of power in the office of the president (*Absolute Power*), and more recently, conspiracies (*The Camel Club*).[17] Sympathetic characters, high-tech and computer machinations, complex story lines with multiple twists make him a good suggestion for many Thriller readers.

Gerritsen, who usually features a sympathetic female protagonist as well as graphic medical detail and more far-fetched plots, crosses between strictly Medical and more Scientific plot emphases. Recent titles feature series characters who blend the medical and investigative arenas, as Boston homicide detective Jane Rizzoli and medical examiner Maura Isles join forces. Police and medical details fill these Thrillers, and the recent *Mephisto Club* even adds an element of the paranormal.[18]

With her series starring an all-women Philadelphia law firm, Scottoline has captured the Legal Thriller market. She combines legal expertise (she is a former lawyer) with investigative details and suspenseful woman-in-jeopardy tales, leavened with witty dialogue and a touch of humor, to create compelling stories of female lawyers fighting for justice. Each novel focuses on one lawyer, but others from the firm also appear. This series offers extensive character detail that also attracts fans.

Silva's stylishly written, compelling stories of unlikely spies have given new life to the espionage end of the Political Thriller. As mentioned earlier, his series character art-restorer Gabriel Allon is a sleeper spy, an Israeli Mossad agent, employed against the most dangerous of Palestinian agents, their enablers, and other anti-Israeli menaces. His tragic past and motivation unfold layer by layer throughout the series.

Classic Thriller writers John Grisham, Robin Cook, and Michael Crichton remain popular. Grisham achieved fame for his David-and-Goliath tales of the underdog lawyer fighting corruption and winning. In recent years, he's expanded his scope to include nonfiction as well. In fact several of his recent best sellers aren't even Thrillers. When he writes about the law, his books are now darker, with characters less black and white, issues more provocative, and a happy ending not necessarily ensured. *The Appeal*, a recent title, combines politics and legal issues in a provocative look at the practice of buying judges.[19]

Cook continues to achieve best-seller status with his fast-paced Medical Thrillers, crusading stories that raise questions of medical ethics as they offer details of the profession. In Cook's Thrillers, the doctors are usually the good guys (and gals), pitted against the soulless, greed-driven health maintenance organizations, the hospitals, and the drug companies. Try *Marker* for a recent example of his best-selling style, as his series characters battle the hospital administration as they try to investigate unnecessary deaths, which almost have to be murder.[20]

Crichton remains the master of Scientific Thrillers, with both *Jurassic Park* and *Prey,* for example, reflecting the obligatory characteristics: crusading hero, story lines out of the news or certainly within the realm of scientific possibility, and fast pacing, not to mention copious scientific details.[21] Dinosaurs brought to life from their DNA rule the former title and swarming microcosms endanger life as we know it in the latter.

WHAT WE KNOW ABOUT FANS

What do these readers expect when they request a Thriller? Having thought about the genre, we understand that most are not looking for novels with complex characters. They expect the plots, with twists and unexpected turns, not the characters, to generate surprises. For the most part, they expect characters to be heroes they can relate to and empathize with and villains they love to hate. Although characters, especially villains, may be caricatures, many characters, good and bad, are drawn from real life. They may be exaggerated, but they are easily recognizable from television and the news.

Pacing is generally fast in Thrillers, and that is another element readers expect. When they request page-turners, these are among those books we suggest. As observers, and perhaps even fans, we know intellectually that all Thrillers are not equally fast-paced. However, we also know that they may seem that way to their fans, as the writers pull the readers into the stories and keep them turning pages.

Plots in this genre should be complex—the more convoluted and surprising the better. These are also stories in which the good guys win, despite the odds and the dangers. Readers do not usually like an author to play with this formula, and we, in exploring the genre, should make note of those who push the boundaries of the formula, so that we can alert fans. Within this formula, readers expect the unexpected. They are looking for frequent plot twists and rapidly changing situations—the out-of-the-ordinary books in which things never go according to plan, for the hero at least. They want to see how the author—and the hero—will handle the problems that inevitably arise. Fans also expect that pulled-from-the-headlines perspective on controversial and newsworthy issues. Thrillers explore many social, political, and ethical questions, and readers like to see them from the insider's point of view that the genre provides.

As we explore the Thriller genre—talking with fans and reading books and reviews—we should also be aware of the pervasive violence. Readers often have a level of violence beyond which they are reluctant to go. If I am aware of a particularly violent scene or that a title tends to be more (or less) violent, I try to make a mental note so that I can share that information with readers for whom it may be an issue.

Readers also seek the frame, those details that form the basis of each of the Thriller types. They demand both jargon and procedures related to the professions. Maps, illustrations, and intricate descriptions add to the appeal of these stories. Detractors may complain about the melodramatic soap opera elements sometimes found in these stories, but fans appreciate characters they care about, clear distinctions between good and evil, and cases in which justice—although not always the law—is served in the end.

Becoming familiar with popular authors is a good place to start in preparing to work with readers. But reading almost anything typical of the genre helps in making contact with readers. Fans of other genres might try authors listed in figure 5.2. Since these authors overlap with other genres, readers (and librarians) can choose a genre they prefer and find a Thriller author who might also satisfy them.

THE READERS' ADVISORY INTERVIEW

Discovering what readers enjoy about a particular author or genre is always difficult, but because Thrillers, like all Adrenaline novels, are so

---

Figure 5.2 *An Introduction to the Thriller Genre*

Thriller Writers to Try, If You Enjoy . . .

Adrenaline:	David Baldacci
	Barry Eisler
	John Grisham
	Lisa Scottoline
Fantasy:	John Twelve Hawks
Historical Fiction:	Ken Follett
	Martin Cruz Smith (*Stallion Gate*)[22]
Horror:	Dean R. Koontz
	John Saul
Humor:	Marne Davis Kellogg
	Donald Westlake
Inspirational:	Tim LaHaye and Jerry B. Jenkins
	Frank Peretti
	Joel C. Rosenberg
Literary:	Daniel Silva
	Scott Turow
Multicultural:	Barbara Parker
Mystery:	John Lescroart
	Stuart Woods
Psychological Suspense:	John le Carré
Romantic Suspense:	Robin Cook
	Gayle Lynds
Science Fiction:	Greg Bear
	Lincoln Child
	Clive Cussler
True Crime:	Joseph Wambaugh
Women's Lives:	Marne Davis Kellogg
	Lisa Scottoline

---

cinematic and have often been made into movies, sometimes we can more easily explore that format with fans. If they are unable to describe titles or authors they enjoy, they can often tell us about movies and we can readily discover what Thriller elements they appreciate. These may simply be subject elements—details of the legal or medical professions—but fans also describe movies in the same way they describe books—by pacing, characterization, story line, frame, tone, and style. We simply listen for those elements and offer a selection of Thrillers that might meet that reader's interests and mood.

And when we are standing at the book stacks with a reader and nothing comes to mind, or a reader asks us about a Thriller that we don't even remember seeing before, we should also remember that this is that occasion when we can ignore the old adage: never judge a book by its cover. Because they often reveal a great deal about the content of Thrillers, we should certainly make the most of the covers—and titles—in identifying Thriller types. As Thriller/Adventure/Suspense expert librarian Michael Gannon suggests, we do not even need much imagination to be successful. A syringe indicates a Medical Thriller; a swastika, likely a World War II Espionage/Political Thriller, while a government seal might suggest a more contemporary Political Thriller; and the words "indictment," "justice," and "evidence" all suggest Legal Thrillers. What could be easier?

Remember too that *Thriller* is a catchall phrase, used across the board by publishers, reviewers, and readers to indicate any of the Adrenaline genres or any fast-paced, suspenseful story. The distinction between suspenseful Thriller and thrilling Suspense, for example, is a very fine one, and frankly not one worth taking time over. Listen to how readers describe books and move them across genres, matching the elements they most prize. The discussion of "Whole Collection Readers' Advisory" and figure 5.3 will help with that process.

Sure Bets

Sometimes a good strategy is simply to describe popular writers who fit generally within the Thriller genre, those Sure Bets that appeal to a wide range of fans within the genre and without. All of the authors discussed in the "Key Authors" section certainly qualify as Sure Bets. Others to be aware of include Greg Bear and Christopher Reich. Bear, perhaps better known for his Science Fiction, has recently written several Scientific Thrillers that appeal to a wide range of fans. *Quantico* mixes the science of Michael Crichton with the political background of Frederick Forsyth's novels for an imaginative, futuristic tale of biological terrorism.[23] Fascinating characters, intricately woven plots laden with scientific details, a suspenseful mood, and a menacing villain add up to an action-packed, cinematic Thriller.

Reich combines the Political with the Financial in his smart Thrillers, which give a sense of the direction of the genre since September 11. The action begins on page one and never lets up, as plot twists, conspiracies, and puzzles lead the hero—and the reader—through layer after layer before the final twist. His award-winning *The Patriots Club* opens as Thomas and his girlfriend Jenny are attacked and Thomas kidnapped and questioned about matters of which he has no knowledge.[24] Then his world falls apart, as he is framed for sexual harassment and murder—and goes on the run. The action and surprises are guaranteed to leave readers breathless.

EXPANDING READERS' HORIZONS WITH WHOLE COLLECTION READERS' ADVISORY

Faced with readers who say they have read everything by an author or in a type they love, we need to remember that the Thriller genre offers extensive crossover, both within the genre and without. (See figure 5.3.)

Figure 5.3 *Expanding Readers' Horizons*

Authors to Take Readers beyond the Thriller Genre

Adrenaline:	Clive Cussler
	Patrick Robinson
Historical Fiction:	David Liss
Horror:	Douglas Preston and Lincoln Child
Mystery:	W. E. B. Griffin (Badge of Honor series)[25]
	Dennis Lehane
	Kathy Reichs
	Randy Wayne White
	Kate Wilhelm
Psychological Suspense:	Jeffry Lindsay
Romantic Suspense:	Nora Roberts
	Elizabeth Lowell
Science Fiction:	Orson Scott Card (Ender series)[26]
	William C. Dietz
	Neal Stephenson

Readers who choose Thrillers for their pacing might enjoy any number of fast-paced titles from other Adrenaline genres, especially Adventure and Suspense. T. Jefferson Parker's stand-alone Suspense novels, Matthew Reilly's high-octane political and military Adventures, or Ridley Pearson's Mystery or Suspense series would make good suggestions.

Medical/Scientific Thrillers contain elements of Suspense, Adventure, Mystery, and even Horror, and thus those genres also offer titles that appeal. For example, Mystery writers Patricia Cornwell and Kathy Reichs offer extensive forensic details that Thriller fans may appreciate. Readers may also find titles of interest among novels dealing with environmental issues and biological or chemical warfare, such as Bear's *Quantico* or Kyle Mills's *Darkness Falls*.[27] This is a popular topic today, and these titles are relatively easy to identify.

Fans who used to read Techno-Thrillers, with their extensive details of military hardware and transport, may also enjoy many authors in the Adventure genre (chapter 2). The Adventure novels of Clive Cussler and the Military Adventures of a fast-paced writer such as Patrick Robinson would also make good crossover suggestions. Watch for the aircraft or submarine on the cover to identify possibilities more easily.

Readers of Legal Thrillers also read true crime and nonfiction accounts of actual trials; Mysteries may appeal to these fans. Although there may be less emphasis on the actual practice of law, the investigation figures prominently in both. Private investigators who also happen to be lawyers or provide extensive legal details are good choices for Legal Thriller fans. (For example, Kate Wilhelm's Barbara Holloway series, beginning with *Death Qualified*, appeals to readers who appreciate a good mystery with abundant legal details.)[28]

Because of the character of most private investigators (P.I.s)—the white knight who operates under his own moral code and solves cases, restoring order and justice to the world—many Mysteries featuring P.I.s appeal to a wide range of Thriller readers, from Legal to Espionage. Thriller readers may also appreciate any story in which the underdog wins against the giant corporation (or other unfeeling, powerful entity), whatever the genre.

TRENDS

The last decade has seen the reemergence of the Espionage or Political Thriller as one of the most popular types, along with the demise of the

Techno-Thriller. As the Cold War languished, so did Political Thrillers, but, unexpectedly, with the end of that era, these Thrillers have attained new popularity. Some writers have mined historical periods but many others have capitalized on current political unrest, especially terrorists, to breathe new life into this Thriller type. As more and more technical elements became de rigueur in Thrillers and other genres, driven especially by familiarity with computer hardware and gadgets, the Techno-Thriller emphasis was simply incorporated into the structure of many Thrillers and indeed of many other genres. Since the rise of Political/Espionage Thrillers corresponds directly with the fall of Techno-Thrillers, it seems possible that the former simply subsumed the latter, with the military emphasis pulled into the political arena.

Thrillers continue to merge with other genres, particularly Suspense and Mysteries, and within the genre as well. The distinct boundaries that once seemed to exist between Legal, Medical, and Political Thrillers, for example, have become so porous that it is almost impossible to talk about them as distinct entities. Fans, too, follow favorite authors as they write and explore new territory within and beyond the genre's confines, and readers pick up on new Thrillers that address contemporary topics that interest them. Thrillers remain topical if diffuse in their focus.

Hard though it may be to believe, even the Thriller genre has been affected by the current popularity of the paranormal as it has infiltrated almost every fiction genre. Douglas Preston and Lincoln Child's Pendergast series has moved from Horror to Thrillers, to Supernatural Thrillers. Also remember Tess Gerritsen's *Mephisto Club* with its brooding, ancient evil and James Patterson's *When the Wind Blows* and *The Lake House,* scientific Thrillers that involve genetically modified, winged children.[29]

Combining elements of suspense, adventure, and intriguing puzzles with professional expertise and jargon, these tales of lawyers, spies, doctors, and others are among the books readers often seek when they ask for page-turners, those fast-paced novels that demand we read them at a rapid rate. These books appear with regularity on best-seller lists; small wonder they are so popular with readers since they feature the thrill of the chase, as beleaguered heroes and heroines fight both to stay alive and to solve the puzzle that has put their lives in danger.

Notes

1. Alan Furst, *The World at Night* (New York: Random House, 1996).
2. Anne Perry, *No Graves as Yet: A Novel of World War I* (New York: Ballantine, 2003); Joseph Kanon, *The Good German: A Novel* (New York: Holt, 2001); Mark Frost, *The Second Objective* (New York: Hyperion, 2007).
3. Elmore Leonard, *Get Shorty* (New York: Delacorte, 1990); Tom Clancy, *The Hunt for Red October* (Annapolis, MD: Naval Institute Press, 1984); John le Carré, *The Spy Who Came in from the Cold* (New York: Coward-McCann, 1963); le Carré, *The Tailor of Panama* (New York: Knopf, 1996).
4. Frederick Forsyth, *The Day of the Jackal* (New York: Viking, 1971).
5. David Baldacci, *The Camel Club* (New York: Warner, 2005).
6. Lisa Scottoline, *Everywhere That Mary Went* (New York: HarperPaperbacks, 1993).
7. Daniel Silva, *The Kill Artist* (New York: Random House, 2000).
8. Lawrence Block, *Hit Man* (New York: Morrow, 1998).
9. Forsyth, *The Afghan* (New York: G. P. Putnam's Sons, 2006); Alex Berenson, *The Faithful Spy: A Novel* (New York: Random House, 2006).
10. le Carré cited above.
11. Chuck Hogan, *Prince of Thieves: A Novel* (New York: Scribner, 2004).
12. Jim Lehrer, *Kick the Can* (New York: Putnam, 1988).
13. Marne Davis Kellogg, *Brilliant* (New York: St. Martin's, 2003).
14. Carl Hiaasen, *Native Tongue* (New York: Knopf, 1991).
15. P. T. Deutermann, *The Cat Dancers* (New York: St. Martin's, 2005).
16. Nelson DeMille, *Night Fall* (New York: Warner, 2004).
17. Baldacci, *Total Control* (New York: Warner, 1997); Baldacci, *The Winner* (New York: Warner, 1997); Baldacci, *Absolute Power* (New York: Warner, 1996); Baldacci cited above.
18. Tess Gerritsen, *The Mephisto Club* (New York: Ballantine, 2006).
19. John Grisham, *The Appeal* (New York: Doubleday, 2008).
20. Robin Cook, *Marker* (New York: G. P. Putnam's Sons, 2005).
21. Michael Crichton, *Jurassic Park* (New York: Knopf, 1990); Crichton, *Prey: A Novel* (New York: HarperCollins, 2002).
22. Martin Cruz Smith, *Stallion Gate* (New York: Random House, 1986).
23. Greg Bear, *Quantico* (New York: Vanguard, 2007).
24. Christopher Reich, *The Patriots Club* (New York: Delacorte, 2005).
25. W. E. B. Griffin, Badge of Honor series, beginning with *Men in Blue* (New York: Jove, 1988).
26. Orson Scott Card, Ender series, beginning with *Ender's Game* (New York: Tom Doherty, 1985).
27. Bear cited above; Kyle Mills, *Darkness Falls* (New York: Vanguard, 2007).
28. Kate Wilhelm, *Death Qualified: A Mystery of Chaos* (New York: St. Martin's, 1991).
29. Douglas Preston and Lincoln Child, The Pendergast series, beginning with *Relic* (New York: Forge, 1995); Gerritsen cited above; James Patterson, *When the Wind Blows: A Novel* (Boston: Little, Brown, 1998); Patterson, *The Lake House: A Novel* (Boston: Little, Brown, 2003).

Part 2

Emotions Genres

6

GENTLE READS

"I just want a nice story."

"They don't write books like they used to!"

If readers have said this to you, you understand the real need we in libraries feel to find Gentle Reads for those who want something other than the often violent and sexually explicit books on the best-seller lists. But how do we know what is gentle enough—or too gentle? And which readers are good candidates for these authors?

This is probably the most difficult genre for librarians and readers—even if we are fans. Helping someone select books that are gentle enough is one part of the problem; trying to remember if there is anything in a book that might offend is the other part of the problem (and then discovering that what we considered innocuous is the one aspect that makes the book too much for a reader). What offends one reader is often what another reader enjoys in a book. And because readers usually do not know what it is they do not want to read about until they come across it in a book we have suggested, our credibility suffers. This can appear to be a no-win situation! Luckily, this category acts as a catchall, a funnel for gentle stories across the genres. The key for readers is that comfortable, gentle quality, and although some books mentioned in this chapter may also fit in other genres, we desperate librarians gather them here—so we have a range of books to suggest to readers who seek that tone and emotional appeal.

A DEFINITION

When we first recognized the need for books of this type at my library, we called the genre Warm Milk. The term came from a conversation a colleague had with a reader. She was looking for books that gave her the same satisfaction and feeling of well-being she felt after drinking warm milk. Charming though that label may be, it is not quite as descriptive as we need in working with the wide range of readers who seek books in this genre. Thus, we transformed it to Gentle Reads, although the feeling these books create remains true to the original description.

Gentle Reads are "feel-good" books. Strictly speaking, they should contain no profanity and no explicit sex or violence, reflect conventional values, and end happily. Beyond that, they are evocative, and, whether they boast contemporary or historical settings, they take the reader back to a gentler, less hurried time. They are cheerful, hopeful stories, told from a peaceful, soothing perspective. Like Horror they appeal primarily to the emotions, but rather than evoking a feeling of fear, they project a comfortable sense of well-being. These are satisfying, old-fashioned stories that reflect an uncomplicated, although not necessarily unsophisticated, lifestyle.

The Gentle Reads genre does not equal Inspirational or Christian Fiction. Although there are certainly authors of Inspirational Fiction who fit within this category, Gentle Reads are more nuanced. To have a list comprising only titles with a religious bent is to do an injustice to, and quite possibly offend, many of the readers of this genre. Although such lists are useful and may supplement our lists of Gentle Reads, they should not be given out interchangeably or discussed as synonymous. Many books within this genre are simply gentle stories with no religious connotation at all. Figure 6.1 lists the characteristics of Gentle Reads.

CHARACTERISTICS AND THE GENRE'S APPEAL

Tone/Mood

The mood projected by these novels is the key to their appeal. These are books that touch the heart. They're cheerful, hopeful stories, told from a peaceful, soothing perspective, and they convey a reassuring sense of well-being. These are feel-good books that transport us back to another time when life was slower and simpler, even if they are books with contemporary settings.

This is not to say that all are happy, carefree stories, but the outlook is ultimately upbeat and optimistic. There may be tragedy, and certainly protagonists may be more reflective than carefree, but in the end all problems are tied up in a satisfying conclusion.

Jennifer Chiaverini's long-running Elm Creek Quilt series demonstrates this particular tone. Throughout the series, characters have faced

---

Figure 6.1 *Characteristics of Gentle Reads*

---

1. Tone is the key in these unpretentious, upbeat, evocative stories that touch the heart. They are "old-fashioned" stories that reflect traditional, rather than modern, values.

2. Language may be colorful, homespun, or even sophisticated, but the style is generally not complex. These novels generally contain no profanity.

3. Characters are comfortable companions, who may also be the source of the humor that lightens the tone of these books.

4. Story lines emphasize relationships among characters, rather than suspense or controversial social issues. Genial humor often underlines these stories, and there is no explicit sex or violence.

5. Settings may be historical or contemporary and are usually in a small town, enclosed community, or rural area. Domestic pleasures often frame these novels.

6. Gentle pacing creates a leisurely story filled with affable characters and no unsettling surprises.

---

difficult times but they have always overcome doubts and tragedies. Both *The Christmas Quilt* and *The New Year's Quilt* tell sweet stories of loss and reconciliation.[1] These are homespun tales, told from the heart and touching on home truths. Readers relate to the introspective characters and their trials as well as to the inspirational (but not necessarily religious) tone.

This is the genre for readers looking for books like they used to find, stories that might deal with issues but ultimately work out satisfactorily; characters one can root for; stories that move at an unhurried pace. *Old-fashioned* is a term sometimes employed to indicate that the story reflects traditional, rather than modern, values.

Style/Language

The traditional values these books endorse require the absence of explicit sex, violence, and profanity. That is also central to this genre. These are "safe" books, and readers do not want to be surprised. Unfortunately, it is increasingly difficult for us as librarians to identify such titles; fewer and fewer books published today meet these strenuous criteria. On the other hand, just because readers appreciate the security of this genre does not mean that they are not willing sometimes to venture farther afield. Suggestions of types of books that go slightly beyond the strict confines of this genre are given in the section "Expanding Readers' Horizons with Whole Collection Readers' Advisory" below.

Stylistically these books are generally not complex; authors do not produce the literary fillips that characterize literary fiction. Colorful, down-home language often fills these stories, but the language might also be more polished. The story lines are straightforward and easy to follow, without the complexities inherent in some other genres. However, we must be careful not to conclude that simply because these are nice, less complicated stories, they are poorly written or unsophisticated. Many of the authors write with a poetic elegance that matches that of much Literary Fiction. Less complicated does not equal lower quality. Kaye Gibbons's lyrical explorations of rural life in the South employ sensitivity and power in describing strong female characters caught up in difficult, sometimes tragic situations. Although she certainly qualifies for inclusion in both the Literary Fiction and Women's Lives and Relationships genres, she also offers a voice that fans of Gentle Reads respond to and respect. Try *Charms for the Easy Life* as an introduction to her work.[2] Here, through the lives of three generations of women, Gibbons evokes the rural South in the first half of the twentieth century in a heartwarming, old-fashioned story.

The pleasures of experimenting with formats have found their way into this genre as well as every other. Epistolary novels and diaries are among the most common forms here, and Mary Ann Shaffer and Annie Barrows's *The Guernsey Literary and Potato Peel Pie Society* offers many pleasures for Gentle Reads fans—the satisfactions of letter writing, characters both quirky and tragic, book clubs, and, despite the undercurrent of misfortune and privation, an uplifting story.[3] Journalist Juliet Ashton, who achieved fame with her humorous wartime (World War II) sketches, is searching for a more serious project, when she receives a letter from a gentleman from Guernsey, hoping for reading suggestions. Their correspondence leads to other characters and their stories in letters of their days under German occupation.

Characterization

These are often ordinary characters in ordinary situations, but the extraordinary can also play a role, as long as the gentle nature of the story remains. Situations need not always be sweetness and light. Sandra Dallas's books reflect hardships in the lives of the characters, and even death plays a role, as in novels by Gibbons and Richard Paul Evans. However, because these tragedies are not sudden or violent, but only part of the natural events, they still fit within the boundaries of this genre. *Heartwarming* and *poignant* are both terms used to describe novels in this genre, and the latter, at least, reflects the range of emotion involved.

Characters, mostly but not always women, are more important than the action or actual events. It is the endearing characters that readers remember and seek in similar titles, as well as the comfortable situations. No matter what the setting, the reader feels at home with the characters and the situations in which they find themselves. That is not to say, however, that these characters are lacking in the wit and sometimes eccentricities that endear them to readers and add humor, or at least a lighter touch, to the stories. Philip Gulley is often praised for the homespun humor of his Harmony series, featuring a Quaker minister in Indiana, as is Clyde Edgerton for his endearing, but quite eccentric, southern characters.[4] Although characters may be familiar and comfortable, they may also be whimsical and charming in less conventional ways.

Story Line

For the most part, not a lot happens in these novels. These are books about the relationships among characters, rather than suspense or controversial social issues. However, because these books overlap with so many genres—especially Women's Lives and Relationships, Romance, and Cozy Mysteries—mildly provocative issues do sometimes figure in. Characters are often struggling to find their place in relationships and beyond. Bad things sometimes happen and their impact must be considered; in the Cozy Mysteries, there has been a murder and the investigative details and results must be reckoned with. Interestingly, the Christian Fiction titles that make up an aspect of this genre are often more likely to present serious, controversial issues than are some other titles. For example, Lynn N. Austin's *A Woman's Place* raises a number of issues and challenges that faced women on the home front during World War II, including racial issues, in this story of four heroines who earnestly live their values at home and in the workplace, a defense plant.[5]

Frame/Setting

The setting, the environment in which the story takes place, is one of the keys to the satisfaction these stories bring. Frames are suggestive and frequently have a timeless quality. These books are often set in small towns, but even if they take place in urban areas, they reflect a close-knit community. Humor may play an important role as well, but even those books without outright humor often display a lighter, more genial touch. Adriana Trigiani's titles demonstrate this. Humor, both outright and underlying, plays a role in all her characters and story lines, whether these are part of her Virginia-based Big Stone Gap series or any of her other titles.

Books may have contemporary or historical settings, and in both cases the details of time and place often add layers to the stories. Crossover Women's Lives and Relationships author Elizabeth Berg's novel of home front Chicago during World War II (*Dream When You're Feeling Blue*) provides a wealth of details of the city and of the history of the period, with women filling jobs that had previously been offered to men only.[6] Kerry Greenwood's Cozy Mystery series set in the Earthly Delights bakery in Melbourne, Australia, is a bit earthy but it should also satisfy Gentle Reads fans. These contemporary stories set around the world from their American readers share many of the pleasures of the genre, as well as an interesting look at Melbourne.

The satisfactions of performing domestic skills—often cooking, baking, and needlecrafts—frequently frame these novels. Greenwood's heroine is a baker, Chiaverini and Macomber infuse their novels with sewing and knitting lore, Fanny Flagg and Sharon Owens may center their characters and stories around restaurants. Macomber's knitting series (beginning with *The Shop on Blossom Street*) stars cancer survivor Lydia Hoffman, who opens the shop to celebrate her recovery.[7] The knitting classes attract a quirky group of characters, young and old, and provide a forum for self-discovery and healing. Home truths are at the core of many of these stories that emphasize homey skills and satisfactions. Quilting, knitting, and even cooking thrive as community activities, and friendships blossom among women involved in these creative enterprises. These are generally not characters involved in solitary quests; they are friends and companions who help one another, whatever the time or place. While these activities also fill novels of Women's Lives and Relationships, here they predominate. Women in Gentle Reads are more likely involved in traditional feminine pursuits. There are fewer doctors and lawyers here. These occupations reflect both the timeless quality of the stories, since these activities are popular now and historically, and the traditional values the books endorse.

Pacing

Another key to the Gentle Reads genre is that these are leisurely paced novels. These comfortable, often meandering stories wash over the reader with their affirming tone and unhurried pace. Eudora Welty, a classic author of the genre, brings her southern charm to bear in all her stories. *Delta Wedding,* for example, evocatively relates the story of the Fairchild family, living on a plantation in the Mississippi Delta in the early 1920s and all involved in the preparations for Dabney's wedding.[8] The story is much more than that, however; it is an intimate examination of the personalities and emotions of all gathered there for this occasion, woven together as only such an inimitable southern storyteller can. Both Nicholas Sparks and Garrison Keillor write novels that fit within this genre and certainly exemplify the leisurely pace that readers associate with Gentle Reads.

KEY AUTHORS

Jennifer Chiaverini's heartwarming, old-fashioned stories of family and friendship typify many reader expectations for this genre. Although mostly contemporary, these tales also offer flashbacks to historical settings. These heartwarming stories are set in a small town in Pennsylvania and center around quilting. Friendship and family are key elements here, and good-spirited friendships, home truths, and conversations direct the story. In the first novel, *The Quilter's Apprentice,* a young married woman takes a job with a reclusive old woman, shunned by friends and family, and with each quilting lesson, the older woman reveals the secrets of her past.[9] Reconciliation and a hopeful future underline these gentle stories.

Mystery writer Alexander McCall Smith has captured a large segment of the Gentle Reads market, especially with his tales of Mma Precious Ramotswe, proprietor of the No. 1 Ladies' Detective Agency in modern day Botswana. Detection is hardly the point in these quiet stories of people and their foibles. Precious and her assistants rely more on their understanding of human nature than on detecting skills to solve crimes that reflect very human issues. No wonder they're so popular with the Gentle Reads crowd; they offer an introduction to an exotic society that turns out to be very familiar in terms of human nature and motivation. *The No. 1 Ladies' Detective Agency* starts the series.[10] Two of his other series, The

Sunday Philosophy Club and 44 Scotland Street, feature similar character-centered, old-fashioned storytelling.

Adriana Trigiani falls at the outside edge of the Gentle Reads spectrum. Her satisfying novels are sometimes romantic and usually reflect issues found in Women's Lives and Relationships. But these humorous, heartwarming, character- and family-centered tales offer a trace of nostalgia for times gone by as well as the positive outlook that pervades Gentle Reads. There may be some sexual situations and some language that may raise eyebrows, but generally readers are so caught up in the characters and tone that these potentially troubling elements pass by unnoticed. Start readers with *Big Stone Gap*, first in the series of the same name.[11] Set in southwestern Virginia, the series explores love, disaster, and redemption in timeless tales.

Debbie Macomber is another writer known for Romances and novels of Women's Lives and Relationships, but Gentle Reads can also claim her. Old-fashioned values and sometimes inspirational elements infuse her novels of women in communities where tragedy may strike but all works out in the end. These are the ultimate feel-good story for many readers. *The Shop on Blossom Street* is the first in her recent Knitting series.[12]

Don't forget the classic authors: Miss Read, D. E. Stevenson, Elizabeth Goudge, and Elizabeth Cadell. Many libraries still own books by these authors, and they continue to find new fans. Miss Read's Thrush Green series explores the quintessential English village and its denizens, as well as the satisfactions and intrigues that provide the daily grist for the mill of gossip (*Thrush Green* is the first).[13] Stevenson's Mrs. Tim, whose antics enliven British military life before and after World War II, still has a satisfied following of readers who read and reread the series, which begins with *Mrs. Tim Christie*.[14] Although she is best remembered for this series, Stevenson has also written other appealing nonseries titles. Goudge wrote both contemporary and historical stories set in the British Isles and Commonwealth. They feature romantic entanglements and family stories that touch the heart. *Green Dolphin Street*, the story of sisters, the man they love, and the directions in which fate moves lives, is a book reread and treasured by fans, a book to be shared with others.[15] Cadell is another author fans of this genre remember fondly. Many readers have told me how her books transported them to other times and places. Try *The Corner Shop* as an example of her romantic stories; there is also an element of mystery as the story plays out.[16]

WHAT WE KNOW ABOUT FANS

Who reads Gentle Reads? When we started trying to identify this audience, we were surprised at the range of readers in all age groups. For many, these are the books for those times we all know when we simply have to have a book in hand and a safe world to escape to. There have been years when, between Thanksgiving and Christmas, we have not been able to find any of Miss Read's books on the shelf! Some readers select Gentle Reads along with a wide range of other genres, while still others may read them exclusively. We do need to be aware, however, that these are not necessarily the books for that proverbial little old lady. We all know many, many older readers who prefer—and request—something very different: a racy Romance or novels of hard-edged Suspense. And although Christian Fiction is certainly not synonymous with Gentle Reads, we know many readers, fans of Gentle Reads and other genres, who appreciate Robin Lee Hatcher's contemporary and historical novels and others by Christian Fiction authors. Fans of Miss Read and Alexander McCall Smith include some of our most sophisticated readers, a fact that confirms the literary standards of fans of this genre and of many of the books that fall within this classification.

We should keep in mind that readers of this genre may read a variety of types and styles of books. Some prefer a more sophisticated story, others something less complicated. Or they are looking for one type today, but they may be seeking something quite different next time. As in every genre, there is a range of writing styles and tone, and we, as readers' advisors, need to be aware of the range in offering possibilities to readers.

When readers describe books that fit within this genre, they usually talk about character-centered books. However, unlike readers of the character-centered novels of Literary Fiction, which often focus on social and moral issues, Gentle Reads readers are generally not requesting such provocative books. Rather, they describe heartwarming, or perhaps nostalgic, stories that portray smaller, often domestic, pleasures. Gentle Reads generally involve a smaller cast of characters and a narrower focus. Their readers seek a more circumscribed story and a community of characters with an emphasis on the personal relationships. They describe evocative stories, and often mention humor, or at least a lighter touch.

Interestingly, although it is often high on their list of likes and dislikes, they are less likely actually to mention the fact that they do not expect explicit sex, violence, or profanity. Just as in the Romance genre it is often difficult to ascertain how much sex readers will tolerate in a book, here, too, they seem reluctant to bring up a matter very dear to their hearts, and often talk in euphemisms: "They don't write books like they used to," or, "I miss those old-fashioned stories." Both of these generally refer to their dismay at the amount of what they consider objectionable that they discover in much modern fiction. We need to listen for these clues that help us direct them to books they will find more satisfying.

Unfortunately, there is no convenient reference book with lists of these authors for our readers. We need to keep a list of authors we come across in reviews, discover in our own reading, or hear about from fans of this genre. Since we frequently borrow these authors from other genres, we need to be vigilant! The best authors for this list are those who write just in this genre, as we can safely suggest any of their books to fans. However, since that is a very small number, we should also keep track of authors of only one book or the one title by an author who also writes in other genres. In the latter case, readers may enjoy the author enough to experiment with the rest of his or her work. When I worked in the library, I was surely not alone in encountering a request for authors in this genre almost every day. This is also the type of book I always looked for to include on general displays or to offer readers whenever it seemed appropriate. Keeping a list is the only way to find authors in this genre when we need them. Figure 6.2 offers additional authors to acquaint readers with Gentle Reads. Here, more than in any other genre, authors may fit in more than one place; they are listed here because they meet the Gentle Reads criteria, even though they may also comfortably fit within Mystery, Romance, Literary Fiction, and other genres.

THE READERS' ADVISORY INTERVIEW

We know what fans expect when they ask for Gentle Reads, and we have some ideas of authors that fit within the genre. But how do we offer them to other readers we think may also enjoy them? As readers talk about what they enjoy in the books they read, we listen for the clues that lead us to this genre: Do they talk about character-centered books that focus on the relationships among characters, rather than on a single protagonist? Upbeat stories? Books that unfold at a leisurely pace? Ordinary characters? A timeless quality? Old-fashioned stories? All of these are clues that Gentle Reads may be a good choice for these readers. As we describe these authors and their books, offering suggestions to readers, we use the same terms in return and highlight the elements they enjoy.

Figure 6.2 *An Introduction to the Gentle Reads Genre*

Gentle Reads Writers to Try, If You Enjoy . . .

Adrenaline:	Gilbert Morris
Fantasy:	Richard Bach
	George MacDonald
Historical Fiction:	Richard Paul Evans
	Robin Lee Hatcher
Humor:	Clyde Edgerton
	Paul Gallico
	Garrison Keillor
	Angela Thirkell
	Adriana Trigiani
Inspirational:	Joseph Girzone
	Philip Gulley
	Jan Karon
Literary:	Kaye Gibbons
	Eudora Welty
Mystery:	Alexander McCall Smith
Romance:	Debbie Macomber
	Robin Pilcher
	Nicholas Sparks
Romantic Suspense:	Barbara Michaels
	Phyllis Whitney
Travel:	Peter Mayle
Westerns:	Brock and Bodie Thoene (Saga of the Sierras)[17]
Women's Lives:	Debbie Macomber
	Sharon Owens
	Rosamunde Pilcher
	Jeanne Ray
	Adriana Trigiani

Patrons who want "guarantees" when we suggest Gentle Reads are one of the most difficult problems we face with this genre. Can we assure them that there is nothing in a particular book that will offend them? How could we possibly know? I think there are two issues involved here. One is that readers simply want to be reassured that it is okay to take the book.

They seem to fear that someone at the circulation desk will laugh at them, or think less of them, for reading this book—whatever it is. This is an apprehension shared by readers of all genres, but it is an easy problem to solve. When they ask us about the book they want to take, we either answer that we have read it or that someone has, or that it got good reviews, and thus assure the reader that it is "safe" to check it out.

The other "safe" issue—whether this book is safe to read or whether it might contain something offensive—is another problem altogether. Although I get this question from adults who have concerns that there not be anything distasteful in what they read, I am even more likely to encounter the question from a parent, seeking a book for his or her teen. We never offer guarantees. If parents have doubts or concerns, we encourage them to read the book first, before giving it to their children. If readers have concerns for themselves, we offer them reviews and tell them simply to close the book and bring it back if it is not to their liking. What offends me in books may not bother another reader at all, and I may skim over something that another reader finds abhorrent. In my experience, no book can be guaranteed safe. When we work with readers of all ages, we offer suggestions and a range of possibilities. We encourage readers to try these and to come back for other suggestions if they are not satisfied. We remind them they do not need to finish every book they start, and we generally fall back on solid readers' advisory techniques as we build a relationship with these readers.

Because Gentle Reads is not a traditional genre, lists of appropriate titles are hard to find. We need to keep lists of authors and titles that have worked for our readers. This is the time to rely on the collaborative nature of readers' advisory and ask other librarians to suggest titles in the genre. That this query has appeared on the readers' advisory electronic discussion list Fiction_L more than once suggests that many of us face readers daily who request the kinds of titles included in the Gentle Reads genre.

One lesson all of us have learned is not to be afraid to look farther afield to find titles that might work. As is evident in both figure 6.2 and figure 6.3 later in this chapter, many authors in other genres write titles that will appeal to Gentle Reads fans. We should watch for these—and keep a list. In fact, many authors have written a "feel-good" book, including Thriller writers John Grisham (*Playing for Pizza*), David Baldacci (*The Christmas Train*), and even James Patterson (*Suzanne's Diary for Nicholas*).[18] These exceptions to their usual writing are interesting and make good suggestions for fans, as long as we give them to readers with the caveat that these titles aren't necessarily typical of these authors' books.

Sure Bets

It will not come as a surprise that there are Gentle Reads authors who appeal beyond the confines of the genre. These authors tell satisfying, heartwarming, old-fashioned stories with memorable characters. What is there not to like?

Sandra Dallas writes Gentle Reads with historical settings, close friendships among strong women characters, and hard times, but these difficult situations are enfolded in ultimately upbeat stories. In *The Persian Pickle Club,* quilting again plays an important role, as a group of women living in rural Harveyville, Kansas, during the Great Depression meet to quilt and socialize.[19] There is trouble here as well, however, and when a long-buried secret is uncovered, the group bands together to protect each other and their families.

Clyde Edgerton, another southerner like Eudora Welty, adds a large dose of humor to his tales of small-town life in the South and West, often adding a touch of mystery as well. Most of his titles work well for Gentle Reads fans, although a few have an edge. Characters reign supreme and the story rambles along, with nothing much happening, but an enjoyable trip is had by all. *Walking across Egypt* is a classic.[20] Mattie Rigsbee, even at seventy-eight, remains independent and only wishes she had grandchildren. When runaway Wesley Benfield enters her life, she does what she has to, even if it means breaking the law, to give him the break he needs.

Terry Kay joins many other authors of Gentle Reads in setting his stories in the past, but again, these poignant, nostalgic stories have a timeless quality. Memories play an important role in many of his novels; looking back to other times—good and bad—creates detailed, resonant stories that remind readers of other, better days. *To Dance with the White Dog* is one of his most beloved.[21] Here Sam Peek, mourning his wife of fifty-seven years who has recently died, returns to his roots to attend his sixtieth class reunion. The dog of the title, perhaps only a figment of his imagination, helps him to reconcile his memories and come to terms with his grief, with death, and with life.

Public radio personality Garrison Keillor has also written several titles for Gentle Reads fans. (And, by all means, collect and share the audio versions of his radio shows; his stories from Lake Wobegon are made for this genre and his audio renditions are excellent.) Since readers are familiar with his affable, and sometimes curmudgeonly, presence on his *Prairie Home Companion* program and his affectionate take on small-town life, they are likely to explore his more provocative novels. *Pontoon: A Lake*

Wobegon Novel is sure to please his myriad fans with the heartwarming story of quirky characters with all their foibles, and it's a good introduction for those who have somehow missed him.[22]

Nicholas Sparks writes serious, often sentimental, sometimes tragic, stories of love. Like Kay's, these are not Romances, although Romance readers may appreciate them. Instead they are timeless stories of love lost and found, and of how people survive loss. *A Walk to Remember* remains popular with readers.[23] This ultimately upbeat story, told from the perspective of forty years later, recounts the unexpected love that blossoms between a high school football hero and the minister's daughter.

While Adriana Trigiani's Big Stone Gap series is always popular, *Lucia, Lucia* remains my Sure Bet.[24] (Not to mention a candidate for one of the best covers ever!) Set in New York City just after World War II, it is the story of an Italian-American community, family, and daughter, and how social changes brought about by the war have improved life in many ways—but not necessarily for everyone. It is a thoughtful look at an interesting woman in a changing time, and it is a good suggestion both for Gentle Reads and Women's Lives and Relationships readers.

Jan Karon's series set in Mitford, North Carolina, remains popular, and for readers who haven't discovered its pleasures, the first, *At Home in Mitford,* is a Sure Bet.[25] These heartwarming tales of Timothy Kavanaugh, an Episcopal priest, have touched the hearts of millions, with their simple stories of faith amid hardships and the joys and sorrows of everyday life. Humor adds to these gentle stories (whenever he quotes scripture, his dog, Barnabas, stops misbehaving and listens attentively), and even though tragedy sometimes accompanies them, there is always the sense that all's right in the world. Although extraordinarily popular with many readers, Karon does not have a universal appeal. Some find the religious emphasis too intrusive, while others complain of "saccharine" characters and plots. This is, of course, one of the dangers with Gentle Reads. For each reader there is a level of gentleness beyond which they do not want to go, and as in all genres, authors appeal to readers for a variety of expected and unforeseen reasons.

No list of Gentle Reads would be complete without Fannie Flagg. Her *Redbird Christmas* is a great suggestion for this audience.[26] When a Chicago businessman is told he hasn't long to live, he locates a small town in Alabama and takes off for the milder climate and the quieter lifestyle. He soon becomes a part of the community's life, almost against his will, and a lot of healing takes place: mended relationships, mended spirits, mended bodies—all through the magic of a cardinal, or redbird, as the locals call it.

EXPANDING READERS' HORIZONS WITH WHOLE COLLECTION READERS' ADVISORY

As should be clear from the previous discussion, Gentle Reads are few and far between; sometimes a single book by an author qualifies; sometimes an author can be counted on to produce a number of novels within the genre. There is also extensive overlap between Gentle Reads and a number of other genres, particularly Romance, Mystery, Literary Fiction, and Women's Lives and Relationships. Just as we watch for books in the Gentle Reads genre, we need to be aware—when we read, when we read reviews, and when we talk with readers—of books from other genres that may please these fans.

For fans of Gentle Reads, the Romance genre offers a number of gentler authors, those who do not generally include explicit sexual encounters, who might appeal. Popular classic Regency Romances by Barbara Metzger and Carla Kelly make good suggestions. Katie Fforde's lighthearted contemporary English Romances are generally "sweet" enough for these readers. Certainly Romances by Christian publishers would work, if readers are interested in that emphasis.

From the Mystery genre we might consider authors such as M. C. Beaton (her Hamish Macbeth series), and numerous other authors of Cozy Mysteries (with the body and any violence well offstage) might work. Try Rhys Bowen's Evan Evans series with its Welsh village police constable (*Evans Above* starts the series); Joan Hess's Claire Malloy mysteries, featuring a bookseller and her daughter (*Strangled Prose* is the first); Dorothy Cannell's zany Ellie Haskell Mysteries, beginning with *The Thin Woman*; and Nancy Atherton's Aunt Dimity series, if your reader does not mind that a ghost is one of the central characters (*Aunt Dimity's Death* is the first).[27]

Not surprisingly, Women's Lives and Relationships offers a number of authors who have strong appeal for fans of Gentle Reads. Newcomer and award-winner Sarah Addison Allen brings gentle stories of community and relationships plus a little magic in her novels, beginning with *Garden Spells*.[28] Maeve Binchy and Marcia Willett write stories of women that are usually gentle enough for these readers. Joan Medlicott's Ladies of Covington Place series and Ann B. Ross's Miss Julia series should also not be forgotten. Others—Joanna Trollope and Elizabeth Berg—may also work, but some of their story lines contain issues (divorce or abuse, for example) beyond what Gentle Reads fans want to read. The style and tone match what they find in Gentle Reads, but the subject matter may be too controversial. Still, these authors are good suggestions with that proviso.

Among Western and Historical writers, don't forget Molly Gloss. *The Hearts of Horses* is particularly evocative of the rural West during World War I.[29] Jeanne Williams is another possibility as an author who combines the West with Historical Fiction. Brock and Bodie Thoene's Christian Historical Fiction might satisfy readers looking for historical story lines, as might Van Reid's Moosepath League series.

Old-fashioned is a phrase to pursue when readers use it in a readers' advisory interview. They, and many of us, think of it in a very positive sense: books that reflect conventional values and mores but tell a good story. Many older authors from a number of genres fit into that category and may make good suggestions for fans of Gentle Reads. From the Adventure genre, both Hammond Innes and Nevil Shute write this type of book, and their stories have many qualities that appeal to fans of this genre. Classic authors of Romantic Suspense—Victoria Holt, Phyllis Whitney, Barbara Michaels, and Mary Stewart—all make good suggestions. Their stories, for the most part not dated, tell of romantic adventures, but they lack the violence and sex that characterize many of the stories in the same genre written today. Even some of the Suspense novels of Mary Higgins Clark may be gentle enough for fans of this genre, although we need to exercise care in suggesting them, allowing readers to see that there may be elements beyond what they enjoy and offering other titles in case Clark does not appeal. Fans of more literary works might appreciate Paulo Coelho's *The Alchemist,* as well as gently reflective titles by May Sarton and Penelope Lively.[30] Figure 6.3 offers authors from other genres who might appeal to fans of Gentle Reads.

TRENDS

If anything, Gentle Reads are more elusive now than in 2001, when the first edition of this book was published. The publishing climate has changed, and books seem to be harder-edged and more explicit than earlier. This, of course, makes it more important to keep the lists of titles when we discover them.

Gentle Reads have been infiltrated by the paranormal, as most other genres have been. Fans love Atherton's Aunt Dimity series, despite the fact that she is a ghost. Many readers accept a wide variety of phenomena as long as the gentle tone, sense of community, and endearing characters remain. Even a little magic seems not amiss in Sarah Addison Allen's novels.

Figure 6.3   *Expanding Readers' Horizons*

Authors to Take Readers beyond the Gentle Reads Genre

Adrenaline:	Mary Higgins Clark
	Hammond Innes
	Nevil Shute
Biography/Memoir:	James Herriot
	Homer Hickam
	Haven Kimmel
Fantasy:	Peter S. Beagle
	T. H. White
Historical Fiction:	Van Reid
	Brock and Bodie Thoene
Humor:	Dorothy Cannell
Literary:	Wendell Berry
	Penelope Lively
	May Sarton
Mystery:	Nancy Atherton
	M. C. Beaton (Hamish Macbeth series)[31]
	Rhys Bowen
Romance:	Katie Fforde
	Barbara Metzger
	Francis Ray
Romantic Suspense:	Victoria Holt
	Barbara Michaels
	Mary Stewart
	Phyllis Whitney
Western:	Molly Gloss
	Jeanne Williams
Women's Lives:	Sarah Addison Allen
	Maeve Binchy
	Neta Jackson
	Joan Medlicott

Christian publishers have expanded their scope. Less didactic titles play an important role among Gentle Reads readers. Julie Klassen's *Lady of Milkweed Manor* is a good example.[32] Set in early nineteenth-century England, it explores the fate of a vicar's daughter, pregnant by an important houseguest and disinherited by her father. Faith issues are subtly and seamlessly interwoven into a romantic novel rich in historical detail.

One last observation about fans of this genre: They are among the most passionate sharers of the books they have loved. They pass treasured titles from one reader to the next among a group they know can be trusted to cherish that author in return. These books have a distinctive emotional element; when readers offer these titles, they are careful to expose themselves only to others whom they believe will also respect the emotions involved. If they share books with us as well, then we know we have earned their trust and respect.

Notes

1. Jennifer Chiaverini, *The Christmas Quilt: An Elm Creek Quilts Novel* (New York: Simon and Schuster, 2005); Chiaverini, *The New Year's Quilt: An Elm Creek Quilts Novel* (New York: Simon and Schuster, 2007).
2. Kaye Gibbons, *Charms for the Easy Life* (New York: Putnam, 1993).
3. Mary Ann Shaffer and Annie Barrows, *The Guernsey Literary and Potato Peel Pie Society* (New York: Dial, 2008).
4. Philip Gulley, the Harmony series, beginning with *Home to Harmony* (Sisters, OR: Multnomah, 2000).
5. Lynn N. Austin, *A Woman's Place* (Minneapolis: Bethany House, 2006).
6. Elizabeth Berg, *Dream When You're Feeling Blue: A Novel* (New York: Random House, 2007).
7. Debbie Macomber, *The Shop on Blossom Street* (Don Mills, ON: Mira, 2004).
8. Eudora Welty, *Delta Wedding* (New York: Harcourt Brace, 1946).
9. Chiaverini, *The Quilter's Apprentice: A Novel* (New York: Simon and Schuster, 1999).
10. Alexander McCall Smith, *The No. 1 Ladies' Detective Agency* (New York: Anchor, 2002).
11. Adriana Trigiani, *Big Stone Gap: A Novel* (New York: Random House, 2000).
12. Macomber cited above.
13. Miss Read, *Thrush Green* (Boston: Houghton Mifflin, 1960).
14. D. E. Stevenson, *Mrs. Tim Christie* (New York: Holt, 1973).
15. Elizabeth Goudge, *Green Dolphin Street* (New York: Coward-McCann, 1944).
16. Elizabeth Cadell, *The Corner Shop* (New York: Morrow, 1967).
17. Brock and Bodie Thoene, Saga of the Sierras, beginning with *The Man from Shadow Ridge* (Minneapolis: Bethany House, 1990).
18. John Grisham, *Playing for Pizza* (New York: Doubleday, 2007); David Baldacci, *The Christmas Train* (New York: Warner, 2002); James Patterson, *Suzanne's Diary for Nicholas* (Boston: Little, Brown, 2001).
19. Sandra Dallas, *The Persian Pickle Club* (New York: St. Martin's, 1995).

20. Clyde Edgerton, *Walking across Egypt* (Chapel Hill, NC: Algonquin, 1987).
21. Terry Kay, *To Dance with the White Dog* (Atlanta: Peachtree, 1990).
22. Garrison Keillor, *Pontoon: A Lake Wobegon Novel* (New York: Viking, 2007).
23. Nicholas Sparks, *A Walk to Remember* (New York: Warner, 1999).
24. Trigiani, *Lucia, Lucia: A Novel* (New York: Random House, 2003).
25. Jan Karon, *At Home in Mitford* (Elgin, IL: Lion Pub., 1994).
26. Fannie Flagg, *Redbird Christmas* (New York: Random House, 2004).
27. Rhys Bowen, *Evans Above* (New York: St. Martin's, 1997); Joan Hess, *Strangled Prose* (New York: St. Martin's, 1986); Dorothy Cannell, *The Thin Woman: An Epicurean Mystery* (New York: St. Martin's, 1984); Nancy Atherton, *Aunt Dimity's Death* (New York: Viking, 1992).
28. Sarah Addison Allen, *Garden Spells* (New York: Bantam, 2007).
29. Molly Gloss, *The Hearts of Horses* (Boston: Houghton Mifflin, 2007).
30. Paulo Coelho, *The Alchemist* (San Francisco: HarperSanFrancisco, 1993).
31. M. C. Beaton's Hamish Macbeth series, beginning with *Death of a Gossip* (New York: St. Martin's, 1985).
32. Julie Klassen, *Lady of Milkweed Manor* (Minneapolis: Bethany House, 2007).

7

HORROR

From classic ghost and vampire tales to hauntings and supernatural visitations, Horror stories, and the thrill they produce, fill our waking and sleeping hours. From ancient times with stories of Lilith and the ghosts of the dead, Horror has always held its own among fiction genres, although the popularity of these stories has waxed and waned throughout the centuries. Horror in literature has been termed mankind's effort to invoke and subdue the demonic. There is a certain pleasure to be derived from the chill that Horror creates, as well as from the relief at being able to close a book to escape its thrall—temporarily at least, as the best of the genre tends to stay with its fans.

A DEFINITION

Many of us recognize Horror from television and movies, even if we are less familiar with the books. Baby boomers grew up on *The Twilight Zone,* with its mix of spooky stories and a supernatural twist, while *The X-Files* has spurred today's surge of interest in this genre (and Science Fiction, too). Teenagers flock to showings of *Scream* and its sequels, as well as to every reincarnation of Jason in the various *Friday the Thirteenth* screenings.

But what constitutes a Horror story? Horror, despite the numerous themes that propel its stories, is one of the most straightforward genres to define and understand on a very basic level. The goal of Horror fiction is to produce fear in readers, sometimes through psychology, sometimes through gory details, and its appeal occurs on a very deep emotional level. It contains a monster of some type, and supernatural elements figure prominently. Thus, Horror certainly includes stories of ghosts, ghouls, werewolves, and vampires of wide variety. The genre runs the gamut from contemporary tales filled with graphic sex as well as gore, to classics such as Bram Stoker's *Dracula,* which creates the loathsome vampire, hunted by those who fear him.[1] What is important is the feeling of foreboding that permeates the novels, the sense of unease as we await the unexpected. Horror novels, then, are stories of nightmares come to life, complete with monsters of various descriptions; and as in all our nightmares, surprise is a crucial element. We never know exactly when the terror will invade our lives. Figure 7.1 lists the characteristics of the Horror genre.

CHARACTERISTICS AND THE GENRE'S APPEAL

Tone/Mood

The atmosphere in Horror novels must, the fans tell us, evoke an emotional response: a chill, a sense of menace, a feeling of supernatural terror. This special atmosphere or setting pervades the novel, and it is what readers are expecting and looking for when they ask us for Horror fiction. Unlike Science Fiction, which appeals first to the intellect, Horror appeals first and foremost to the emotions, and primitive ones at that. The point

---

Figure 7.1   *Characteristics of Horror*

1. A nightmare mood dominates these novels and creates a feeling of menace, evoking a strong emotional response from the reader. A dark tone and a sense of foreboding characterize these stories.

2. Monsters of some kind frame the stories, along with supernatural and paranormal phenomena. Graphic violence, strong language, and explicit sex often enhance the effect of the supernatural and the impact of the stories.

3. Endings are unresolved. Although it may be beaten down temporarily, the horror lives on.

4. Language is rich in adjectives and description, generally of the evil that threatens. These sharply imagined images intensify the readers' reaction.

5. Protagonists are often haunted, shattered individuals. Antagonists are always sinister and often monsters in some form, whether real or imaginary.

6. Unexpected appearances and attacks, designed to jolt the reader, accelerate the pacing and keep the story moving quickly.

of a good Horror story is to evoke an emotional and spiritual response in the reader: true fright.

In Horror all elements (story line, characterization, pacing) help create this sense of menace and contribute to this emotional impact. These novels are infused with this mood. Readers never escape this feeling, at least not for long. In fact, many Horror novels highlight the horrific or supernatural element by employing different typefaces, such as bold type, capitals, or italics. (This is a technique Stephen King frequently uses to emphasize and underline the horrific.) There may also be a prologue that creates this horrific atmosphere right from the beginning. In Sarah Langan's *The Missing*, a prologue related in first person establishes an immediate connection with the reader and builds a strong sense of foreboding as it tells of a chemical fire which may have released more than mere chemicals.[2] Our interest is piqued and we simply wait, anxiously, to see what will happen next.

It goes without saying that the bleak and disturbing tone of much Horror fiction also reflects and enhances this dark atmosphere. Even though Horror novels are decidedly dark, readers find in them a surprising amount of humor, albeit grim. There are often puns and plays on words that amuse fans, and some authors are noted for their macabre humor. Christopher Moore's award-winning *A Dirty Job* illustrates this with the madcap humor of this mock epic featuring an obsessive new father who, because he sees death taking his wife's soul, must become a Death Merchant himself.[3] That is, he collects soul vessels from the dying to be used by the soulless. Luckily he is aided in his efforts by the quirky cast of characters who live and work in the building that houses his secondhand store, not to mention hell hounds and assorted minions of Death. Clive Barker's *Mister B. Gone* achieves similar levels of hilarity with his tale of a magic-deprived Renaissance-era demon whose advice to the reader is simple: burn this book.[4]

Horror titles range from the Storyteller end of the genre, where the sense of foreboding and menace build slowly and graphic gore likely appears only toward the end (although the suggestion of terrible things happening creates the uneasiness that drives the plot), to the Visceral end where violence occurs early on and the intensity never flags. Explicit sex and violence, as well as profanity, play a role in all these novels across the genre.

Frame/Setting

Horror conventions and characters—werewolves, ghosts, vampires, and more—have been borrowed by so many genres (Fantasy, Romance, Mystery, even Literary Fiction) in recent years that it's no longer possible to identify the genre by the type of characters and background. However, what remains true is that Horror is populated by monsters of some kind, and they are usually supernatural. In some Horror novels we meet these monsters in all their depravity in the first few pages, while in others, tension builds as a sense of foreboding signals their arrival later in the novel.

In addition, it is important to recognize that Horror novels usually contain graphic violence and themes of sensuality and sexuality that seem to go hand in hand with creating this menacing atmosphere. These elements may be offensive to readers new to Horror who are not expecting them. For fans, this heightened level of gore and sex simply add to the visceral quality they expect. For a taste of this style, try Richard Laymon, known for his disturbing and graphically gory tales. In *Island*, originally published in 1995 but more recently reprinted (like many of Laymon's titles), shipwrecked survivors become the victims of a bloodthirsty maniac.[5]

Because the setting and atmosphere are so important, they are often very detailed. If there is a haunted house, you will know where all the windows are, what wall and floor coverings are there, how it smells, sounds—and, especially, how it feels. If you have read any of Clive Barker's Horror novels, you know that the descriptive details give you a clear picture of the setting, whether in the real world or the horrific. In *Coldheart Canyon* the description of the room of tiles, supposedly created by the devil's first wife Lilith, resonates throughout the story.[6] In fact, the setting and atmosphere may be described more completely and vividly than the characters. You can feel and sense the evil, sometimes even before you see it. There is no question that Hill House, from Shirley Jackson's classic psychological ghost story, *The Haunting of Hill House,* embodies the appropriate sense of dread and disquiet long before the actual horrific incidents occur; its very description reflects the menace the house contains.[7] A reader coming upon such descriptions, and influenced by the mood they create, would have no doubt about what lies ahead for the protagonist—and for himself as a reader.

Story Line

The presence of the supernatural pervades these stories and sets Horror apart from other genres. Not only does it affect the mood and tone of the story, it influences the story line as well. In fact, story lines in the Horror genre do not necessarily flow in a logical order, due to the influence of the supernatural. This does not bother fans, as it is part of what they expect to find in these books. However, this is one of the reasons why Horror may not be as satisfying to fans of other genres, such as those who enjoy Mysteries, for example, where loose ends are tied up and justice triumphs. In Horror, the supernatural leads to the unexpected. Horror deals with the unexplained and unexplainable. H. P. Lovecraft was among the first authors in the genre to suggest that there is a parallel universe of unimaginable horrors that occasionally finds ways to break through into our own. (Try *The Dunwich Horror* and subsequent stories featuring the dreaded Necronomicon by the mad Arab Abdul Alhazred.)[8] Classic contemporary authors, including King ("The Mist") and Dean R. Koontz (*The Bad Place*), have also used this theme.[9]

The ending of a Horror novel is crucial to its appeal and also sets these novels apart from those in other genres. In Horror novels readers do not know how the story will end, and this is a direct contrast to many other genres, especially Mystery and Romance, in which readers can often predict the ending after the first few pages. (Readers do not know the details of each novel's conclusion, but in Romance, they understand that the couple in question will resolve the issues that keep them apart; and in Mysteries, justice will be done, with the murderer apprehended.) In Horror novels, the endings themselves are often vague, sustaining the menacing atmosphere rather than tying loose ends together. The horror has been beaten down for now, but it is not dead. The evil is still lurking. Although the monster may have been killed, its egg remains, left unseen. In Scott Smith's chilling title *The Ruins,* a group of college students on vacation visit an archeological site, lured there by a carnivorous vine that mimics familiar voices and entraps them.[10] In the end they realize that there is no rescue, no escape, and we readers understand that the ruins and that deadly vine remain, patiently awaiting their next victims.

Until recently there were rarely sequels in Horror fiction, even though most of the novels end as if the author is planning one. (One of the few early examples of a sequel is *The Reliquary,* by Douglas Preston and Lincoln Child, which follows the enormously popular *Relic.*[11] Even though this sequel would probably appeal more to fans of Medical/Scientific Thrillers, it does end with the possibility that some of the horror has survived. Later titles in the series move away from Horror and into the Adrenaline genres.) However, even Horror has succumbed to the pressure evident in other genres to provide an ongoing series. Jonathan Maberry's Pine Deep series, Gary Braunbeck's Cedar Hills series, F. Paul Wilson's Repairman Jack, and Dean R. Koontz's Odd Thomas series all demonstrate the current popularity of series.[12] Each novel constitutes an adventure and follows the general characteristics of the genre, although the ongoing characters are more fully developed than in most single-title Horror novels.

Style/Language

Certainly profanity and excesses typify the language of Horror novels, but there are other features as well. As with all the Emotion genres, Horror novels are rich in adjectives and descriptions. One need only look to Koontz's Odd Thomas series or his novel *The Taking* to see that lush prose style.[13]

Other writers employ distinct styles that display their skills as they intensify the horrific elements. Mark Z. Danielewski's *House of Leaves* is a stylistic tour de force.[14] It's a novel within a novel, with a story line in the elaborate footnotes that threatens to overwhelm this tale of a discovered manuscript which is the commentary on a documentary film about a house that is bigger inside than its outer dimensions would suggest. Without a strictly linear plotline, this layered novel plays with stories and dimensions, language and narrative style. The excesses typical of Horror appear in both story and style in this elaborately executed haunted house tale.

The plotline of Toby Barlow's *Sharp Teeth* may be more straightforward, but stylistically it is also interesting.[15] Written in blank verse with the ends of lines looking disconcertingly like teeth, this modern werewolf tale takes readers inside werewolf society. While the poetry is lyrical and image-rich, the tone is dark and the language edgy. Like any good Horror novel, this is the stuff of nightmares.

Max Brooks's stylish mockumentary *World War Z: An Oral History of the Zombie War* takes a more playful though deadpan approach.[16] Think Studs Terkel crossed with the author's father Mel Brooks for a sense of this account by the survivors of Earth's battle against the zombies and an ironic look at society.

In Horror readers also see the influence of graphic novels, as Horror themes and characters continue to infiltrate graphic novels and illustrations find their way into Horror novels. Although it is not a graphic novel, Mike Mignola's *Baltimore; or, The Steadfast Tin Soldier and the Vampire* is filled with illustrations that heighten the impact of the horrific. Mignola employs old-fashioned language and cadence as Lord Henry and his comrades attempt to vanquish the vampire plague unleashed by the Great War.[17] In *Welcome to Lovecraft,* the first title in their Locke and Key series, artist Gabriel Rodriguez's exceptional illustrations rival Joe Hill's haunting prose for excellence in setting the disturbing mood.[18] Fans will find adaptations of the works of classic Horror authors H. P. Lovecraft and Edgar Allan Poe, as well as modern graphic novel classics by Alan Moore and Neil Gaiman.

Diaries and e-mails update Bram Stoker's classic *Dracula* in *Fangland.*[19] John Marks reimagines the story in the modern-day world of television broadcasting with a style that harkens back to the original. Dan Simmons's *The Terror* refers to the ship of that name, as well as to the horror that stalks the explorers of Sir John Franklin's arctic expedition in the 1840s.[20] Journal entries set the story in its time, as do the nineteenth-century style and vocabulary.

Characterization

What about characters in Horror novels? They are usually haunted, shattered individuals or in some way vulnerable; these are people who are out of control. There are not many happy-go-lucky characters in Horror fiction. (And if they do appear, they are unlikely to survive the first fifty pages!) The character of the villain or evil force is always sinister; these are monsters in some form. In fact, the villains do not need to be realistic, just plausible, unlike other genre fiction that insists on realistic characters, even among the bad guys.

One of the most interesting features of characterization in Horror is how point of view can help readers' advisors separate Horror from hard-edged Suspense, which generally has a different readership. In serial killer novels, the readers find the point of view of both the killer and the detective, and they know what each is thinking and doing. Although there can still be grisly moments, these are expected, because we know the killer and his plans. This knowledge makes all the difference in how readers react to the story. There may be exceptions, but generally speaking, Horror fans do not often find serial killer novels satisfying in exactly the same way; in hard-edged Suspense, they know too much and lose the desired element of total surprise. Also, endings in Suspense tie things up, with the good guys in control, while Horror offers open, unresolved endings. In

Suspense, as opposed to Horror, the characters are generally more in control and heroes survive. In Horror, their fate is uncertain (even protagonists die, a fate that is anathema in many other genres), and they seem to have little control. Also, as the evil is generally unknown, its appearances are jarring and unexpected. (Even if the evil has been identified, its appearance is unpredictable and can precipitate an electric moment of adrenaline rush.)

Within Horror novels, point of view can create very different types of novels, depending on whether it is the innocent's point of view or the evil's point of view that the reader follows. An example of a novel told from the evil's point of view is Anne Rice's classic *Interview with the Vampire*.[21] Here we see the action from the vampire's point of view, and that intensifies the atmosphere and the reader's relationship to the story and characters. Horror novels in which the reader sees the action from the evil's point of view often have a very different, more disturbing feel. By contrast, the characterization in Horror novels by King allows the reader to identify with the protagonists—often ordinary people caught up in an extraordinary situation—and to empathize with them and their plight. We are pulled in by the sympathetic characters, rather than distanced by the viewpoint of the sinister protagonist. Both have the intended effect of books in this genre, but that effect is achieved quite differently in each case.

Pacing

The pacing helps create and sustain Horror's unique atmosphere. Pacing in Horror novels is often erratic, with scenes of calm followed, without warning, by more intense scenes. These unexpected qualities and sudden changes add to the menacing nature. Readers expect to get a jolt at irregular, unpredictable intervals in Horror novels. These differ from those we find in a genre such as Suspense, where readers know more than the protagonists and thus anticipate these episodes. But because in Horror these interludes occur erratically and unexpectedly, thus capturing the essence of living in a nightmare, there is a very real sense that the pacing is out of control, and, by inference, so are characters and plot.

KEY AUTHORS

Stephen King remains the name to know in the Horror genre and among popular fiction writers in general, as he is an outspoken advocate of genre fiction and story in its many forms, including audiobooks and e-books.

Few would question King's preeminent popularity and productivity. His first Horror novel, *Carrie,* was published in 1974 and he continues to make his mark on the Horror genre.[22] Under his real name as well as his pseudonym, Richard Bachman, King has written more than forty Horror novels, as well as a few Dark Fantasy novels, and even a few mainstream novels (for example, *Dolores Claiborne* and *The Girl Who Loved Tom Gordon,* although even they contain the suggestion of the supernatural).[23] King's books are generally characterized by sympathetic, although certainly haunted, protagonists; a seemingly normal environment into which the horror intrudes; and usually a long buildup to the horrific situation. His writing ranges from the more Storyteller end of the genre, with a slow and steady buildup to the intensely horrific ending written as King, to the more Visceral, with violence and depravity in the first pages, written as Bachman.

Ramsey Campbell, another popular and award-winning author, brings an English perspective, often drawing his setting and characters from his native Liverpool. His stories and prose have a dreamy quality, and his books often make good crossover for fans of Psychological Suspense. Like King he extracts Horror from the ordinary and everyday, usually in urban settings. A recent title, *The Grin of the Dark,* tilts at the sinister aspects of the movie industry and clowns, both popular Horror themes, but with his inimitable twist.[24]

Joe Hill, Stephen King's son, shows signs of assuming his father's mantle with his assured and terrifying take on the genre. His award-winning *Heart-Shaped Box* features a nightmare tone, graphic violence, relentless dread, paranormal events, and characters who are surprisingly sympathetic.[25] A heavy-metal superstar, now in retirement, collects obscure, macabre objects; however, the ghost he buys over the Internet turns out to be the spirit of his late girlfriend's stepfather—who is both very real and very angry. To date Hill has also published an acclaimed collection of ghost stories and a graphic novel.

Peter Straub has co-written several Horror novels with Stephen King, but he stands as a key author in his own right. His early novel *Ghost Story* remains a classic book and film.[26] More recently *Lost Boy Lost Girl* demonstrates his skill at creating creepily atmospheric tales of growing terror.[27] Here a haunted house becomes the focus for a writer's battle against supernatural serial murderers. Straub's work is characterized by horror that springs from the everyday, small town settings, hauntings, and a style that pays homage to the masters of the genre.

WHAT WE KNOW ABOUT FANS

What do we know, and need to know, about fans of the Horror genre? We know that they expect the unexpected. They demand characters, events, and situations that surprise them. They read Horror because they enjoy being frightened. Atmospheric stories appeal to them; authors need not necessarily be literary stylists, but they must tell a story infused with a creepiness, a growing dread of the outcome. How much blood and guts they can tolerate varies, as discussed below. However, fans of the Horror genre read to be frightened, to confront their personal nightmares, or to experience the terror they had not even imagined before. Their favorite writers are those who meet these expectations.

Fans of Horror likely know more about forthcoming titles and popular authors than we do. Like Romance, this is a genre that is not always reviewed in the library literature, in part, perhaps because titles are often published by small presses and as paperbacks. In addition, some of the most popular titles among readers have been passed by word of mouth; they are cult books that we may not have heard about. If we make an effort to solicit suggestions from fans of the genre, we can often keep up to date on the most recent titles, as well as authors whose work we should collect. Ask fans also for useful websites and blogs that follow the genre.

Figure 7.2 lists Horror writers you might want to try if you enjoy one of these other genres. Going from a genre we already read and appreciate to an author of Horror who writes similarly may help us understand and better appreciate the Horror genre.

THE READERS' ADVISORY INTERVIEW

The most important question to consider in working with readers is not how graphic and violent the Horror is, but how early that element appears in the book. Those Horror readers who really do not like a lot of gore can tolerate much more if it occurs later in the novel, once they know the characters and are engrossed in the story. (This is the same phenomenon that occurs with the amount of sex in Romances; sex too soon or too graphic early in the book may be off-putting to some readers. If it occurs later in the novel and between a couple who care about each other, it is less likely to offend, no matter how graphic.)

Intensity is a closely related issue. Many authors at the Storyteller end of the genre build the sinister mood more slowly, while examples of the

Figure 7.2 *An Introduction to the Horror Genre*

Horror Writers to Try, If You Enjoy . . .

Adrenaline:	Bentley Little
	F. Paul Wilson (Repairman Jack series)[28]
	John Saul
	Dan Simmons
Biography/Memoir:	Stephen Marlowe (*The Lighthouse at the End of the World*)[29]
Fantasy:	Kelley Armstrong (Women of the Underworld series)[30]
	H. P Lovecraft
Gay/Lesbian:	Poppy Z. Brite
	Chelsea Quinn Yarbro (Saint-Germain series)[31]
Historical Fiction:	Barbara Hambly (*Those Who Hunt the Night*)[32]
	Chelsea Quinn Yarbro
	Dan Simmons (*The Terror*)[33]
History:	Andrei Codrescu (*The Blood Countess*)[34]
	Brian Stableford (David Lydyard trilogy)[35]
Humor:	Christopher Moore
Inspirational:	Frank Peretti
Literary:	M. R. James
	Mark Z. Danielewski
Multicultural:	L. A. Banks
	Koji Suzuki (*Ring*)[36]
Mystery:	Tanya Huff
Natural History:	Douglas Preston and Lincoln Child (Pendergast series)[37]
Psychological Suspense:	Ramsey Campbell
	Edgar Allan Poe
	Peter Straub
Romance:	Laurell K. Hamilton
Saga:	Anne Rice (Vampire Chronicles)[38]
Science Fiction:	Max Brooks (*World War Z*)[39]
True Crime:	John Farris
Women's Lives:	Kelley Armstrong

Visceral end are often more intense early on. Each reader has a comfort level, and the easiest way to discover it is to offer a range of suggestions that reflect the diversity of the Horror genre. This is a genre that relies on an emotional impact, and although readers may not have a firm grasp of what they are looking for, they are generally able to reveal their preferences as they react to possibilities. Each of us has a level of creepiness and gore beyond which we do not want to go, and to work successfully with readers, we need an idea of the range of possibilities the genre offers so we can present them to readers.

Now, how can we best help readers find what they are looking for? In a slight twist on the general readers' advisory technique, I ask readers to tell me the scariest parts of books they have enjoyed. Armed with this information, I can make suggestions that are more likely to fit within those parameters. In offering suggestions, I try to contrast these types of Horror and let the reader choose. Do they like those that start out fairly normally but then things start to go awry? Or do they prefer to be thrown right in the middle of a horrific situation?

We keep mental (or physical) lists of authors and titles to follow up on these questions. For example, John Saul, Stephen King, Peter Straub, Joe Hill, and Dean R. Koontz build the horror and atmosphere more slowly, while authors such as Clive Barker (especially in his earlier titles) and Brian Lumley, as well as Anne Rice (her classic Horror titles beginning with *Interview with the Vampire*)[40] and Brian Stableford, tend to present the horrific elements much earlier.

If the readers are not certain which they might enjoy, I describe several and offer possibilities. Collections of short stories, especially ones that run the gamut of appeal, are also a good suggestion for readers. Just as they can help staff become better acquainted with Horror, they offer readers a chance to sample the range of the genre. In my experience, many genre readers do not necessarily like short stories, but this is not true in Horror. Because the genre depends so heavily on atmosphere, Horror lends itself well to this format.

We should also remember the classic Horror writers, as they often make good suggestions, especially for readers who want to experiment. Readers new to the genre may not have discovered Shirley Jackson, H. P. Lovecraft, M. R. James, and Daphne du Maurier, and they might be pleased to see that stories by these classic authors are still accessible—and chilling.

Remember, too, that some Horror readers have particular subject interests. They may say they like anything with vampires or witches or whatever.

For these, we use reference tools to identify titles. However, even though readers may come first with subject requests, they often discover, as they read more, that they really prefer a particular mood, the special atmosphere that evokes that emotional chill from a certain type, not subject, of a book.

When we talk with readers, we describe books in terms of that atmosphere, how it makes the reader feel, how it pulls readers into the horror (either immediately or more slowly), how readers relate to characters and share their plight or observe them from a distance. We offer authors and titles based on their responses to these descriptions.

Teenagers constitute a very large section of the Horror audience. I am not certain why Horror has such a strong appeal for this age group. It may be because there are often teen protagonists. Certainly, there is a suspension of societal rules; kids are often in charge, solving problems and fighting evil, without assistance from adults. Teens, like the rest of us, enjoy Horror for the chill it evokes. And they read everything, from titles written for teens to those aimed at an adult audience.

We do need to exercise caution, however. Just because Horror is popular with young adults, we should not automatically assume it is the genre to suggest to someone who simply wants a good read. We need to be aware of the amount of sex in some Horror novels, especially in those that start out with violence, but even in others. Sometimes titles that feature teen protagonists also have strong sexual themes.

Sure Bets

Because a number of readers have preconceived notions about the Horror genre, it is not as easy to identify and share Sure Bets. They simply do not have the universal appeal of some books in other genres. This does not prevent us from putting examples of the best on display and in readers' hands, but the appeal is not always so obvious and automatic.

Koontz's *Odd Thomas* and its successors in his series please a wide range of readers, because they offer a rather naive and sympathetic protagonist, a wealth of paranormal elements, and an edgy and dangerous mood that builds in intensity.[41]

King, of course, as an author whose books always reach the best-seller lists, is the mainstay of our Sure Bets. I like to give readers unfamiliar with his work *The Shining*, which I still consider one of his best.[42] The size is not so daunting, and the Horror builds delightfully. *Bag of Bones* is another title on my Sure Bets list.[43]

Even though it was originally published in 1991, Robert McCammon's *Boy's Life* continues to attract readers.[44] (In fact, one of my local high schools has added it to their summer reading list!) Winner of both the World Fantasy and Bram Stoker awards, this coming-of-age story delves into the terrifying secrets of a seemingly sleepy small Alabama town in the 1960s.

After twenty-seven years of writing Horror, Anne Rice has changed directions completely and now writes Historical Fiction with a decidedly Christian emphasis. Still, *Interview with the Vampire* remains a genre classic and a Sure Bet for readers who like to explore the face of evil.[45]

EXPANDING READERS' HORIZONS WITH WHOLE COLLECTION READERS' ADVISORY

Suggesting other Horror writers to a fan of the genre is one thing, but we should also remember that almost none of us reads exclusively in a particular genre and that readers are always excited at the prospect of discovering other writers that might meet their needs and interests. Thinking in terms of crossing genres is important for us as readers' advisors, too. Just because someone mentions one genre does not mean that is the only possibility for us to pursue.

Horror offers several directions for exploration. The crossover works in terms of both the themes explored in Horror and the appeal and tone of Horror novels. For example, fans of stories of vampires, werewolves, and other beasts of the night will find, perhaps unexpectedly, series in the Romance genre that may interest them. Sherrilyn Kenyon and Christine Feehan both offer brooding tales of werewolves and vampires and settings familiar to Horror fans. Susan Krinard's lyrical werewolf and vampire novels (*Prince of Wolves*, et al.) make good suggestions for fans.[46]

Several writers of Horror also write Dark Fantasy. Fans of the Horror novels of King, Koontz, and Dan Simmons, to name a few of these authors who write in more than one genre, might also enjoy the Fantasy these authors write. Other fantasy writers, especially Jim Butcher and Charlie Huston, incorporate Horror themes and conventions. Wizard (Butcher) or vampire (Huston) detectives in dangerous urban areas might be just the thing for a Horror reader interested in a change of pace.

Some crossover is less obvious and is based on appeal rather than theme. Horror readers appreciate darkly atmospheric tales and do not always require the presence of the supernatural. Although, as I mentioned earlier, fans are unlikely to enjoy serial killer novels for the same reasons they like Horror, there may be novels of hard-edged Suspense, Thriller, or Mystery that appeal to them, given their dark atmosphere and bleak tone, not to mention the explicit violence. Writers such as Tess Gerritsen may have enough atmosphere and gore, with touches of the supernatural, to satisfy Horror readers. Chelsea Cain's disturbing novels—in terms of both graphic violence and psychological distress—might also be good suggestions, as might Michael Gruber's chilling novels. Don't forget Jeffry Lindsay's Dexter books for Christopher Moore fans, or Peter Abrahams's unnerving novels of Psychological Suspense.

In moving readers across the Dewey Divide to nonfiction, we should keep in mind that books about the occult may make an interesting suggestion for Horror fans. Biographies of Horror writers—whose lives were sometimes as tangled as their stories—and Horror movie stars and producers offer other possibilities. Certainly out-of-control science topics work well, as might a title such as Mary Roach's *Stiff: The Curious Lives of Human Cadavers*.[47] What more could someone interested in the dead and undead want? Fairy Tales, which form the basis for some Horror novels, are also a good bet, as are the numerous Urban Legends books and almost anything about Parapsychology and the Supernatural.

Other possibilities come to mind as we consider what it is that Horror readers enjoy—and more specifically what the reader standing in front of us mentions—and think about what we know about the characteristics of other genres and what they have to offer. We should also remember that there will be a wealth of titles for Horror readers in our graphic novel collections. Figure 7.3 lists additional authors to take readers beyond Horror.

TRENDS

Is Horror dead? Some would argue that the genre has all but disappeared in recent years, rationalized by science or religion so that it's gone underground. (That's surely temporary, since one of the main tenets of Horror is that the evil is beaten down—but never quite destroyed. It simply lies dormant, waiting to rise again.)

It's hard for Horror to survive when reality is so frightening. When nanotechnology and insidious weapons of mass and individual destruction dominate our news—and especially titles on the best-seller lists—is there still room for Horror? For example, King's recent novel, *The Cell*, offers a dark and scary story about zombies—monsters of a sort, but monsters created by science.[48] There's graphic violence, a Horror requisite, but

---

Figure 7.3 *Expanding Readers' Horizons*

Authors to take Readers beyond the Horror Genre

Adrenaline:	Chelsea Cain
	Michael Crichton
	Tess Gerritsen
	Michael Gruber
Fantasy:	Jim Butcher
	Neil Gaiman
	Charlie Huston
Historical Fiction:	Elizabeth Kostova (*The Historian*)[49]
Literary Fiction:	Bret Easton Ellis
	Joyce Carol Oates
	Chuck Palahniuk
Mystery:	Tana French
Natural History/Science:	Richard Preston
Psychological Suspense:	Peter Abrahams
	Dennis Lehane (*Shutter Island*)[50]
Romance:	Christine Feehan
	Sherrilyn Kenyon
	Susan Krinard
Romantic Suspense:	Nora Roberts (Sign of the Seven series)[51]
Science Fiction:	Greg Bear
	Scott Sigler (*Infected*)[52]
Travel:	Michael Norman and Beth Scott (Haunted series)[53]
True Adventure:	Jason Hawes and Grant Wilson (*Ghost Hunting*)[54]
True Crime:	John Douglas
	Mark Olshaker

---

the supernatural element seems to be missing. The victims are zapped; their brains are wiped clean and new connections are made. Blame evolution, not the supernatural. This novel, and many others published by Horror writers and marketed as Horror, may be horrific, but not the traditional Horror of the past.

Short stories don't seem as much affected, but the novel seems to be on the wane. Horror will come back, just as it did in the 1960s. Not dead, only resting. In fact short stories remain an important part of the genre, and they're a good introduction to writers if readers aren't interested in committing to reading an entire book. Published in book collections and in magazines, these short stories offer intense indication of an author's style and themes.

One reason that Horror seems to be disappearing from the mainstream is that many publishers are small presses. Only major authors—King, Koontz, Hill, Straub, Campbell—are published in hardcover by mainstream publishers. Much of the best of the genre's writing, and certainly many new authors, are offered by small publishers who specialize in this genre and often Fantasy as well. Unfortunately, their books are not as consistently reviewed in library review journals. Watch the websites and blogs for more information and to keep up to date in the genre.

In addition to their overlap with Thrillers, Horror also has infiltrated Fantasy, Mystery, and Romance, as noted above. Readers who appreciate supernatural elements or a particular Horror character or convention can often find that in these genres as well. Now that figures from Horror have become key elements in Paranormal Romances and Mysteries—some serious but others humorous takes on the horror genre—it's hard to think about vampires or werewolves in quite the same way.

Horror authors continue to write across the genres as well. King, Koontz, Barker, and Straub all dabble in Fantasy, and Campbell in Psychological Suspense. Neil Gaiman's *American Gods* won awards from the Fantasy, Science Fiction, and Horror genres, and his Sandman series of graphic novels combines Fantasy and Horror.[55] Joe Hill and Tom Piccirilli have both won Thriller awards for their Horror Novels. This trend will likely continue, but it allows us to see the endless crossover connections and often leads readers from other genres into Horror.

Horror is another genre, like Romance, that has yet to achieve legitimacy among critics. Its growing popularity in the mass media, however, bespeaks the place it holds among fans. Horror is also a genre that attracts extreme opinions. Fans love it—or types of it—while others look at it with distaste and pride themselves in never having sampled it—and never wanting to! (This latter reaction is unfortunate, as some of our best storytellers have specialized in this genre and have written Horror that transcends the reservations of the most intransigent anti-Horror group.)

In their guide to the genre, Anthony J. Fonseca and June Michele Pulliam write, "Horror allows us to experience the emotion of fear in a controlled setting."[56] Reading Horror stories and viewing Horror films provide us with an opportunity to face down monsters vicariously, to confront the evil and walk away unharmed. We can always close the book if the story becomes too frightening.

NOTES

1. Bram Stoker, *Dracula* (London: Constable, 1897; New York: Doubleday and McClure, 1899).
2. Sarah Langan, *The Missing* (New York: Harper, 2007).
3. Christopher Moore, *A Dirty Job* (New York: Morrow, 2006).
4. Clive Barker, *Mister B. Gone* (New York: HarperCollins, 2007).
5. Richard Laymon, *Island* (New York: Leisure Books, 2002).
6. Barker, *Coldheart Canyon* (New York: HarperCollins, 2001).
7. Shirley Jackson, *The Haunting of Hill House* (New York: Viking, 1959).
8. H. P. Lovecraft, *The Dunwich Horror* (New York: Bart House, 1945).
9. Stephen King, "The Mist," in *Skeleton Crew* (New York: Viking, 1985); Dean R. Koontz, *The Bad Place* (New York: Putnam, 1990).
10. Scott Smith, *The Ruins* (New York: Knopf, 2006).
11. Douglas J. Preston and Lincoln Child, *The Reliquary* (New York: Forge, 1997); Preston and Child, *Relic* (New York: Forge, 1995).
12. Jonathan Maberry, Pine Deep Trilogy, beginning with *Ghost Road Blues* (New York: Pinnacle, 2006); Gary Braunbeck, Cedar Hills series, beginning with *Graveyard People* (Shrewsbury, MA: Earthling, 2003); F. Paul Wilson, Repairman Jack series, beginning with *The Tomb* (New York: Whispers, 1984); Koontz, Odd Thomas series, beginning with *Odd Thomas* (New York: Bantam, 2003).
13. Koontz, *The Taking* (New York: Bantam, 2004).
14. Mark Z. Danielewski, *House of Leaves* (New York: Pantheon, 2000).
15. Toby Barlow, *Sharp Teeth* (New York: Harper, 2008).
16. Max Brooks, *World War Z: An Oral History of the Zombie War* (New York: Crown, 2006).
17. Mark Mignola, *Baltimore; or, The Steadfast Tin Soldier and the Vampire* (New York: Bantam, 2007).
18. Joe Hill, *Welcome to Lovecraft* (San Diego: IDW, 2008).
19. John Marks, *Fangland* (New York: Penguin, 2007).
20. Dan Simmons, *The Terror: A Novel* (New York: Little, Brown, 2007).
21. Anne Rice, *Interview with the Vampire* (New York: Knopf, 1976).
22. King, *Carrie* (Garden City, NY: Doubleday, 1974).
23. King, *Dolores Claiborne* (New York: Viking, 1993); King, *The Girl Who Loved Tom Gordon* (New York: Scribner, 1999).
24. Ramsey Campbell, *The Grin of the Dark* (New York: Tor, 2008).
25. Hill, *Heart-Shaped Box* (New York: Morrow, 2007).
26. Peter Straub, *Ghost Story* (New York: Coward, McCann, and Geoghegan, 1979).
27. Straub, *Lost Boy Lost Girl: A Novel* (New York: Random House, 2003).
28. Wilson cited above.
29. Stephen Marlowe, *The Lighthouse at the End of the World: A Tale of Edgar Allan Poe* (New York: Dutton, 1995).
30. Kelley Armstrong, Women of the Underworld series, beginning with *Bitten* (New York: Viking, 2001).

31. Chelsea Quinn Yarbro, Saint-Germain Cycle, beginning with *Hotel Transylvania* (New York: St. Martin's, 1978).
32. Barbara Hambly, *Those Who Hunt the Night* (New York: Ballantine, 1988).
33. Simmons cited above.
34. Andrei Codrescu, *The Blood Countess: A Novel* (New York: Simon and Schuster, 1995).
35. Brian Stableford, David Lydyard Trilogy, beginning with *The Werewolves of London* (New York: Carrol and Graf, 1992).
36. Koji Suzuki, *Ring* (New York: Vertical, 2003).
37. Preston and Child, The Pendergast series, beginning with *Relic* (cited above).
38. Anne Rice, The Vampire Chronicles, beginning with *Interview with the Vampire* (cited above).
39. Brooks cited above.
40. Rice cited above.
41. Koontz cited above.
42. King, *The Shining* (Garden City, NY: Doubleday, 1977).
43. King, *Bag of Bones* (New York: Scribner, 1998).
44. Robert McCammon, *Boy's Life* (New York: Pocket Books, 1991).
45. Rice cited above.
46. Susan Krinard, *Prince of Wolves* (New York: Bantam, 1994).
47. Mary Roach, *Stiff: The Curious Lives of Cadavers* (New York: Norton, 2003).
48. King, *The Cell* (New York: Scribner, 2006).
49. Elizabeth Kostova, *The Historian* (New York: Little, Brown, 2005).
50. Dennis Lehane, *Shutter Island* (New York: Morrow, 2003).
51. Nora Roberts, Sign of the Seven Trilogy, beginning with *Blood Brothers* (New York: Jove, 2007).
52. Scott Sigler, *Infected* (New York: Crown, 2008).
53. Michael Norman and Beth Scott, Haunted series, beginning with *Haunted Wisconsin* (Sauk City, WI: Stanton and Lee, 1980).
54. Jason Hawes and Grant Wilson, *Ghost Hunting: True Stories of Unexplained Phenomena from the Atlantic Paranormal Society* (New York: Pocket Books, 2007).
55. Neil Gaiman, *American Gods* (New York: Morrow, 2001).
56. Anthony J. Fonseca and June Michele Pulliam, *Hooked on Horror: A Guide to Reading Interests in Horror Fiction* (Englewood, CO: Libraries Unlimited, 1999), xv.

8

ROMANCE

Imagine the following familiar scenario. On one side of the service desk we have a Romance reader, who is looking for a new book by her favorite author. Or perhaps she has read everything by that author, and she's looking for some new authors. She is a little wary of approaching library staff, because many people, and perhaps especially the librarians she has encountered, seem to deplore her reading taste. She knows, in a general way, what she likes about Romances: the independent heroines, the happy ending, and, especially, the feeling of satisfaction she gets from the Romances she reads. However, she may not be able to put these emotional responses into words. She may be embarrassed to ask about Romances and describe the kind of Romances she likes—perhaps the ones with explicit sex—and is certainly uneasy about asking for assistance.

On the other side of the desk, we have the librarian. Unless we librarians are Romance readers as well, what we feel when faced with a fan of the genre has been put succinctly by one of my staff: genuine fear. It's not just Romance, of course; every time we seek to assist readers in genres in which we are not well read, we feel uncomfortable and inadequate. How on earth can we help readers if we know little or nothing about the genre they love?

Unfortunately, a patron's discomfort plus a librarian's fear do not produce a satisfactory readers' advisory interview, no matter what the genre. All too often, this scenario reflects reality, although an increasing number of librarians have discovered the appeal of this vast genre and have more success working with readers.

A DEFINITION

It's no easy task to define a genre so large and diverse that it accounts for the largest share of the consumer book market.[1] This immense genre covers a wide range of books—from contemporary to historical, racy to gentle, realistic to paranormal, and much in between. Still, definitions help us focus our energies, come to terms with the genre, and better understand its fans.

In *Romance Fiction: A Guide to the Genre,* Kristin Ramsdell defines Romance as "a love story in which the central focus is on the development and satisfactory resolution of the love relationship between the two main characters, written in such a way as to provide the reader with some degree of vicarious emotional participation in the courtship process."[2] These are the two keys to Romance fiction: first, the plot revolves around the love relationship and its happy ending; all else that happens is secondary. Other genres certainly rely on romantic themes, and Romance readers may enjoy those too. In books that fall within the Romance genre, however, the romantic relationships are the focus of the novels. Secondly, these stories are told in such a way that the reader is involved in the outcome of the Romance; the reader participates on an emotional level and experiences genuine satisfaction at the emotionally satisfying conclusion. Certainly we may feel an emotional involvement with the characters in books in other genres, but here the reader's participation in the story is essential. We experience the story emotionally, and this makes our satisfaction in its outcome hard to explain to someone unfamiliar with the genre. In school we are neither taught nor expected to appreciate stories on this emotional level. The satisfaction that fans experience with Romances (as well as the others in this Emotions group) depends so heavily on the emotional connection that the appeal is hard to explain to nonfans and difficult even for fans to acknowledge and verbalize. See figure 8.1 for characteristics of the genre.

CHARACTERISTICS AND THE GENRE'S APPEAL

Tone/Mood

Romance appeals first to our emotions. This is one of the reasons fans find this genre (as well as Women's Lives and Relationships, Gentle Reads, and Horror) so difficult to talk about: it is almost impossible for them to characterize what it is that they enjoy. How does one describe the effect of that

---

Figure 8.1 *Characteristics of Romances*

---

1. The evocative, emotional tone draws readers in, and they participate in this love story and read toward the emotionally satisfying, happy ending.

2. Characters are easily identifiable types. Men are rugged, strong, distant, and dangerous; women are strong, bright, independent, and often beautiful.

3. The story features either a misunderstanding between the protagonists or outside circumstances that force them apart, followed by the satisfactory resolution of their romantic relationship. Social and moral issues may play a role in the story lines of Romances, although they are always secondary and do not interfere with the happy ending.

4. Engaging details of time and place attract readers, and these historical, cultural, and social particulars often frame the stories.

5. Although Romances usually can be read fairly quickly and are called fast-paced by their fans, they can also be stopped and started easily, without losing the story line.

6. Language plays an important role in setting the stage. The language of a Romance is instantly recognizable, with extensive use of descriptive adjectives to delineate characters, setting, and romantic or sexual interludes.

---

satisfyingly evocative, romantic tone? Readers expect to be drawn in, to identify with the characters and their relationship, to experience these stories, and it is this tone that prompts the vicarious emotional participation on the part of the reader. The tone may be upbeat throughout or may include darker moments, but the end always produces a satisfactory resolution.

This emotional pull provides the foundation for the success of many Romance writers. These are stories about the creation of families, and readers feel the power of love on all levels: parents to children, among siblings and friends, and with lovers. This tone may be difficult to define, but fans recognize it and respond to the atmosphere it creates. Readers tell us they get a special feeling from reading Romances, that they read these books to experience that emotional satisfaction of being part of a love story.

Certainly the tone in Romances may vary from book to book. Some are lighthearted, like Cathie Linz's romantic comedy series set in Rock Creek and Serenity Falls and featuring quirky and sometimes flamboyant characters, small town atmosphere, and sizzling sex (*Good Girls Do* is the first).[3] Others, like Jennifer Crusie's laugh-out-loud *Faking It,* combine a lighthearted tone with an insightful yet poignant look at families and relationships.[4] In others, especially some of the Paranormal Romances, the mood may be dark and dangerous, even though the conclusion provides the requisite happy ending. Christine Feehan's popular Dark series as well as her tales of the Drake sisters feature ominous secrets and deadly adversaries which create this dark mood.[5]

Characterization

Characters rather than plot twists drive Romances. In a Romance the lovers must come to understand themselves and their relationships with each other. As readers, we see interior as well as exterior aspects of these characters, and we respond to them and their developing relationship. In her Contemporary Romances Susan Elizabeth Phillips explores complex family relationships and the difficult concepts of guilt, forgiveness, and grief. Although these affect the protagonists and force them to mature, these themes do not detract from the power of the Romance. In fact, it is because of the environment the Romance creates, one in which the characters feel safe sharing their deepest emotions, that healing finally comes.

This growth, however, is not limited only to Romances with a serious side. In almost all, the characters are forced to change, to relinquish preconceptions about themselves (often their lack of self-worth) and their partners before they are able to embrace the romantic union readers demand. For example, in Loretta Chase's *Your Scandalous Ways,* heroine Francesca Bonnard was divorced by her husband, now an English lord but in reality a traitor.[6] Shunned by society and forced to leave England, she has created a new career as an elegant courtesan. When world-weary spy James Cordier is sent to steal the letters that will incriminate her ex-husband, he must accept his love for her, a fallen woman, and she must learn to trust a man despite the betrayal that ruined her.

That characters are written to a pattern is important, too, as it is in most genres from Adventure to Women's Lives and Relationships. The women are bright, independent, strong, and, perhaps surprisingly, not always beautiful but certainly interesting and articulate. The men must be strong, distant, and always dangerous, because the stronger the hero, the greater the victory when the heroine brings him to his senses and his knees. Conquering a gentle, affectionate, mild-mannered, sensible hero simply is not as satisfying, either for the heroine or for the reader.

The best also include well-developed, interesting, and often quirky secondary characters. For example, Feehan focuses on one Drake sister in each of the series titles, but the others appear throughout, their pre- or post-stories interwoven into the fabric of the current sister's dilemma. *Magic in the Wind* is the first.[7]

One last important point about characterization is that we almost always get the point of view of both protagonists. This allows us to experience their inner dilemmas and follow their thoughts as they work out their relationship. This is not just her story; it is his as well. Romances are almost never written first-person; the reader and author require the third-person perspective to create the full picture, to reveal easily the inner thoughts and struggles of both characters. For example, Mary Balogh's *Simply Magic* offers the perspective of both teacher Susanna Osbourne and wealthy nobleman Peter Edgeworth, thus providing an intimate look at the thoughts of both characters as they evaluate their feelings and their relationship.[8]

Story Line

The focus of the story line in the Romance is the romantic relationship and its happy conclusion. All else that happens may be interesting, but it is secondary to this resolution. By the way, we can always identify a Romance by that first kiss, which is like no other. The hero awakens passions in himself and the heroine that they have never experienced before. We may know earlier that they are destined to fall in love, but the kiss confirms their connection—for us and for them. If you read Romances, you know what I mean.

Marriage does not always occur within the story itself; however, hero and heroine recognize and affirm their love, and the suggestion of marriage at some point is almost de rigueur. If this recognition and affirmation of love do not occur, the book is not a Romance—or certainly not a satisfying one. Many of Nicholas Sparks's and Danielle Steel's titles are romantic, but not Romances. Robert James Waller's *The Bridges of Madison County* is the classic example of a romantic book that is not a Romance.[9] Although critics and reviewers called this popular title a Romance, fans of the genre did not agree. In Romances the lovers are not separated at the conclusion of the novel, and that ending gives Waller's book a completely different feel.

This is not to say that Romances are limited to this narrow story line. Many add elements of adventure, intrigue, or mystery to their stories. Lauren Willig develops Romance story lines in both the present day and late eighteenth century in her popular series featuring a researcher studying a group of English spies who were contemporaries of the Scarlet Pimpernel. Linda Lael Miller adds action and adventure to her popular Western Historical Romances. Other authors offer intriguing insights into occupations (chocolatier in Jennifer Greene's *Blame It on Chocolate,* children's book author and illustrator in Susan Elizabeth Phillips's *This Heart of Mine,* and futuristic zombie hunter in Linnea Sinclair's *Down Home Zombie Blues*).[10] These details are, however, pleasant extras. The point of the story line is the culmination of the romantic relationship. In the Romance, the hero and heroine will resolve their difficulties and discover their love. We read Romances because we find it so satisfying to participate in the courtship process. We read them for the emotional high they provide.

In her scholarly study of the Romance genre, *Dangerous Men and Adventurous Women,* Jayne Ann Krentz writes in an essay with Linda Barlow that "her future happiness and his depend on her ability to teach him to love."[11] The plot is structured around this process, although in more recent titles, it may be the hero providing the instruction, or the teaching may be mutual as both hero and heroine learn to love and trust in their love. In Stephanie Laurens's racy Regency-set Romances, the hero is almost always placed in the role of persuading the heroine to accept his offer, although she may be the one who ultimately teaches him how to love.

Although Romances guarantee a happy ending, with the love relationship resolved, many also explore provocative moral and social issues. Kathleen Eagle addresses abuse as well as American Indian issues, while Virginia Kantra tackles a range of controversial topics from child and spousal abuse to alcoholism and racial discrimination. Even Regencies, including Mary Jo Putney's *The Rake* and several titles by Mary Balogh and Carla Kelly, address the social ills of that time (early nineteenth century), from alcoholism and other addictions to the difficulties facing returning veterans and the problems of workers and factories.[12] In addition, countless Romances deal with the role of women in society and efforts throughout history to improve their plight. Social issues and taboos have long found a forum in all types of Romances—Historical, Contemporary, Paranormal, and Inspirational.

Frame/Setting

Readers often have decided preferences for the time frame in which romances are set. Whether the background details writers provide are just wallpaper or elaborate and authentic, they attract particular readers simply because they portray the past, the present, the future, or some alternate reality that involves multiple time periods and travel between.

For example, in Regency Romances the setting among the *ton* (the elite upper class) in London with the parties, clothes, and carriages is as important for fans as is the witty banter between hero and heroine and the Regency jargon that fills the pages. Readers of Contemporary Romances appreciate the emphasis on heroines and their professional lives, reflecting the importance placed on this dual role for women by society today. Alternate Reality Romances cover a broad spectrum of Romances: Futuristic (set in future times with the feel, if not the detail, of Science Fiction), Paranormal (featuring supernatural and magical elements, including vampires, ghosts, etc.), and Time Travel (with protagonists who move to and from time periods, sometimes transporting other characters as well). Fans look for trademark characteristics of each type, with the classic Romance story line set against that frame.

Other writers place their novels in particular recognizable areas—Debbie Macomber's Pacific Northwest, Eagle's contemporary and historical western landscapes, Dorothea Benton Frank's low country of South Carolina. For some the setting is a generic urban, small town, or rural area, but in all cases these details add to the mood the author creates with her story and underline the character's progress toward that happy ending.

Still others employ the career and hobby frames popular in many genres. Protagonists may be involved in the art world, or crime (as thieves and detectives), business, medicine, and journalism. Hobbies, too, provide interesting backgrounds that intersect with occupations and attract readers with the details that range from the more common (cooking, needlecrafts) to the obscure (belly dancing).

Pacing

Fans tell us that Romances are fast reading. Because they are character-centered, Romances rely more on dialogue than description. This affects the reading experience, and the books feel as if they read quickly. Although a variety of events may take place, the stories are constructed so they can be put down when a reader is interrupted. When that reader picks it up again, she falls right back into the story.

Style/Language

Writers use language to create the romantic tone and emotional attraction readers seek. One can identify a Romance in the first few pages, just by observing the way the story is constructed and the language used.

Romances are descriptive, and writers rely on adjectives to describe characters and places, as well as to set the mood. The vocabulary sets the tone and the stage for the Romance. In fact, writers such as Nora Roberts and Sandra Brown, who now write harder-edged Romantic Suspense instead of the Romances that established their reputations, have kept much of their Romance-reading audience, in part because they have retained the language of the Romance, even though their more suspenseful books no longer fit within the Romance genre. In their novels of Romantic Suspense, the descriptions of character and place pull the readers into the story, allowing them to "see" the action, to participate fully in the story. The books feel and read like Romances, even though the focus is different and the action more violent.

KEY AUTHORS

Among current Romance authors every librarian—and reader—should know are Susan Elizabeth Phillips (Contemporary), Julia Quinn (Historical), and Sherrilyn Kenyon (Paranormal).

Award-winning and *New York Times* best-selling writer Susan Elizabeth Phillips is one of the foremost writers of Contemporary Romance. Interesting heroines with more depth than may at first appear, unexpected heroes (often active men involved in sports with as much brain as brawn), sparkling dialogue, a heartwarming tone, explicit sex, and a generally lighthearted approach—even if controversial issues are introduced and resolved—characterize Phillips's writing. Her recent award-winning title, *Natural Born Charmer*, exemplifies her passionate, tender, and insightful style.[13] It opens with down-home football star Dean Robillard driving his flashy sports car down a back road in Colorado when he comes upon a very irritated but attractive young woman—in a beaver costume! Sparks fly between the two, as they work out their differences, shed their emotional baggage, and accept their future as family. These romantic resolutions may be rocky, but they are also humorous and touching.

Julia Quinn also writes award-winning Romantic Comedy, but with a historical setting. She is best known for her series featuring each of the eight Bridgerton siblings and their romantic entanglements. Intelligent conversation and wicked banter, explicit but always joyful sex, and close relationships among family and lovers characterize these stories, filled with dangerous yet vulnerable heroes and bright heroines. Set in the early nineteenth century, these novels use Regency society as a backdrop, and the mysterious Lady Whistledown's society papers, an intriguingly anonymous but accurate gossip sheet, frame the story and add to the humor. But they are romances above all and offer intelligent but not always beautiful heroines matched with handsome heroes, who possess an unexpected softer side. In *The Duke and I*, the first title in the series, Daphne, who has always been a friend to men of the *ton* yet never sought as a romantic interest, traps a duke who harbors a dark secret into a loving relationship and marriage.[14]

Representing Paranormal or Alternative Reality Romances, Sherrilyn Kenyon projects a darker tone. With a doctorate in history, she draws on her knowledge of ancient Greece in creation of her universe in her enormously popular Dark-Hunter series. But there is also humor: one hero is a were-leopard and the corresponding heroine is allergic to cats. Complex characters, brooding heroes and strong heroines, a rich universe of linked characters who appear in titles throughout the series, verbal battles, satisfying relationships, edgy story lines with steamy passion, a strong sense of place, and deadly dangers fill these novels. The first in the Dark-Hunter series, *Fantasy Lover*, provides a good introduction to Kenyon's style and themes.[15] Julian of Macedon, a former Greek general, has been cursed to remain a love slave for eternity—or so it seems until he falls in love with Grace Alexander, the only woman who might be able to free him.

What happened to Nora Roberts, you might ask? Once the mainstay of Romance readers and library collections, Roberts now writes contemporary and paranormal Romantic Suspense almost exclusively. As one of the first authors to make the move to Romantic Suspense, she has carried many of her fans with her. Her new titles continue to employ Romance themes. There is a clash between the resourceful, passionate heroine and the strong man who listens and protects but who also respects her independence. These are fast-paced stories with a full measure of sexual tension and often, explicit sex. Relationships among family members, friends, and lovers form the core of her plots, with secrets and treasures often adding an interesting frame. However, since Suspense now rivals Romance for primacy in her novels, she is covered in chapter 3, "Romantic Suspense," with the Adrenaline genres, as are Jayne Ann Krentz (who also writes Historical Romantic Suspense as Amanda Quick), Sandra Brown, and other former Romance stalwarts.

WHAT WE KNOW ABOUT FANS

Every Romance reader, whether she has actually formulated it or not, has her own definition of the genre, based on the books she has read and enjoyed. One of our tasks in the interview is to listen to her description to discover how she defines the genre. However, there are some characteristics that all fans acknowledge.

First, readers do not expect to be surprised by the resolution of a Romance novel. They know the outcome of the story from the start; that is one of the reasons they have chosen a book in this genre. Fans of all genres find a specific formula that satisfies them and select books that fit that particular pattern. In a Mystery we expect the crime to be solved and justice to triumph. Here, in Romance, hero and heroine will resolve their difficulties and affirm their love. Fans read Romances because they find participating in the courtship and resolution so satisfying. Although they may tolerate a few twists or surprises in the general formula, for the most part they are not looking for something new and different. They seek the simple satisfaction of having their expectations fulfilled through the Romance formula.

Secondly, as in other genres, readers want to read everything by authors they enjoy and all titles in a series. In the Romance genre, series do not generally exist in the same form as they do in many other genres. Because Romances end with the satisfactory resolution of the romantic entanglement between hero and heroine, their story has been told, and further chapters or a new book featuring these characters would hardly be a Romance. On the other hand, the author may choose a family or a group of friends and successfully match each set of characters. Then couples from previous Romances can appear in later titles to help further that story, and readers get a glimpse of their continued happiness and the growth of their families. These are usually referred to as "linked" Romances, and it behooves every librarian to keep track of these, as publishers are not always thoughtful or savvy enough to include series information—titles and the correct reading order—in all volumes of the series.

Patrons read in many different ways. That is a characteristic shared by readers in all genres, and Romance is no exception. Some read by author and want everything an author has written (from our collections and then on interlibrary loan, wherever we can find the titles). Then they want someone else who writes just like the author they love. Some fans follow publishers' series and read only Harlequin NASCAR or Silhouette Desire, and they want to find them all and perhaps even read them in order. Some read just Romances and like to be introduced to Romance authors they have not yet discovered. Others will enjoy a range of books that feature strong romantic themes, even if they fall outside the genre. Possibilities for that third group are discussed in detail below, in the section "Expanding Readers' Horizons with Whole Collection Readers' Advisory."

There is another kind of reader we meet: one who has not admitted to herself, or to anyone else, that Romance describes the kind of book she enjoys. This genre-denial syndrome is especially common in a genre such as Romance, which has received such bad press from reviewers and librarians alike. All of us have been in a position of sensing a reader might enjoy exploring another genre, based on what he or she enjoys reading, but have been frustrated by genre labels. One patron, for whom I had suggested titles for years, was talking one day about Historical Fiction and Adventure. I suggested the novels of Patricia Veryan, knowing they combined the two, as well as some of the mystery elements this reader had long enjoyed. She was converted, quickly reading everything Veryan wrote. Had I called these Romances, as they properly are, she would have never attempted one. I still would not call her a Romance reader, but I know she has explored the genre, discovering other authors whose books provide the elements she enjoys. Many of us, especially voracious readers, find ourselves exploring—and enjoying—genres we never thought we would read. With Romances, however, the stigma of being perceived as a fan seems to leave readers open to mockery—or so they believe. Not all readers are ready to acknowledge they may read and enjoy Romances, and they should not be forced into that admission. As we do with every genre, we readers' advisors need to be able to distinguish the books that might be classified as Romance, as well as those that appeal to fans of the genre, and to recognize this genre when readers describe it.

Fans understand that publication in this genre is primarily in paperback, and they expect titles by their favorite authors to be purchased and made available, preferably cataloged and inter-shelved with hardcover titles. While librarians often have concerns about the value of paperbacks in a collection, readers do not. Many hardcover best-selling authors in all genres began their career published only in paperback, so Romance paperbacks should be treated in the same way we treat Science Fiction, Fantasy, and Mystery: popular genres with a high volume of titles in paperback.

As in all genres, the key to understanding the popularity of Romance is to read. If you are not a Romance fan, try some of the authors in figure 8.2, which lists Romance authors you may enjoy if you read in other genres. It should also help in introducing readers to the genre.

Figure 8.2 *An Introduction to the Romance Genre*

Romance Writers to Try, If You Enjoy . . .

Adrenaline:	Joanna Bourne
	Loretta Chase (*The Lion's Daughter*)[16]
Fantasy:	Susan Carroll
	Christine Feehan
	Virginia Kantra
	Sherilynn Kenyon
	Lynn Kurland
Gay/Lesbian:	Eric Jerome Dickey
	Emma Donoghue (*Landing*)[17]
	E. Lynn Harris
	Steve Kluger (*Almost like Being in Love*)[18]
	Michelle Sawyer
	Bob Smith (*Selfish and Perverse*)[19]
Gentle Reads:	Katie Fforde
Historical Fiction:	Katy Medillio Cooper
	Georgette Heyer
	Barbara Woods
Horror:	Susan Krinard
	Stephanie Meyer
Humor:	Jennifer Crusie
	Susan Elizabeth Phillips
	Julia Quinn
Inspirational:	Karen Kingsbury
	Francine Rivers
	Lori Wick
Multicultural:	Maria Castillo
	Kathleen Eagle
	Beverly Jenkins
	Francis Ray
Mysteries:	Stephanie Laurens
Romantic Suspense:	Christine Feehan
Saga:	Francis Ray (Graysons of New Mexico series)[20]

Figure 8.2 *An Introduction to the Romance Genre (cont.)*	
Science Fiction:	Jayne Castle
	Susan Grant
	Robin D. Owens
	Linnea Sinclair
Westerns:	Kathleen Eagle
	Leigh Greenwood
	Linda Lael Miller
Women's Lives:	Katie Fforde
	Kristin Hannah
	Susan Wiggs

THE READERS' ADVISORY INTERVIEW

How then do we conduct the readers' advisory interview with Romance readers? Of what special information do we need to be aware? What techniques do we need to implement to serve this audience well? What do we need to know to help readers when they ask for a Romance?

There are three vital pieces of information we need to discover: what does this particular reader mean by Romance? Does the reader want a book set in a particular time period or with Paranormal elements? And, finally, how much sex does the reader want—or how much will she tolerate?

First, what does the reader mean when she talks about Romances? Every reader has a different sense of what kind of books the term Romance includes. A major difficulty we often experience with a reader is not knowing exactly what she is looking for when she says she reads Romances. Does she mean a paperback Harlequin Historical or something more like a Danielle Steel novel? Romances or a romantic novel? Although we librarians may need definitions to gain an understanding of the genre, we learn to put those aside when we work with readers. If a reader says Steel writes Romances, we need to identify other "Romance" writers who write just like her. (In this book, authors similar to Steel are discussed in chapter 9, "Women's Lives and Relationships.") Posing the traditional initial readers' advisory request, "Tell me about a book you have enjoyed," usually elicits a response that allows us to get a sense of this reader's definition of a Romance. Our familiarity with authors across the genre—or any lists we have created to assist us—then allows us to make appropriate suggestions.

The next factor to consider is the time frame. Does the reader prefer a contemporary or a historical setting? Some readers enjoy both, but most have preferences, often strong ones, about what they are in the mood to read. Obtaining this information is straightforward, at least. I simply ask, "Do you prefer a book set in the past or in the current day?" Another similar question might identify readers of Alternate Reality Romances, but that information will likely have come out when they described Romances they enjoy.

Finally, the crucial piece of information we need to discover when we talk to readers is the amount of sex they want in their Romances. By this, I do not simply mean whether they want a lot of sex or very little and how graphically it is described. Sometimes one very explicit interlude leaves readers feeling this is a very sexy book, even if that was an isolated occurrence. The real point is the intensity and frequency of the sexual encounters, and whether they occur at the beginning, before the reader really knows the heroine and hero, or farther along in the story. Often if the sex comes later, it feels different than books in which there is graphic sex right from the first few pages. If the sex is later and between a couple seen by readers as "made for each other," it is less likely to offend or even really be noticed, almost regardless of how graphic. We are often surprised by readers who say they are looking for books without a lot of sex, like those by Susan Elizabeth Phillips or Stephanie Laurens, when we know that explicit sexual interludes figure prominently in novels by these authors. This is a phenomenon I am unable to explain, even though I have encountered it with regularity in speaking with readers. It may have something to do with the reader's perception of the heroine. If she engages in sexual activity too early in the story, before we know and care about her, we may be more likely to view her as promiscuous. That perception creates a different tone in the story, and for many readers it is not as satisfying.

How much sex a reader expects in a Romance may be the hardest information to discover; it's the one thing readers are least likely to want to talk about. We cannot simply ask patrons about this directly; they do not have a vocabulary to answer us, even if we could discover just how to phrase the question. Queries of this sort are simply too embarrassing, and because readers cannot come up with words for what they want, we have to provide them with a vocabulary and alternative choices as we suggest a range of authors.

I listen for clues when the reader describes books or authors she enjoys. If I am unsure, I offer a variety of titles. I might talk about *gentler* or *more innocent* Romances to indicate those without a lot of sex. Often classic

Regencies fit the bill, early titles by Nora Roberts, or some of the paper-back category Romances (Harlequin Romance, for example, is labeled *Tender* by the publisher), or romantic novels by authors such as Maeve Binchy or Sharon Owens.

To indicate the other end of the spectrum, I might talk about *racier* Romances, by which I mean more risqué Romances in which sex may be explicit and perhaps frequent. Many of these, especially those by Laurens and Quinn, also feature a sense of fun and a lighter touch, which readers who enjoy these authors expect. When I describe this kind of book, I might conclude by saying it's a little racier, like the books by an author whose name I know the reader will recognize and thus understand. I like the term *racy* because it is not pejorative and can be used for authors with both contemporary and historical settings. This language allows me to provide information about the books and authors and then let the reader make choices from the range I have offered.

Having said this, I do want to add that I am sometimes surprised at the diversity of books people read. We need to be careful not to stereotype readers. A sweet, grandmotherly lady might adore Robin Schone or other very explicit authors, and she may find the gentle Romances far too tame for her taste. Readers are really looking for that satisfaction Romances give them, and for some, sex too soon or too much sex destroys that feeling. The atmosphere and when sex occurs can make all the difference.

We should keep in mind those elements that readers tell us they appreciate: the strong, bright, independent women pitted against powerful, distant, and dangerous men; the classic conflict between the two, and the ultimate resolution of their differences, with the heroine always victorious (although both really win when she is triumphant); and, most important, the evocative, emotional tone that allows us to be drawn in and to experience this love story with its inevitable happy ending. This is what readers are seeking when they ask for Romances.

Now for the hard part of the readers' advisory interview. Judging from my personal experience, when we come face to face with a Romance reader, we have only about five seconds to make a connection with the reader. This may sound absurd, but we have no more than a few seconds in which to let this reader know that we understand Romances and their appeal. This is not the time to be aloof. Romance readers are accustomed to being looked down upon, and we need to learn ways to indicate immediately that we have read in this genre, that we are someone they can talk with about their favorites. This kind of pressure can be a little intimidating.

The good news is that even having read just one or two Romances and having thought about their appeal, we have a basis on which to make that connection. Readers do not expect us to be fans; they expect us to be fellow readers and to appreciate what they enjoy, whatever that is. We are simply required to smile and invite the readers to share information about the kind of book they are seeking. Acknowledging that we have read Romances breaks the ice and allows us to continue a conversation with the reader. I find readers much more willing to talk to me if they know I have read in this genre they love.

Once we librarians start reading Romances and making contact with patrons, we find more and more Romance readers coming to us for assistance. We do a lot more indirect readers' advisory: we might suggest books for one patron, who does not take them, only to find them taken by someone else who was standing there, or have that third person join in the conversation. The more readers we help, the more we are inspired to read, because readers give us excellent suggestions of what is popular, and thus the more we learn about the genre.

Sure Bets

In addition to the key authors mentioned above (Susan Elizabeth Phillips, Julia Quinn, and Sherrilyn Kenyon) many authors have titles that can be counted as Sure Bets with broad appeal beyond Romance readers. Sometimes the title may be older, but since we in libraries keep popular books, this only helps us promote our collections.

One such title is Jennifer Crusie's *Bet Me,* a sexy Contemporary Romance filled with quirky characters, humor, and witty dialogue.[21] Statistician Minerva Dobbs is on the rebound after her stodgy boyfriend dumps her. When she thinks she hears gorgeous Cal take a bet that he can bed her within the month, she decides to show him! Unfortunately, or surely fortunately for both, their instant dislike softens into true affection in this fairy tale leavened by the whimsical acts of interfering family and friends.

Loretta Chase has a number of Sure Bet titles, especially good for readers who like historical settings, charming characters, and laugh-out-loud dialogue, which I often find I must copy in my notes and which makes me smile again, even years later. In *Not Quite a Lady,* twenty-seven-year-old Lady Catherine finally meets her match in the youngest son of the aristocratic Carsington family.[22] Like Lady Catherine's father, Darius is a man of science, whose father has given him a choice: marry an heiress or make a small, languishing estate pay within a year. Of course, Lady Catherine is on the neighboring estate, and her father knows and respects Darius already. It's a great love story filled with both the passion and redemptive nature of true love. But there's also sparkling verbal sparring and double entendres; quirky secondary characters complement the story.

On a more serious note, Julie Klassen's *Lady of Milkweed Manor*, demonstrates that Inspirational Romances often address serious issues while telling compelling stories.[23] When the daughter of a vicar finds herself pregnant, she is sent to Milkweed Manor, a home for unwed mothers. Her struggles, and those of the other unwed mothers, reveal a Regency England very different from that portrayed in Regency Romances. Faith themes are seamlessly integrated into Charlotte's story of sacrifice and eventually finding her true love.

Katie Fforde's Contemporary Romances, set in England, attract a number of readers, in part because of her deftly humorous touch but also perhaps because her heroines range in age from twenties to forties; they aren't just young women. *Wild Designs* offers an older heroine in Althea, a divorced mother confronting the problems of three teenagers, a difficult younger sister, and an impossible ex-husband.[24] Having lost her job, her only hope, winning a gardening competition, is dashed as the vacant greenhouse where she has been secretly growing plants is purchased by the attractive and rich Patrick. Fans of Romances will have no difficulty envisioning the story to its happy conclusion, but Althea's dilemmas appeal to readers beyond the confines of that genre, as she addresses the family and personal issues that affect women of her age and position.

Francis Ray writes both Contemporary and Inspirational Romances with multicultural characters (American Indian and African American) and thus pleases a wide range of readers. Ethnic heritage plays an important role in these novels, including her sagas about the Grayson and Falcon families, as do geographic details of the American Southwest, where she sets these stories. The inspirational message is key in her popular *Any Rich Man Will Do*, which stars a young woman who has lost everything— and gets a second chance.[25]

Do not forget classic Romance writers like Georgette Heyer, whose titles are being reissued in paperback. Even our well-worn hardcover copies circulate extensively, and as a fan of audiobooks, I can vouch for the pleasures provided by that format. *The Talisman Ring* is a Georgian romp featuring two couples (one young and romantic, the other more staid), Adventure, Mystery (the plot hinges on the discovery of a stolen ring), and a perfidious villain.[26] The delightful dialogue leaves readers laughing out loud, and more than one has told me this is not necessarily the best book to be reading on a commuter train, if one cares what fellow passengers think.

EXPANDING READERS' HORIZONS WITH WHOLE COLLECTION READERS' ADVISORY

Many books outside the Romance genre appeal to Romance readers. Those who seek a satisfying love relationship in Romances may also find this as a secondary theme in a range of genre and nongenre fiction, from Mystery and Science Fiction to award-winning Literary Fiction. Romantic stories in all genres appeal to Romance readers, and the readers may not consciously recognize the difference between these and those that fit within the stricter confines of the genre. They may like a range of books that include romantic relationships, and their reading tastes may cut across all genres. What appeals to them may be the successful resolution of the romantic entanglements, and some days they will choose Romances for this fulfillment; on others they may seek that satisfaction in titles from other genres.

Lois McMaster Bujold's long-running Vorkosigan series, beginning with *Shards of Honor,* for example, can be enjoyed as Romance or Science Fiction or both.[27] Some readers may relate to the fast-paced action of this Science Fiction adventure set in a future time and on other worlds. Others may find the development of the romantic relationship between Betan commander Cordelia Naismith and her Barayarran captor, Captain Aral Vorkosigan, the main attraction. Both appeals are legitimate, and thus this title proves an excellent suggestion for readers in both genres. Catherine Asaro's novels set in the Skolian Empire are also a good suggestion (*Primary Inversion* is the first), as are her stand-alone, near-future Science Fiction novels like *The Veiled Web*, about a Latina American dancer, a Middle Eastern computer scientist, and the Internet as artificial intelligence.[28]

There are any number of Fantasy authors who also rely heavily on the romantic tone, if not actual Romance, in creating their stories. Both Bujold and Asaro have Fantasy series that also appeal to Romance fans. Asaro's Aronsdale Trilogy and Bujold's Sharing Knife series are both good suggestions, as are Anne Bishop's darkly erotic Black Jewels trilogy and her more traditional Tir Allain Trilogy.[29] In addition, Laurell K. Hamilton's series featuring vampire hunter Anita Blake and her would-be lover (and master vampire) Jean-Claude demonstrates crossover from the Horror genre.

Guilty Pleasures starts the series.[30] Fantasy/Horror/Mystery writer Charlaine Harris has achieved fame recently for her southern vampire novels, recently adapted for television. Despite the distinctly unfamiliar romantic background, Romance fans will likely find the characters and themes they enjoy, not to mention the humor. *Dead until Dark* is the first.[31]

Novels of Women's Lives and Relationships offer other examples. These are closely related to the Romance genre, and many of the most popular are written by authors who made their reputations as writers of Romances. These novels, instead of focusing on the romantic entanglements of the protagonists, cover a broader scope and concentrate on the details of women's lives and their relationships, romantic and otherwise. Chick Lit author Meg Cabot adds a large measure of Romance to her novels, as does newcomer Sarah Addison Allen. Kathleen Gilles Seidel, a Rita Award–winning Romance author, now writes intriguing novels that focus more on women's lives, as do Deborah Smith and Barbara Samuel.

Some readers enjoy Mysteries with a strong romantic interest, such as those by Elizabeth Peters. (Her first Amelia Peabody mystery, *Crocodile on the Sandbank,* focuses on the romantic relationships of Amelia and her friend Evelyn with the Emerson brothers, and *He Shall Thunder in the Sky* features the romantic entanglements of Amelia's son Ramses.)[32] Carrie Bebris revisits Jane Austen's Elizabeth and Fitzwilliam Darcy, casting them as newlywed detectives.[33]

Since several popular Romance authors now write Romantic Suspense, their titles make excellent crossover suggestions. Nora Roberts, Elizabeth Lowell, Jayne Ann Krentz, and Linda Howard have kept their romantic themes and language and added large measures of Suspense. Their titles continue to attract readers from both genres. Other Adrenaline genres—Thrillers and Suspense—are represented by additional former Romance writers, Karen Robards and Lisa Gardner, whose new titles contain less romance but still convey the tone Romance readers appreciate. Gayle Lynds is another good suggestion.

Across the Dewey Divide in the nonfiction collection, titles dealing with relationships might make good suggestions for displays along with Romance titles. Biographies of romantic figures from history, memoirs detailing successful relationships, and subjects dealing with the creations of families are good bets for Romance readers (and for fans of Women's Lives and Relationships as well!). Readers' advisors should be open to the possibility of exploring other genres in helping these readers. See figure 8.3 for additional suggestions.

Figure 8.3 *Expanding Readers' Horizons*

Authors to Take Readers beyond the Romance Genre

Adrenaline:	Lisa Gardner
	Gayle Lynds
	Karen Robards
Fantasy:	Anne Bishop
	Melanie Rawn
	Jennifer Roberson
Gentle:	Rosamunde Pilcher
	Nicholas Sparks
Historical Fiction:	Jennifer Donnelly
	Elizabeth Chadwick
	Brenda Rickman Vantrease
Horror:	Laurell K. Hamilton
	Chelsea Quinn Yarbro
Literary:	Jane Austen
Mystery:	Carrie Bebris
	Elizabeth Peters
	Gillian Roberts
Romantic Suspense:	Kay Hooper
	Linda Howard
	Iris Johansen
	Elizabeth Lowell
	Jayne Anne Krentz/Amanda Quick
	Karen Robards
	Nora Roberts/J. D. Robb
Saga:	Cynthia Harrod-Eagles (Kirov Saga)[34]
Science Fiction:	Catherine Asaro
	Lois McMaster Bujold
	Sharon Shinn
	Judith Tarr
Western:	Jo-Ann Mapson
Women's Lives:	Sarah Addison Allen
	Meg Cabot
	Barbara Delinsky
	Kathleen Gilles Seidel

TRENDS

More recently popular in other genres, the paranormal has long been a standard feature in Romance. Alternate Reality Romances remain hot, and magical and supernatural themes play significant roles in many contemporary and historical titles. In fact, authors known primarily for their historical or contemporary Romances have also begun publishing titles that add elements from the paranormal. Mary Jo Putney's Guardian series is a recent example.[35] Janet Evanovich, a Romance author before writing her best-selling Mystery series starring Stephanie Plum, has returned to her roots with a number of short Romance titles featuring Stephanie and the mysterious, magical Diesel. (He first appears in *Visions of Sugar Plums*.)[36] Alternative Reality Romances remain extremely popular with special emphasis on the paranormal: vampires, werewolves, witches, magic, and more. Perhaps in contrast there seem also to be more and more Inspirational Romance lines and more titles published, both Contemporary and Historical.

While genre blending continues in Romance, a more obvious trend is the number of authors leaving the genre to write in related genres. Krentz, Linda Howard, and Roberts now write Romantic Suspense (often with large measures of Paranormal) exclusively; Kristin Hannah, Susan Wiggs, and Barbara Samuel/Ruth Wind, once staples of Romance, now write novels of Women's Lives and Relationships. While they are not described in this chapter but in the others focusing on their new genres, they have all taken fans with them and thus expanded the reading universe for many who once considered themselves solely Romance readers. In fact, readers may not be as aware of the gradual change in styles and focus among these authors, and fans still consider them as their favorite Romance authors. We should too, and should feel comfortable offering them a wide range of authors from these genres that might appeal.

Romantic comedy continues to dominate the genre—in all types of Romances. Whether Historical, Contemporary, or Alternative Reality, comedy features prominently across the genre, and these books, which often play with genre conventions, tend to attract readers who may not consider themselves Romance fans. Susan Elizabeth Phillips, Julie Kenner, and Julia Quinn are among the authors to know.

Just as other genres are becoming edgier, so many Romances are now more sensual, bordering on the erotic. Regencies, which used to be considered "safe" for all readers, may now include as much sex as the racy Historical Romances they used to contrast with. Alternative Reality Romances have long been edgier and that trend continues. In fact, several Romance publishers have added lines that support this trend. These are not Erotica, books in which sex is the focus; here Romance remains the central issue, but there are more sexy encounters, more graphically described. Classic authors include Susan Johnson, Bertrice Small, Thea Devine, and Robin Schone. Among newer authors try Jade Lee, Jennifer Ashley, Emma Holly, and Jamie Sobrato.

Romance has long been a rich field for multicultural Romances, and African American themes remain strong; many publishers have specific lines devoted to these titles. Zane combines two trends with erotic novels featuring African American characters. Rochelle Alers, Brenda Jackson, Francis Ray, and Sandra Kitt remain multicultural authors to collect. Other authors to watch include male authors, long thought to be an anomaly among Romance writers: Eric Jerome Dickey, E. Lynn Harris, and Omar Tyree write Romance and Urban Fiction popular with a wide audience, regardless of race or gender. Of course, African American culture is not the only one emphasized in the genre, and we continue to see a wider range of Romances that broaden readers' experience. In fact, Harlequin even has lines published in Spanish to address that growing audience. (Interestingly, despite the emphasis on exploring cultures, most titles seem still to be set in the United States and British Isles.)

Recently publishers have launched lines of Romance graphic novels, a format that especially suits edgier, speculative Romances. E-books are another popular format for Romance readers and writers. In fact, Romance writers were among the earliest adapters of this technology. No longer constrained by the dictates of traditional commercial publishing and physical merchandising, these authors are among the most innovative in their choice of themes and portrayal of characters and conflicts. Additionally, their readers enjoy the luxury of purchasing from the comfort of their own homes and downloading the stories to portable devices as well as to their home computers.

⊣⧛ ⧚⊢

Romance readers are an audience worth cultivating. They are voracious readers and often committed supporters and users of the library. Because many Romances are quite short, fans read a lot of them. The typical Romance reader often has a wide range of interests, and this group includes some of our most sophisticated readers. It is not uncommon to see the same reader preparing to check out a handful of category Romances, P. D. James, some Science Fiction, and perhaps an Anne Tyler or John Updike.

Romances are fantasies, and their readers recognize them as such, just as readers of Mystery, Science Fiction, Western, Thriller, and other genres recognize their favorites as fantasies. In the particular fantasy explored in each Romance, the woman always wins—and perhaps that is what makes the Romance so subversive. These are stories of women who are defined by what they do, not just by what they are. Best-selling Romance author Patricia Gaffney summarizes the genre's appeal: "Dress it up with ghosts, angels, werewolves, leprechauns; mix it up with murder, kidnapping, comedy, time machines—it doesn't matter. If the core is a believable story about two people finding and committing to each other for life, if it touches our emotions, if it rings true and makes us laugh, cry, and celebrate the miracle of human intimacy, it's romance."[37]

NOTES

1. *Romance Writers Report* 28 (September 2008), 34.
2. Kristin Ramsdell, *Romance Fiction: A Guide to the Genre* (Englewood, CO: Libraries Unlimited, 1999), 5.
3. Cathie Linz, *Good Girls Do* (New York: Berkley Sensation, 2006).
4. Jennifer Crusie, *Faking It* (New York: St. Martin's, 2002).
5. Christine Feehan, Dark series, beginning with *Dark Prince* (New York: Love Spell, 1999); Drake Sisters series, beginning with *Magic in the Wind* (New York: Berkley, 2005).
6. Loretta Chase, *Your Scandalous Ways* (New York: Avon, 2008).
7. Feehan cited above.
8. Mary Balogh, *Simply Magic* (New York: Delacorte, 2007).
9. Robert James Waller, *The Bridges of Madison County* (New York: Warner, 1992).
10. Jennifer Greene, *Blame It on Chocolate* (Don Mills, ON: HQN, 2006); Susan Elizabeth Phillips, *This Heart of Mine* (New York: Morrow, 2001); Linnea Sinclair, *Down Home Zombie Blues* (New York: Bantam, 2007).
11. Jayne Ann Krentz, ed., *Dangerous Men and Adventurous Women: Romance Writers on the Appeal of Romance* (Philadelphia: University of Pennsylvania Press, 1992), 17.
12. Mary Jo Putney, *The Rake* (New York: Topaz, 1998).
13. Phillips, *Natural Born Charmer* (New York: Morrow, 2007).
14. Julia Quinn, *The Duke and I* (New York: Avon, 2000).
15. Sherrilyn Kenyon, *Fantasy Lover* (New York: St. Martin's Paperbacks, 2002).
16. Chase, *The Lion's Daughter* (New York: Avon, 1992).
17. Emma Donoghue, *Landing* (Orlando, FL: Harcourt, 2007).
18. Steve Kluger, *Almost like Being in Love* (New York: Perennial, 2004).
19. Bob Smith, *Selfish and Perverse* (New York: Carroll and Graf, 2007).
20. Francis Ray, Graysons of New Mexico series, beginning with *Until There Was You* (Washington, DC: BET, 1999).
21. Crusie, *Bet Me* (New York: St. Martin's, 2004).
22. Chase, *Not Quite a Lady* (New York: Avon, 2007).
23. Julie Klassen, *Lady of Milkweed Manor* (Minneapolis: Bethany House, 2007).
24. Katie Fforde, *Wild Designs* (New York: St. Martin's, 1997).
25. Ray, *Any Rich Man Will Do* (New York: St. Martin's Griffin, 2005).
26. Georgette Heyer, *The Talisman Ring* (London, ON: Heinemann, [1936]).

27. Lois McMaster Bujold, *Shards of Honor* (New York: Baen, 1986).
28. Catherine Asaro, *Primary Inversion* (New York: Tor, 1995); Asaro, *The Veiled Web* (New York: Bantam, 1999).
29. Asaro, Aronsdale Trilogy, beginning with *The Charmed Sphere* (New York: Luna, 2004); Bujold, Sharing Knife series, beginning with *Beguilement* (New York: Eos, 2006); Anne Bishop, Black Jewels Trilogy, beginning with *Daughter of the Blood* (New York: Roc, 1998); Bishop, Tir Allain Trilogy, beginning with *The Pillars of the World* (New York: Roc, 2001).
30. Laurell K. Hamilton, *Guilty Pleasures* (New York: Ace, 1993).
31. Charlaine Harris, *Dead until Dark* (New York: Ace, 2001).
32. Elizabeth Peters, *Crocodile on the Sandbank* (New York: Dodd, Mead, 1975); Peters, *He Shall Thunder in the Sky* (New York: Morrow, 2000).
33. Carrie Bebris, Mr. and Mrs. Darcy Mysteries, beginning with *Pride and Prescience; or, A Truth Universally Acknowledged* (New York: Forge, 2004).
34. Cynthia Harrod-Eagles, Kirov Trilogy, beginning with *Anna* (New York: St. Martin's, 1991).
35. Mary Jo Putney, Guardian series, beginning with *A Kiss of Fate* (New York: Ballantine, 2004).
36. Janet Evanovich, *Visions of Sugar Plums* (New York: St. Martin's, 2002).
37. Patricia Gaffney, "Coming Out of the Closet and Locking It Behind Us," in *North American Romance Writers*, ed. Kay Mussell and Johanna Tuñon, 92.

9

WOMEN'S LIVES AND
RELATIONSHIPS

One of the most popular annotated booklists at my library is one devoted to books written by women authors about women and their lives. If the popularity of our booklists is any indication of what women read, we know that many women—in my library at least—are requesting books that generally deal with Women's Lives and Relationships. These books that explore concerns faced by women in a specific age group or by women in general do not fall easily into a genre. Sometimes readers seek a lighthearted book in this vein; at other times they look for a title that deals more seriously with an issue; at times a soap opera approach satisfies their need to escape the reality of their lives; and at other times they seek something more provocative. All of these are stories that appeal to the emotions. Fortunately for librarians and readers alike, this is a market publishers have recognized and worked to meet, providing a wide range of titles that deal with the concerns and joys found in women's lives.

A DEFINITION

Although some call this genre Women's Fiction, I find that term too limiting, as it could suggest to the uninitiated that this is all that women read. Or that this is what women should read. Or what we should suggest to any woman who asks for assistance. We know that just as there is no single type of fiction all men read—no comparable Men's Fiction—there is no one genre all women read. However, the popularity of these books suggests that we find a way to group them. Therefore, this genre is called Women's Lives and Relationships throughout this chapter.

These are books that explore the reaches of women's lives; that deal with the dynamics of relationships with family, friends, and lovers; that may or may not end happily (although they do generally end with issues resolved or the resolution suggested); that examine the issues women confront in their lives (at home and at work) and the distinctive way in which women deal with these concerns. Written almost exclusively by women for a primarily female audience, these are stories that chart the courses of their lives. They deal with real problems and real solutions. They provide their readers a glimpse into the way others have confronted dilemmas similar to those they face themselves, as well as into lifestyles and problems very different from their own.

They overlap with books in other genres, with titles that feature strong women and emphasize the same kinds of relationships and struggles with issues; this crossover and how to use it to help readers find more of the types of books they enjoy are discussed below. See figure 9.1 for characteristics of the genre.

Figure 9.1   *Characteristics of Novels of Women's Lives and Relationships*

---

1. While the mood may be thoughtful or humorous, tragic or romantic, these novels offer a generally optimistic outlook. Stories provide an intimate glimpse into the lives of the protagonists and exert an emotional pull.

2. The protagonist is female, as is the author. Protagonists may have a support group composed of female, and sometimes male, family members and friends.

3. Story lines reflect the issues affecting women's lives and portray women facing difficult situations. Universal female themes—family conflicts, family relationships, work versus family, friendships—and how the protagonists react to these issues focus the plot. Difficulties are generally resolved satisfactorily (or solutions are put in place), and endings are usually hopeful, if not happy.

4. The setting is usually contemporary; these are books about today's women and the problems they face. Interesting careers and hobbies add intriguing backgrounds to the novels.

5. The writing style may range from elegantly poetic to more prosaic, from conversational to humorous. Unusual formats—letters, e-mail, instant messages (IMs), diaries—are often employed to tell these personal stories.

6. Pacing is generally unhurried. Fans talk of these as compelling reads, which pull readers in and involve them with the protagonist's story.

CHARACTERISTICS AND THE GENRE'S APPEAL

Tone/Mood

Titles in this genre offer an intimate glimpse into the lives of protagonists. While the tone ranges from more melodramatic to realistic or provocative, it sets up the emotional link that readers want and expect.

This contrast is easy to see by comparing Plum Sykes's ironic look at the jet-setting, glamorous New York life for her smart young women getting married and then divorced (*Bergdorf Blondes* and *The Debutante Divorcée*) with the more domestic and unpretentious treatment of a young divorced woman in Judith Ryan Hendricks's *Bread Alone* and *The Baker's Apprentice*.[1] Each author creates a distinct and identifiable tone that satisfies its audience.

This is not to say that one is better than the other, but simply that each has a different tone and possibly readership. Both deal with a similar topic and feature characters of approximately the same age, but with different purposes in mind. Fans recognize the distinction, and although they may read and appreciate both books, they do not see them as the same kind of book. That rather ephemeral distinction clouds much of our consideration of genre fiction, but in this genre, which approaches basic truths in women's lives, it becomes clearer that authors, by their intention and direction, create a range of books that deal with similar, always difficult and emotional topics. Some readers may never want to go beyond a more casual look at an issue, and they choose particular books because they know they can count on authors to meet their expectations. Others are disappointed if authors do not explore issues, reflecting, often poetically, on the possibilities. Tone is a vital consideration in this genre.

However, as I suggested earlier, this tone also runs the gamut. Elinor Lipman and Jennifer Weiner tell their stories with large measures of wit and humor. Danielle Steel and Fern Michaels rely on more sentimental devices. Readers would not choose Meg Cabot's or Sophie Kinsella's romps and expect to find the style and tone similar to Jodi Picoult's thoughtful and edgy consideration of very serious topics. Each author has her fans, and readers may read a variety of types to meet different needs.

Characterization

These are novels written by women, and they explore the lives of female protagonists while they focus on her relationships with family, friends, and lovers. The story line may follow a single character and examine the ways in which she relates to others and attempts to make sense of her life, or they may explore a group of women, usually friends, and the interrelated issues of their lives and friendships. If there is a single protagonist, she is supported by a group of friends and family, usually female, although male characters sometimes take on this nonromantic responsibility. Whether with one heroine or several, these novels are character-centered.

As in most other genres, there are often series that may focus on a single woman or a group. Ann B. Ross's popular Miss Julia novels follow the antics of the heroine, a woman on the far side of age seventy, in a small southern town (*Miss Julia Speaks Her Mind* starts the series).[2] Diane McKinney-Whetstone's unique series highlights African American women in the same Philadelphia community in different decades from the 1940s to the twenty-first century (*Tumbling* is the first).[3] Maeve Binchy frequently writes of a group of characters whose lives intertwine. Her characters tend to be disparate, brought together by an event, and multigenerational, and they form a family of sorts by book's end. (In *Whitethorn Woods* she assembles her characters to stop a by-pass and save a well in a small Irish town.)[4]

Story Line

Novels in this genre examine themes of concern special to women. Generations of families, family relationships and friendships, issues with health and career, and women triumphing over adversity and reconstructing their lives are among those considered.

Many are domestic and celebrate the pleasures of hearth and home. Marisa de los Santos's *Belong to Me* explores domestic dramas—death and birth—with lyrical, image-rich prose.[5] This sprawling story examines how life changes people and how people change with life's vicissitudes, as it reveals the complex intertwining of lives in a neighborhood in which wife and mother Cornelia is dying. The big issues—love, trust, family—center around home life. Others portray women in the workforce. Heather Swain's *Luscious Lemon* combines both as chef Ellie Manelli tries to juggle the demands of home and work when she discovers she is pregnant.[6] Anna Quindlen's *Rise and Shine* is the story of radio celebrity Meghan Fitzmaurice, who adds a string of profanities to the end of an interview, thinking she is off the air.[7] How she copes with the loss of her job, and how that changes the dynamic in her relationship with her younger sister who idolized her, makes an absorbing story.

Provocative issues drive the novels of many of these authors, and even among those, the tone differs. Jodi Picoult's novels may stretch the genre boundaries, but her edgy focus on family issues makes this genre a logical spot to consider her. In *My Sister's Keeper* her young female protagonist raises intriguing questions about the nature of family and the role of family members.[8] Her own birth was genetically engineered so that she would be a perfect match for her older sister who suffers from a rare form of leukemia. Elizabeth Berg raises similarly important issues in many of her novels, but she does so more gently. Abuse, terminal illness, and betrayal are among the topics she considers. In *Dream When You're Feeling Blue,* a World War II novel set in home front Chicago, she takes on the changing role of women.[9] Pearl Cleage (also an accomplished playwright) can be counted on to tackle a wide range of racial and social issues in her lyrical novels of the African American community. *I Wish I Had a Red Dress* centers on a rural enclave outside Detroit and examines the lives of women who learn to be responsible for themselves.[10]

Novels in this genre revolve around healing and discovering solutions to problems many women share. "Family" in the broadest sense pervades these stories. Children, siblings, spouses, parents, and the extended family of friends people these novels. These are stories of relationships and of coping with problems and issues. Although frequently domestic, these stories are as noncompartmentalized as the lives of the women they describe. Family, friends, work, and home must all fit together into a woman's life, and the focus of the novel may be on the way the protagonist must handle all to avoid disaster. The conflicts arising from juggling work and home responsibilities are at the heart of many of these stories, and compromise is the key to the resolution. Novels of Women's Lives and Relationships reflect universal themes that highlight the strength and resilience of the heroine but often also set up conflicts that demand thoughtful reconciliation and resolution.

Frame/Setting

Currency of issues constitutes part of the appeal of this genre. Themes address problems women face today. Although some Historical Fiction may also reflect women's issues, as in Catherine Cookson's studies of the plight of nineteenth-century women in rural England, these do not have the same impact and immediacy for fans as contemporary titles. Readers may read and enjoy both, but they look to modern-day stories of Women's Lives and Relationships for different reassurances and satisfactions.

Fascinating background details related to geographical setting, careers, and hobbies frame these stories. Sarah Addison Allen's charming *Garden Spells* plays up the atmosphere of its Southern setting and adds an element of magic.[11] Sarah Bird's *Flamenco Academy* explores the history of the flamenco dance, its roots in gypsy culture, and the landscape of New Mexico.[12] Berg often takes readers to Chicago and its suburbs, while Binchy leads them to Dublin and other Irish locales. Books and book groups are a popular frame, used to great effect by Karen Joy Fowler (*The Jane Austen Book Club*), Lorna Landvik (*Angry Housewives Eating Bon Bons*), and Virginia Ironside, whose sassy and curmudgeonly protagonist is defiantly against book clubs (*No, I Don't Want to Join a Book Club: Diary of a Sixtieth Year*).[13] Mary Kay Andrews draws on the worlds of antiques and cooking, and many authors dabble in the world of the rich and famous (Louise Bagshawe, Candace Bushnell, Diane Johnson, and Sykes, among others).

Style/Language

Writing style is a factor in all genres. Here, the writing styles range from Margaret Drabble's literary prose and intelligent dialogue to the more conversational style of Meg Cabot's smart dialogue and descriptions. Although some readers choose authors based on writing style, for others, language is but the means to tell the story of women and their lives. Readers choose among a range of styles, sometimes indiscriminately, or so it seems, just as they do in all genres (except perhaps Literary Fiction, in which style is often of primary importance), finding the story and the characters that resonate with them and suit their mood. A romantic tone characterizes the style of many of these authors—Steel, Rosamunde Pilcher, Cabot, and Kinsella, among them. Others, for example Barbara Kingsolver and Alice Hoffman, are appreciated equally by fans of Literary Fiction as consummate stylists who deal with provocative issues.

This genre also displays a wide range of styles and formats. Epistolary novels are particularly popular, and the letters are as likely to be e-mail and IMs as the more traditional variety. Cecilia Ahern's *Rosie Dunne* chronicles the story of a lost love through letters, while Kinsella intersperses her first Shopaholic novel (*Confessions of a Shopaholic*) with increasingly sharp notes from heroine Becky's bank manager.[14] Cabot's *Every Boy's Got One* reproduces memorabilia from the heroine's honeymoon trip, including the airplane menu and passport.[15] Picoult has even incorporated illustrations in her novel *The Tenth Circle,* as one of the characters is a graphic novelist.[16]

Pacing

Finally, the pacing of these novels tends more toward the leisurely unfolding or unhurried, generally lacking the elements of suspense or adventure that might move the story more quickly. Still, readers speak of them as compelling reading, books that pull them in and keep them engaged. The sense of the pacing, of moving forward through the problems faced by the protagonist and her friends, likely feels brisker than is reflected by the actual turning of pages. The format can also make the pacing seem quicker. Short e-mails and IMs and short chapters speed the reader through the book. For example, Alice Kuipers's use of notes on the refrigerator to tell her story of a mother's battle with cancer in *Life on the Refrigerator Door: Notes between a Mother and a Daughter* transforms the book into a literal page-turner.[17]

KEY AUTHORS

Identifying important names in the genre opens a Pandora's box of possibilities. There are those who write a more conversational prose versus those with a more literary style, those who write more humorously versus those who take a more serious approach, the sentimental versus the realistic schools, and much in between.

Elizabeth Berg has long had broad appeal in many of our libraries—even before Oprah discovered her. Her character-centered books play out domestic dramas on a small stage. She elegantly and poignantly depicts women's emotional lives and relationships in lyrical prose and addresses universal themes—marriage, friendships, parents, and family. Her resilient protagonists are always compassionately depicted. Most of her books project a timeless quality; she emphasizes emotions and relationships more than time lines, and this means that even older titles remain popular. *Open House,* Oprah's Book Club selection, still resonates with readers. Divorced Samantha reinvents herself and discovers happiness in this comfortable, lightly humorous story.[18]

Jennifer Weiner appeals both to younger readers (fans of the ever popular Chick Lit) as well as to older. Her characters, usually in their thirties or slightly older, are smart, often plus-sized, and engaging, and they deal with issues related to juggling family and work. There may be an element of Mystery introduced (*Goodnight Nobody*), but generally these are witty, thoughtful, heartwarming stories that explore friendships and family relationships.[19] *Good in Bed* established her reputation in 2001, and *Certain Girls* continues the story of her heroine Cannie Krushelevansky, née Shapiro, as she faces a new challenge, her daughter's bat mitzvah, and thus adds a complex mother-daughter relationship to the tale.[20]

Irish writer Maeve Binchy continues to charm readers. Often told as short stories braided together into a novel form, Binchy's character-centered books touch a chord that resonates across the Atlantic. Her Irish women face universal situations similar to those of their American counterparts, and they deal with them in similarly traditional ways. Binchy's stories are evocative, descriptive of both geography and character, and although they do not always produce happy endings, stories are resolved in a way that leaves readers satisfied. *Whitethorn Woods,* mentioned above, employs her distinctive style with interwoven, layered stories.[21]

Jodi Picoult writes intelligent, provocative novels of Women's Lives and Relationships with far-reaching implications. Often emphasizing the spiritual and psychological aspects of characters and issues alike, Picoult writes serious, intriguing, and insightful dramas that raise difficult questions. *My Sister's Keeper* is a particularly poignant introduction to her style.[22]

Once the unrivaled benchmark in this genre, Danielle Steel remains popular, but she is no longer universally loved and read as she was in the 1980s. Her books feature strong female characters, timeless values (love for children, home, and family), a romantic and often sentimental tone, rich-and-famous elements (brand names, designer labels, etc.), and, as expected, the issues that women face in their lives, from divorce and breast cancer to problems with children. She writes stories that are both touching and satisfying about women who face tragedy and emerge stronger. Try *Safe Harbour,* a recent title that portrays Ophelie, the quintessential Steel heroine—gentle, kind, decent, honest, and compassionate—paralyzed by grief following the deaths of her husband and son in an airplane crash.[23] It is her daughter Pip who manages to shake her out of her lethargy, and, with the help of a lonely divorced father, her recovery is ensured.

For many, Sophie Kinsella's Shopaholic series characterizes the Chick Lit phenomenon. Not the first of its type but perhaps the first series, Kinsella's novels star Becky Brandon née Bloomburg, a twenty-something Londoner who can't manage her own finances but who writes articles on managing one's money for a respectable financial magazine! The series starts with *Confessions of a Shopaholic,* and although marriage and a baby have tamed her financial instability, she's always game for a bargain.[24] Kinsella also writes popular stand-alone titles that feature humor, witty dialogue, naive heroines, and rich and famous backgrounds.

WHAT WE KNOW ABOUT FANS

Readers are primarily women, and they may read a range of authors from Danielle Steel to the more literary and provocative Jodi Picoult. These are readers who appreciate stories of women facing difficulties in their everyday lives and coming to terms with them, often with the help of friends who are almost always other women. These readers seek stories that reflect both the domestic and professional aspects of women's lives, as well as the way in which women have always been required to juggle the demands of these two worlds. Issues are usually resolved in these stories, a fact that makes them immensely satisfying. Even though we know these are "just" books, the fact that solutions can be found offers hope to readers. Problems may not always be solved neatly, but possible solutions are presented and the characters begin on the path toward working out the difficulties. These are generally hopeful stories, featuring a range of women and situations that explore the dilemmas that often shape women's lives. That is what readers expect.

Readers may be attracted to protagonists of roughly their own age, as those characters face issues similar to the ones readers themselves confront in their own lives. This breakdown provides a good place to start when exploring the range of authors in this genre, and it makes these authors and their books easier to describe to readers. However, I would be the last to advocate pigeonholing readers—or writers—in this fashion. The themes that direct these stories are timeless and ageless. The best appeal to readers of all ages, and all fans find at some point a similar interest in these authors and their characters, no matter what their own age or that of the protagonists.

Among those authors who often feature protagonists in their twenties and thirties are Judy Baer, Meg Cabot, Emily Giffin, Jane Green, Erin Hilderbrand, Marian Keyes, Sophie Kinsella, Ann Maxted, Mameve Medwed, and Alisa Valdes-Rodriguez. The younger protagonists might be sassy, feisty heroines or more contemplative, quiet observers of the world. Just out of school and beginning careers, these women face the problems arising from leaving one's family and living on one's own, resolving career obstacles, finding mates (or deciding not to), and generally sorting out their futures. These authors often view the world with a humorous, sometimes irreverent eye. This is the original Chick Lit.

As the protagonists move into their thirties, their stories address issues of husbands and young families, along with careers and sustaining friendships, a slightly different focus and often a less frantic tone. In *The Blue*

Bistro, Hilderbrand blends elements of rich-and-famous (Nantucket during the summer season means the glamour of the beautiful people), enticing food (the heroine works at a restaurant), a touch of nostalgia (the restaurant will close at the end of the season) into a comfortable, heartwarming story of a young woman recovering from a bad relationship and getting a new start.[25]

Characters in their forties and fifties star in the novels of Elizabeth Berg, Pearl Cleage, Claire Cook, Kristin Hannah, Lorna Landvik, Elinor Lipman, and Anne Rivers Siddons. Although these protagonists may have children, they are usually older or grown and away. Regaining relationships with husband and friends and confronting the specter of death (of parents, peers, or children) are the themes that dominate these stories. Lee Smith's recent novels also feature women in this age group. Her evocative southern settings enhance the flavor of these leisurely paced stories of family and friends. In *The Last Girls* four college friends meet on a Mississippi riverboat to spread the ashes of one of their group.[26] In 1965 as coeds they made a similar trip on a raft they built, and flashbacks to that trip as well as the stories of each of the friends combine to create a nostalgic tale of enduring friendships.

Older protagonists, in their sixties and above, also find their stories told in this genre. In fact, publishers have discovered a market for this age group, and these novels are increasingly popular and available. Sarah Challis, Joan A. Medlicott, Jeanne Ray, Ann B. Ross, and Marcia Willett are all good suggestions for readers. Medlicott's *The Ladies of Covington Place Send Their Love* is the first of a series featuring three women of a certain age making their way on their own and creating a community.[27] Home truths, along with a mix of memories and everyday events, fill these stories of women working out the last third of their lives.

Some authors who have written for several years—Steel, Binchy, Nancy Thayer—tend to place their heroines near their own current age. Margaret Drabble is a master of this. Many of us read of the lives of her younger protagonists in the 1970s and later followed through the lives of the more mature women who people her titles in the twenty-first century. (If you are interested in experimenting, start with an early novel from the 1970s—the award-winning *The Millstone* perhaps, with its story of an unwed mother—and continue through her recent *The Sea Lady,* which features a woman academic looking back over her life and choices.)[28] This sense of following an author through similar periods in our lives is a real draw; we feel we know each other and face similar problems. Reading earlier titles brings back earlier days in our own lives, while later titles by those authors may be harbingers of our own futures. That these authors seem to chart our own lives is part of their enormous, satisfying appeal.

It is clear from the previous descriptions of authors and titles that other genres overlap with Women's Lives and Relationships, and themes from those genres may play a role in these stories. On the other hand, if you are a fan of another genre but want to explore novels of Women's Lives and Relationships, it is useful to find authors that reflect the elements you enjoy in genres you currently read. Figure 9.2 offers suggestions of authors to try.

THE READERS' ADVISORY INTERVIEW

Women's Lives and Relationships is another genre that readers do not generally request by name. In fact, readers might be surprised to discover that we consider this a genre. They may come to the desk and offer the names of some of these authors as ones they have read and enjoyed, or they may describe a book about relationships and coping, and this seems a logical genre to explore with them. They may also talk about some of the genres covered in this book, and the suggested links to writers of novels about Women's Lives and Relationships will give them new directions to explore. The key for us is, of course, to listen to which authors they enjoy and how they describe them. Are they looking for the more literary or popular authors? More serious treatment or less? And we must develop ways to pose these questions, or offer authors and titles, so that we do not offend this audience by denigrating their favorite authors and the themes that have touched them.

Novels of a young woman's coming of age often fit in with novels of Women's Lives and Relationships. They, too, explore universal and timeless issues dealing with friends and family, love and loss. While helping younger readers to deal with these issues, they also take older readers back to that time in their own pasts and remind them of how they felt, producing satisfaction in a wide range of readers. Recent titles to consider include *Sweetwater Creek,* Siddons's novel of a young girl's coming to terms with her mother's death and her father's lack of interest.[29] This is a bittersweet, timeless tale told in lyrical prose of a girl who discovers her talent and her niche. In contrast, Gail Godwin's *Queen of the Underworld* is a sophisticated story told in polished prose of a young journalist's first job working in Miami in the summer of 1959, a time when Cuban exiles were

---

Figure 9.2   *An Introduction to the Women's Lives and Relationships Genre*

Writers of Women's Lives and Relationships to Try, If You Enjoy . . .

Adrenaline:	Jane Heller
	Susan Isaacs
Fantasy:	Sarah Addison Allen
Gay/Lesbian:	Kris Radish
Gentle:	Rosamunde Pilcher
Historical Fiction:	Sandra Dallas
Horror:	MaryJanice Davidson
Humor:	Meg Cabot
	Sophie Kinsella
	Elinor Lipman
Inspirational:	Judy Baer
	Robin Lee Hatcher
	Neta Jackson
	Beverly Lewis
Literary:	Gail Godwin
	Alice Hoffman
Multicultural:	C. C. Medina
	Marsha Mehran
	Francis Ray (Invincible Women series)[30]
	Alisa Valdes-Rodriguez
Mystery:	Mary Kay Andrews
	Susan Isaacs
Romance:	Kristin Hannah
	Barbara Samuel
	Deborah Smith
Saga:	Amy Tan
Western:	Jo-Ann Mapson

---

flooding Miami to escape Castro, and the bustling city was a far cry from her stifling home and family in North Carolina.[31]

The best solution to the problem of helping readers is to create lists of popular writers in this genre, including a range of age groups and tone. Displays of such titles seem to be enduringly popular in libraries, and because there are so many authors that fit in this genre, lists and authors for displays are relatively easy to discover.

Sure Bets

Many of Elinor Lipman's titles work for a wide range of readers. She adds humor to her tales of the fates of her female protagonists, and because they are often timeless stories, rather than tied to specific events, her older titles remain popular. For example, imagine that your birth mother finally reveals herself to you, and she is a cross between Oprah and Sally Jessie Raphael. That is what happens to April Epner in *Then She Found Me*.[32] How that discovery affects her job as a teacher (Latin, no less), her relationship with her adopted parents (Holocaust survivors), and her own budding romance, as she researches the several stories about her birth father, makes a diverting but thoughtful story. This is a novel of contrasting relationships, sophisticated and witty dialogue, and home truths about what it is to be a parent.

Lorna Landvik's *Angry Housewives Eating Bon Bons* is surely the quintessential Women's Lives and Relationships book.[33] Even the title is enticing. Here, through good times and bad, friendship sustains the neighbors whose book group originally brings them together. Book group choices frame each section with a description of the title and date read, and the chapters reflect the voices of the different women as they reveal secrets of the past and present and resolve the issues that affect the group individually and as a neighborhood. A heartwarming, humorous, and comfortable tone underpins more than thirty years of friendship.

Sarah Addison Allen is a rising star in this genre, and her award-winning *Garden Spells* is a book that readers cannot help but share with others.[34] It features the Waverley Sisters and their magical gifts. Caterer Clare has always lived in the family home in Bascomb, North Carolina, and she has built up a business based, at least in part, on her magical way with herbs; she knows exactly what to add to cure what ails one. When wayward Sydney (who cuts hair to perfection) and her daughter Bay (who knows where things belong) return, the women must reconcile their relationship and come to terms with their gifts. This is a charming, magical story, stylish and upbeat.

In a somewhat darker vein, Sarah Bird's *Flamenco Academy* tells of a friendship we know from the first will end in disaster.[35] Two young women discover flamenco in college in New Mexico, and the dance and culture draw them together and apart. Rae is the *metronom*, the cadence of the dance, and she possesses the precise technique as well as the soul of the dance. In contrast, Didi is all charisma, showmanship, and emotion. Bird explores their friendship, their professional relationship as two halves of a whole, and the culture and romance of the dance. This is a bittersweet story filled with heart.

Jeanne Ray is another author for the Sure Bets list. Her stories of women over fifty and the challenges they face please a wide range of readers. Her novels range from the more romantic *Julie and Romeo,* which presents sixty-year-olds in a Shakespearean spin-off of sorts with dueling florist families in present-day Boston, to *Eat Cake* and *Step-Ball-Change,* family-centered tales of difficult times told with humor and grace, not to mention a cast of quirky yet believable characters.[36]

EXPANDING READERS' HORIZONS WITH WHOLE COLLECTION READERS' ADVISORY

Readers of novels of Women's Lives and Relationships find much they enjoy in related genres. As is clear above, many titles in this genre have romantic themes; others fit closely with Literary Fiction or Gentle Reads. All draw in readers with their compelling stories that touch the emotions. But there are also authors in other genres, Mysteries for example, that deal with many of the same issues, adding Mystery trappings to the story. Gail Bowen is such an author. Her series features Canadian professor and widow Joanne Kilbourn. Although these focus on serious, often very disturbing, crimes, they also highlight Jo and her family—two daughters (the younger one, an artistic prodigy, adopted after her mother, a close friend of Jo's, is murdered) and two sons—and her difficult romantic relationships. The sense of motherhood and family pervades these stories so completely that I have yet to give them to another mother who has not found them intensely satisfying. (Not that one has to be a mother to enjoy these, but that connection is especially strong.) This is also a clear case when it is better not to start with the first title, which is not the strongest. *Love and Murder* provides a good introduction to the characters and the family.[37]

Although closely related to many in the Romance genre, novels of Women's Lives and Relationships have a broader emphasis than the romantic entanglements of their characters. Romance may be an element in these books, but the focus is on the bigger picture of women's lives and the problems they face, how they meet crises and resolve them. In fact, a number of authors—Kathleen Eagle, Kristin Hannah, Susan Wiggs—write in both genres. Englishwoman Katie Fforde writes Romances that are also a very good bet for these readers, especially since she writes of heroines ranging from twenty-something to decades older. Readers may find the elements they seek in Romances by these authors, whose themes include a strong sense of family relations and women's roles without an overpowering Romance.

Literary Fiction authors Anita Shreve, Isabel Allende, Diana Abu-Jaber, Joanne Harris, and Anne Tyler also address issues of interest to readers of this genre. In fact, many of the authors who write books centering on women and their issues are extremely difficult to slot into specific genres. Shreve, Tyler, and Sue Miller probably fit better as Literary Fiction authors, because their provocative novels explore beyond women's issues. Abu-Jaber also offers the Middle Eastern-American perspective, while Chris Bohjalian remains one of the few male authors who consistently provides an authentic woman's perspective. On the other hand, an elegant stylist such as Alice Hoffman certainly meets the literary criteria, but her stories seem to place her more comfortably in Women's Lives and Relationships than in Literary Fiction. Luckily, patrons are not hindered by our attempts to group authors by genre. They read the ones they enjoy, whether those authors' books seem to fall into one genre or another. Our task is to help them discover similar authors, no matter what genre we find them in.

Gentle Reads proves a treasure trove for fans of Women's Lives and Relationships. Crossover authors Debbie Macomber and Adriana Trigiani make good suggestions. Historical fiction writers who focus on the roles of women are also good possibilities. Try Margaret George, Jewel Parker Rhodes, and Lisa See—especially her popular book group title, *Snow Flower and the Secret Fan*.[38] Feminist authors of Fantasy and Science Fiction—Rosalind Miles, Marge Piercy, Sheri S. Tepper—provide provocative options for fans.

Among nonfiction topics, memoirs by women and biographies of famous women might work for these readers. Two fascinating biographies of the role of American first ladies—Margaret Truman's *First Ladies* and Cokie Roberts's *Founding Mothers: The Women Who Raised Our Nation*—are interesting possibilities to put in readers' hands or add to a display.[39] Certainly titles dealing with family relationships, with women and identity, and with women's roles should be added to lists and displays. Books on style, rich and famous celebrities and fashions, as well as books devoted to domestic pleasures such as needlecrafts, cooking, and decorating, all provide background material for readers in this genre to explore.

Our graphic novels collections also provide numerous suggestions for these fans, not the least of which are Alison Bechdel's and Marjane Satrapi's memoirs. See figure 9.3 for additional suggestions.

Figure 9.3   *Expanding Readers' Horizons*

Authors to Take Readers beyond the Women's Lives and Relationships Genre

Biography/Memoir:	Alison Bechdel
	Sarah and A. Elizabeth Delany
	Marjane Satrapi
Fantasy:	Rosalind Miles
Gentle Reads:	Debbie Macomber
	Adriana Trigiani
Historical Fiction:	Margaret George
	Jewel Parker Rhodes
	Lisa See
History:	Jung Chang (*Wild Swans: Three Daughters of China*)[40]
	Ellen Hampton (*Women of Valor*)[41]
	Elizabeth M. Norman (*We Band of Angels*)[42]
Literary:	Diana Abu-Jaber
	Christopher Bohjalian
	Joanne Harris
	Anne Tyler
Mystery:	Gail Bowen
	Julia Spencer-Fleming
Romance:	Katie Fforde
Science Fiction:	Marge Piercy
	Sheri S. Tepper
Style and Lifestyle:	Jill Connor Browne
True Adventure:	Kira Salak

TRENDS

Books in this genre cross lines of age and ethnic background in ways that books in other genres may not do as easily. Readers appreciate Multicultural novels, both to learn how issues that affect women are played out differently in other cultures and to recognize themselves and their problems in books set outside their ken (for example, in the universal themes of mothers and daughters in Amy Tan). In recent years, the genre has become international in scope, although few of the foreign titles have yet to appear in the United States. Examples of multicultural Chick Lit include Kim Wong Keltner, who chronicles the Chinese American experience; Anjali Banerjee and Bharati Mukherjee who do the same for South-Asian Americans; and Monica Ali who writes about Pakistani women in England. This trend shows no sign of waning.

The paranormal has found a niche in this genre too. Of course, Alice Hoffman has long written magical stories of women's lives and authors such as Sarah Addison Allen continue that tradition. Others move farther afield. MaryJanice Davidson, for example, has taken the characters traditionally found in Horror and applied them to Women's Lives and Relationships—specifically to the life of newly dead Betsy Taylor, a former model now destined to be queen of the vampires. (The Horror genre may not survive such encroachment!) Her issues may not be typical of those faced by most women, but readers find them no less amusing.

Chick Lit remains the most popular type of Women's Lives and Relationships. Multicultural, Inspirational, serious and silly, all treatments attract readers of all ages and backgrounds. Lad Lit—books from the male point of view exploring men's issues by writers such as Nick Hornby—doesn't seem to have caught on. Women read it, but men don't seem as anxious to examine their inner lives in this format.

Women's Lives and Relationships attracts writers from other genres. Romance writers have written in this genre and stayed or moved back to Romances. Writers of Gentle Reads sometimes experiment with edgier books that fit here. Certainly women's issues appear in many genre titles, mostly written by women. We watch for these to expand our own and our readers' knowledge of the wealth of available titles.

Because the themes of these novels potentially touch more than 50 percent of our readers, novels of Women's Lives and Relationships have a broad appeal. Although readers may not read these exclusively, they often like to sample them when they come to the library. These authors, in their various guises, are often good suggestions for readers looking for something new. Depending on how the reader describes what she enjoys—or what she is looking for today—a variety of these authors may be satisfying.

Novels of Women's Lives and Relationships strike an emotional chord with a range of female readers, whether they read extensively in this particular genre or not. These are books that are often passed by word of mouth, hand to hand, from one reader to another. They meant something to one reader going through a difficult time and are offered to another in similar circumstances. Like Gentle Reads and Romances (not to mention Horror and many Mysteries), there is a strong emotional element to these books, and the ways in which the protagonists cope often offer a pattern to follow—and provide hope—that obstacles can be overcome.

NOTES

1. Plum Sykes, *Bergdorf Blondes* (New York: Miramax, 2004); Sykes, *The Debutante Divorcée* (New York: Hyperion, 2006); Judith Ryan Hendricks, *Bread Alone* (New York: Morrow, 2001); Hendricks, *The Baker's Apprentice* (New York: Morrow, 2005).
2. Ann B. Ross, *Miss Julia Speaks Her Mind* (New York: Morrow, 1999).
3. Diane McKinney-Whetstone, *Tumbling* (New York: Morrow, 1996).
4. Maeve Binchy, *Whitethorn Woods* (New York: Knopf, 2007).
5. Marisa de los Santos, *Belong to Me* (New York: Morrow, 2008).
6. Heather Swain, *Luscious Lemon* (New York: Downtown Press, 2004).
7. Anna Quindlen, *Rise and Shine* (New York: Random House, 2006).
8. Jodi Picoult, *My Sister's Keeper* (New York: Atria, 2004).
9. Elizabeth Berg, *Dream When You're Feeling Blue* (New York: Random House, 2007).
10. Pearl Cleage, *I Wish I Had a Red Dress* (New York: Morrow, 2001).
11. Sarah Addison Allen, *Garden Spells* (New York: Bantam, 2007).
12. Sarah Bird, *Flamenco Academy* (New York: Knopf, 2006).
13. Karen Joy Fowler, *The Jane Austen Book Club* (New York: Putnam, 2004); Lorna Landvik, *Angry Housewives Eating Bon Bons* (New York: Ballantine, 2003); Virginia Ironside, *No, I Don't Want to Join a Book Club: Diary of a Sixtieth Year* (New York: Viking, 2007).
14. Cecelia Ahern, *Rosie Dunne* (New York: Hyperion, 2005); Sophie Kinsella, *Confessions of a Shopaholic* (New York: Delta Trade Paperbacks, 2001).
15. Meg Cabot, *Every Boy's Got One* (New York: Avon, 2005).
16. Picoult, *The Tenth Circle* (New York: Atria, 2006).
17. Alice Kuipers, *Life on the Refrigerator Door: Notes between a Mother and Daughter; A Novel in Notes* (New York: HarperCollins, 2007).
18. Berg, *Open House* (New York: Random House, 2000).
19. Jennifer Weiner, *Goodnight Nobody* (New York: Atria, 2005).
20. Weiner, *Good in Bed* (New York: Pocket Books, 2001); Weiner, *Certain Girls* (New York: Atria, 2008).
21. Binchy cited above.
22. Picoult cited above.
23. Danielle Steel, *Safe Harbour* (New York: Delacorte, 2003).
24. Kinsella cited above.
25. Erin Hilderbrand, *The Blue Bistro* (New York: St. Martin's, 2005).
26. Lee Smith, *The Last Girls* (Chapel Hill, NC: Algonquin, 2002).
27. Joan A. Medlicott, *The Ladies of Covington Place Send Their Love* (New York: St. Martin's, 2000).
28. Margaret Drabble, *The Millstone* (New York: Morrow, 1965); Drabble, *The Sea Lady: A Late Romance* (Orlando, FL: Harcourt, 2006).
29. Anne Rivers Siddons, *Sweetwater Creek* (New York: HarperCollins, 2005).
30. Ray, Invincible Women series, beginning with *Like the First Time* (New York: St. Martin's Griffin, 2004).
31. Gail Godwin, *Queen of the Underworld* (New York: Random House, 2006).

32. Elinor Lipman, *Then She Found Me* (New York: Pocket Books, 1990).

33. Landvik cited above.

34. Allen cited above.

35. Bird cited above.

36. Jeanne Ray, *Julie and Romeo* (New York: Harmony Books, 2000); Ray, *Eat Cake* (New York: Shaye Areheart Books, 2003); Ray, *Step-Ball-Change* (New York: Shaye Areheart Books, 2002).

37. Gail Bowen, *Love and Murder* (New York: St. Martin's, 1993). Originally published as *Murder at the Mendel*, 1991.

38. Lisa See, *Snow Flower and the Secret Fan* (New York: Random House, 2005).

39. Margaret Truman, *First Ladies* (New York: Random House, 1995); Cokie Roberts, *Founding Mothers: The Women Who Raised Our Nation* (New York: Morrow, 2004).

40. Jung Chang, *Wild Swans: Three Daughters of China* (New York: Simon and Schuster, 1991).

41. Ellen Hampton, *Women of Valor: The Rochambelles on the World War II Front* (New York: Palgrave Macmillan, 2006).

42. Elizabeth M. Norman, *We Band of Angels: The Untold Story of American Nurses Trapped on Bataan by the Japanese* (New York: Random House, 1999).

Part 3

Intellect Genres

10

LITERARY FICTION

Many readers and librarians may be surprised to see Literary Fiction categorized as a genre. Surely such an act is a form of blasphemy! Literary Fiction readers, a group that includes many librarians, tend to see their favorite authors as the epitome of literary standards and style. The authors who write Literary Fiction win the highest accolades available to writers (except, perhaps, best-seller status). It hardly seems fair to link them with genre fiction.

Although readers may not recognize this as a genre, even if they read Literary Fiction, it helps librarians to do so. As with all genres, certain elements characterize the books that these readers seek. When we consider this as a genre, with identifiable characteristics and a particular pattern of writing, it is far easier to help those readers seeking more books that attain the literary standards they desire.

A DEFINITION

If Literary Fiction is a genre, how do we define it? All genres have a literary dimension, novels that are better written, that are acknowledged for their style and elegance, even though they still fit within that particular genre. The implications of this are useful for us as readers' advisors, as we quickly learn that readers who appreciate more literary titles may enjoy them whether they are classified as Mysteries, Science Fiction, or any other genre.

Literary Fiction is critically acclaimed, often award-winning, fiction. These books are more often character-centered rather than plot-oriented. They are thought-provoking and often address serious issues. These are not page-turners, per se, although their fans certainly find them engrossing and compelling reading. As defined in *Readers' Advisory Service in the Public Library,* these are "complex, literate, multilayered novels that wrestle with universal dilemmas."[1] These are books that appeal first to the mind rather than to the heart and the emotions. Like others in the Intellect genres, Literary Fiction novels present dilemmas that please their readers, whether through singular characters, avant-garde style, or an intellectual approach to serious issues. Figure 10.1 lists the characteristics of Literary Fiction.

Figure 10.1   *Characteristics of Literary Fiction*

---

1. Literary style is important. Authors and readers pay attention to words and how they are woven together with elegant, often poetic language. The structure of the novel itself may be more complex, even experimental, and these novels may play with the conventions of other genres.

2. Characters emerge as more important than story lines, and the philosophical questions central to these books are often explored more through character than through story. Characters, even secondary characters, are multi-dimensional and often act in ways that are unpredictable.

3. Story lines are thought-provoking. Literary Fiction operates in the realm of ideas as well as practicalities, and these novels often consider universal dilemmas. Endings are often open or ambiguous.

4. Pacing is slower, as these are usually densely written books. Complex characters and/or story lines, as well as imaginative language and style, force readers to read more slowly in order to understand the layers of embedded meaning. There is generally more description than dialogue.

5. The tone of Literary Fiction may be dark because of the seriousness of the issues considered, but Literary Fiction may also be humorous—either light or satirical in mood. Atmosphere may carry meaning or function as a component of the writing style.

6. Although frame is less important than in some genres, these layered stories often lend themselves to elaborately portrayed background details.

CHARACTERISTICS AND THE GENRE'S APPEAL

Style/Language

Language and writing style are primary keys to the appeal of books and authors in this genre. When talking with fans of Literary Fiction, it becomes almost impossible for us as librarians not to describe books as *well written*, because by any literary standards, they are. Still, it is better to discover other words to describe these novels: *elegantly written, lyrical,* and perhaps *layered* are terms that provide the same information about the use of language and style without the chance of misunderstanding by readers.

Fans of Literary Fiction prize complex language and interesting styles. Words are important in their own right; how an author says something is almost as important as what is said. Knowing this, we understand better the range of books that might appeal to fans of this genre and, more important, what will not. Language runs the gamut from the spare, unadorned prose of Ha Jin's *A Free Life* to the slangy jargon of Mark Haddon's autistic narrator in *The Curious Incident of the Dog in the Night-Time* to the lyrical, evocative, yet sometimes brutal language of Cormac McCarthy in his postapocalyptic novel, *The Road*.[2] Although language and tone may vary greatly throughout the genre, they must also be appropriate to the topic and sense of each novel.

This is also a genre that allows greater leeway in regard to style, and prose styles are often more complex and experimental. Stories may be told through stream of consciousness, letters, diaries, or alternating points of view among the characters, to mention just a few possibilities. (Some are even illustrated or employ other creative features. For example, Jonathan Safran Foer included photographs in his September 11 novel, *Extremely Loud and Incredibly Close*, while Haddon's *Curious Incident* uses only prime numbers to number the chapters.)[3] Because style and use of language are so important to fans, authors are more comfortable experimenting with literary forms in this genre in which the understanding that there is no set pattern is the pattern. Examples of these varying styles include the stream of consciousness jazz riffs of Haruki Murakami (*After Dark*), the magical realism of Nobel Prize–winner Gabriel García Márquez (*One Hundred Years of Solitude*), the Möbius strip backward and forward in time of Audrey Niffenegger's *The Time Traveler's Wife*, the story-within-a-story device frequently employed by Literary Fiction authors like Ian McEwan in *Atonement,* or simply the unconventional style of Thomas Pynchon, with picaresque stories, wordplay and puns, and encyclopedic knowledge (*Gravity's Rainbow* won the National Book Award).[4]

Literary Fiction writers also experiment with the conventions of other genres, creating novels that appeal to a broader range of readers. For example, Kate Atkinson's series starring millionaire private investigator Jackson Brodie begins with *Case Histories* and stylishly blends elements of the Mystery genre into her Literary Fiction novels.[5] Michael Chabon also borrows from Mystery genre conventions as well as Science Fiction's use of Alternate History in *The Yiddish Policemen's Union*, which follows a policeman in Jewish Alaska (their post–World War II homeland).[6] His *Gentlemen of the Road*, on the other hand, spoofs the Adventure genre with its madcap historical tale, originally titled "Jews with Swords."[7]

Characterization

Readers who love character-centered stories turn frequently to Literary Fiction. Here, introspective, in-depth character studies allow readers to watch them develop. Relationships among characters are important, too, as they are in genres such as Women's Lives and Relationships and Romances. Penelope Lively's character-centered novels are a good example. Unique but always believable, these interesting lives focus Lively's compelling stories. In the recent *Consequences*, for example, she provides an intimate look at the lives of three generations of engaging and independent women and their family legacy.[8]

While we relate to some characters, we step back and observe others. Literary fiction relies more on shades of gray between accessible and distant characters than do many other genres. The characters who inhabit these literary stories are not always sympathetic, and, as in Psychological Suspense, they are not always people readers want to know. Tom Wolfe's *The Bonfire of the Vanities* remains a classic example of a novel essentially devoid of sympathetic characters.[9] Arthur Phillips's *The Egyptologist* employs two obsessed and unreliable narrators: the archaeologist of the title and an Australian detective trailing him in an attempt to charge him with murder.[10] Readers can only stand back and watch their demise against Gothic trappings and historical details from the 1920s.

Secondary characters often play crucial roles in these complex dramas, and they emerge almost as fully realized as the protagonists. Amy Bloom's *Away*, an immigrant's tale, features a female Ulysses who doesn't quite make it home (to the Ukraine) but who creates her own home in the end.[11] Rich in characters, this novel also reveals the fate of all with whom heroine Lillian interacts, as she flees from pogroms in Russia to New York City and then attempts the reverse journey to find her daughter in Siberia, this time crossing the United States and Canada's Yukon to the Bering Strait.

Story Line

In the story lines of Literary Fiction, authors probe a range of themes. Like its counterparts in Science Fiction and Thrillers, for example, Literary Fiction tends to deal with serious, provocative topics. Several authors have explored the implications of the terrorist attacks of September 11, and as should be expected in this genre, in vastly different ways. Don DeLillo's *Falling Man* creates both the immediacy of the event and its aftermath as it affects a survivor and his family, while Foer's *Extremely Loud and Incredibly Close* follows the perspective of a young boy whose father was a victim and includes parallels to the bombings of Dresden and Hiroshima.[12] Through characters rather than politics they explore the implications and effects of this event.

These are novels that explore universal dilemmas, and the truths they expose lift the stories from the bounds of the subject classification. John Updike's *The Terrorist* is not simply another terrorism tale set in the New York City area or a reaction to the events of September 11.[13] It is, instead, a stylish psychological character study that provides a glimpse into the world of the terrorist, here an intriguing, naive hero. Updike's thoughtful approach, coupled with his graceful, elegant prose, elevates this layered novel beyond what one might expect from the title and subject (Terrorism—Fiction). Literary Fiction presents a world in which there are no easy choices and no clear-cut good and evil. The story line almost always takes the reader beyond the basic plot into the world of larger issues and broader implications.

Endings in Literary Fiction are often inconclusive. Authors tantalize the readers with options but do not always indicate which eventuality occurs. Our understanding of the characters allows us to make our own choices. In Ian McEwan's *On Chesil Beach* the narrative moves beyond the crucial event—the failed wedding night—to follow the characters in later life, but these are characters whose lives extend beyond the page, and their futures may be suggested but not resolved.[14] Since Literary Fiction is about possibilities and imaginative futures, it comes as no surprise that many authors choose not to tie up loose ends. In other genres, these open endings might suggest the possibility of a sequel; here, they only underline the extent to which the characters live on beyond the confines of the novel.

Although I have suggested that the story line of Literary Fiction is not the genre's greatest strength, there is no denying that many of its practitioners are, above all, storytellers. From Philip Roth and John Updike to Margaret Atwood and Joyce Carol Oates, these are authors who tell great stories, and to that basic frame they add intriguing characters, breathtaking prose, and provocative points of view.

Pacing

Whether longer books or shorter, Literary Fiction is almost never deemed fast-paced. Authors pride themselves on the layers of meaning in their works, and as the words themselves are important, readers read more slowly to savor the language and discover the author's message. The novels of Richard Powers exemplify this. Although they tell interesting stories that move right along, it is impossible to read them quickly. We are held back by the pleasure of the language, the speculations provoked by the layered plot, and the quirkiness of the characters. In *The Echo Maker* parallel identity crises, lyrical passages describing the sand hill crane migrations, and excerpts from works of naturalists frame this powerful story that journeys from a brain injury after an accident to the philosophical contemplation of identity.[15] This stimulating, erudite novel fascinates and holds the reader spellbound. A quick read of a novel so rich is likely physically, and certainly mentally, impossible.

Tone/Mood

The tone of Literary Fiction is often darker, as befits the serious themes with which much of it is concerned. Khaled Hosseini's novels of his native Afghanistan, *The Kite Runner* and *A Thousand Splendid Suns*, offer heartbreaking tales of adversity and violence.[16] Murakami's *After Dark* features disenfranchised characters who connect only for the night.[17] The seductive language and jazz-like riffs on ideas enhance the moody, dreamy, alienated, melancholy tone of the novel. The lighthearted, however, also has its place in this genre. From the imaginative playfulness of T. Coraghessan Boyle (*Talk Talk*) and John Irving (*The World According to Garp*) to the outrageous, slapstick writing of Kurt Vonnegut and Zadie Smith, among others, humor, although often ironic, abounds in this genre, and it is frequently used as a means to explore serious issues.[18]

Frame/Setting

In addition to the illustrations, photographs, and quirky typographical devices employed by some authors, detailed backgrounds are as popular in this genre as they are in every other. From the magic of Joanne Harris's provocative tales (especially *Chocolat* and *The Girl with No Shadow*) to the sensual delights of food—its tastes, textures, and aromas—in Diana Abu-Jaber's novels (*Crescent*), background frames entice and charm readers.[19] Among the most common frames are historical details from one or sometimes several periods. Geraldine Brooks's *People of the Book* begins as a rare book restorer examines a priceless manuscript.[20] Each discovery—a wine stain, a hair—takes the reader back in time, tracing the provenance backward and revealing the stories of the owners as well as the cultural and social milieu of each age. Stories of the characters and their relationships, from the conservator on, also figure prominently. These historical details and the backstories of each character enrich this novel, which also considers complex political and religious issues.

KEY AUTHORS

In this genre, no single author currently dominates the scene. There are, however, a number of authors with whom we should be familiar. Oprah Winfrey has done a great deal to promote fine writing with her author choices for her on-air book club. Nobel laureate Toni Morrison, long appreciated by fans of the genre, has been given a much broader exposure, and rightfully so. In her award-winning *Song of Solomon* and *Beloved*, as well as in her other novels, Morrison charts the lives of African American women past and present.[21] However, her books resonate with readers of all races, and her literary style and technique reinforce her insightful stories.

Certainly John Updike deserves mention here with accessible Literary Fiction authors. With his quartet of novels plotting the state of the United States as seen through the life of Harry Angstrom (*Rabbit, Run* is the first of this series, each published a decade apart), Updike has secured his reputation as one of the premier writers of this genre.[22] However, it is his extensive oeuvre that continues to amaze, challenge, and satisfy readers. From his early, myth-based *The Centaur*, which fuses fantasy and reality, to his sweeping novel of American history and society, *In the Beauty of the Lilies*, Updike remains both popular and stimulating.[23]

The popularity of Britain's McEwan and Zadie Smith, Canada's Margaret Atwood and Michael Ondaatje, Africa's J. M. Coetzee, Turkey's Orhan Pamuk, and Japan's Murakami alongside America's Don DeLillo, Louise Erdrich, and Michael Chabon reminds us that Literary Fiction is international, encompassing important and requested authors from around the globe.

WHAT WE KNOW ABOUT FANS

What do we know about Literary Fiction readers? We know that they often read reviews. Rather than look for which authors are on the best-seller lists, they seek the ones well reviewed in prestigious newspapers and magazines. They want to see the *New York Times* "Editor's Choice" list, because these are among the titles they would more frequently like to read. (It should be noted, however, that Literary Fiction titles reach the best-seller lists every year. Recent examples include Khaled Hosseini's *A Thousand Splendid Suns;* Junot Díaz's Pulitzer Prize–winning novel, *The Brief Wondrous Life of Oscar Wao;* and Jhumpa Lahiri's short story collection, *Unaccustomed Earth*.)[24]

Within the boundaries of style, these readers may read a surprising variety. They consider themselves adventurous readers, and, in fact, they may be interested in exploring books from other genres, as long as the titles are up to their literary standards. If they see us as readers of Literary Fiction, they may want to know what we have read and enjoyed recently. And unlike most readers, who, when they ask if we have read a book, simply want to know if it is okay for them to take it, these readers truly want to hear what we thought of books we have read.

These readers always appreciate lists of award-winning titles and authors. They like to evaluate books that have won awards for themselves: do these award-winners really meet their standards? Reference resources that keep us up to date on these winners are particularly useful with this audience. We also keep track of interesting lists of "best" authors for these readers, as they like to sample the best and see how these authors fare according to their personal standards. Be prepared for the fact that these readers keep their own lists, both of new titles and classics they may have missed, and they always welcome new titles to add to these lists.

Literary Fiction readers prefer books that demand more from them. The style, the language, and the issues considered may all require an intelligent reader willing to invest some time and effort in unraveling the puzzle these books often present. Basically, fans of this genre are looking for other elegantly written, acclaimed novels that they can discuss with their circle of friends who share similar reading tastes.

These are readers who will want to read everything by an author they have enjoyed, but they do not want to read the same book over and over. Again, the pattern of this genre is that there is not a concrete pattern. In fact, some authors write very different kinds of books with almost everything they publish. Michael Chabon, Jane Smiley, Jonathan Lethem, and Joyce Carol Oates do this consistently; almost every title explores new literary dimensions or presents the story in a different way. It should also be noted that authors of Literary Fiction are not particularly prolific. Unlike writers in other genres, whom one can count on for at least a book a year, these authors usually do not publish every year, and every new title is anticipated by their fans.

These are also readers who choose books more frequently for style and literary quality and are thus more likely to read across genres than many other readers, who choose more by other appeal elements. They enjoy a range of books of high literary quality even if they are on widely different topics from a range of genres. Martin Cruz Smith, with his bleak and layered Thrillers, may be appealing, as might Ruth Rendell's psychological explorations. (Figure 10.3 below offers suggestions that take fans of Literary Fiction beyond the confines of the genre.) Figure 10.2 lists additional Literary Fiction writers to try if you are new to Literary Fiction and a fan of these other genres.

THE READERS' ADVISORY INTERVIEW

When Literary Fiction readers ask for assistance and tell us about authors they have read and appreciated, they are likely not looking for another author exactly like the authors they mention; they are usually looking for another acclaimed author with an interesting, or perhaps similar, style. They like to experiment. They also like to discuss why they did or did not like a book, what the author should have done, or why the book did not work for them. Although I generally discouraged staff from giving personal recommendations to readers, I was sometimes forced to make an exception with this group. If we do make personal recommendations,

Figure 10.2 *An Introduction to the Literary Fiction Genre*

Literary Fiction Writers to Try, If You Enjoy . . .

Adrenaline:	Don DeLillo
Biography/Memoir:	Isabel Allende
	T. Coraghessan Boyle
	Nancy Horan
Fantasy:	Isabel Allende
	Alice Hoffman
	Gabriel García Márquez
Gay/Lesbian:	James Baldwin
	David Leavitt
	Sarah Waters
Gentle:	Eudora Welty
Historical Fiction:	Geraldine Brooks
History:	E. L. Doctorow
	Gore Vidal
Horror:	Jonathan Carroll
Humor:	Jonathan Safran Foer
	Michael Malone
	Richard Russo
Inspirational:	Charles Williams
Multicultural:	Junot Díaz
	Louise Erdrich
	Jhumpa Lahiri
	Gloria Naylor
	Zadie Smith
Mystery:	Kate Atkinson
	Michael Chabon (*The Yiddish Policemen's Union*)[25]
Natural History:	Wendell Berry
Psychological Suspense:	Henry James
	Arthur Phillips
Romance:	Amy Bloom (*Away*)[26]
Saga:	Sandra Cisneros (*Caramelo*)[27]
	Louise Erdrich
	Joyce Carol Oates (*We Were the Mulvaneys* and *The Falls*)[28]

Figure 10.2 *An Introduction to the Literary Fiction Genre (cont.)*

Science Fiction:	Margaret Atwood
	Kazuo Ishiguro (*Never Let Me Go*)[29]
	Doris Lessing
	Philip Roth (*The Plot against America*)[30]
Travel:	Paul Theroux
True Adventure:	Herman Melville
	Arturo Pérez-Reverte
True Crime:	Kathryn Harrison
	Matthew Pearl
Western:	Jim Harrison
	Craig Johnson
	Cormac McCarthy
	Larry McMurtry
Women's Lives:	Diana Abu-Jaber
	Margaret Drabble
	Toni Morrison

---

however, we can expect these readers to come back and discuss the books with us. They are almost never embarrassed to tell us they did not like a book—and why. Unlike most fiction readers, they do not have to like the book to find it satisfying. Furthermore, they see this discussion with other readers about how the book affected them as an integral part of their enjoyment of Literary Fiction.

Like other genre fans, Literary Fiction readers want to read everything a favorite author has written. When they are ready to go on to someone new, they may want a current title by another provocative author or they may want to fill in with classic authors. Lists of classic titles everyone should read are good suggestions to use in working with these readers. Readers of this genre also appreciate short stories, and prizewinning collections offer numerous examples of authors whose novels—or collections of stories—they might explore. Remember that many of these prizewinning authors also publish short stories in magazines specifically oriented toward the short story (*Zoetrope*) and more general magazines such as *The New Yorker* and *The Atlantic,* as well as the *New York Times' Magazine.* Readers may have discovered their shorter work and want to explore further, while other readers may appreciate the opportunity to sample among the magazines' pages, which may lead them to fiction and nonfiction of interest.

Fans of Literary Fiction, like readers of other genres, recognize the attraction of thematic links among books. Readers of this genre might not consider Dan Brown's enormously popular *The Da Vinci Code* up to their elevated standards, yet the popularity of that title spawned a wealth of titles, including more literary ones that might very well appeal to their pleasure in intricately plotted puzzles related to books or other artifacts and their intriguing provenance.[31] From Ian Caldwell and Dustin Thomason's *The Rule of Four* (a secret encoded in a rare Renaissance text) and Javier Sierra's *The Secret Supper* (clues to a clandestine cabal hidden in Da Vinci's painting) to Matthew Pearl's atmospheric *The Dante Club* (a new translation of Dante's *The Divine Comedy* sparks murders that refer to the poem, and Boston's nineteenth-century literary elite investigate), these span the centuries and please readers who appreciate contemporary or historical tales or a mix of the two.[32] They may not fall strictly within the genre, but they are thematically and stylistically interesting enough to appeal and to spur discussion.

International and Multicultural authors often have a particular appeal for fans of Literary Fiction. For International authors to be published in the United States, they must have attained a certain literary standard, and that guarantees interest from these readers. Among these writers some of the most interesting literary experiments are carried out, and that, too, is a draw for fans of this genre. Unique, challenging, and thoughtful titles from these authors should be noted and shared with fans of Literary Fiction. Isabel Allende's diverse titles are a good suggestion for many fans. Latin America and nineteenth-century Spanish America provide the backgrounds for many of her novels, which range from haunting (*House of the Spirits*) to amusing and swashbuckling (*Zorro*).[33] She often layers historical details with strong women characters to tell evocative, dramatic tales. Chinese American Ha Jin has written evocatively about his native China as well as his adopted country, and Cuban American Oscar Hijuelos explores the clash of cultures, often humorously. East Indian and East Indian-American/English writers—Jhumpa Lahiri, Bharati Mukherjee, Vikram Seth, V. S. Naipaul, and Anita Desai—offer fascinating glimpses into a foreign culture as well as into the process of acculturation. Kazuo Ishiguro, Orhan Pamuk, Michael Ondaatje, Ursula Hegi, and Nadine Gordimer explore their native countries and cultures and beyond. Australia has also provided a wealth of authors for Literary Fiction fans, including Thomas Keneally, Geraldine Brooks, and Peter Carey.

Book discussion titles are often gathered from this genre, and those lists make good suggestions for Literary Fiction readers—just as favorites among the Literary Fiction crowd often make excellent choices for book discussions.

Sure Bets

Discovering Sure Bets is both easier and more difficult in this genre. Although there are perhaps fewer authors with a wide-ranging popular appeal, readers who appreciate one author in this genre will likely enjoy others, as well as literary stylists in other genres. Those authors who have appeared on the best-seller lists are good suggestions—David Guterson, McEwan, Atwood, as well as Anne Tyler, Chabon, Richard Russo, and Alice Hoffman.

Jane Smiley is an author whose writing typifies Literary Fiction, and she is a popular choice for a wide range of readers. At my library at least, it was with the publication of two novellas, *Ordinary Love* and *Good Will*, in 1989, that she gained a real following among readers who appreciate her skill at language and exploring difficult topics.[34] Even now we give these haunting, psychological stories to readers, and they come back hungry for more. Readers may love or hate her work, but they always want to read and discuss her books—another indication of both her popularity and her status as a writer of provocative material.

Michael Chabon's award-winning fiction continues to gain fans. Whether he is writing about the history of comic books (*The Amazing Adventures of Kavalier and Clay*), skewering academia (*Wonder Boys*), or playfully rewriting history (*The Yiddish Policemen's Union*), Chabon's intriguing characters, layered plots, and fluid style attract a wide range of readers across genres.[35]

EXPANDING READERS' HORIZONS WITH WHOLE COLLECTION READERS' ADVISORY

We can turn to almost any genre and find titles that fans of Literary Fiction will enjoy. Historical Fiction has a great deal to offer Literary Fiction readers who appreciate historical settings. The late Dorothy Dunnett, with her Historical Adventures set in renaissance Europe, classical quotations, and generally pleasing literary references, is a good choice. Another author to suggest is Sharon Kay Penman. Her detailed examinations of the people and the times (both in her Mystery series in the court of Eleanor of Aquitaine and in her historical novels set primarily in thirteenth- through fifteenth-century England and Wales) satisfy and fascinate readers. Other suggestions include Michael Shaara's intimate and evocative account of the Civil War (*The Killer Angels*), Margaret George's compelling biographical portraits (*The Memoirs of Cleopatra*), and Steven Pressfield's character-centered explorations of ancient Greece (*Gates of Fire* is the first).[36]

In Science Fiction, Ursula K. Le Guin and Neal Stephenson are both good choices. Le Guin consistently explores philosophical and intellectual issues, while Stephenson's virtuoso blend of language and ideas, not to mention his pyrotechnics-rich alternative history series, attracts readers from many genres. For their great facility with and inspired use of language, Mary Doria Russell and Gene Wolfe must also be included here. Certainly Russell's *The Sparrow* offers readers the ideas and characters fans of Literary Fiction demand, and Wolfe's several series (especially the Book of the New Sun, which begins with *The Shadow of the Torturer*) challenge and fascinate readers.[37]

Adrenaline offers a number of elegant Thriller writers, including Dunnett (mentioned above), Arturo Pérez-Reverte, Daniel Silva, and Martin Cruz Smith. Although their novels are more quickly paced than those of Literary Fiction writers, they all interpose difficult issues in elegantly written novels. Pérez-Reverte creates sophisticated literary puzzles peopled by complex characters and driven by image-rich, evocative prose. Silva is best known for his elegantly written but explicitly violent tales of Mossad agent and art-restorer Gabriel Allon, while Smith's reputation was established with *Gorky Park* and sequels, featuring beleaguered Russian policeman Arkady Renko.[38]

Literary Fiction readers might also appreciate authors from the Horror genre. Classic author M. R. James (*Ghost Stories of an Antiquary*) wrote chilling tales, and their antiquarian settings and evil forebodings still resonate with readers today.[39] A new entry, Toby Barlow's *Sharp Teeth*, sets a tale of packs of werewolves in contemporary Los Angeles in a haunting verse novel.[40] In Psychological Suspense, Minette Walters and Ruth Rendell are both excellent crossover suggestions. The Mystery genre, too, has many authors that appeal to readers who like elegantly written, layered puzzles. Among the best are P. D. James's series featuring Adam Dalgleish and James Lee Burke's haunting, atmospheric detective stories set in the South.

Another genre with extensive crossover is Women's Lives and Relationships. Many strong female writers tell stories of women, and those authors might fit easily in either genre. Anita Shreve, Jane Hamilton, and others from chapter 9 would be good suggestions for fans of Literary Fiction.

As we consider Whole Collection Readers' Advisory, we can readily identify a number of nonfiction authors who appeal to readers of Literary Fiction. Azar Nafisi's *Reading "Lolita" in Tehran: A Memoir in Books* offers elegant writing, a unique perspective, and literary criticism—elements that appeal strongly to Literary Fiction fans.[41] Award-winning writers of History and Biography, such as David McCullough and Robert A. Caro, are also good suggestions.

True crime hosts a treasure trove of possibilities with fiction crossover authors Truman Capote and Norman Mailer, as well as Erik Larson. His *Devil in the White City: Murder, Magic, and Madness at the Fair That Changed America* and *Thunderstruck,* which links murderer Edward Crippen and Marconi of telegraph fame, offer fascinating glimpses into historical crimes.[42]

Fans of science and geology will be interested in the writings of Stephen J. Gould and Diane Ackerman, as well as John McPhee, literary stylists all. And for armchair travelers there are Bill Bryson, Michael Palin (certainly one would expect a way with words from an ex-Python!), and Paul Theroux. (Both Palin and Theroux have written fiction as well.) Bryson is also a good bet for language buffs, as is Lynne Truss, whose popular *Eats, Shoots and Leaves: The Zero Tolerance Approach to Punctuation* pleased novices and experts alike.[43]

Don't forget another format: graphic novels. Art Spiegelman's histories (*Maus*) and other titles, fiction and nonfiction, should appeal to Literary Fiction fans who appreciate elegant style, unique format, and provocative story lines.[44] Alison Bechdel would be another good choice. See figure 10.3 for a list of authors that might appeal to readers of Literary Fiction.

TRENDS

In many ways, Literary Fiction is becoming more mainstream, with more and more authors achieving best-seller status and the genre expanding to cross with other popular genres. Increasingly, titles by non-English-speaking writers, as well as writers from other English-speaking countries, are gaining attention and winning awards. Literary Fiction continues to embrace experimental and Multicultural titles, and that, too, expands its horizons. Short stories remain an important aspect of the genre, and short story writers such as Alice Munro and Raymond Carver have gained greater attention as their work moves to film. And as graphic novels come

Figure 10.3 *Expanding Readers' Horizons*

Authors to Take Readers beyond the Literary Fiction Genre

Adrenaline:	Arturo Pérez-Reverte
	Daniel Silva
	Martin Cruz Smith
Biography/Memoir:	Robert A. Caro
	Azar Nafisi
	May Sarton
Fantasy:	Jasper Fforde
	Neil Gaiman
Gentle:	Phillip Gulley
	Alexander McCall Smith
Historical:	Margaret George
	Sharon Kay Penman
	Steven Pressfield
History:	Doris Kearns Goodwin
	David McCullough
	Art Spiegelman
Horror:	Toby Barlow
	Michael Cadnum
	M. R. James
Language:	Bill Bryson
	Lynn Truss
Mystery:	James Lee Burke
	P. D. James
	Fred Vargas
Natural History:	Annie Dillard
	Stephen J. Gould
	Oliver Sachs
Psychological Suspense:	Minette Walters
	Ruth Rendell/Barbara Vine
Saga:	James Michener
Science Fiction	Michael Flynn
	Neal Stephenson

Figure 10.3 *Expanding Readers' Horizons (cont.)*

Travel:	Bill Bryson
	Michael Palin
	Paul Theroux
True Adventure:	John Krakauer
True Crime:	Truman Capote
	Erik Larson
	Norman Mailer
Western:	Ivan Doig
	Larry McMurtry
Women's Lives:	Kaye Gibbons
	Barbara Kingsolver

of age, their authors are producing more titles that appeal to Literary Fiction readers and increasing the ranks of fans of both genre and format.

For decades Literary Fiction made up the core of our libraries' fiction collections. It was the collection readers felt comfortable asking for—and the one librarians could safely "recommend" to any reader. Although no longer the most popular genre, Literary Fiction has lost none of its appeal for fans, who continue to challenge librarians to find them books that offer elegantly written, thought-provoking explorations of universal themes.

Notes

1. Joyce G. Saricks, *Readers' Advisory Service in the Public Library,* 3rd ed. (Chicago: American Library Association, 2005), 32.
2. Ha Jin, *A Free Life* (New York: Pantheon, 2007); Mark Haddon, *The Curious Incident of the Dog in the Night-Time* (New York: Doubleday, 2003); Cormac McCarthy, *The Road* (New York: Knopf, 2006).
3. Jonathan Safran Foer, *Extremely Loud and Incredibly Close* (Boston: Houghton Mifflin, 2005).
4. Haruki Murakami, *After Dark,* trans. Jay Rubin (New York: Knopf, 2007); Gabriel García Márquez, *One Hundred Years of Solitude,* trans. Gregory Rabassa (New York: Harper and Row, 1970); Audrey Niffenegger, *The Time Traveler's Wife* (Orlando, FL: Harcourt, 2003); Ian McEwan, *Atonement* (New York: Nan A. Talese/Doubleday, 2002); Thomas Pynchon, *Gravity's Rainbow* (New York: Viking, 1973).
5. Kate Atkinson, *Case Histories* (New York: Little, Brown, 2004).

6. Michael Chabon, *The Yiddish Policemen's Union* (New York: HarperCollins, 2007).
7. Chabon, *Gentlemen of the Road: A Tale of Adventure* (New York: Del Rey, 2007).
8. Penelope Lively, *Consequences* (New York: Viking, 2007).
9. Tom Wolfe, *The Bonfire of the Vanities* (New York: Farrar, Straus, and Giroux, 1987).
10. Arthur Phillips, *The Egyptologist: A Novel* (New York: Random House, 2004).
11. Amy Bloom, *Away: A Novel* (New York: Random House, 2007).
12. Don DeLillo, *Falling Man: A Novel* (New York: Scribner, 2007); Foer cited above.
13. John Updike, *The Terrorist* (New York: Knopf, 2006).
14. McEwan, *On Chesil Beach* (New York: Nan A. Talese/Doubleday, 2007).
15. Richard Powers, *The Echo Maker* (New York: Farrar, Straus, and Giroux, 2006).
16. Khaled Hosseini, *The Kite Runner* (New York: Riverhead Books, 2003); Hosseini, *A Thousand Splendid Suns* (New York: Riverhead Books, 2007).
17. Murakami cited above.
18. T. Coraghessan Boyle, *Talk Talk* (New York: Viking, 2006); John Irving, *The World According to Garp* (New York: Dutton, 1978).
19. Joanne Harris, *Chocolat* (New York: Viking, 1999); Harris, *The Girl with No Shadow* (New York: Morrow, 2008); Diana Abu-Jaber, *Crescent* (New York: Norton, 2003).
20. Geraldine Brooks, *People of the Book* (New York: Viking, 2008).
21. Toni Morrison, *Song of Solomon* (New York: Knopf, 1977); Morrison, *Beloved: A Novel* (New York: Knopf, 1987).
22. Updike, *Rabbit, Run* (New York: Knopf, 1960).
23. Updike, *The Centaur* (New York: Knopf, 1963); Updike, *In the Beauty of the Lilies* (New York: Knopf, 1996).
24. Hosseini cited above; Junot Díaz, *The Brief Wondrous Life of Oscar Wao* (New York: Riverhead Books, 2007); Jhumpa Lahiri, *Unaccustomed Earth* (New York: Knopf, 2008).
25. Chabon cited above.
26. Bloom cited above.
27. Sandra Cisneros, *Caramelo; or, Puro Cuento* (New York: Knopf, 2002).
28. Joyce Carol Oates, *We Were the Mulvaneys* (New York: Dutton, 1996); Oates, *The Falls: A Novel* (New York: Ecco, 2004).
29. Kazuo Ishiguro, *Never Let Me Go* (New York: Knopf, 2005).
30. Philip Roth, *The Plot against America* (Boston: Houghton Mifflin, 2004).
31. Dan Brown, *The Da Vinci Code: A Novel* (New York: Doubleday, 2003).
32. Ian Caldwell and Dustin Thomason, *The Rule of Four* (New York: Dial, 2004); Javier Sierra, *The Secret Supper: A Novel*, trans. by Alberto Manquel (New York: Atria, 2006); Matthew Pearl, *The Dante Club: A Novel* (New York: Ballantine, 2006).
33. Isabel Allende, *House of the Spirits*, trans. by Magda Bogin (New York: Knopf, 1985); Allende, *Zorro: A Novel*, trans. by Margaret Sayers (New York: HarperCollins, 2005).
34. Jane Smiley, *Ordinary Love* and *Good Will* (New York: Knopf, 1989).
35. Chabon, *The Amazing Adventures of Kavalier and Clay* (New York: Random House, 2000); Chabon, *Wonder Boys* (New York: Villard, 1995); Chabon cited above.
36. Michael Shaara, *The Killer Angels* (New York: McKay, 1974); Margaret George, *The Memoirs of Cleopatra* (New York: St. Martin's, 1997); Steven Pressfield, *Gates of Fire: An Epic Novel of the Battle of Thermopylae* (New York: Doubleday, 1998).
37. Mary Doria Russell, *The Sparrow* (New York: Villard, 1996); Gene Wolfe, *The Shadow of the Torturer* (New York: Simon and Schuster, 1980).
38. Martin Cruz Smith, *Gorky Park* (New York: Random House, 1981).
39. M. R. James, *Ghost Stories of an Antiquary* (Freeport, NY: Books for Libraries Press, 1969).

40. Toby Barlow, *Sharp Teeth* (New York: Harper, 2008).

41. Azar Nafisi, *Reading "Lolita" in Tehran: A Memoir in Books* (New York: Random House, 2003).

42. Erik Larson, *The Devil in the White City: Murder, Magic, and Madness at the Fair That Changed America* (New York: Random House, 2003); Larson, *Thunderstruck* (New York: Crown, 2006).

43. Lynne Truss, *Eats, Shoots and Leaves: The Zero Tolerance Approach to Punctuation* (New York: Gotham Books, 2004).

44. Art Spiegelman, *Maus: A Survivor's Tale I; My Father Bleeds History* (New York: Pantheon, 1986).

11

MYSTERIES

Many of us in libraries find that Mysteries are the most popular genre among readers. (It would not surprise me if a poll of public librarians revealed that this is their favorite as well!) Mystery bookstores, websites, and reference resources abound. As has been the case since the genre's nineteenth-century beginnings, readers have been fascinated by the character of the detective. Exploring the lives of these sleuths—their past and present, relationships, and friendships—has become, for many readers, as important as solving the Mystery. Series dominate all aspects of the genre, from hard-boiled private investigators (P.I.s) to amateur detectives in Cozies (cases without sex, violence, and profanity) and in Contemporary as well as Historical Mysteries. Despite this fascination with the detectives' lives, the key to Mysteries remains the puzzle, carefully laid out for both detective and readers to solve, and the more intricate and clever the puzzle and its solution, the more these appeal to our intellects.

A DEFINITION

Mysteries are constructed around a puzzle; the author provides clues to the solution but attempts to obscure some information so that the mystery cannot be solved too easily. We, along with the detective, are drawn into the puzzle in an attempt to solve it. This puzzle involves a crime, usually murder, and, of course, a body. There is an investigator (or a team of investigators), amateur or professional, who solves the question of "whodunit." The Mystery tracks this investigation, with its concomitant exploration of victim's, murderer's, and detective's lives.

Straightforward as that sounds, defining a Mystery is as convoluted and problematic as the cases posed in the genre. Many libraries, mine included, have a separate section for Mysteries and thus a working definition, however vague, so we can decide whether to catalog a book in Mystery or Fiction. At least, that is the expectation. However, as Mysteries become more and more difficult to identify, problems arise. At my library we have Michael Connelly in Fiction, along with Ridley Pearson and Stephen White. Yet there is a body in each of these and an investigation that reveals the identity of the killer as well as the motive for the crime. The first two even feature police detectives. Why do we not catalog them as Mysteries?

At one time, Mystery titles were under three hundred pages, and you could tell at a glance that this (or a Western or other genre book) fit in the genre collection, rather than in Fiction. Now that Mysteries are as long as or longer than many mainstream novels, the distinction becomes more difficult. The answer to what belongs in the Mystery collection is that there is no definitive answer; there is often no clear-cut distinction between Mysteries (and much other genre fiction) and mainstream novels. We make our best guess, based on how a book is reviewed, whether we have others by that author or in that series, and, most important, where we believe readers expect to find the book.

Novels that fall within the Mystery genre follow a particular pattern: A crime is committed. An investigator pursues the clues, interviewing suspects and drawing conclusions. The crime is solved, and the culprit is brought to justice. In the hands of skilled writers in the genre, this bare-bones plot outline can become so much more. Figure 11.1 identifies characteristics of Mysteries.

CHARACTERISTICS AND THE GENRE'S APPEAL

Story Line

The crime and subsequent investigation form the heart of the story line in this genre and create the puzzle that attracts readers. Because the crime is almost always murder, I use that term in this discussion. There should be a murder and an investigation, not to mention a body, for a title to qualify as a Mystery.

Within this framework, authors offer an enormous variety. Some focus on the intricacies of the puzzle. For some readers, the goal is to solve the puzzle before the investigator. They want the writer to play fair, present the clues, and allow them a chance to solve the Mystery. (Do not offer

---

Figure 11.1 *Characteristics of Mysteries*

---

1. The solving of a crime, usually a murder, drives the plot, and the detective, along with the reader, sorts through the available clues to discover the solution. Readers and the detective understand "whodunit" and why by the book's conclusion.

2. The story focuses on the investigator or an investigative team. Mysteries are often written as a series, following the investigator through several cases. Secondary characters, whether suspects or supporting characters in the investigation, play an important role in the appeal of the Mystery and may also be series characters.

3. The frame in which the Mystery is set—whether a physical location or fascinating background details—plays a crucial role in its appeal.

4. The mood of Mysteries ranges from dark and gritty to lighthearted and witty with a multitude of variations in between.

5. The broad scope of the genre, embracing countries around the world and involving widely differing classes of characters and historical periods, demands a range of language and narrative styles.

6. Since all Mysteries move toward the solution of the puzzle, pacing is relentless and compelling, sometimes slowed by details of time and place, but always moving inexorably toward the solution.

---

these readers Agatha Christie's classic puzzle *The Murder of Roger Ackroyd*.[1] Christie tricks the reader with a totally unexpected twist at the end, and those who expect authors to play fair will not be pleased.) Other authors add strong elements of suspense and intrigue, often threatening the characters with considerable danger throughout the investigation. William Kent Krueger's fans expect his protagonist, Cork O'Connor, to battle bad guys and the dangerous landscape of the Upper Peninsula, with his life constantly in danger, as he seeks solutions to crimes. Still others focus on particular social issues and weave them into their stories, as does Donna Leon in the cases of Commissario Guido Brunetti of the Venetian Questura. (*Death at La Fenice* is the first in this series that often exposes corruption in both the police and the government.)[2]

Many Mysteries are more than straightforward puzzles written to a pattern. Most involve layers of information about the plot and characters; these must be peeled away, with secrets revealed one by one, until the solution is discovered. P. D. James's complex, layered novels of detection follow the exploits of Scotland Yard Commander Adam Dalgleish and are read by fans of Mysteries as well as those who appreciate character-driven Literary Fiction.

The issue of justice is one that is considered throughout this genre, because the administration of justice is at the heart of the solution of the Mystery. Legal justice is not always an option, however, and when it is not, investigators have been known to take the law into their own hands, to see that justice is effected, even if it means operating outside the law. P.I.s especially are notorious for taking this approach. (Their personal moral code is discussed below with that subgenre.) However, even police detectives and amateurs have been known to bring about justice of a sort, outside of the law. An example is the mercurial Kathleen Mallory in Carol O'Connell's series (*Mallory's Oracle* is the first).[3] Unorthodox, but very successful, methods are the hallmark of the investigative style of this New York Police Department detective.

Characterization

Since the point of Mysteries is to examine the clues and solve the puzzle, the character of the investigator plays a major role, and these two appeal elements—characterization and story line—intertwine as the crime is solved. While some read to solve the mystery before the detective, others like to participate in the investigation and in the lives of the investigators. In fact, the character of the investigator often determines the appeal of the Mystery to the reader and is the basis of the subgenres considered below. With the ever-increasing popularity of series, these readers find much to their liking. Many tell us they read as much to see what is happening in the characters' lives as to appreciate the clever Mystery plot. No wonder authors occasionally despair and do nasty things to their characters if they feel they are not appreciated for their intricate plots! The quintessential example of murder-by-author is, of course, Sir Arthur Conan Doyle's attempt to do in Sherlock Holmes at Switzerland's Reichenbach Falls in *The Memoirs of Sherlock Holmes*.[4] He was then forced to resurrect the detective in *The Return of Sherlock Holmes*, thus allowing Laurie R. King, almost a century later, to pull him back into the fray with her series featuring Holmes and Mary Russell, beginning with *The Beekeeper's Apprentice*.[5]

Characterizations in Mystery are treated differently than they are in other genres. In Adventure, for example, we do not necessarily want to follow Dirk Pitt's life; we simply want to know what will happen next in this adventure, and he is our guide. In Horror we respond to what the protagonist experiences—we share the same emotions—but we do not necessarily want more details of his life. In Romances we only follow the characters until they tie the knot, so to speak; then we expect new characters and a new love story, although fans are always pleased when characters reappear in secondary roles and offer an update to their lives. In Mystery, however, fans want to know far more about the characters, whose personal lives we discover over the course of the series. Although authors may tire of a particular character, most authors do not resort to Doyle's solution of killing off his detective. More frequently today's authors embark on another series and let a character rest for a time—or permanently. Robert B. Parker, for example, after years of recounting the adventures of Spenser, his Boston P.I., has expanded in several directions with a Western series (Virgil Cole and Everett Hitch), a police detective series (Jesse Stone), a female P.I. series (Sunny Randall), and several historical stand-alone novels. Other authors of long-running series slowly allow us to see more of their character's past. In Leon's Venetian series we discover more of Brunetti's history and extended family, as the author creates a more realistic and personable hero, plagued by doubts and concerns beyond his official duties. Readers readily relate to these fully realized characters.

Although the protagonist is certainly an important draw for fans, even secondary characters are more important in Mysteries than in many other genres. The sidekick, who appears from book to book, often plays a key role in solving the case and in attracting readers. A classic example is Archie Goodwin, general factotum and dogsbody for the reclusive Nero Wolfe. Although there may be no doubt that it is through Wolfe's superior brain power that the Mysteries are solved, there is also no denying that it is Goodwin's hard work gathering and presenting clues that sets up the solution. (Try *Too Many Cooks* to sample Rex Stout's style and the relationship between the humorous Goodwin and the often crotchety Wolfe.)[6] Fans would certainly feel the loss of recurring secondary characters Grandma Mazur and Lula in Janet Evanovich's enormously popular series featuring bounty hunter Stephanie Plum (*One for the Money* is the first).[7] Much of the genre's appeal derives from the interaction with secondary characters, as is the case in Parker's Spenser series as well as in Robert Crais's Mysteries featuring Elvis Cole and his unusual sidekick, Joe Pike. (*The Watchman*, the eleventh in the series, tells Pike's story.)[8]

One last characteristic of all these investigators is that they enjoy solving crimes. Their interest is piqued by the puzzles they encounter, and they enjoy matching wits with wily murderers. Like their readers, fictional detectives devote their minds and energies to these mysteries, whether they're paid or not, whether they're on the job or off. The lure of the puzzle drives them, just as it entrances fans.

Frame/Setting

Frames flourish in the Mystery genre, and they contribute to the appeal of this Intellect genre; readers often comment on how much they learn about places as well as fascinating trivia about treasures, professions, issues, and more. Easiest to identify is the setting, either a specific geographical place or a time period in a particular place. Ellis Peters's Brother Cadfael series, set in twelfth-century Shrewsbury, England, established the standard for this technique, with many readers enjoying the glimpse of the times as well as the elaborate puzzles. Anne Perry has continued the tradition with her several series set firmly in the Victorian and World War I eras. The late American Mystery writer Tony Hillerman offers similar satisfaction with his Mysteries, which are framed by the Native American culture and customs of the contemporary American Southwest. Try *Thief of Time* for a taste of his work.[9]

Some authors set Contemporary Mysteries in specific locales and attract readers who enjoy the geographic details and feel of a place, along with their puzzle. In Sara Paretsky's V. I. Warshawski novels, set in Chicago and the surrounding suburbs, we locals can plot her course as V. I. pursues clues. Los Angeles comes alive in the hands of Michael Connelly, as police detective Harry Bosch uncovers murders, while Cynthia Harrod-Eagles's Bill Slider traverses London and surrounding counties, offering detailed information about the geography as well as the people. Nevada Barr takes readers to national parks around the United States with her park ranger Anna Pigeon and her adventures. There are exotic locales as well; with the increased popularity of Scandinavian Mysteries, readers travel effortlessly with Henning Mankell to Sweden (and Africa), to Oslo and more remote Norway with Karin Fossum's Konrad Sejer, and even to Reykjavik in Arnaldur Indridason's police detective series featuring Erlendur Sveinsson. Even more exotic and perhaps dangerous is John Burdett's Bangkok in the company of police detective Sonchai Jitpleecheep in his series beginning with *Bangkok 8*.[10] Just the thing for readers who want more than a tourist's overview!

Other authors focus on the occupations or hobbies of the sleuths, usually amateur detectives, and the details—about almost everything from scrapbooking to sports—add interest and variety to the plots. Diane Mott

Davidson popularized the cooking Mystery (recipes included) specialty begun by Virginia Rich with her Eugenia Potter series (*The Cooking School Murders* is first).[11] Davidson's series featuring caterer Goldy Bear (*Catering to Nobody* starts the series), put gourmet cooking and Mysteries with recipes on the map.[12] Among amateur detectives, we have herbalists and gardeners (Susan Wittig Albert's China Bayles and Ann Ripley's Louise Eldridge), actors—including those who also create greeting cards (Harley Jane Kozak's Wollie Shelley), journalists (Edna Buchanan's Britt Montero), antique and rare book dealers and scouts (John Dunning's Cliff Janeway and Sharon Fiffer's Jane Wheel), ancient and medieval physicians (Ruth Downie's Gaius Petreius Ruso and C. L. Grace's Kathryn Swinbrooke), clergy (Julia Spencer-Fleming's Clare Fergusson and Margaret Coel's Father John O'Malley), psychics (Charlaine Harris's Harper Connelly and Jacqueline Winspear's Maisie Dobbs), forensics experts (Kathy Reichs's Temperance Brennan in Quebec and North Carolina and Ariana Franklin's twelfth-century expert in the art of death, Adelia Aguilar), and almost any profession and hobby imaginable. In the course of the Mystery, readers learn almost as much about the profession or hobby of the detective as they do about the investigation, and for many readers, this is an important satisfaction.

Tone/Mood

Within the vast reaches of the genre, there is surely a Mystery for every mood. We may think of Mysteries as dark and dangerous, but Amateur Detective stories are frequently lighthearted and even gentle in their approach to crime. There are examples of humor across the genre, in Police Procedurals (the black humor of Burdett and the puns and wordplay of Marshall Karp); Private Investigators (Lisa Lutz and her quirky family of P.I.s, as well as Parker and Crais); and Amateur Detectives (Donna Andrews, Rhys Bowen and many more). But there are also sinister tales throughout. Spencer-Fleming's thoughtful series featuring amateur sleuth and Episcopal priest Clare Fergusson offers fans of dark tales a similar gritty, edgy feel that we have come to expect from P.I.s (Loren D. Estleman and Marcia Muller) and Police Detectives (Peter Robinson and Michael Connelly). Fans who appreciate a particular tone can find examples across the genre.

Still other writers frame their Mysteries with a singularly evocative tone. Jacqueline Winspear sets her atmospheric stories in London between the world wars. They project a darkly expressive tone as she traces the cases of psychic/detective Maisie Dobbs, haunted by her experiences in the war as well as her sense of evil lurking in postwar London and the despair faced by returning soldiers.

Style/Language

Many readers prize the distinctive styles that characterize these titles. From the bleak and lyrical cadence of Ireland in Benjamin Black's Quirke Mysteries and the colorful but spare Scots accents of Ian Rankin's Inspector John Rebus series to McCall Smith's lyrical prose with a distinctive Botswanan cadence, language plays an important role for many readers in their appreciation of the genre. While some fans look for the sophisticated banter of Elizabeth Peters's Amelia Peabody series and the smart dialogue that fills Phryne Fisher's adventures by Kerry Greenwood, others appreciate Mysteries with the jargon and idioms from around the world provided by the growing number of Mysteries in translation.

Style plays a role too, and Mysteries may include excerpts from journals and diaries, as well as kidnappers' notes and murderers' confessions. Current technology flavors contemporary Mysteries with e-mails and instant messages as well as blogs providing clues and background information.

Pacing

Pacing is the hallmark of many genres (especially those in the Adrenaline section), but the importance of a particular pace is less of an issue in Mysteries. Although there is considerable difference in the pacing of specific books, from the detailed, involved, literary Mystery novels of James to the flying farces of Joan Hess and much in between, readers do not frequently mention pacing as a reason for reading Mysteries in general or a particular author—although it may be one of the subconscious reasons they prefer one over another. However, they may want to know where a book falls on the pacing range. The bigger books are generally more involved and slower paced, although Elizabeth George's Mysteries, for example, were slower moving even before the page count trebled. The investigative details necessarily slow the story, make it move at a pace slower than a book filled primarily with adventure, suspense, or humor, but the fascination with the characters draws readers on and makes the pacing less noticeable.

Mystery readers accept that books in this genre are not necessarily fast-paced, although they certainly are compelling, because we want to discover who committed the crime and how the solution will be reached.

KEY AUTHORS AND SUBGENRES

Key Authors

Among the authors every Mystery reader recognizes are Janet Evanovich, Michael Connelly, P. D. James, Alexander McCall Smith, and Robert B. Parker. Always on the best-seller lists, these writers represent various subgenres but also possess qualities that entice fans who might generally read another type of Mystery or a different book altogether. Evanovich sets her humorous Mysteries in New Jersey, where bounty hunter Stephanie Plum, often assisted by her eccentric friends and relatives, brings bail-bond jumpers to justice—and frequently finds herself involved in a more serious Mystery. Evanovich is unique in that she combines aspects of all three subgenres in her Mysteries: the whimsy of the Cozy Amateur (although there is certainly considerable violence), the authority of the police (because, as a bounty hunter, she is a representative of the court), and the investigative style of a rather inept P.I.

Connelly's writing focuses primarily on series police detective Harry Bosch, although he also has excellent single titles. Bleak, atmospheric, violent scenes characterize his stories, as well as damaged heroes, suspenseful story lines, and often elegant prose. This series, with Harry Bosch often investigating on his own, appeals as much to fans of the Private Investigator Mysteries as of the Police Detectives, where he technically fits.

The award-winning P. D. James has written more than a dozen best-selling Mysteries that follow the exploits of Scotland Yard Commander Adam Dalgleish. She is critically acclaimed for her beautifully complex prose, thoughtful character studies, complex puzzles, and philosophical reflections on the nature of evil.

McCall Smith's adventures of Botswana's Mma Precious Ramotswe and her No. 1 Ladies' Detective Agency have captured the imagination of a wide range of readers of both Mysteries and Gentle Reads (with the Botswanan community dubbed the African Mitford). These stories are a bit light on the traditional Mystery elements, as Mma Ramotswe and her able assistants solve crimes that reflect very human issues, and her techniques rely more on her understanding of human nature than on her detective skills, as did Agatha Christie's Miss Marple's methods. Readers appreciate their gentle stories and the bits of culture and custom that accompany the detection.

Parker has one of the longest-running series, still popular with a wide range of readers who return every year to devour the exploits of P.I. Spenser, his associate Hawk, and his longtime love Susan Silverman. Descriptive scenes of Boston and the Northeast, witty dialogue, strong and sympathetic characters, action and building tension, stories that pull readers into the characters and the problems they face—all characterize his books.

Subgenres of Mysteries

The character and specific type of investigator or detective are key to the way readers select Mysteries. The story line may control how the characters act, but the personality of those characters directs the book and its appeal to readers. Thus, the most straightforward way to examine the Mystery genre is to focus on these investigator types. As discussed below, however, there is also a particular feel that cuts across these types and may draw readers from one type to another. The types of investigator described here are the private investigator, police detective, and amateur detective. Even here the subgenre lines tend to blur. There are Police Detective Mysteries that feel like (and will appeal to fans of) Amateur Detective Mysteries (those by Louise Penny and Rhys Bowen, for example); Police Detective stories that feel more like those of private investigators (Michael Connelly's); and Cozy amateurs who get a P.I. license midway through the series (M. C. Beaton's Agatha Raisin). Rather than causing problems, this overlap tends to open up new subgenres for readers to explore.

PRIVATE INVESTIGATORS

Today's P.I.s grew out of the tradition established by classic authors Raymond Chandler and Dashiell Hammett in the 1930s and 1940s, when Philip Marlowe, Sam Spade, and the Continental Op employed their nononsense investigative techniques to solve crimes. This is primarily an American phenomenon, and some of today's most popular characters are direct descendants of this hard-boiled tradition, while others are decidedly more soft-boiled. Figure 11.2 lists additional characteristics of P.I.s.

P.I.s explore cases that, even if they do not start out as murder, usually lead there. Characters in these stories are often series characters, and we

---

Figure 11.2   *Characteristics of Private Investigators*

---

1. Investigations are carried out step by step and are usually narrated first-person by the protagonist.

2. Investigators operate under a personal moral code, which may not follow the rule of law.

3. Settings are usually urban. The tone is often dark, and many novels highlight serious social issues.

4. Books often have a hard edge and deal with more violent situations, sometimes in explicit detail.

5. Protagonists may be men or women, and their adventures are usually part of an ongoing series.

---

build a relationship with them and their associates over time through the series. P.I.s are traditionally self-reliant loners who operate independently (although some of today's most popular P.I.s have sidekicks). They differ from amateur detectives in that they are hired to perform the investigation and paid for work; in addition, they usually have some training, skills, and a license they may lose if they cross the police too often.

Another characteristic these protagonists share is a personal moral code under which all operate. Like medieval knights or Western heroes, they are on the side of truth and justice—although they understand that truth may not always be discovered (and proven) or justice meted out if one stays within the confines of the law. None of them is likely to let a little thing like the law stop them, and although they are licensed and generally work within the law, they are not above bending it discreetly (or otherwise) to solve a case. Because they have no actual authority to interview suspects, they sometimes pose as members of the police to question suspects, and if they believe legal justice may fail to be effective, they are not above devising a method of their own to mete it out, as Spenser frequently demonstrates in Parker's series. This ability to take justice into their own hands, to administer it more effectively than even officers of the law often can, makes them very appealing characters. Who would not want to be part of the team that knows what is right and is able to bring it about?

P.I.s usually work on only one case at a time. If there are more cases in the story, they are usually linked in some fashion by the end. Social questions are often highlighted. Parker frequently raises concerns about women and children; Sara Paretsky is known for tackling corporate and government issues and industries, from waste disposal and big medicine to insurance; Jacqueline Winspear addresses issues related to veterans of World War I in her late 1920s series set in London. Operating outside of the law, with techniques unavailable to the police, these P.I.s make good use of their consciences in working to right social injustice.

The tone of these Mysteries is usually dark, even though the dialogue may be witty. Considering that many P.I.s are not only burned-out policemen, but also alcoholics and recovering alcoholics—for example, Ken Bruen's Jack Taylor and James Lee Burke's Dave Robicheaux—the bleak tone should not be a surprise. On the other end, Crais (Elvis Cole), Parker (Spenser), and Lutz (Spellman family) are known for their one-liners that often lighten a tough situation. Ultimately, however, P.I.s do not match the Amateur Detective subgenre for humor, and they generally present a darker tone.

These Mysteries are almost always narrated first-person. This technique affects our perception of and feeling for the characters as well as the tone of the book. We are privy to the protagonist's thoughts as well as actions; it is as if the character is talking to us, and thus the feel is more personal. This approach reinforces the manner in which we follow the investigation step by step, because we are literally walking in our detective's shoes. However, the first-person voice also affects the tone; if the character is a recovering alcoholic, the book reflects the problems he has seen and his bleaker worldview.

As in all Mysteries, geographical setting is an important part of the frame. P.I.s tend to operate in an urban environment. Even though Burke's Cajun detective Robicheaux tries to isolate himself in rural Louisiana, he is always found by those who seek his skills, and the action generally takes place in town or at least deals with urban rather than rural crime. A good example is his dramatic and elegiac *The Tin Roof Blowdown*, in which Robicheaux investigates a crime committed in New Orleans during Hurricane Katrina.[13]

Not only are the settings urban, they are also generally quite detailed. These authors pride themselves on the accuracy of both the geographical details and the feel of the place—the customs and people—as well. Laura Lippman's Baltimore and its denizens come alive in her series featuring journalist-turned-P.I. Tess Monaghan. She clearly loves her city and its unique citizens, and her Mysteries explore the city and area's landmarks as well as the dark streets (*Baltimore Blues* is the first).[14]

Key Authors

One of the best known and most popular of current Mystery writers, Sue Grafton is an author whom librarians ignore at their peril. Although some fans may only know her as the author who writes that alphabet series, they request every book as soon as they think it is time she published another. Kinsey Millhone, originally an investigator for an insurance agency and later a P.I., captured the attention of Mystery fans and rode the wave of women Mystery writers to fame and fortune. *"A" Is for Alibi* was published in 1982, and fans are already worrying what she will do after she reaches Z.[15] Kinsey is a loner, although over the years, she has collected a group of friends who serve as family. She is ready for anything—she even keeps a little black dress crumpled up in the trunk of her compact car, just in case she needs to dress more professionally on a case. Clever plotting, gritty stories, a sassy heroine, and a strong sense of place set Grafton apart. Kinsey introduces herself in the first few paragraphs of each book, so the reader can start almost anywhere in the series and feel connected to the story and character. Try *"K" Is for Killer, "N" Is for Noose,* or *"O" Is for Outlaw* for typical examples of her style and range.[16] Interestingly, she has kept her series set in the 1980s, and the omission of modern standard electronic equipment—cell phones and computers—give these an almost retro feel.

Other important American authors of P.I. Mysteries include Robert Crais, Laura Lippman, and Marcia Muller. Crais offers dark humor and smart dialogue although his books address serious issues. His Los Angeles–based Elvis Cole is a good bet for fans of Parker's Spenser series. Both feature witty dialogue, caring detectives, difficult issues, and strong, silent sidekicks. *Sunset Express* is one of his best and a good introduction to the series.[17]

Lippman's series focuses on Baltimore and environs. Like Parker and Crais, her Mysteries offer witty dialogue, complex story lines, difficult social issues, and a strong sense of time and place. *No Good Deeds* places Tess in a tough situation as she investigates the murder of an assistant district attorney.[18] Her live-in boyfriend Crow has rescued a boy from the streets who may be involved in the murder, and to save him, Crow and the boy disappear, leaving Tess to face the investigation's dangers alone.

Marcia Muller's Sharon McCone, the first female P.I., remains one of the genre's best examples. Based in San Francisco, the tough yet vulnerable McCone investigates cases from Nob Hill to the underbelly of San Francisco society. Suspense, investigative detail, and likeable series characters make her Mysteries good suggestions for many readers. As in all series we learn about the detective bit by bit; however, *Till the Butchers Cut Him Down* provides significant background detail.[19]

The P.I. as detective, as described here, is a fairly recent phenomenon; however, there are a number of Mysteries with historical settings that would certainly appeal to fans of this type. A pair of authors has brought new life to ancient Rome with their series featuring P.I.s. Both Lindsey Davis and Steven Saylor probe issues in Roman society through the characters and investigations of their detectives. In Davis's series Marcus Didius Falco is a P.I. in the time of Vespasian (AD 69–79); his investigations lead him to the far reaches of the Roman Empire (Germany, Spain, and beyond). Described as "Columbo in a toga," Falco adds an element of humor to the history in these stories.[20] The series begins with *The Silver Pigs*.[21] Saylor, on the other hand, offers Gordianus the Finder in a series set more than one hundred years earlier during the Roman Republic. Suspense, intrigue, and detailed historical setting characterize this series, of which *Roman Blood* is the first.[22]

POLICE DETECTIVES

Although the most famous of the classic detectives may never have been police detectives, the subgenre certainly has had its day. In books, radio (those of us lucky enough to have grown up listening to *Dragnet* know how effective a medium radio can be), television (from *Dragnet* to *Hill Street Blues*, *Prime Suspect*, and *NYPD Blue* to *Law and Order* and the ubiquitous and multiple *CSI* series and *The Shield*), and the movies (*Dirty Harry*, *Lethal Weapon*, and *Beverly Hills Cop*, for example, not to mention *L.A. Confidential*, with its noir outlook and feel), the police story has long been popular. See figure 11.3 for characteristics of Police Detective/Police Procedural Mysteries.

**Figure 11.3   *Characteristics of Police Detective/
Police Procedural Mysteries***

---

1. Either the department as a whole or particular members (almost always detectives) provide the focus for these Mysteries.

2. Details of police departments and police work figure prominently, and the details of the investigative procedures enhance the story.

3. Settings may be urban, suburban, or small town. Details of the setting, a strong sense of place, are often important.

4. The police team or department is generally engaged in working on multiple cases, usually unrelated to each other, and these are not necessarily all solved.

That the protagonists are members of police departments clearly distinguishes this subgenre from the P.I. and Amateur Detective stories. As policemen (and -women) they have the force of the law on their side—to investigate cases, to question witnesses, to incarcerate possible felons. But they are also likely overwhelmed by office politics and a heavy caseload. In Police Detective Mysteries we get the details of the investigation, as well as the inner workings of the department, from the police perspective.

Because they also involve official investigators who play by the rules, it is possible to include forensics Mysteries here as well. Patricia Cornwell's long-running series featuring medical examiner Kay Scarpetta started the craze for this type of police detective with *Postmortem* in 1990.[23] Kathy Reichs's Temperance Brennan and Bill Bass and Jon Jefferson's Dr. Bill Brockton (Bass is the founder of the original Body Farm) fit comfortably in the Mystery genre, while Karin Slaughter's Sara Linton and Jeffery Deaver's quadriplegic criminalist Lincoln Rhyme straddle the line with Adrenaline novels.

Police Detective Mysteries generally involve more than one case. There may be a principal case that is being investigated, but there will be other cases as well, and these may be related to the principal case, or not, and they may be solved, or not. While P.I.s and amateur detectives can devote all their time to a single case, police detectives must juggle their cases in ways that provide interesting opportunities for writers. On the other hand, police detectives work as part of a team, never alone. Police detectives are paired with a partner, with whom they share the details of the investigation. These stories are related by a third-person narrator, so we readers have the benefit of more information from a variety of characters to use in solving the cases.

In their investigations police detectives should play by the rules. They have the authority to question suspects but only within strict guidelines. They have all the department's resources at their fingertips—if they can only call in enough favors to have those resources devoted to the case they are working on. Evidence must be handled in a prescribed manner to be admissible in court. All hinges on the precision of the investigation, with little room for ingenuity or alternative approaches. Having said that, I would add that there are always exceptions, authors who push the borders of the genre beyond the traditional confines. Here Connelly's Harry (really, Hieronymus) Bosch of the Los Angeles Police Department, a Vietnam vet who has little respect for the rules of law and less for authority, stands out. Complex, suspenseful plots, a bleak atmosphere, and a knight-errant hero who prefers to work alone characterize these award-winning

Mysteries. In *Closers* he's back at the LAPD in a new department that focuses on cold cases.[24]

Even more than P.I.s, police detectives are likely to be placed in perilous situations, such as armed encounters with dangerous criminals. There is a difference in the amount of violence in American Police Detective Mysteries versus those set in England and Europe, mirroring the differences in the societies in real life. The American stories have more violence and more gunplay than their British and Continental counterparts. The British stories are certainly often bleak but not necessarily as violent, although Ian Rankin's John Rebus Mysteries grow increasingly, dark, problematical, and dangerous. They also display a serious concern for social issues, as in Deborah Crombie's Duncan Kincaid and Gemma James series.

On the American side, violence and gunplay may replace or figure alongside the frequently bleak mood of the Police Detective Mysteries. Linda Fairstein's New York policemen and Alexandra Cooper, head of Manhattan's Sex Crimes unit; Parker's Jesse Stone in a small Massachusetts town; Michael McGarrity's Kevin Kerney in Santa Fe, all feature this dark tone.

Not all Police Detective Mysteries are bleak and violent, however. Series from both continents reflect a large measure of humor—in dialogue and situation—as well as an upbeat, or at least lighter, tone. For example, England offers Colin Dexter's series, set in Oxford and popularized by the television renditions, with Inspector Morse's uncanny intuition, irascible personality, and dogged investigating, as well as M. C. Beaton's Hamish Macbeth, a constable in the Scottish Highlands, whose unorthodox techniques, intuition, and rather eccentric personality likely appeal more to fans of Cozy Amateur Detective Mysteries than of police stories. American Joan Hess gives us another small-town series with its unique feel—Police Chief Arly Hanks and Maggody, Arkansas—about as far from the mean streets as one can get. Texan Bill Crider offers a lighter touch in his Sheriff Don Rhodes series. Tony Hillerman's series, set in the American Southwest on Native American reservations, also qualifies as a Police Detective Mystery, even though there is less interaction within the department, and because of the lack of staff, officers are often out on their own. Although his books do not offer much humor, they do display a more human touch. Violence is not absent, but it does not dominate these thoughtful mysteries, rich in character, geography, culture, and Native American tradition. It is interesting to note that these lighter Police Detective Mysteries seem almost closer to Amateur Detective stories in feel and appeal, and as many readers of Amateur Detective Mysteries are as likely to read them as are fans of Police Detective stories.

This mood distinction seems to reflect geography: Urban police stories are more likely bleak and more violent; those set in small towns are generally lighter, with the details of the crime filtered through the cozy feel of the town and its personalities. Louise Penny's Three Pines series, set in a small Quebec town, fits this profile, as the Montreal detective called to investigate the murders almost becomes part of the close-knit community. Archer Mayor's series set in Vermont and Craig Johnson's Wyoming-based Sheriff Walt Longmore stand out as exceptions. Set in a more rural environment, at least away from major cities, a gentler mood might be expected. In fact, they deal with serious issues of narcotics and drug trafficking, spousal abuse, racism, and violence. This is not the small-town life one would expect in such a bucolic setting. *The Ragman's Memory* is a good example of Mayor's excellent character development, complex mystery, strong sense of place, and menacing villains.[25]

Many of the newer Mystery series from around the world feature police detectives. The Scandinavian authors mentioned earlier focus on police detectives and the procedures unique to their countries. On the other side of the world are Australians Peter Temple (Joe Cashlin) and Garry Disher (Hal Challis). There are also long-running Historical and Contemporary series set in India (H. R. F. Keating), Italy (Leon and Magdalen Nabb), Israel (Batya Gur), Japan (Laura Joh Rowland), Egypt (Michael Pearce), China (William Marshall and Robert van Gulik) and Canada (L. R. Wright) to name just a few of the variety of settings for police procedurals.

Key Authors

Within the Police Detective Mysteries there are those that focus on the department as a team and those that feature a single investigator and assistant, and the authors that best exemplify this distinction are also key authors in the subgenre. The late Ed McBain's 87th Precinct Mysteries typify the former. Set against the background of a bustling big-city police department (not unlike New York City's), these Mysteries play out with an ongoing cast of characters. We know them from the first paragraph, thanks to McBain's skill in providing thumbnail sketches of the players and their roles. Although Steve Carella emerges as a hero of sorts, it is in fact the interplay of the whole department that makes the series. Try *Hark!*, one of the last in this long-running series. It features the return of the devious Deaf Man.[26]

On the other hand, in James's Scotland Yard, we know few of the characters more than superficially. These are the stories of Commander Adam Dalgleish; other characters figure peripherally, but the stories are his and thus have a feel quite different from McBain's departmental team. Here, elegant prose, descriptions, deeper psychological analysis of the suspects, and insights into Dalgleish's own nature and investigation make these Mysteries slower-paced; they are stories to savor as we do more literary novels.

The distinction between an emphasis on the department as a whole and the investigations of one or two detectives makes an enormous difference in the feel of the story. The story of the busy inner workings and juggling of cases in a police department contrasts with a single character, and perhaps an assistant, who has the backing and credentials of the police but is essentially investigating on his or her own. The latter type crosses over with both P.I.s and Amateur Detective Mysteries in terms of feel and appeal.

Police detectives also appear less frequently in Historical Mysteries, primarily because in most countries organized police departments didn't exist before the mid-eighteenth century. Bruce Alexander, however, covers London in a series that features famous London jurist Sir John Fielding, who created the Bow Street Runners, London's first police force. *Blind Justice* is the first.[27] Robert van Gulik and Laura Joh Rowland take readers farther afield—to the Far East—with series set in ancient China and medieval Japan. Although Gulik's Judge Dee is not exactly a police detective, he represents the law, such as it was, solves cases, and administers justice with the authority of a modern police department. (Try *The Haunted Monastery* to explore his style.)[28] Rowland's series, featuring Sano Ichiro and set in seventeenth-century Japan, is full of interesting details of the samurai period. *Shinju* is the first.[29]

AMATEUR DETECTIVES

Amateur detectives are more likely to view their cases as puzzles. (See figure 11.4.) They become intrigued with something that does not quite fit in the details of a murder, and they go off on their own to investigate, outside the official investigation but sometimes paralleling it. Or they may themselves be suspects in a case and they investigate to clear their names. They often have a contact in the police force, as did Lord Peter Wimsey in Dorothy Sayers's successful series of Mysteries that spanned the 1920s and 1930s. Peter's brother-in-law, along with other connections in Scotland Yard, supported his investigations and profited from his findings. Successful amateur detectives, as Lord Peter certainly was, build a reputation and are often sought for assistance in investigating a case, just as P.I.s are. The difference, of course, is that the amateur detectives are not licensed nor do they charge a fee for their efforts. (However, both amateur detectives and P.I.s are looked down upon by the police detectives.)

Figure 11.4 *Characteristics of the Amateur Detective*

---

1. These detectives are not professionals who have been specially trained in detecting techniques; they are more likely to "fall into" a case (often involving someone they know) than to be asked to investigate, and they are usually engaged in only one case at a time.
2. Amateurs have another job or a hobby which occupies their time and the details of which supplement the Mystery.
3. Mysteries featuring amateurs are usually gentler, although there is a range of violence, as well as tone.

Although they have never been formally trained in police-type investigations, amateur detectives tend to be skilled at turning up clues that the police manage to miss. (This may be one of the reasons the police dislike them so!) In Cozies (a gentle type of Amateur Detective Mystery discussed below), these amateur detectives tend to rely more on intuition and their knowledge of human nature, rather than any structured investigation, to discover the true nature of the crime and the criminal. Dorothy Cannell's romps, featuring the inimitable Ellie Haskell, provide a heroine detective who happens on murders in the best Cozy tradition and solves them just as expeditiously. *The Thin Woman* starts the series, in which overweight Ellie Simons falls into murder—and love—attending a family reunion.[30] Joanne Fluke's Hannah Swensen Mysteries, set in a small Minnesota town, project the same comfortable, amusing tone. *Chocolate Chip Cookie Murder* is the first.[31]

Frames, often focused on the profession or hobbies of the investigators, are important in these stories. Jonathan Gash's Lovejoy is an antiques dealer who, as a "divvy," possesses skills to determine accurately whether something is authentic or a fake. Lovejoy's extensive knowledge of antiques, not to mention his slightly off-color opinions, have made him a popular amateur detective who is not above carrying out a good scam himself. *The Grail Tree* is the first of this long-running series, which has also been imported from British television.[32] Newer series featuring antiques by Sharon Fiffer, Jane K. Cleland, and Lyn Hamilton have taken advantage of the popularity of this frame.

Methods of detection vary widely in this subgenre. Some amateurs take their cases and investigations more seriously, following clues with the precision of the best of P.I.s, as does psychologist Alex Delaware in Jonathan Kellerman's series. As with most amateurs, Delaware has a police connection (LAPD detective Milo Sturgis), but many cases are solved by Delaware's step-by-step analysis and investigation, as well as his intellectual approach and psychological insight into the crimes and criminals. *Monster* is an excellent example of his technique.[33] Others casually fall into a puzzle, into trouble, and into a solution, as does Donna Andrews's Meg Langslow, blacksmith and detective. *Murder, with Peacocks,* the first in her series, highlights the humor and eccentric characters.[34]

Key Authors

Popular writers of Amateur Detective Mysteries include Julia Spencer-Fleming, Lilian Jackson Braun, John Dunning, and Edna Buchanan. Spencer-Fleming's series, set in an Adirondack town in upstate New York, features Episcopal priest Clare Fergusson. In these dark and moody Mysteries, Clare wrestles with matters of faith, the complexities of her friendship with unhappily married police chief Russ Van Alstyne, and the disturbing crimes that plague her congregation and town. Fans read these as much for the graceful prose and layered mystery as to follow the complicated lives of the protagonists. *In the Bleak Midwinter* is the first.[35]

Lilian Jackson Braun, author of The Cat Who Mysteries, continues to delight fans of both sexes with the antics of two Siamese cats, Koko and Yum Yum, and their owner, journalist and later philanthropist Jim Qwilleran, as he solves cases in the rural North Country. *The Cat Who Could Read Backwards* is the first in the long-running Cozy series.[36]

John Dunning's Cliff Janeway Mysteries satisfy many readers' interest in books and the rare book business. But this Denver-based dealer and amateur sleuth also demonstrates the darker and more dangerous side of this subgenre, with violence a typical feature in his cases. His sleuth's previous career as a police detective gives him those skills and Dunning's own career as an antiquarian book dealer adds to the authenticity of the series. *Booked to Die* is the first.[37]

Edna Buchanan's investigator, Britt Montero, represents another kind of amateur detective. Not really a detective, Britt, who works for a Miami newspaper, comes upon murder through her job of investigating a news story or incident. Buchanan, a Pulitzer Prize–winning reporter, gives her heroine extensive reporting skills, as Britt goes for the story but often comes up with murder. *Contents under Pressure* is the first of this series.[38]

The Cozy, referred to several times throughout this chapter, represents a particular, and currently very popular, type of Amateur Detective Mystery. In these the body is traditionally offstage, and neither death nor any other violent episode is explicitly described. The protagonist, often a woman, solves the Mystery through intuition and knowledge of human nature. These often feature small-town settings, and gossip—as well as casually talking with suspects who are friends and neighbors—plays an important role in providing the information necessary to solve the crime. Fingerprints, markings on the bullet, and autopsy reports (even if they did have access to them) are seldom as crucial in an environment in which one can learn, with a few carefully considered and well-placed questions, just who was leaving the victim's house on the evening in question. Generally speaking, Cozies feature quirky characters; a sense of community (generally small-town or at least enclosed); and an upbeat, often quite humorous tone, which emphasizes amusing dialogue and human foibles. In addition, amateur detectives in Cozies likely have some connection with the police; in many cases, the protagonist's boyfriend or husband is on the force. Because they usually contain more dialogue than other Mysteries, Cozies are usually faster-paced and shorter.

Although protagonists in Cozies are generally women, there are inevitably exceptions. A popular example is Lawrence Block's Bernie Rhodenbarr series, which takes place in Manhattan (rather than in a small town). Burglar and secondhand book dealer Bernie seems always to get caught with a body in a home he only meant to rob, and thus, he is forced to investigate to save his own skin. The series opens with *Burglars Can't Be Choosers*.[39]

Although suspension of disbelief is certainly a necessary qualification to enjoy Cozies, these are neither simple nor for the simpleminded. Many popular Historical Mysteries are Cozies, and like those by Sharon Kay Penman, are acclaimed for their attention to historical detail. Even the lightest of Cozies offers a wry look at human nature and either an interesting frame or an exploration of social issues on some level.

Mysteries featuring amateur detectives, and particularly Cozies, have come into their own in the last decades. Although they may not dominate the best-seller lists, they support the growing habit of readers who like the "English Village Mystery" or a "nice" Mystery, with a puzzle, interesting characters, and the body well offstage. Certainly, there seem to be more writers of Amateur Detective Mysteries than of either of the other two subgenres, and the Cozy titles often make good crossover suggestions for fans of Gentle Reads.

For many of us, Elizabeth Peters is the benchmark Cozy Mystery writer. Her Mysteries have entertained and educated millions of readers since *The Jackal's Head* appeared in 1968.[40] She has written more than thirty Mysteries (nonseries and in three series) and nearly thirty novels of Romantic Suspense under the pseudonym Barbara Michaels. Named a Grandmaster by the Mystery Writers of America in 1998, her reputation is ensured.

Peters's Mysteries feature a variety of themes and frames, but because the author herself is an Egyptologist, things Egyptian remain a prominent feature. She writes a series set in turn-of-the-twentieth-century Egypt featuring Amelia Peabody Emerson and her Egyptologist husband, Radcliffe. These are basically humorous Cozy Mysteries, with little explicit violence, sex, or strong language, but Peters takes justified pride in the accuracy of the historical setting and details of the excavations of the tombs, as Victorian Egyptologists unearth the treasures of the pharaohs. Each entry in the series is set in a specific time and reflects actual historical events. The first, *Crocodile on the Sandbank,* is set in the 1880s.[41]

As are all Mysteries, those featuring amateur detectives tend to be descriptive of time and place, whether contemporary or historical. Mysteries in this subgenre lend themselves to historical topics to a greater extent than either of the other two subgenres, because neither police departments nor true P.I.s play much of a role in history before the middle of the eighteenth century. Following in Peters's footsteps with medieval and Elizabethan settings are a plethora of writers including Sharan Newman, Margaret Frazer, Edward Marston, Elizabeth Eyre, and Fiona Buckley. On this side of the Atlantic, Abel Jones's series of military Mysteries investigated by Owen Parry makes a good suggestion.

Mystery writers set their adventures of amateur detectives around the world, primarily in historical settings. Series to note include Kerry Greenwood's featuring woman-of-the-world Phryne Fisher solving mysteries in 1920s Australia and the prolific P. C. Doherty's medieval English, ancient Egyptian, and Alexander the Great Mysteries.

WHAT WE KNOW ABOUT FANS

Personally, I despair of ever reading enough Mysteries to work with the range of fans who ask for suggestions. Although fans of some genres are elusive and must be sought out and roped in before they will talk with us, it seems as though many Mystery fans are comfortable with their genre of choice and believe everyone else reads and enjoys Mysteries and should be able to suggest more that are just like their favorite authors. This is no small task, considering the breadth of this genre. Lists, displays, reviews, and the comments of other readers (staff and patrons) are all invaluable in preparing us to work with readers and helping us when we have actual readers in tow.

What do we know about Mystery fans? Aside from the fact that they tend to be voluble, Mystery readers like series. They follow series characters from case to case and are always on the lookout for the next book in that series as well as additional series that have the same appeal. They want to read series in order, and they frankly don't care if an individual title gets a less-than-favorable review; they expect the library to buy it anyway. Keeping lists of read-alike suggestions for popular authors is always a good idea. Identifying what makes the author popular and then discovering other authors who share those characteristics are the place to start.

Many readers follow a series because they like the detective. This means that fans of a Cozy series might also be interested in a P.I. if the characters are similar. Other readers want a type—they may like Police Detective Mysteries and will read all we can give them, or they may be interested in P.I.s set in a particular location, or they may want Mysteries of any kind that have a particular frame—art or gardening, for example. Reference resources tend to be much more helpful in identifying authors to satisfy these readers.

The issue of series brings up another problem: paperbacks. Many series begin as paperbacks and then continue in hardcover. Luckily, more and more review journals consider paperbacks along with hardcovers, because if we miss purchasing the early titles in a series, we may never be able to fill them in. Treat paperbacks carefully and catalog them so that they stay in the collection, available to fans who discover the series later.

Some readers read to discover the answer to "whodunit," preferably before the detective reaches his own conclusions. Others read for the frame or the characters. It helps if we have thought about these different appeals, so that we are ready when readers come to us for assistance and describe what they enjoy.

As Mystery fans know, more and more Mysteries are set in specific locations and may be popular in that area, even if they are not as popular elsewhere. Although the benchmark in your community may be Robert B. Parker or Janet Evanovich, there may be popular local authors whose books you must consistently purchase—often in multiple copies. Because we cannot buy everything, we need to listen to what readers enjoy and request and gear our collections as much as possible to their interests. If you are not a Mystery reader, you might try some of the suggestions in figure 11.5.

Figure 11.5 *An Introduction to the Mystery Genre*

Mystery Writers to Try, If You Enjoy . . .

Adrenaline:	Loren D. Estleman
	Bill James
	William Kent Krueger
Biography/Memoir:	Bruce Alexander
	Max Allan Collins
Fantasy:	Christopher Fowler (Bryant and May Mysteries)[42]
	Charlaine Harris
	Kim Harrison (*Dead Witch Walking*)[43]
Gay/Lesbian:	Ellen Hart
	Laurie R. King (Kate Martinelli series)
	Mark Richard Zubro
Gentle:	Alexander McCall Smith
Historical Fiction:	P. C. Doherty
	Sharon Kay Penman (Eleanor of
	Aquitaine series)[44]
	Anne Perry
History:	Ariana Franklin
	Frank Tallis
Horror:	Charlie Huston
Humor:	Lawrence Block (Burglar series)
	Janet Evanovich
	Eric Garcia
Inspirational:	Randy C. Alcorn
	Terri Blackstock
	G. K. Chesterton
Literary:	James Lee Burke
	P. D. James
Multicultural:	Edna Buchanan
	Carolina Garcia-Aguilera
	Craig Johnson
	Walter Mosley
	Barbara Parker
Natural History:	Nevada Barr

(cont.)

Figure 11.5 *An Introduction to the Mystery Genre (cont.)*

Psychological Suspense:	Caleb Carr
	Carol O'Connor
Romance:	Elizabeth Peters
Romantic Suspense:	April Henry
Saga:	Elizabeth Peters (Amelia Peabody series)[45]
Travel:	Nevada Barr
	Carolyn Hart
True Adventure:	Dick Francis
True Crime:	Louise Penny
Western:	C. J. Box
	Michael McGarrity
	Owen Parry
Women's Lives:	Gail Bowen
	Joan Hess (Claire Malloy series)[46]
	Julia Spencer-Fleming

THE READERS' ADVISORY INTERVIEW

One problem we always face in working with readers who want to explore such a large and diverse genre is how to zero in on good suggestions. When fans ask for Mysteries, we verify first that they are asking for books with a puzzle: a crime, an investigation, and a solution. Then, depending on whether they are in the mood for a P.I., Police Detective, or Amateur Detective Mystery, we might offer a variety of types and characters.

A very useful strategy is to ask the Mystery fan to describe the kind of detective she enjoys. The response is usually very revealing, and the question is far easier to pose and to answer than to query if they like Police Procedurals or Amateur Detective Mysteries, terms they may not even clearly understand or use themselves. Readers may talk about the loner working on a case, or the step-by-step police investigation, or the little old lady who stumbles into cases. These descriptions give us valuable clues as to the type and tone of Mystery we might suggest.

Tone is another important aspect to keep in mind, because it strongly affects the appeal of the Mystery. We listen to the way readers describe the books they enjoy. If they emphasize the lighter tone, they may enjoy a range of Mysteries, from the breezy Cozies of Susan Wittig Albert's herbal

Mysteries (*Thyme of Death*) to Janet Evanovich's rather incompetent bounty hunter, or the humorous Police Detective Mysteries of Rhys Bowen and Joan Hess.[47] Fans of a darker tone might also cut across the subgenres with Julia Spencer-Fleming (amateur detective), Dennis Lehane (P.I.), and Michael Connelly (police detective). Fans of elegantly written, more literary Mysteries should be made aware of P. D. James, certainly, but they may also enjoy authors such as Elizabeth George and James Lee Burke. Readers looking for books that match a particular mood and tone are often willing to read outside the boundaries of the familiar, and thoughtful suggestions are always appreciated.

Readers also ask for Mysteries by frame. They enjoy cooking Mysteries, or ones that include literary puzzles. They may appreciate a certain geographical setting, or they might like a particular historical period. All these can be found through relatively straightforward searches in the numerous book and web reference sources.

We can also draw conclusions from the way readers talk about the story line and style of the Mystery. Readers who talk about investigative details are more likely to appreciate Police Detective and P.I. Mysteries. On the other hand, readers who hint more at intuition and extensive frame will likely prefer Amateur Detective stories, perhaps even Cozies.

As should be obvious from the preceding discussion, setting and frame are increasingly important. Readers who mention local details and urban environments should be steered first toward urban Police Detective and P.I. Mysteries, while those who talk about villages and enclosed communities will surely want to consider Cozies. Listening to how readers talk about Mysteries they have enjoyed in the past and using the framework of the genre and subgenres discussed earlier allow us to offer suggestions that help readers more readily discover the kinds of Mysteries they are in the mood to read.

One last point to consider is where to start a reader in a series or with a new author. Some readers insist on reading the first book in a series; if I know that is not the author's best and am unable to dissuade them, I simply tell them that even if they are not enamored of it, they should try another, the one I believe best represents the author's style and story line. The first in a series is not always the best—Robert B. Parker's *The Godwulf Manuscript* is a good example of a first mystery that fails to capture the essence of the series characters and style.[48] If we are offering an unfamiliar author to a reader, we should make every effort to suggest a representative title. If a reader enjoys a series, he will read all the titles; the key is to hook him with that first book. We watch for good examples of an author as we read, read reviews, and talk with patrons. When we find a reference source that makes such recommendations, we should cherish it and share that information with colleagues and readers.

Sure Bets

It is always helpful to have in mind—or even better, written down—the names of those authors who work consistently for a large number of readers who enjoy Mysteries and related titles. If you do not keep a list now, you should start. Every library's clientele is different; your readers will enjoy authors whom mine may not appreciate as much. Watch for the authors that your readers talk about and reserve.

Laurie R. King writes two excellent Mystery series featuring female detectives. Her series titles starring an aging Sherlock Holmes and his young wife Mary Russell have the dual satisfaction of the continuing adventures of a classic detective as well as the intriguing addition of a younger, female partner. *The Beekeeper's Apprentice* starts the series and might be suggested to fans of the Holmes oeuvre, readers of Historical Mysteries, and others who simply appreciate intricately conceived and executed puzzles.[49] King's other series stars Kate Martinelli in contemporary San Francisco and explores both the professional and personal life of her lesbian police detective. Like Mary Russell, Martinelli is intelligent and courageous, and King's attention to emotional and professional development in both these characters allows them to struggle against and overcome the strictures of their times. *A Grave Talent* is the first.[50]

Another author with a wide-ranging appeal is Nevada Barr, whose National Park Service ranger-protagonist Anna Pigeon is appreciated by both male and female readers. Because Pigeon is posted to different parks around the country, Barr is able to give readers an insider's look into the parks, their history and geography, as well as the particular issues relevant to that locale. In addition to braving natural dangers inherent in her job and solving a murder in each book, Anna must also fight her personal demons. Barr has created a very human, down-to-earth amateur detective, who will appeal especially to readers of female P.I. Mysteries by Sue Grafton and Marcia Muller. Suggest a title based on a national park that interests the patron, or try *Hunting Season,* a great accompaniment, especially in the audio version, while driving the Natchez Trace Parkway.[51]

All the authors previously mentioned in this chapter have been popular with readers at my library, and all are good candidates for displays, lists, and other promotion. For example, Anne Perry has two long-running series that combine elements of amateur detective with a police department in the Pitt series and with a P.I. in the William Monk series. Her first series features Inspector Thomas Pitt and his aristocratic wife, Charlotte, in Mysteries that explore the serious social and class issues in Victorian England. Although Thomas is part of London's police force, that organization plays a very small role, and the Mysteries are solved as frequently by Charlotte, accompanied by an eccentric cast of secondary characters, and her snooping, as by actual police investigation. (In the first, *The Cater Street Hangman*, Charlotte and Thomas meet and fall in love, amid the investigation of her sister's murder.)[52] The second series features William Monk, a policeman who has lost his memory in an accident. As he struggles to regain his memory and his career, he works as a P.I. of sorts, assisted by, among others, Hester Latterly, a nurse who trained with Florence Nightingale in the Crimean War and who has her own forthright ideas of the role of nurses and women in general in Victorian society. This series opens with *The Face of a Stranger*.[53] These Historical Mysteries feature bleak, evocative, atmospheric mysteries that also delve into the underside of Victorian society, just as many contemporary P.I.s probe today's society.

EXPANDING READERS' HORIZONS WITH WHOLE COLLECTION READERS' ADVISORY

Because none of us can accurately identify all the Mysteries in our collection and then carefully catalog them in a separate collection, we need to be aware of the range of books outside the genre that appeal to Mystery readers. So many genres overlap with Mysteries, in terms of all the appeal elements, that the possibilities are almost infinite—if we open up our own minds and those of readers to see these possibilities.

Investigators appear in many genres in addition to Mystery, and readers who enjoy that type of character may enjoy reading outside the genre to find the same satisfaction. Legal Thrillers feature the same investigative techniques, although the outcome may not be the arrest of a murderer, and the focus is often on the trial. In fact, many Adrenaline authors might appeal to Mystery readers, among them Harlan Coben, John Lescroart, and John Grisham. Romantic Suspense offers J. D. Robb's Eve Dallas series and Iris Johansen's Eve Duncan series, with the forensic details and puzzles.

There is also a group of books that features police departments, and perhaps even detectives, but does not feel like Mysteries to readers.

Authors like Stephen J. Cannell (*The Tin Collectors*), William Caunitz (*One Police Plaza*), Michael Grant (*Line of Duty*), W. E. B. Griffin (Badge of Honor series, beginning with *Men in Blue*), T. Jefferson Parker (*The Blue Hour*), and Joseph Wambaugh (*The Golden Orange*) have written books, even series, that have more Suspense and Thriller elements than do straightforward Mysteries.[54] This distinction causes us to put their books in Fiction rather than Mystery, as they seem to fit in with Police Thrillers. Although crimes are committed and investigations take place, the feel and pattern of the stories are not the same as in Mysteries dealing with the same issues: the puzzle and its solution are not necessarily the point of these stories. Still, this group might appeal to readers interested in police investigative techniques and details.

We place authors in genres where we think the readers are most likely to discover them, but the blurring of the borders of the genres is becoming a fact of life. Fans of the P.I. subgenre might consider Laurell K. Hamilton's Anita Blake, Vampire Hunter series (now also available as a graphic novel) or the Fantasy/Paranormal Romance series starring Meredith Gentry. Don't forget Steven Brust's Vlad Taltos Fantasy series.[55]

Nonfiction collections also offer treasures for Mystery readers. History and True Crime sections provide background for true crime-based Mysteries, and Biography can add to the depth of characters based on historical personages.

See figure 11.6 for additional possibilities that lead readers beyond the borders of the Mystery genre.

TRENDS

The most obvious trend in the Mystery genre today is the genre's expansion around the globe. Certainly there have long been Mysteries set in foreign climes, but now Mysteries by authors from around the world are finding readers here. Rich in characters, setting, culture, and language, these also offer a glimpse into the social issues of the country and the crime-solving techniques.

Paranormal elements have become increasingly popular here, as in most genres. Detectives may be vampires or werewolves, vampire and demon hunters, shamans or psychics; ghosts investigate crimes or assist susceptible humans. Animals, from cats and dogs to dinosaurs, speak and investigate or offer their insightful observations into the nature of crimes and the identity of criminals. While many of these are humorous in tone, others are deadly serious.

Figure 11.6 *Expanding Readers' Horizons*

Authors to Take Readers beyond the Mystery Genre

Adrenaline:	Harlan Coben
	John Grisham
	John Sandford
Fantasy:	Steven Brust
	Laurell K. Hamilton (Meredith Gentry series)
Gentle:	Ann B. Ross
	Sandra Dallas
History:	James L. Swanson (*Manhunt*)[56]
Horror:	Jim Butcher
	P. N. Elrod
	Laurell K. Hamilton (Anita Blake series)[57]
Literary:	Umberto Eco (*The Name of the Rose*)[58]
	Martin Cruz Smith
Psychological Suspense:	Patricia Highsmith
Romance:	Jennifer Crusie
	Stephanie Laurens
Romantic Suspense:	Iris Johansen (Eve Duncan series)[59]
	J. D. Robb
Science Fiction:	Isaac Asimov (Robot series)[60]
True Crime:	Bill Bass and Jon Jefferson (*Death's Acre*)[61]
Western:	Loren D. Estleman (Page Murdock series)[62]

Historical Mysteries remain among the most popular and they include more and more countries and cultures and offer historical/cultural/social details, as noted above in the descriptions of each subgenre. Both Historical Fiction and Mystery readers choose these authors and their books for the details of a particular historical period, as well as for the puzzle and the characters.

The Mystery genre has long supported a variety of ethnic writers. There are sleuths of almost every conceivable background. Interested readers will find gay and lesbian investigators (Joseph Hansen's David Brandstetter, an insurance investigator, was one of the first to achieve widespread popularity), Hispanic (Edna Buchanan's Britt Montero), American Indian (Aimee Thurlo's Ella Clah as well as Dana Stabenow's

Kate Shugak), and Asian (from Laura Joh Rowland's seventeenth-century samurai Sano Ichiro to Leslie Glass's April Woo and S. J. Rozan's Lydia Chin, in New York). African American writers and characters are particularly prominent and range from Walter Mosley's Easy Rawlings to Eleanor Taylor Bland's suburban Chicago homicide detective Marti MacAlister.

It should come as no surprise that a Mystery writer excels at summing up the genre. In *Blood Work*, writer Michael Connelly describes Mysteries as follows: "Everything is ordered, good and bad clearly defined, the bad guy always gets what he deserves, the hero shines, no loose ends. It's a refreshing antidote to the real world."[63] This is what readers look for, the pattern they seek when they request Mysteries.

NOTES

1. Agatha Christie, *The Murder of Roger Ackroyd* (New York: Dodd, Mead, 1926).
2. Donna Leon, *Death at La Fenice: A Novel of Suspense* (New York: HarperCollins, 1992).
3. Carol O'Connell, *Mallory's Oracle* (New York: Putnam, 1994).
4. Sir Arthur Conan Doyle, *The Memoirs of Sherlock Holmes* (1893; reprint, New York: Ballantine, 1975).
5. Doyle, *The Return of Sherlock Holmes* (New York: A. Wessels, 1907); Laurie R. King, *The Beekeeper's Apprentice; or, On the Segregation of the Queen* (New York: St. Martin's, 1994).
6. Rex Stout, *Too Many Cooks* (New York: Farrar and Rinehart, 1938).
7. Janet Evanovich, *One for the Money* (New York: Scribner, 1994).
8. Robert Crais, *The Watchman: A Joe Pike Novel* (New York: Simon and Schuster, 2007).
9. Tony Hillerman, *Thief of Time* (New York: Harper and Row, 1988).
10. John Burdett, *Bangkok 8* (New York: Knopf, 2003).
11. Virginia Rich, *The Cooking School Murders* (New York: Dutton, 1982).
12. Diane Mott Davidson, *Catering to Nobody* (New York: St. Martin's, 1990).
13. James Lee Burke, *The Tin Roof Blowdown* (New York: Simon and Schuster, 2007).
14. Laura Lippman, *Baltimore Blues* (New York: Avon, 1997).
15. Sue Grafton, *"A" Is for Alibi: A Kinsey Millhone Mystery* (New York: Holt, 1982).
16. Grafton, *"K" Is for Killer* (New York: Holt, 1994); Grafton, *"N" Is for Noose* (New York: Holt, 1998); Grafton, *"O" Is for Outlaw* (New York: Holt, 1999).
17. Crais, *Sunset Express* (New York: Hyperion, 1996).
18. Lippman, *No Good Deeds* (New York: Morrow, 2006).
19. Marcia Muller, *Till the Butchers Cut Him Down* (New York: Mysterious Press, 1994).
20. Emily Melton, review of *Last Act in Palmyra* by Lindsey Davis, *Booklist*, March 15, 1996, 1242.
21. Lindsey Davis, *The Silver Pigs* (New York: Crown, 1989).
22. Steven W. Saylor, *Roman Blood* (New York: St. Martin's, 1991).
23. Patricia Cornwell, *Postmortem* (New York: Scribner, 1990).
24. Michael Connelly, *Closers* (New York: Little, Brown, 2005).
25. Archer Mayor, *The Ragman's Memory* (New York: Mysterious Press, 1996).

26. Ed McBain, *Hark! A Novel of the 87th Precinct* (New York: Simon and Schuster, 2004).
27. Bruce Alexander, *Blind Justice* (New York: Putnam, 1994).
28. Robert van Gulik, *The Haunted Monastery* (New York: Scribner, 1969).
29. Laura Joh Rowland, *Shinju* (New York: HarperPaberbacks, 1996).
30. Dorothy Cannell, *The Thin Woman: An Epicurean Mystery* (New York: St. Martin's, 1984).
31. Joanne Fluke, *Chocolate Chip Cookie Murder: A Hannah Swensen Mystery* (New York: Kensington, 2000).
32. Jonathan Gash, *The Grail Tree* (New York: Harper and Row, 1979).
33. Jonathan Kellerman, *Monster* (New York: Random House, 1999).
34. Donna Andrews, *Murder, with Peacocks* (New York: Thomas Dunne Books, 1999).
35. Julia Spencer-Fleming, *In the Bleak Midwinter* (New York: Thomas Dunne Books, 2002).
36. Lilian Jackson Braun, *The Cat Who Could Read Backwards* (New York: Dutton, 1966).
37. John Dunning, *Booked to Die: A Mystery Introducing Cliff Janeway* (New York: Scribner, 1992).
38. Edna Buchanan, *Contents under Pressure* (New York: Hyperion, 1992).
39. Lawrence Block, *Burglars Can't Be Choosers* (New York: Random House, 1977).
40. Elizabeth Peters, *The Jackal's Head* (New York: Meredith Press, 1968).
41. Peters, *Crocodile on the Sandbank* (New York: Dodd, Mead, 1975).
42. Christopher Fowler, Bryant and May Mysteries beginning with *Full Dark House* (New York: Bantam, 2004).
43. Kim Harrison, *Dead Witch Walking* (New York: HarperTorch, 2004).
44. Sharon Kay Penman, Eleanor of Aquitaine series, beginning with *The Queen's Man: A Mystery* (New York: Holt, 1996).
45. Peters cited above.
46. Joan Hess, Claire Malloy series, beginning with *Strangled Prose* (New York: St. Martin's, 1986).
47. Susan Wittig Albert, *Thyme of Death* (New York: Scribner, 1992).
48. Robert B. Parker, *The Godwulf Manuscript* (Boston: Houghton Mifflin, 1973).
49. King cited above.
50. King, *A Grave Talent* (New York: St. Martin's, 1993).
51. Nevada Barr, *Hunting Season* (New York: G. P. Putnam's Sons, 2002).
52. Anne Perry, *The Cater Street Hangman* (New York: St. Martin's, 1979).
53. Perry, *The Face of a Stranger* (New York: Fawcett, 1990).
54. Stephen J. Cannell, *The Tin Collectors: A Novel* (New York: St. Martin's, 2001); William Caunitz, *One Police Plaza* (New York: Crown, 1984); Michael Grant, *Line of Duty* (New York: Doubleday, 1991); W. E. B. Griffin, *Men in Blue* (New York: Jove, 1991); T. Jefferson Parker, *The Blue Hour* (New York: Hyperion, 2000); Joseph Wambaugh, *The Golden Orange* (New York: Morrow, 1990).
55. Laurell K. Hamilton, Anita Blake series, beginning with *Guilty Pleasures* (New York: Ace, 1993); Hamilton, Meredith Gentry series, beginning with *A Kiss of Shadows* (New York: Ballatine, 2000); Stephen Brust, Vlad Taltos series, beginning with *Jhereg* (New York: Ace, 1983).
56. James L. Swanson, *Manhunt: The Twelve-Day Chase for Lincoln's Killer* (New York: HarperPerennial, 2007).
57. Hamilton cited above.
58. Umberto Eco, *The Name of the Rose*, trans. by William Weaver (San Diego: Harcourt Brace Jovanovich, 1983).
59. Iris Johansen, Eve Duncan series, beginning with *The Face of Deception* (New York: Bantam, 1998).
60. Isaac Asimov, Robot series, beginning with *I, Robot* (New York: Doubleday, 1950).

61. Bill Bass and Jon Jefferson, *Death's Acre: Inside the Legendary Forensic Lab of the Body Farm Where the Dead Do Tell Tales* (New York: G. P. Putnam's Sons, 2003).

62. Loren D. Estleman, Page Murdock series, beginning with *The High Rocks* (Garden City, NY: Doubleday, 1979).

63. Connelly, *Blood Work* (Boston: Little, Brown, 1998), 131.

12

PSYCHOLOGICAL SUSPENSE

Imagine almost any Alfred Hitchcock film that you have enjoyed, and you understand the attraction of Psychological Suspense. These are books that play with our minds, that create a frisson of unease, that blend the creepiness generated by the Horror genre with the tension inherent in Suspense. These are stories that appeal to a range of readers—and filmmakers—and don't fit easily in any related genre into which we try to slot them.

Many genres lend themselves to comparisons between book and film representations, and Psychological Suspense is no exception. Hitchcock is the film master of this genre, but many examples of film noir—those dark, atmospheric, artistic explorations of madness and corruption—please fans of these books as well. Like the movie versions, novels of Psychological Suspense cast the reader in the role of fascinated observer, almost a voyeur, as we compulsively follow these tales of elegantly twisted plots and minds, of obsession and sometimes revenge, and of characters trapped in their own personal nightmares.

A DEFINITION

If ever there were a group of books that is neither fish nor fowl, this is surely it. Called Suspense, Thrillers, Horror, Mystery, and sometimes just Psychological Fiction, these titles are genre orphans. I have arbitrarily chosen *suspense* as the operative noun, because that term implies the building excitement these books generate, even though they are not fast-paced in the same way that Suspense genre titles are.

Much fiction, especially Literary Fiction, draws on psychological theories and motivations to propel the story and define the characters. In Psychological Suspense that tradition is clearly evident, but these stories center on the psychological impact. Although not truly Suspense, that term emphasizes the impact of these books, with their building tension and claustrophobic feel. Novels of Psychological Suspense create worlds of unease and potential disaster in which characters explore their options and their obsessions, while the reader observes from the outside. In this way they fit firmly in the genres that appeal to the intellect. Masters of the genre create disturbing tales of unbalanced minds, and as we readers observe in morbid fascination, we are pulled into their nightmare worlds. These are puzzles that explore the mind and its inner workings in troubling tales of heart-racing suspense.

These are novels that produce a chill. They play with our minds in very disturbing ways and leave us wondering about characters, as well as the resolution of the plot. In many ways, these books are closer to Horror and to that genre's effect on readers, rather than to Suspense or Thrillers. Because they often portray characters beset by guilt for imagined or accomplished acts, these stories inexorably draw readers into those nightmares. The internal, psychological monsters created by these authors engender a sense of uneasiness that can be just as disquieting as that produced by the monsters of the Horror genre. These nightmare stories, by writers such as Ruth Rendell/Barbara Vine, evoke a very chilling terror that is more interior but no less harrowing than that produced by Horror.

These books are not clinical studies of particular psychoses. Diagnosis is not the issue in these stories, nor is treatment. Thus, some authors who deal with psychological motivations, such as Jonathan Kellerman and Stephen Walsh White in their popular Mystery series, really do not fit within this genre. Although their books are certainly psychological, they are far more clinical than the titles that exemplify Psychological Suspense. They deal with identification of neuroses and the crimes that often relate to affected victims; thus, the tone is different as well. Novels of Psychological Suspense deal with the psyche, and there is a sense that there is no cure for or solution to the psychological difficulties. The fact that these neuroses may not even be recognized or acknowledged pervades these stories and drives both characters and plot. See figure 12.1 for a list of the genre's characteristics.

CHARACTERISTICS AND THE GENRE'S APPEAL

Story Line

These novels play with our minds. They depict the slow but sure discovery that something is dreadfully wrong in this seemingly normal world and

---

Figure 12.1 *Characteristics of Psychological Suspense*

---

1. Elaborately constructed plots are the hallmark of these stories, which are characterized by frequent twists (both mental and plot), surprises, and layers of meaning. Endings may be unresolved.

2. These books create a world of mental nightmares, and that chilling, disturbing tone drives the stories and keeps the readers off balance.

3. The interior workings of the mind—even madness—frame these stories, and leave readers on edge, straddling the line between sanity and unreason.

4. Protagonists are often misfits, who may or may not be sympathetic characters. Readers observe the characters rather than participate in their predicaments.

5. Writing style is important in creating this disturbing mood, and these novels are often elegantly written.

6. The pacing is more measured and the physical action less intense than in Suspense novels. These are often densely written novels with more description than dialogue.

---

that the demons that haunt the protagonist (and disturb us as observers) are surely psychological. Henry James's classic "The Turn of the Screw," with its chilling tale of a young governess's tenuous grip on reality, exemplifies this tradition.[1] Sometimes it is not until the very end that we, and the protagonist, recognize that this unsettling feeling that has plagued us throughout is really something more, and certainly more terrible, than we imagined.

Tangled plots and layered stories characterize Psychological Suspense. Although there is less physical action, there are no fewer twists of plot, and authors pride themselves on the levels of meaning they create. We readers either add layer upon layer of information to discover the truth of the disturbing situation, or we peel these layers away as we delve deeper and deeper into the story. Several titles by Thomas H. Cook demonstrate this layering technique. He creates haunted protagonists, forced to explore lurid secrets that expose their own pasts as well as the mysteries they investigate. In *Into the Web* an English professor at a small California college comes home to face his dying father in Kingdom County, West Virginia, and the repercussions of an old crime.[2] More sympathetic than many protagonists of Psychological Suspense, Roy Slater wrestles with mental as well as physical demons in this complicated, layered, and atmospheric story of families and their secrets.

As in Literary Fiction, the endings of Psychological Suspense may be unresolved. This adds to the unease generated by the story: Authors raise troubling issues, create disturbed and disturbing characters, and then leave the reader to wonder at the outcome. In her neo-Gothic novel *The Keep* Jennifer Egan not only spins a story within a story, but leaves the reader unsure of the outcome of both plotlines.[3] In one thread, cousins reunite at a crumbling castle in central Europe, ostensibly to rebuild it but perhaps to reenact one's betrayal by the other in their youth, and in the other, a convict presents the first story in a prison writing class. The question of what is real and what is "story" is only one of the unsettling questions that makes this so compelling and leaves the reader wondering about the veracity of characters as well as events.

Tone/Mood

The tone created by the author is almost as important as story in driving the action. Authors create mental nightmares, with much of the action in the mind, and that haunted feeling keeps both protagonists and readers off balance. Words such as *moody, claustrophobic, bleak, edgy, evocative, ominous,* and *foreboding* describe this menacing atmosphere. Carol Goodman consistently develops story lines with this haunting quality and strong sense of foreboding. In *The Lake of Dead Languages,* for example, the atmosphere dominates the intricately plotted tale.[4] Goodman offers crimes and tragedies, past and present, and interweaves these stories set in a private school in upstate New York to create a real sense of menace for Jane, a former student who returns to her old school as a Latin teacher, only to be forced to confront secrets from her past which impinge on the present. The key to the unease inherent in books in this genre is found in the way the author creates the atmosphere. These are often stories of nightmares and madness. *Unsettling* is another term frequently used to describe them.

Frame/Setting

Since these novels explore the inner workings of the often unstable protagonist's mind, madness often frames the stories. The protagonist may start out in the normal world of everyday, but something goes awry, and we watch as he is trapped, mentally at least, in a nightmare world that may be inescapable. Madness, whether overt or initially undetected, often plays an essential role in Psychological Suspense, and it draws the reader into that fine line between sanity and madness. Best known for his writing in other genres, Mystery writer Dennis Lehane delved into Psychological Suspense with *Shutter Island*.[5] Moody and atmospheric, the masterful novel creates a strong sense of foreboding as two U.S. marshals search for a patient missing from a mental hospital for the criminally insane. Readers know from the beginning that there is more to the story than this investigation, but even at the end, with its startling conclusion, we may not be certain exactly what has happened. Dreams and nightmares, the possibility of illegal research, and the dangers of an approaching hurricane all add to a devastatingly complex, mind-bending reading experience—not to mention the question of which character is really mad.

Characterization

Protagonists in this genre are not the well-rounded, likeable heroes of other fiction, but misfits, sometimes as much antiheroes as heroes, and they may not be particularly sympathetic. Writers, however, pull us into their lives and their dilemmas. We stay on the fringes of the action, observing their efforts rather than participating in their plights. The appeal of the characters is intellectual, focusing on the question of what they might do next, rather than an emotional connection.

Classic Psychological Suspense author Patricia Highsmith frequently underlines the reader's ambivalent feelings toward the protagonist. In *The Talented Mr. Ripley,* for example, we feel uneasy with the protagonist from the very first, and by the last scene, when we realize both that he has escaped detection and that this amoral "hero" will continue on the path he has set for himself, we are aware of a terrible sense of foreboding.[6] We may not enter his consciousness, but we are certainly victims, mentally at least, of the nightmare he has created—one that lives on beyond the story and that we are powerless to stop. In his series starring a troubled forensic psychologist, Keith R. Ablow has created another type of antihero protagonist. Frank Clevenger battles a wide range of addictions as well as inner demons as he aids police in their investigations. His introspective musings and sometimes unorthodox methods make this a compelling but disturbing series. *Denial* is the first.[7]

Style/Language

The writing style employed in Psychological Suspense is often elegant and seldom pedestrian. As are writers of Literary Fiction, with which this genre overlaps, these authors are stylists. Every word is important, and they carefully choose how sentences are framed. In many cases, these are shorter books; the sense of menace is encased in a spare, often poetic prose style. The style effectively sets the tone of these books and draws readers in. Authors often differentiate characters and mood by typeface, and diaries, journals, or e-mail and instant messages may be used to underline the menace. In Joyce Carol Oates's *Zombie*, the protagonist, a convicted child molester, offers crude drawings and random capitalization that reflect his unbalanced mind.[8] Oates often writes with a psychological twist, but this novel in particular is a compelling example of the unstable character and edgy style that typify the genre. *Zombie* feels like Diane Arbus's photography, although more violent. Like Arbus, Oates builds on the banal and ordinary; resulting depictions are slightly askew but others, like this, are clearly disturbing.

Pacing

Pacing in this genre is measured. Mental activity, rather than physical action, drives these stories, and as a result the plot may move slowly, but the books remain compelling, engrossing reading. Highsmith is a master of this style. In the much-imitated *Strangers on a Train*, two men meet by accident and, as strangers might do in those circumstances, tell their darkest secrets.[9] Unluckily for the unsuspecting Guy, Bruno has a solution to Guy's problematic marriage: If each kills the person who is creating insuperable problems in the other's life, each will commit the perfect crime and never be caught. Unfortunately, such a scheme never works quite as planned, and here murder creates a spiraling nightmare in which Guy becomes trapped. Suspense, although slower paced than exemplars of that genre, figures prominently, but action is limited. What grips the reader is the sense of how out of control the story, started with so straightforward an act, quickly becomes. The dark, menacing atmosphere pervades the story, as does the sense that the outcome is inescapable. And unlike the Adrenaline genres, here Guy fights more for his soul than his life. Highsmith's writing parallels the movies of Alfred Hitchcock and the classic stories of Edgar Allan Poe.

KEY AUTHORS

Ruth Rendell stands out as an exemplar of this genre. Although she has also written an award-winning Mystery series featuring Inspector Wexford, her Psychological Suspense, written both in her own name and her pseudonym Barbara Vine, sets the standard for the genre. Claustrophobic, intimate glimpses into lives ruled by obsession and characters in crisis, these haunting stories remain with us long after we close the book. Her novels often feature two or three separate story lines, each with its own dysfunctional protagonist, and their convergence can only lead to disaster. *13 Steps Down* is a recent example of her skill.[10] Elderly Gwendolyn Chawcer rents a room in her crumbling house to Michael "Mix" Cellini, a seemingly ordinary repairer of exercise equipment, who is obsessed with both John Reginald Halliday Christie, an infamous murderer in post–World War II London, and with a contemporary supermodel. What makes this such a chilling study of the mind of a murderer is the matter-of-fact tone in which the tale is related. Both protagonists are haunted by ghosts, real or imagined, and by dreams that invade reality. Rendell's well-crafted stories create worlds of menace and danger where obsession reigns among the mundane.

Other popular authors worth exploring in this genre include Peter Abrahams, Carol Goodman, Jeffry P. Lindsay, and Minette Walters. Twists dominate Abrahams's hypnotic novels; plot twists and twisted characters drive crime stories that are interior and chilling. In *End of Story* the naive heroine and budding author Ivy Seidel takes a position teaching a writing class for prison inmates, only to become infatuated with one.[11] Convinced that talented Vince Harrow could not be guilty of the terrible crimes for which he is incarcerated, she begins investigating—and finds herself in terrible danger. Readers have seen Harrow's facade peeled away layer by layer and we recognize the menace and danger long before she does, which adds to the chilling effect of the novel. Secrets from the past, cinematic plots, and obsessive characters fill Abrahams's nightmarish novels.

Goodman writes an image-rich prose filled with mythical and magical allusions. Favorite themes involve the existence of evil, magic, and myth contrasted with reality, along with a fascination with secrets from the past. In *The Seduction of Water,* myth and reality blend in stories within a story, as heroine Iris Greenfeder pursues secrets from her famous mother's past.[12] It all begins when she assigns her adult English class to take a personally important fairy tale and retell it. As an example, she retells the selkie myth her mother so often shared with her, and this spurs her to return to the upstate New York hotel where her mother died and where Iris plans to write her biography. The secrets she uncovers prove more dangerous than she expects.

In a lighter vein (although dominated by very black humor) Lindsay explores the life and times of Dexter Morgan, a detective and splatter analyst for the Miami police department. Dexter is, in fact, a serial murderer of serial murderers. He gets his information from the police department and only pursues the really bad guys. Amusing in a very twisted way, his first-person accounts reveal the curious workings of a very devious and amoral mind, and these novels play with our minds and our perceptions of morality. *Darkly Dreaming Dexter* is the first of these novels, which have become the basis of a popular television series.[13]

Although many of us classify her as a writer of Mysteries, Minette Walters also fits with writers of Psychological Suspense. Her powerful, atmospheric stories blend the puzzle of a Mystery with elements of Psychological Suspense: open endings, complex but unbalanced characters, psychological implications, and an elegant style that leaves the reader distanced, forced to play observer. In *The Chameleon's Shadow* a British veteran of the war in Iraq struggles to overcome the effects of a terrible brain injury and facial mutilation.[14] Although we certainly sympathize with Charles Acland, there's also that niggling possibility that in his less lucid moments he is the serial murderer terrorizing London. As do many of Rendell's novels, this work lacks an omniscient narrator, so we see events from multiple perspectives, and we're never quite certain where truth lies. This adds to the nightmare quality of the story and its telling. Although Walters's books often feature a mystery to be solved, they focus more on the psychological, and the mystery is simply one of the elements that make up these unsettling novels.

WHAT WE KNOW ABOUT FANS

Readers of Psychological Suspense appreciate dark stories with psychological undertones. Although they may call these books Psychological Novels or Psychological Suspense, fans may also refer to them as Mysteries, Thrillers, Suspense, or Horror. When they talk about what they enjoy, however, we recognize the books they seek. They expect books that grip them with intense, interior stories and elegant prose, and provide disturbing, open endings.

These are also readers who may read a range of books across genres to find the elements they seek. They are likely familiar with the psychological slant of titles in Mystery, Thrillers, Suspense, Horror, and Literary

Fiction and, like readers of Literary Fiction, may be willing to experiment with new authors as long as their expectations and standards are met.

Fans appreciate well-drawn characters that they can observe from afar. Although they like details of lives and predicaments, they do not expect to be drawn in, to sympathize or even empathize with characters, as in some genres. These readers enjoy being observers of others' lives and obsessions. They expect to be distanced from the characters so that they might watch them, evaluate their strategies, and speculate on their success or failure, especially because so many of these novels are unresolved at the end.

Atmospheric stories also appeal to these readers. They anticipate a carefully drawn, detailed setting that also hints at a darker mood. Books in this genre are often leisurely paced, in part because the detailed setting and mood slow the action, which itself is often interior. Plot isn't as important as quirkiness—in characters and story lines—and readers prize the exquisite, atmospheric chill produced by these novels.

Although twisted plots are often a characteristic of these story lines, readers also look for the intensity that underlines the mood and action. These are not generally fast-paced, but they do exert a tremendous pull on readers. Seldom graphically violent, they more often suggest gruesome ends than show them. Readers look for the building of tension and the layers of meaning that make these such powerful and gripping stories.

Popular, recurring themes are revenge and secrets from the past which reemerge to haunt, and often imperil, the protagonist. Titles published recently that reflect an increased interest in Gothic have more in common with Psychological Suspense and Horror than with Romance and Romantic Suspense. Readers' advisors can safely suggest Jennifer Egan's *The Keep* with its gloomy setting in an old castle plus a ghost; Carol Goodman's *The Drowning Tree,* with its isolated setting, mysterious events, and menacing landscape; Diane Setterfield's *The Thirteenth Tale* with its supernatural elements and secrets from the past; or Dan Simmons's *The Terror,* historical adventure with a distinct Gothic twist, to a range of Psychological Suspense fans.[15] Currently a common theme developed by authors in this genre involves prison writing programs. It's easy to see how this theme lends itself to this genre—haunted, dysfunctional characters, dark and gloomy settings, stories in which the reader is never certain where the truth lies. Popular authors Goodman (*The Seduction of Water*) and Abrahams (*End of Story*), as well as Egan (*The Keep*), have all employed this motif to create edgy, layered tales. Keep an eye out for individual reviews as well as themes that suggest titles that might be good choices for these fans.

See figure 12.2 for authors of Psychological Suspense who might introduce this genre to readers of other genres.

THE READERS' ADVISORY INTERVIEW

When we work with readers, we always ask them to describe books they have enjoyed and listen for clues in preparing to suggest possible titles. In Psychological Suspense especially, we can listen for particular words that suggest that this is the genre readers want. Do they describe disturbing books that deal with obsessions? Do they mention layers of meaning? Do they allude to a haunting quality? If so, titles in this genre would be a good choice. However, sometimes readers will do better describing films that reflect this genre's appeal. Asking about film interests as well as books often leads us into good crossover suggestions—and highlights both our book and film collections.

Figure 12.2   *An Introduction to the Psychological Suspense Genre*

Psychological Suspense Writers to Try, If You Enjoy . . .

Adrenaline:	Peter Abrahams
Fantasy:	Jonathan Carroll
Historical Fiction:	Thomas H. Cook
Horror:	Jennifer Egan
	Stephen King (*Misery* and *Gerald's Game*)[16]
	Joyce Carol Oates (*Zombie*)[17]
Humor:	Jeffry P. Lindsay (Dexter series)
Inspirational:	Charles Williams
Literary:	Carol Goodman
	Ruth Rendell
Mystery:	Keith R. Ablow
	Michael Robotham
	Minette Walters
Romantic Suspense:	Carol Goodman
True Crime:	Val McDermid
Women's Lives:	Nicci French (*Beneath the Skin*)[18]
	Philippa Gregory (*The Little House* and *Zelda's Cut*)[19]

Many titles are labeled Psychological Suspense, but most of these focus on psychologists as characters, rather than the atmosphere and dysfunctional characters that make up titles in this genre. Since this is not a recognized genre, most readers won't request it by name. Only through their descriptions of the types of books that they enjoy are we tipped off to their interest. Classic authors, from M. R. James to Patricia Highsmith, are often good suggestions. Don't forget Daphne du Maurier, one of whose short stories became Hitchcock's "The Birds," and her *Rebecca* should be on every fan's must-read list.[20] Short story collections, especially those that cross with Dark Fantasy and Horror, are also a good source of these unsettling tales.

Keeping a list of authors who write in this genre is the best fail-safe—and the best preparation to work with readers. The Sure Bets below, as well as the other authors discussed in this chapter, make a good place to start.

Sure Bets

In this, as in all genres, there are authors who appeal consistently to fans and are good suggestions for others whom we suspect may also enjoy the genre. Philippa Gregory, better known for her popular historical novels, has also written Psychological Suspense. *The Little House* is an excellent example of her skill in presenting a young wife and her domineering mother-in-law, with a satisfying twist at the end.[21]

Val McDermid writes an unsettling Mystery/Suspense series featuring criminologist Tony Hill and police detective Carol Jordan, and while titles in this series might appeal to Psychological Suspense readers, her stand-alone titles are Sure Bets. In the award-winning *Place of Execution* a young girl has disappeared from her home in a small town in northern England in the early 1960s.[22] The inspector assigned to the case is obsessed by it, but despite his efforts, he never discovers her fate. Then thirty years later a journalist revisits the case, and writes a "true crime" take on the murder, stirring up simmering tensions in the closed community and exploring layers of secrets past and present. Intriguing characters and an atmospheric setting add to this memorable story.

Michael Robotham writes genre-blending novels of Mystery and Psychological Suspense with his series featuring a British psychologist diagnosed with Parkinson's disease and a hard-boiled British cop. Neither character is always likeable, or necessarily to be trusted, but they form a sort of alliance as they work through cases to which both are drawn. The first, *Suspect*, follows psychologist Joe O'Loughlin, who is falsely accused in a murder case.[23] His inner musings, along with the edgy atmosphere and strong sense of foreboding, should please genre fans.

EXPANDING READERS' HORIZONS WITH WHOLE COLLECTION READERS' ADVISORY

Every reader in every genre reaches the point when that genre does not offer enough of interest. They are ready for a change, but they may not want to range too far afield. That is when we examine the genre and think about ways that it links to other genres and to authors within those genres.

As is clear from the previous discussion, there is extensive crossover appeal to other genres for fans. Readers of Psychological Suspense find numerous writers of Mysteries who meet their requirements. Suggest Caleb Carr's murky tales set in turn-of-the-century New York City (*The Alienist*), Elizabeth George (*A Great Deliverance*), and P. D. James (especially *Original Sin*) with their dark, psychological stories of detection.[24]

Many writers in the Adrenaline genres might please readers. A range of Thrillers should satisfy, from the classic, interior stories of Graham Greene and John le Carré to those of someone like Mo Hayder, whose *Pig Island*, although faster-paced than most Psychological Suspense, provides manipulative characters, a strong sense of foreboding, disturbing relationships, and a satisfying twist at the end.[25] Dean R. Koontz's *Intensity* and *Velocity* are also much faster-paced, but they, too, offer the introspective characters and chilling tales that keep readers off balance.[26] Serial killer novels often cross over with Psychological Suspense, even though the pacing is usually at odds. However, there is no denying that Thomas Harris's *Hannibal* would be of interest to readers of Psychological Suspense.[27] Hannibal Lecter, the looming menace whose presence pervades *The Silence of the Lambs*, is the hero here (or, more appropriately, the antihero), and the manner in which Harris manipulates readers, pulling us into the story so that we sympathize with the man we know we should despise, will fascinate fans of Psychological Suspense.[28]

Literary Fiction, with its elegantly written and often provocative plots, offers other possibilities. *The Ghost*, a departure for Robert Harris, who is better known for his historical novels, provides a moody consideration of a recent British prime minister and the ghostwriting of his memoirs.[29] Harris plays with the idea of ghost—there's the original ghostwriter, his replacement, and the ghosts of the prime minister's alleged crimes—and establishes a chilling tale of politics. Many of the novels of Joyce Carol Oates and Haruki Murakami will also resonate with fans of this genre. Some of the Science Fiction written by the provocative philosophical writers—Roger Zelazny, Robert Silverberg, and Gene Wolfe, for example— also provide the psychological emphasis, the elegant prose, and the open endings fans of this genre prize. And certainly Anne Rice's earlier Horror titles would be a possibility, with their interior glimpses into the minds and lives of vampires and ghouls.

In nonfiction too, there are authors who may appeal to Psychological Suspense fans. Since so many novels focus on crimes and criminals, True Crime is a good suggestion. Writers such as Ann Rule and Erik Larson, who explore the minds and motives of the criminals as well as the crimes, might satisfy readers. Susan Orlean's *The Orchid Thief*, an elegant, true tale of obsession and natural history makes a good suggestion, as does the movie version.[30] Speaking of obsession, Augusten Burroughs's fascinating memoirs are another possibility.

See figure 12.3 for additional authors to suggest to take readers beyond the genre.

TRENDS

In this genre—which is essentially an amalgamation of others—genre blending continues to dominate. Novels of Psychological Suspense overlap with Horror, Thrillers, Suspense, and Romantic Suspense, as well as Literary Fiction. Elements may also drive some nonfiction, as in True Crime investigations, in which the psyche of the killer is as important as the crime.

Many popular authors dabble in this genre. Suspense writer Laurie R. King and Mystery author Kate Wilhelm have several novels that should appeal to fans of Psychological Suspense. Suggest King's *Keeping Watch* and Wilhelm's *The Deepest Water*.[31] Stephen King's *Misery* and *Gerald's Game* are also good suggestions.[32] Not only will the individual titles please fans, the suggestions may introduce them to the other works by authors whom they might enjoy.

Fans of Psychological Suspense value these carefully crafted stories for their spare, elegant prose. Not a word or image is ever wasted. As in the

---

Figure 12.3 *Expanding Readers' Horizons*

Authors to Take Readers beyond the Psychological Suspense Genre

Adrenaline:	Thomas Harris
	Mo Hayder
	Greg Iles
	Dean R. Koontz
	Val McDermid (Tony Hill and Carol Jordan series)[33]
Biography/Memoir:	Augusten Burroughs
	John Lahr (*Prick Up Your Ears: The Biography of Joe Orton*)[34]
Fantasy:	Stephen King (Dark Tower series)[35]
History:	Ludovic Kennedy (*10 Rillington Place*)[36]
Horror:	Shirley Jackson
	Anne Rice
Literary:	Ian McEwan
	Arthur Phillips
Mystery:	Caleb Carr
	Elizabeth George
	P. D. James
	Carol O'Connell
	Fred Vargas
Natural History:	Susan Orlean
Romantic Suspense:	Kay Hooper
Science Fiction:	Gene Wolfe
	Roger Zelazny
Travel:	John Berendt
True Crime:	Erik Larson
	Ann Rule
Women's Lives:	Alice Sebold

---

best short stories, every piece is important and adds a layer of knowledge and tension for the reader. And although style is certainly important to readers, they relish the twist at the end even more. Much is not really as it appears in novels of Psychological Suspense, and its many fans enjoy both the presentation and the unraveling of the puzzle, which leads into the troubled minds of the protagonists.

NOTES

1. Henry James, "The Turn of the Screw" (New York: Heritage Press, 1949).
2. Thomas H. Cook, *Into the Web* (New York: Bantam, 2004).
3. Jennifer Egan, *The Keep* (New York: Knopf, 2006).
4. Carol Goodman, *The Lake of Dead Languages* (New York: Ballantine, 2002).
5. Dennis Lehane, *Shutter Island* (New York: Morrow, 2003).
6. Patricia Highsmith, *The Talented Mr. Ripley* (New York: Vintage, 1992). Originally published in New York by Coward-McCann, 1955.
7. Keith R. Ablow, *Denial* (New York: Pantheon, 1997).
8. Joyce Carol Oates, *Zombie* (New York: Dutton, 1995).
9. Highsmith, *Strangers on a Train* (New York: Harper, 1950).
10. Ruth Rendell, *13 Steps Down* (New York: Crown, 2004).
11. Peter Abrahams, *End of Story: A Novel of Suspense* (New York: Morrow, 2006).
12. Carol Goodman, *The Seduction of Water* (New York: Ballantine, 2003).
13. Jeffry P. Lindsay, *Darkly Dreaming Dexter* (New York: Doubleday, 2004).
14. Minette Walters, *The Chameleon's Shadow* (New York: Knopf, 2008).
15. Egan cited above; Goodman, *The Drowning Tree* (New York: Ballantine, 2004); Diane Setterfield, *The Thirteenth Tale* (New York: Atria, 2006); Dan Simmons, *The Terror* (New York: Little, Brown, 2007).
16. Stephen King, *Misery* (New York: Viking, 1987); King, *Gerald's Game* (New York: Viking, 1992).
17. Oates cited above.
18. Nicci French, *Beneath the Skin* (New York: Mysterious Press, 2000).
19. Philippa Gregory, *The Little House* (New York: HarperCollins, 1996); Gregory, *Zelda's Cut* (New York: St. Martin's, 2000).
20. Daphne du Maurier, *Rebecca* (Garden City, NY: Doubleday, 1938).
21. Gregory cited above.
22. Val McDermid, *Place of Execution* (New York: St. Martin's Minotaur, 2000).
23. Michael Robotham, *Suspect* (New York: Doubleday, 2005).
24. Caleb Carr, *The Alienist* (New York: Random House, 1994); Elizabeth George, *A Great Deliverance* (New York: Bantam, 1988); P. D. James, *Original Sin* (New York: Knopf, 1994).
25. Mo Hayder, *Pig Island* (New York: Atlantic Monthly Press, 2006).
26. Dean R. Koontz, *Intensity* (New York: Knopf, 1995); Koontz, *Velocity* (New York: Bantam, 2005).
27. Thomas Harris, *Hannibal* (New York: Delacorte, 1999).
28. Harris, *The Silence of the Lambs* (New York: St. Martin's, 1988).
29. Robert Harris, *The Ghost* (New York: Simon and Schuster, 2007).
30. Susan Orlean, *The Orchid Thief* (New York: Random House, 1998).
31. Laurie R. King, *Keeping Watch* (New York: Bantam, 2003); Kate Wilhelm, *The Deepest Water* (New York: St. Martin's Minotaur, 2000).
32. King cited above.
33. McDermid, Tony Hill/Carol Jordan series, beginning with *The Mermaids Singing* (New York: HarperCollins, 1995).
34. John Lahr, *Prick Up Your Ears: The Biography of Joe Orton* (New York: Knopf, 1978).
35. Stephen King, Dark Tower series, beginning with *The Gunslinger* (West Kingston, RI: Donald M. Grant, 1982).
36. Ludovic Kennedy, *10 Rillington Place* (London: Victor Gollancz, 1961).

13

SCIENCE FICTION

Science Fiction is a genre that strikes fear in the hearts of many librarians. If we do not read it, this genre seems as strange as the beings that populate the pages of its books. And Science Fiction readers often seem an exclusive club, into which it is hard for a nonfan to gain admission.

Upon further exploration, however, we are likely to find this a genre rich in both physical and intellectual adventure, with something to offer a wide range of readers. This vast genre, with roots in the nineteenth century, is respected by fans and others for its intellectual underpinnings, and its diversity offers a variety of interesting directions for readers to pursue. From Romance to Mystery and beyond, Science Fiction is an unexpected treasure trove of crossover authors and titles.

A DEFINITION

Although it seems that every genre overlaps others at some point, this problem is so pronounced with Science Fiction that even the experts disagree when they try to do something as basic as define it. When it comes to deciding whether or not a book fits within this genre (or Fantasy, the genre with which it most frequently overlaps), everything is up for grabs. One problem is that many of the genre's popular practitioners—Orson Scott Card, Lois McMaster Bujold, Ursula K. Le Guin, and C. J. Cherryh, to name a few—write both Science Fiction and Fantasy. Card suggests, facetiously, we might use cover art to differentiate between Science Fiction and Fantasy. If there are rivets on the cover, the book is Science Fiction. If there are trees on the cover, it is Fantasy.[1] An interesting approach, but it likely says more about publishers and their covers than about the genres! Another difference suggested by Science Fiction fans is that Science Fiction is the left brain reaching out to the right brain (logic reaching toward the artistic) while Fantasy is the opposite. Unfortunately, neither distinction is particularly helpful when we are working with patrons or cataloging books.

As a basic definition, it is probably safe to say that Science Fiction posits worlds and technologies which *could* exist. Science, rather than magic, drives these speculative tales, and the science must be accurate and true to key axioms of Newtonian (classical) and relativistic physics. The following explanations of the characteristics of the genre will expand on this definition. Of course, each reader will bring his or her own definition to any discussion of books that fall within the Science Fiction genre—especially in this genre in which readers are vocal and opinionated. See figure 13.1.

CHARACTERISTICS AND THE GENRE'S APPEAL

Story Line

Science Fiction is speculative fiction that appeals to the reader's intellect. As Betty Rosenberg suggested in the first edition of *Genreflecting*, "Science fiction has been labeled a fiction of questions: What if . . . ? If only . . . ? If this

---

Figure 13.1 *Characteristics of Science Fiction*

---

1. This is speculative fiction, frequently set in the future. It explores moral, social, intellectual, philosophical, and/or ethical questions against a setting outside of everyday reality.

2. Setting is crucial and invokes otherness of time, place, and/or reality. Both the physical setting of the story and the inherent technical and scientific detail create this essential frame.

3. From the jargon of Cyberpunk to the lyrical language of some classic tales, Science Fiction offers a range of styles and language crafted to suit the story line and to reinforce the intellectual and speculative nature of the genre.

4. Titles reflect a wide range of tone or mood from dark to comic. Tone is often used to disorient readers and to highlight the issues considered.

5. Authors use characters to underscore issues and atmosphere. Aliens and otherworldly creatures emphasize the otherness of these stories.

6. The focus of the story drives the pacing. If there are more adventure elements and physical action, the pacing is usually faster; if ideas are emphasized more, the book generally unfolds at a more leisurely pace.

goes on . . . ?"[2] Questions such as these characterize the premise behind these books. As speculative fiction, these books consider moral, social, and ethical issues while exploring philosophical, technical, and intellectual questions. Science Fiction is a fertile ground for the discussion of challenging and often controversial issues and ideas, and authors use it expressly for that purpose. Science Fiction introduces an almost overwhelming richness of concepts and ideas. Other fiction genres may also raise difficult questions, but in Science Fiction, authors take a precept, perception, or idea and explore it, often in a setting outside our own world or in a future time, but certainly out of everyday contexts. For example, on one level Orson Scott Card's *Ender's Game* is a coming-of-age story set in the future.[3] The reality of the story is much more, as Ender unknowingly plays a key role in the war to save the human race and the planet from invaders. A further level requires the reader to consider philosophical issues, such as moral and social questions about society, as well as more general questions about power and authority. Subsequent titles in the series have an even greater philosophical emphasis. As is the case with much Science Fiction, this is a book to be read and appreciated on many levels.

Although telling a good story is clearly the aim of most books in all genres, here the authors emphasize creating inviting stories in which to make the ideas they promote interesting and accessible. Some titles are cinematic, and readers can readily imagine these books as movies or television series, as, in fact, some of them are. Look at Lois McMaster Bujold's series featuring Miles Vorkosigan, physically weak and deformed, who must continually prove his military prowess and acumen to keep his position as a rising military leader on Barrayar. This ongoing series features Bujold's characteristic wit and even romantic touches, as we follow Miles's exploits, always confident that he will survive threats to his reputation as well as his life.

In others, ambiguity is the key. Questions are raised, but there are seldom clear-cut answers to what is right and what is wrong. Even the ending may be uncertain, with issues and questions left unresolved. Characters face difficult, sometimes impossible, choices, as is certainly the case in Mary Doria Russell's *The Sparrow,* which features a Jesuit priest/scientist, "safely" returned from another planet but mutilated physically, mentally, and emotionally, his core beliefs and motivations shredded by the different reality and worldview he has been forced to experience.[4]

Removing readers from what is safe and known forces them to think differently when considering the available possibilities, to see things as they might be—to consider "what if," not just what is or what they know.

This otherness of time, place, or reality is crucial to the appeal of Science Fiction. The reader is taken from the known world to the unknown, to another world or time. Kay Kenyon's Entire and the Rose series (*Bright of Sky* is the first) is not just another Adventure tale, although that is certainly part of its appeal.[5] Set both on our world in the future and on another world where the dangers, denizens, and politics all create an atmosphere foreign to our understanding, this series requires its Earth-based hero—and readers—to see worlds differently and to develop new strategies to face the exotic landscape and dangers.

As a consequence of this speculative nature, Science Fiction also affirms the importance of Story in our lives and the importance of imagination in the survival of the species. In *Great Sky River* Gregory Benford speculates that only "dreaming vertebrates" know life holds more than just existence.[6] We are part of that group, and these writers imagine our dreams and those of other species and validate their importance in our lives. Small wonder that much Science Fiction deals with the idea of dreams and dreaming as a true means of communication or as an actual parallel reality.

Science Fiction is often series-centered. Because of the complexity of the worlds and cultural situations they conceive, authors tend to use them more than just once, creating continuing characters that people that world, or at least setting further adventures within their unique environment. The special problems created for libraries in terms of retaining all within a series and keeping up on series are discussed below.

Frame/Setting

Science Fiction is consistently evocative and visual. It is not surprising that the Golden Age of Science Fiction, its first real flush of popularity, was also the age of radio, a time when listeners were accustomed to using their imagination to visualize settings, characters, and events. In Science Fiction, authors create and populate new and alternative worlds, and they have to be able to describe the alien nature of the worlds they create and the beings that inhabit them to place us there.

It goes without saying that technical and scientific details are also an important part of the genre's appeal. However, there is a great deal of current Science Fiction in which hard science, hardware, and technology, although important, do not dominate the novels as they did in the 1950s, when scientifically accurate technology was the key to most Science Fiction. It came as a surprise to me to realize that one need not have an extensive scientific background to understand and enjoy much of what is currently being written in the genre. Even writers of so-called Hard Science Fiction add enough plot and frame to make their novels understandable to the science-challenged, following the tradition largely established by Isaac Asimov, who had a gift for integrating ideas into stories that could be appreciated on several levels. In the same vein, Robert Charles Wilson relies heavily on scientific detail in his award-winning *Spin* and its sequel *Axis,* but the stories also depend on richly developed characters (including inscrutable aliens) and plot elements familiar to Thriller readers so that scientific knowledge is not crucial in appreciating these titles.[7]

Style/Language

Readers of Science Fiction shouldn't be surprised to discover the diverse styles employed by writers in this genre. For example, in Cyberpunk (those cynical tales of a negative high-tech future in which humans are not necessarily the highest life-forms, science may not be our salvation, and somehow the universe has gone awry), which emerged in the late 1980s, language was idiomatic, jargon-filled, and often incomprehensible to the uninitiated at first glance. The otherness of the worlds or futures in which these books were set was underlined by the disorienting effect of the language. In fact, the use of language seemed sometimes to create a kind of word game or wordplay, another aspect of Cyberpunk's appeal. We have to be "in the know" to understand and relate to the language. Neal Stephenson, the natural heir to William Gibson and the Cyberpunk tradition, is known both for his unique style and flamboyant language. He artfully combines Literary Fiction's language and style with Historical and Science Fiction in his Baroque Cycle, which explores scientific thought and personages in the early eighteenth century (*Quicksilver* is the first).[8]

Writing styles run the gamut in this genre. In *The Carpet Makers* Andreas Eschbach employs a stylized language that gives the feel of a parable to his far-future tale.[9] Octavia E. Butler's elegant, lyrical writing contrasts with Robert Sawyer's more conversational, sometimes slapdash style. All relate fascinating science fiction tales, but readers may be more attracted to the language and style of one and less fond of another.

Tone/Mood

There is a wide range of tone in this "otherness" in which Science Fiction is set. There's the adjective-rich, romantic tone of Catherine Asaro and Anne McCaffrey, the wacky exuberance of Douglas Adams and the humor of Robert Asprin, the jaunty tone of Joe Haldeman's *The Accidental Time Machine,* contrasted with the dramatic, thoughtful tone projected in the novels of Kathleen Ann Goonan and Kim Stanley Robinson.[10]

As does the language in some Science Fiction, the tone also plays on the genre's appeal to the intellect. Tone may disorient (or reorient) readers, taking them outside their comfort zones and forcing them to reimagine situations and events in other contexts. In Ian McDonald's *Brasyl,* for example, the edgy, violent, bleak tone flows through all three time periods—1732, 2006, and 2030—and intensifies the effect of the issues raised in this nonlinear story.[11] Conversely, emulating the tone of Victorian-era authors helps bring readers into the world and times of Tarzan in Philip José Farmer's fictional biography, *Tarzan Alive: A Definitive Biography of Lord Greystoke.*[12]

Characterization

Science Fiction focuses on ideas and setting. The moral, social, and philosophical questions considered in the genre are woven into the story line and are often pursued through the action, situations, and events rather than through characters. Although attention is paid to characterizations in the more literary end of the genre, generally the issues, story, and frame are emphasized more. In his numerous Alternative History series, Harry Turtledove creates an elaborately detailed alternate Earth, rich in characters that are not quite right and story lines that are just a little off from what we know to be fact. The intellectual satisfaction of sorting out his puzzles is great, and readers marvel at the universe he has created, but despite the somewhat familiar characters, these novels are about ideas, not people.

On the other hand, the variety of characters makes Science Fiction an excellent source of books about "others." Whereas other genres have expanded to include multicultural protagonists as well as gay and lesbian characters, Science Fiction has long been a place to find these characters—

and almost any type one can imagine. Characters may not dominate here, but they certainly come in a wide enough variety of sizes, shapes, colors, motivations, histories, and beliefs to appeal to and to intrigue a broad spectrum of readers. And, as in Mysteries, readers follow characters throughout a series.

Pacing

Action in Science Fiction may be interior (more philosophical or psychological) or exterior, with more action and adventure elements included. Pacing is usually determined by the amount of action. Titles in which there is more physical action are usually seen as fast-paced by fans. Others may be described as *engrossing* or *compelling,* but the emphasis on more interior action and speculation may mean that they are actually read at a slower pace. To get a sense of this distinction, compare the popular Honor Harrington series by David Weber, which moves at a brisk pace with action spurring the reader on, to Octavia E. Butler's densely written, provocative Parable series, in which the philosophical emphasis makes the books engrossing but slows the reader's pace.[13]

KEY AUTHORS

Although it is important for us to be familiar with classic authors—Isaac Asimov, Arthur C. Clarke, Robert Heinlein—whose writing still influences readers and writers alike, it is to current authors that we look for new directions in the genre. While classic, established, and newer authors are mentioned throughout this chapter, two newer authors, Kathleen Ann Goonan and Richard K. Morgan, stand out as representative of interesting and contrasting directions in the genre. Goonan, perhaps best known for her series of four books that explore the effects of nanotechnology and a nanotech plague on humanity, gracefully merges hard science with lyrical prose, creating dark, character-focused stories that explore ethical questions in a science-dominated world. Her award-winning Alternate History, *In War Times,* offers a sympathetic hero caught up in a complex tale that begins on the eve of the attack on Pearl Harbor in 1941.[14] Soldier Sam Dance, an expert in electronics and jazz, receives plans for a machine that could end this war—and all wars—and transform human nature. The novel features enough science to satisfy that audience but the importance of the character and story make this a good suggestion for general readers as well.

Goonan drew from her father's World War II diaries in creating Dance's fictional diary, and these details add depth to the character and his task.

Richard K. Morgan's cinematic novels combine adventure, futuristic violence, complex issues, and a dark, almost noir tone. *Thirteen* features a genetically engineered fighting machine as the protagonist.[15] His mission is to destroy the remaining hybrid hit men, but he is now a man made to kill who doesn't want to play anymore. The influence of Cyberpunk is unmistakable. This moody, unsettling story includes the relentless action-filled pacing of a man on a mission as well as thoughtful and insightful analysis of his nature and his purpose.

Don't forget the continuing popularity of those prolific authors who fall between the classic and new poles. Anyone desiring an appreciation of the genre should become familiar with Ursula K. Le Guin (*The Lathe of Heaven*), Connie Willis (*Doomsday Book*), Orson Scott Card (*Ender's Game*), Kim Stanley Robinson (Mars trilogy), Lois McMaster Bujold (Vorkosigan series), and Neal Stephenson (*Snow Crash*).[16]

WHAT WE KNOW ABOUT FANS

Fans of Science Fiction are among the most elusive yet outspoken readers who use our libraries. Elusive, because they often spurn our offers of assistance and certainly our suggestions; outspoken, because they know what they are seeking and they feel it is unlikely that we can offer them new directions—unless they see us as fellow fans (and far too few of us qualify in that role). If we are able to make contact, however, we find them voluble on this subject. They know what they like—the "good" Science Fiction—and ignore, or even reject, everything else. They expect us to have new titles by their favorite authors as soon as they learn about them (which may be long before they are even written) and demand that we have all in a series that they enjoy. "Out of print" and "unavailable" are terms that do not exist in their vocabulary.

This means that we librarians need to be diligent and persistent in seeking out and then keeping all titles in a series. Science Fiction book clubs and some publishers help by reprinting these volumes, but obtaining and retaining all titles in a series remain difficult. Because many early titles, and some titles in current series, have been published only in paperback, the issue of keeping copies becomes even more problematic, although Science Fiction paperbacks do tend to stay in print longer than their counterparts in the Romance genre. However, if your library is small and your shelf space is limited, do try to have the first few and the most recent in popular series. Science Fiction readers are old hands at using interlibrary loan to feed their reading habits—and it's a nice way for library staff to develop a working relationship with these somewhat elusive patrons.

Asked to share suggestions for what should be added to our collections, Science Fiction fans are always ready to provide long lists of titles, authors, and series that every self-respecting library should own. If we ask for suggestions to develop our collection, we do so at our peril. This technique should not be risked unless we have a healthy budget and shelf space to support extensive additions to our collection!

The shared worlds of the Science Fiction and Fantasy genres create another problem for libraries. Do we catalog additions to the endless Star Trek series under the names of individual authors or under the series? If you do the former, you must not have many readers asking for the newest book in the series or for a particular title by number! It only took us a few weeks one summer, working with teen after teen, ourselves new to the Science Fiction collection and exploring that series, to convince us that the only hope was to catalog and shelve all series under the series name, rather than the individual authors, so they would be shelved together. Now readers can easily find all within a series—and so can we!

Knowing something about Science Fiction, even if we have only read one or two books, makes us more comfortable talking to fans and makes them more comfortable relating to us. They see that we understand what it is that they love in this genre. As in every genre, we need to encourage fans to talk to us. We ask them about the authors they currently enjoy reading and of what other books or authors a particular title reminds them. Fans are usually effusive when asked about the authors they enjoy.

Although it may be difficult to suggest titles to fans, especially if we are not fans ourselves, it takes no more than a cursory exploration of the genre to discover titles and series that might be of interest to fans of other fiction genres. Many Science Fiction titles might appeal to readers of other genres who would never think of choosing Science Fiction on their own. (When we suggest them, however, we do better if we describe their appeal first and the ways in which they parallel a reader's taste before revealing that they are Science Fiction. Genre labels both attract and repel readers; connections made without the encumbrance of labels often help readers see beyond the genre classification to the appeal of the book.) Those librarians who are not Science Fiction fans might approach the task of becoming familiar with the genre this way as well. See figure 13.2.

Figure 13.2 *An Introduction to the Science Fiction Genre*

Science Fiction Writers to Try, If You Enjoy . . .

Adrenaline:	William C. Dietz
	L. E. Modesitt
	Richard K. Morgan
	David Weber
Biography/Memoir:	Steven Brust and Emma Bull (*Freedom and Necessity*)[17]
Fantasy:	Lois McMaster Bujold
	Ursula K. Le Guin
	Andre Norton
Gay/Lesbian:	Samuel R. Delany
	Joanna Russ
Gentle Reads:	Andre Norton
Historical Fiction:	Connie Willis
	Kage Baker (*In the Garden of Iden*)[18]
History:	Michael Flynn (*Eifelheim*)[19]
Horror:	Kate Wilhelm (*The Dark Door*)[20]
Humor:	Douglas Adams (Hitchhiker series)[21]
	John Scalzi
Inspirational:	Jerry Jenkins
	Madeleine L'Engle
	C. S. Lewis
	Bill Myers
Literary:	John Crowley
	William Gibson (*Neuromancer*)[22]
	Michael Swanwick (*Vacuum Flowers*)[23]
	Gene Wolfe
	Roger Zelazny (*The Dream Master*)[24]
Mystery:	Isaac Asimov (Robot books)[25]
	Paul Levinson (Phil D'Amato series)[26]
	Richard K. Morgan (Takeshi Kovacs series)[27]
	Timothy Zahn (Frank Compton series)[28]

(cont.)

Figure 13.2   *An Introduction to the Science Fiction Genre (cont.)*

Multicultural:	Andreas Eschbach
	Nalo Hopkinson
	Linda Nagata
Natural History:	Greg Bear (Darwin series)[29]
	Michael Crichton
	Kim Stanley Robinson
Psychological Suspense:	Mark Budz (*Till Human Voices Wake Us*)[30]
	Jack Finney (*Invasion of the Body Snatchers*)[31]
	Stanislav Lem
Romance:	Catherine Asaro
	Susan Grant
	Sharon Shinn
Saga:	C. J. Cherryh
	Frank Herbert
	David Weber
True Crime:	Robert Asprin and Linda Evans (Time Scout series)[32]
	Harry Turtledove (*The Man with the Iron Heart*)[33]
Westerns:	Bruce Boxleitner (*Frontier Earth: Searcher*)[34]
Women's Lives:	Octavia E. Butler
	Marge Piercy
	Pat Murphy

THE READERS' ADVISORY INTERVIEW

Working with fans in Science Fiction is a little different than in other genres. As I mentioned earlier, fans of Science Fiction tend to be among the most knowledgeable and opinionated readers I have encountered. They often have definite ideas about what they like and do not like, and although they may listen politely, they are not usually interested in our suggestions. (Admittedly, it is difficult to suggest to fans of any genre, unless we are also fans; they have always read more than we have. However, fans in most other genres don't seem as adamant about their taste as these.) On the other hand, Science Fiction fans are always very happy to share suggestions of authors and titles every civilized reader should have read. Thus, the dialogue with these readers is slightly different from that with readers looking for suggestions and ideas. (Their attitude may have been fostered by the sometimes-too-clear evidence that we librarians really do not know and appreciate the authors they love. They may have reason to distrust our offer of assistance.)

As always when we talk with readers looking for suggestions, the key is to get them to tell us what they enjoy most in the books they have read. For readers who talk about characters and action, I might suggest the novels of classic authors such as Frank Herbert and Isaac Asimov or of newer writers such as David Weber, Lois McMaster Bujold, and Richard K. Morgan. Those who describe Science Fiction more in terms of the ideas or the mood are more likely to enjoy Ursula K. Le Guin, Philip K. Dick, Kathleen Ann Goonan, and Gene Wolfe.

Movies and television series also make a useful jumping-off point in exploring what someone is in the mood to read. There are tie-ins written as companions to many television series and movies, and many current novels and classics have been the basis of recent dramatizations.

In Science Fiction, short stories remain a popular form—among fans, critics, and authors. Short story collections also provide a good introduction to the genre for nonfans (librarians and readers alike), and award-winning or critically acclaimed anthologies are good purchases for libraries, especially those on a tight budget. Readers can then pursue single titles by authors they enjoy through interlibrary loan. Collections of Nebula Award stories and *The Year's Best Science Fiction* are particularly good examples, but many thematic collections are published every year.[35]

Science Fiction attracts teen readers as well as adults. This may be because of the strong adventure element in many novels or because many authors choose teen protagonists. As in Horror, Science Fiction often features teenagers in control of their lives and their destinies. Unlike Horror, there is generally less graphic sex and violence here, especially in pre-twenty-first-century novels, and these may be "safer" reading in that sense—but not if parents are concerned that these younger readers might be led into new ways of thinking and seeing the world. Another important appeal may be that these stories also examine ideas—social, political, philosophical—in varying degrees of intensity. Readers appreciate the opportunity to probe the issues they see in the world, even if, in Science Fiction, they are set in a context outside their own. Orson Scott Card's Ender series, as well as several by Willis, Herbert's classic *Dune,* and most of Lois McMaster Bujold's Vorkosigan series, feature adolescent protagonists, but based on what appeals to the teen reader, any of the authors and titles already discussed might make good choices.[36]

Unless we are longtime fans of the genre or have a truly excellent source of prepublication information, we find it almost impossible to make suggestions to fans. Many have read for years and know more about the genre than we can ever hope to discover. A useful technique is to pump readers for information about the genre and favorite authors and use their suggestions to discover authors that might appeal to readers new to the genre or to fans of other genres. Fans like to be acknowledged but not necessarily assisted. On the other hand, if they have been away from the genre for a few years, they like to be made aware of new authors they may have missed. We occasionally have readers who come home from college with time to read again, and they like to be updated on trends in the genre. In general, this group is genuinely interested in learning about new authors linked to their favorites, so once we've developed an ongoing relationship with Science Fiction fans, we can cultivate them by paying particular attention to reviewers' comments about newer or first-time novelists. Reference sources can help them—and us—keep up to date.

While we certainly keep and promote Science Fiction classics, they may not be quite the draw for younger readers that they are for adults who want to reread old favorites. Each generation honors its own classic authors, and in this genre especially, ideas may be outdated, a fact which will put off some readers. We make classic titles available, but we must also keep an eye out for the next generation of classics.

Sure Bets

As in all genres, there are Science Fiction titles that appeal to a wide range of readers, even those who read outside this genre. Two that come immediately to mind are Card's *Ender's Game* (described above) and Mary Doria Russell's *The Sparrow*. In Russell's novel, scientists have identified signals from a planet in another galaxy: music, a sure sign of sentient life. And because they have access to money and personnel, Jesuit scientists mount a mission to make first contact, but only one returns. As the book opens we meet the damaged space traveler, and then, through a series of flashbacks interspersed with real time, we learn the terrible story of his mission. Layer upon layer the story builds, and we discover the harrowing truth of the group's experiences during their stay on the planet. Through the character of Father Emilio Sandoz we see what happened, and, in our reaction to him and his plight, we explore the book on a deeper level. We see into his mind and share his anguish as the story unfolds and the truth emerges. This title makes an excellent choice for a library book discussion.

Despite its size, Herbert's *Dune* is surprisingly accessible and enjoyed by a wide range of readers who simply appreciate a good Adventure story—and can ignore the sandworms if they seem too preposterous. Herbert wrote several Dune titles, and his son Brian, joined by Kevin J. Anderson, continues the series. Ray Bradbury's chilling *Fahrenheit 451* reaches readers on other levels beyond the Science Fiction themes, as does Walter M. Miller Jr.'s classic, *A Canticle for Leibowitz,* which combines black humor with the details of a postapocalyptic world.[37] The recent upsurge in interest in Alternate Histories makes Harry Turtledove's many series as well as Neal Stephenson's Baroque Cycle excellent suggestions. And if humor is the universal language, Piers Anthony, Roger Zelazny, Douglas Adams, and Spider Robinson offer a range of possibilities.

EXPANDING READERS' HORIZONS WITH WHOLE COLLECTION READERS' ADVISORY

Just as there are many Science Fiction authors who might appeal to nonfans, so there are a number of interesting directions in which we might steer Science Fiction fans seeking to explore other genres. First, keep in mind that many Science Fiction writers also write in other genres. The greatest crossover is with Fantasy; authors such as Bujold, Card, and Le Guin have popular series and fans in both. Other authors—Anne McCaffrey and Marion Zimmer Bradley—sit on a fine line between Science Fiction and Fantasy. They say they write Science Fiction but in my library at least, their books, with the almost magical dragons and laran, appeal more to Fantasy readers than to fans of Science Fiction. Still other authors, Chelsea Quinn Yarbro and Dan Simmons, for example, write Science Fiction and Horror.

There is much in Literary Fiction to appeal to Science Fiction aficionados. Haruki Murakami, Thomas Pynchon, and William Burroughs are good suggestions for fans of Cyberpunk and cutting-edge Science Fiction, as these authors also feature experiments with words and interesting, provocative language. The very nature of Literary Fiction with its provocative story lines parallels much of Science Fiction, and many authors cross over easily. Michael Chabon's *The Yiddish Policemen's Union* and its playful reimagining of genre conventions might also make an interesting suggestion as an Alternate History Mystery.[38]

Romance and Romantic Suspense offer a surprising amount of crossover as well. Just as Romance readers read Science Fiction for the satisfying love interest as well as for the strong, well-developed female protagonists,

Science Fiction readers who appreciate these elements are beginning to find authors they enjoy in the Romance genre. With the increased popularity of Alternate Reality Romance novels, this trend continues to grow. Suggest Linnea Sinclair's space-set military romances and J. D. Robb's Romantic Suspense with a futuristic detective story (*Naked in Death* is the first).[39] Diana Gabaldon's popular Time Travel/Alternate History Romance series starting with *Outlander,* which follows a twentieth-century nurse drawn back to eighteenth-century Britain and America, may also work for some readers.[40]

Science Fiction's world-building emphasis makes it a good candidate for the Landscape genres, especially Fantasy. Readers who appreciate the emphasis on the details of the author's world in Science Fiction might also relate to the equally careful constructions of Fantasy worlds by writers such as Raymond E. Feist and Robert Jordan.

In addition to crossover with appeal elements from Science Fiction to other genres, there is also crossover of themes. Militarism is one of the popular themes of Science Fiction that readers will find in many other genres, especially Thrillers. Weber or Morgan fans will find much to appreciate in Techno-Thriller writers such as Dale Brown. Those fascinated with postapocalyptic literature should certainly try Cormac McCarthy's chilling take on this theme, *The Road,* or Jim Crace's *The Pesthouse.*[41] Many Medical and Scientific Thrillers overlap with Science Fiction; readers should be aware of authors such as Greg Bear and Michael Crichton, as well as F. Paul Wilson. Nanotechnology is another rich field for Science Fiction and Thrillers, not to mention quirky peripheral titles like MaryJanice Davidson's Gorgeous series featuring a bionic female spy.[42] Artificial intelligence, a frequent Science Fiction theme, also appears in Thrillers (Greg Iles's *The Footprints of God* and Dean R. Koontz's *Demon Seed*), and even Donna Andrews's humorous Turing Hopper Mystery series (starting with *You've Got Murder*).[43]

Nonfiction may make a good match for some readers, especially those who seek the facts behind the scientific speculation posited in this genre. Since Science and Science Fiction both seem to move at warp speed, readers may be astonished to discover that their favorite authors are just a step or two ahead of scientists at some points and at other times their work builds on recent scientific discoveries. Accessible Science writers such as Richard Rhodes, Stephen J. Gould, and Stephen Hawking delve into the implications of scientific discoveries. See figure 13.3 for more suggestions.

Figure 13.3 *Expanding Readers' Horizons*

Authors to Take Readers beyond the Science Fiction Genre

Adrenaline:	Dale Brown
	Michael Crichton
	Clive Cussler
	Stephen Spruill
Biography/Memoir:	Richard Feynman
Fantasy:	Orson Scott Card
	Raymond E. Feist
	Robert Jordan
Historical Fiction:	Gore Vidal
History:	Dava Sobel
Horror:	Max Brooks (*World War Z*)[44]
	Richard Matheson
Literary Fiction:	Michael Chabon
Natural History/Science:	David Bodanis
	Richard Rhodes
Psychological Suspense:	Tess Gerritsen
Romance:	Jayne Castle
	Susan Grant
	Lyndsay Sands
	Linnea Sinclair
Romantic Suspense:	Linda Howard (Raintree trilogy)[45]
	J. D. Robb
Westerns:	Ishmael Reed (*Yellow Back Radio Broke-Down*)[46]
Women's Lives:	Margaret Atwood

TRENDS

Science Fiction remains a vital genre, adapting to scientific discoveries and political events. Environmental concerns have long been championed in this genre, and that trend continues. Kim Stanley Robinson continues to set the standard for raising ecological issues, but other writers such as Anne McCaffrey and Elizabeth Ann Scarborough in their Twins of Petaybee novels and John Barnes in his Century Next Door series have also addressed these problems.[47]

Artificial intelligence (AI) and nanotechnology are current popular themes that fascinate readers and writers alike. From Asimov's robots to Iain M. Banks's sophisticated—and unusual—computers and ships, writers have imagined a fascinating race of thinking machines that help and hinder mankind. Goonan's Nanotech Cycle and Thriller-writer Michael Crichton's *Prey* and others point up the dangers, while Catherine Asaro explores the possibility of human/AI cooperation and even the development of romantic relationships in her near-future suspense titles (*The Veiled Web, The Phoenix Code, Sunrise Alley,* and its sequel *Alpha*).[48] Other authors to know include David Marusek, Kage Baker, Neal Stephenson, and John Barnes.

Interest in Alternate Histories remains high. Although some books that explore this topic are really Fantasy because they employ magic (Card's popular Alvin Maker series, considered in chapter 14, "Fantasy," is a prime example), most Alternate History novels fit here, in recognition of their speculative nature. "What would have happened if . . ." is the question these authors pose. This popular theme has been explored by a range of authors from contributors to the Star Trek series, who often play with Earth's history on other worlds (John Vornholt's *Masks,* part of the Star Trek, the Next Generation series, is one example) to Dick's award-winning *The Man in the High Castle,* a searching story of America's prospects if Germany and Japan had won World War II and partitioned the country.[49] Another practitioner of this type of Science Fiction is Harry Turtledove, who popularized these stories among general readers with his novels of victory by the South in the Civil War (*The Guns of the South: A Novel of the Civil War*).[50] His Great War series is an excellent example of his style and use of history. His recent World War II series, beginning with *Into the Darkness* and featuring dragons and magic, is more Fantasy than Science Fiction.[51]

Genre blending is rife here, as in other genres. Crossover with Fantasy, Mystery, Romance, Thrillers, and Horror adds interesting elements to all these genres and attracts fans from across the spectrum. Authors continue to write in many genres, and when they return to Science Fiction, they bring ideas that influence the direction of the genre.

Space Opera and Military Science Fiction are also experiencing a resurgence of popularity. Weber, Asaro, Elizabeth Moon, Bujold, Brian Herbert, William C. Dietz and Linnea Sinclair are authors to remember.

Graphic novels offer new possibilities for Science Fiction, as well as a means of renewing interest in classic titles and themes. Graphic novelists have reinterpreted a broad range of titles from the cartoon superheroes and media series (X-Files and Star Wars) to classic titles (Philip K. Dick's *A Scanner Darkly*) and original titles (Frank Miller's Sin City, Alan Moore's Watchmen series, Brian Vaughan's Y the Last Man series).[52]

Science Fiction offers an amazing range of appeal, from adventure and relationships among characters facing philosophical and ethical questions on one end, to the elegant style, fully realized characters, and strong speculative bent on the other, and much in between. In general Science Fiction engages the reader's intellect. It deals with "why," with philosophical speculation, as well as with "where," with a futuristic setting outside of the usual—with alien beings as well as alien and unorthodox concepts. It cherishes the unexpected, in terms of setting, characters, and plot, and it is generally thought-provoking and prides itself on its ability to raise challenging questions. The most successful examples can challenge the reader to question his or her concept of reality.

NOTES

1. Orson Scott Card, untitled luncheon speech at Public Library Association Preconference, March 28, 2000.
2. Betty Rosenberg, *Genreflecting* (Littleton, CO: Libraries Unlimited, 1982), 173.
3. Card, *Ender's Game* (New York: Tom Doherty, 1985).
4. Mary Doria Russell, *The Sparrow* (New York: Villard, 1996).
5. Kay Kenyon, *Bright of Sky* (Amherst, NY: Pyr Books, 2007).
6. Gregory Benford, *Great Sky River* (New York: Bantam, 1987).
7. Robert Charles Wilson, *Spin* (New York: Tor, 2005); Wilson, *Axis* (New York: Tor, 2007).
8. Neal Stephenson, *Quicksilver* (New York: Morrow, 2003).
9. Andreas Eschbach, *The Carpet Makers* (New York: Tom Doherty, 2005).
10. Joe Haldeman, *The Accidental Time Machine* (New York: Ace, 2007).
11. Ian McDonald, *Brasyl* (Amherst, NY: Pyr Books, 2007).
12. Philip José Farmer, *Tarzan Alive: A Definitive Biography of Lord Greystoke* (Garden City, NY: Doubleday, 1972).
13. David Weber, Honor Harrington series, beginning with *On Basilisk Station* (Riverdale, NY: Baen, 1993); Octavia E. Butler, Parable series, beginning with *Parable of the Sower* (New York: Four Walls Eight Windows, 1993).
14. Kathleen Ann Goonan, *In War Times* (New York: Tor, 2007).
15. Richard K. Morgan, *Thirteen* (New York: Del Rey, 2007).
16. Ursula K. Le Guin, *The Lathe of Heaven* (New York: Scribner, 1971); Connie Willis, *Doomsday Book* (New York: Bantam, 1992); Card cited above; Stephenson, *Snow Crash* (New York: Bantam, 1992).
17. Steven Brust and Emma Bull, *Freedom and Necessity* (New York: Tor, 1997).
18. Kage Baker, *In the Garden of Iden: A Novel of the Company* (New York: Harcourt Brace, 1998).
19. Michael Flynn, *Eifelheim* (New York: Tor, 2006).
20. Kate Wilhelm, *The Dark Door* (New York: St. Martin's, 1988).

21. Douglas Adams, Hitchhiker series, beginning with *The Hitchhiker's Guide to the Galaxy* (New York: Harmony Books, 1979).

22. William Gibson, *Neuromancer* (New York: Berkley, 1984).

23. Michael Swanwick, *Vacuum Flowers* (New York: Arbor House, 1987).

24. Roger Zelazny, *The Dream Master* (Boston: Gregg Press, 1976).

25. Isaac Asimov, Robot series, beginning with *I, Robot* (Garden City, NY: Doubleday, 1950).

26. Paul Levinson, Dr. Phil D'Amato series, beginning with *The Silk Code* (New York: Tom Doherty, 1999).

27. Richard K. Morgan, Takeshi Kovacs series, beginning with *Altered Carbon* (New York: Ballantine, 2003).

28. Timothy Zahn, Frank Compton series, beginning with *Night Train to Rigel* (New York: Tor, 2005).

29. Greg Bear, Darwin series, beginning with *Darwin's Radio* (New York: Ballantine, 1999).

30. Mark Budz, *Till Human Voices Wake Us* (New York: Bantam, 2007).

31. Jack Finney, *Invasion of the Body Snatchers* (New York: Universal-Award House, 1955).

32. Robert Asprin and Linda Evans, Time Scout series, beginning with *Time Scout* (Riverdale, NY: Baen, 1995).

33. Harry Turtledove, *The Man with the Iron Heart* (New York: Del Rey, 2008).

34. Bruce Boxleitner, *Frontier Earth: Searcher* (New York: Ace, 2000).

35. *The Year's Best Science Fiction* (New York: St. Martin's, 2000).

36. Frank Herbert, *Dune* (Philadelphia: Chilton Books, 1965).

37. Ray Bradbury, *Fahrenheit 451* (London: Hart-Davis, 1954); Walter M. Miller Jr., *A Canticle for Leibowitz* (Philadelphia: Lippincott, 1959).

38. Michael Chabon, *The Yiddish Policemen's Union: A Novel* (New York: HarperCollins, 2007).

39. J. D. Robb, *Naked in Death* (New York: Berkley, 1995).

40. Diana Gabaldon, *Outlander* (New York: Delacorte, 1991).

41. Cormac McCarthy, *The Road* (New York: Knopf, 2006); Jim Crace, *The Pesthouse* (New York: Nan A. Talese/Doubleday, 2007).

42. MaryJanice Davidson, Gorgeous series, beginning with *Hello, Gorgeous!* (New York: Kensington, 2005).

43. Greg Iles, *The Footprints of God* (New York: Scribner, 2003); Dean R. Koontz, *Demon Seed* (New York: Bantam, 1973); Donna Andrews, *You've Got Murder* (New York: Berkley Prime Crime, 2002).

44. Max Brooks, *World War Z: An Oral History of the Zombie War* (New York: Crown, 2006).

45. Linda Howard, Raintree Trilogy, beginning with *Raintree: Inferno* (New York: Silhouette, 2007).

46. Ishmael Reed, *Yellow Back Radio Broke-Down* (Normal, IL: Dalkey Archive Press, 2000).

47. Anne McCaffrey and Elizabeth Ann Scarborough, The Twins of Petaybee series, beginning with *Changelings* (New York: Del Rey, 2006); John Barnes, Century Next Door series, beginning with *Orbital Resonance* (New York: Tor, 1991).

48. Michael Crichton, *Prey* (New York: HarperCollins, 2002); Catherine Asaro, *The Veiled Web* (New York: Bantam, 1999); Asaro, *The Phoenix Code* (New York: Bantam, 2000); Asaro, *Sunrise Alley* (Riverdale, NY: Baen, 2004); Asaro, *Alpha* (Riverdale, NY: Baen, 2006).

49. John Vornholt, *Masks* (New York: Pocket Books, 1989); Philip K. Dick, *The Man in the High Castle* (New York: Putnam, 1962).

50. Turtledove, *The Guns of the South: A Novel of the Civil War* (New York: Ballantine, 1992).

51. Turtledove, *Into the Darkness* (New York: Tor, 1999).

52. Dick, *A Scanner Darkly* (New York: Pantheon, 2006).

Part 4

Landscape Genres

14

FANTASY

Fantasy may be the most ubiquitous of the genres, as there are fantasy elements in most fiction, almost regardless of how realistic the story is. It is also an ancient form, the genre of myth and legend, as well as of the fairy tales and stories of our childhood. This is the world of faerie, and magic, sorcery, and enchantment all live on in Fantasy.

Like Westerns and Historical Fiction, Fantasy novels create specific landscapes. These are world-building books, and it is important that readers be able to see, hear, and feel the worlds in which the authors place them. Fantasy novels tell a wide range of stories, but the success of each is dependent upon the author's skill in creating a believable, albeit magical, world populated by characters to whom readers relate.

A DEFINITION

Like Science Fiction, with which it is most frequently linked, Fantasy is not easily defined in a single phrase or two. If Science Fiction emphasizes ideas, then Fantasy delves more into relationships. The stories it tells appeal more to the emotions than to the intellect. As does Science Fiction, Fantasy deals with otherness of time or place; settings may be contemporary or historical but something is out of kilter—the train platform in Eva Ibbotson's *The Secret of Platform 13* or the talisman that aids nurse Kitty McCulley in Elizabeth Ann Scarborough's *The Healer's War*.[1] Fantasy exists in a world that most people believe never could be, while Science Fiction worlds are those we accept as possible, even if improbable. Science Fiction generally offers something radically new and different, but Fantasy frequently takes a familiar story, legend, or myth and adds a twist, a new way of looking at things that brings it to life again. The key to Fantasy, however, is the presence of magic. If there is no magic, the story may fit in the Horror, Science Fiction, Romance, Historical Fiction, or Adventure genres. When magic is integral to the story, it must be Fantasy.

Although Fantasy most frequently overlaps with Science Fiction, there are significant links to Horror, Romance, and Adventure as well. Both Fantasy and Horror draw on everyday fears and feature realms and creatures that are larger than life and often not of this world. However, while Horror creates a nightmare situation in which characters strive to survive and temporarily defeat the evil, Fantasy is more affirming, giving protagonists a chance to win the battle against the dark and permanently end the reign of evil. Like Fantasy, Science Fiction presents a challenging unknown, but, unlike Fantasy, it offers technical explanations and ways to "know," to discover through science and empirical tests. One finds alternate realities in both Fantasy and Science Fiction, but in Fantasy these alternate universes and histories depend on magic, while in Science Fiction the roots are logical, not magical. Horror and Fantasy share an intuitive approach to the world, in contrast to the rational outlook of Science Fiction. Like Romance, Fantasy may have a romantic tone, and some stories certainly project the same emotional appeal, but magic supplants the romantic interest as the most important element. Adventure abounds in many types of Fantasy, but again it is secondary to the magical nature of the story. Figure 14.1 delineates the characteristics of the Fantasy genre.

CHARACTERISTICS AND THE GENRE'S APPEAL

Frame/Setting

In fantasy, it is clear from the start that things are not as the reader knows them from his own experience. The presence of magic or enchantment is the element that most clearly distinguishes Fantasy from other genres. The amount differs throughout the genre, but its presence, to some extent at least, ensures that readers understand they are in a Fantasy world. Magic may manifest itself in the existence of a magical sword or magical powers; there may be creatures that readers know can exist in none but a magical world; or there may be a feeling of otherness, a sense of enchantment that grows throughout the story. Just as Merlin practices magic in the myriad Arthurian tales, so do the fey folk of Charles de Lint's Urban Fantasy stories conjure up this otherworldliness that magic engenders. The presence of magic may be explicit, as in Arthurian stories and de Lint, or it may

---

Figure 14.1 *Characteristics of Fantasy*

---

1. Detailed settings depict another world, often Earth, but out-of-time or invisible to most people. Magic frames the story.

2. Story lines feature Good versus Evil, as protagonists battle and ultimately conquer the malevolent forces—although victory does not come easily or cheaply. Titles are frequently part of a series with a continuing story told over several books.

3. Mood ranges from humorous to dark, but it is ultimately optimistic. Despite this, a melancholy tone pervades much of the genre even when victory is achieved.

4. Characters, clearly defined as good or bad, often attain special magical gifts, and the story lines explore ways to discover one's own potential, magical or otherwise. Even good characters will find themselves challenged, both physically and ethically. Characters may include mythical creatures—dragons, unicorns, elves, wizards—as well as more familiar ones.

5. In general, books start slowly as the author sets the scene, presents the challenge, and introduces the cast—frequently involving a group of diverse characters who are brought together solely to fight a new or resurging evil in an unfamiliar world. Pacing increases later as more adventure elements appear.

6. From the stylized language of High Fantasy to the jargon of Urban Fantasy, language and style run the gamut. Language creates verbal pictures of characters and landscape, and illustrations sometimes enhance both adult and children's Fantasy.

---

simply be hinted at and expanded as the story develops. In Neil Gaiman's *Anansi Boys,* unless the reader is familiar with the trickster hero and specifically the West African legend of the Spider that frames the novel, this may simply seem a quirky coming-of-age tale.[2] Along with hero Fat Charlie Nancy, we gradually learn of his divine ancestry as the tale takes on a mythic dimension. Enchantment or magic may take unexpected forms, but if it drives the plot, this is Fantasy.

The emphasis on landscape and the creation of a fantasy world are crucial in this genre. Detailed settings ground the stories. These authors, referred to as *world builders,* create elaborate, easily visualized settings for their stories, whether for a single title or a series. Among these are classic authors such as Lloyd Alexander (The Chronicles of Prydain, of which *The*

Book of Three is the first), Ursula K. Le Guin (Earthsea Trilogy, beginning with *A Wizard of Earthsea*), and J. R. R. Tolkien's Lord of the Rings (*The Fellowship of the Ring* is the first of his trilogy).[3] Newer series by authors like Patricia Wrede (Lyra series, beginning with *Raven Ring*) and David Anthony Durham's Acacia series (*The War with the Mein* comes first) follow in this tradition.[4] Others use contemporary real-world settings, but alter them slightly to create that sense of otherwordliness. In Charles de Lint's Newford the real and unreal worlds intersect, and some characters live in both.[5]

Fantasy also features stories of alternate or parallel worlds. Unlike the alternative worlds discussed in chapter 13, "Science Fiction," here magic plays an important role and distinguishes these series from the speculative ones discussed there. Jasper Fforde's infinitely inventive series starring literary detective Tuesday Next in an alternate England features puns and endless literary references, as the heroine makes her way in and out of books that come alive, along with characters who have a fascinating existence outside the novels with which they're associated. *The Eyre Affair* is the first in this ongoing series.[6] Closer to home, Emma Bull has recast familiar Western themes in an alternate West peopled by familiar characters—Doc Holliday and Wyatt Earp—as well as young Jesse Fox, who possesses magical powers. There's humor here too, but provocative issues add to the thoughtful tone, as Bull's novel compels readers to rethink the Old West and its heroes. *Territory* is the first in this projected pair of novels.[7] Alternate medieval worlds offer common ground for many popular Fantasy series, including classics like Tolkien's Ring series, as well as Katherine Kurtz's Deryni Chronicles series.[8] Even alternate Napoleonic eras frame two popular Fantasies—Susanna Clarke's award-winning *Jonathan Strange and Mr Norrell* and Naomi Novik's Temeraire series, starting with *His Majesty's Dragon* and featuring sentient dragons.[9] All these create worlds that mirror our own but include a fascinating magical twist that makes them "other" Even though it is not a parallel world, the map of Piers Anthony's Xanth, which bears a startling resemblance to Florida, tends to make us more comfortable with the location, this "other" Florida. To these vaguely familiar settings we bring our own understanding of time and place, and the authors build on that knowledge in creating their magical worlds.

Another popular setting is developed in Urban Fantasy, which tends to be darker, despite the fact that it is sometimes characterized as elves on motorcycles! The emphasis on societal issues, power or its absence, and general urban blight contributes to the bleaker nature of these stories.

The classic Urban Fantasy author is Charles de Lint. Try *Memory and Dream*, part of his Newford series, as an introduction to this landscape.[10] A young artist's paintings release ancient spirits into the modern world with unpleasant results. Other well-regarded authors of Urban Fantasy include China Miéville (the New Crobuzon series—*Perdido Street Station* is the first) and Emma Bull, whose award-winning *War for the Oaks* recounts a war among fairies in modern-day Minneapolis.[11] Consider also Jim Butcher's Dresden Files, beginning with *Storm Front.*[12] Harry Dresden is a professional wizard and supernatural investigator who operates in an alternate Chicago in these dark though witty stories. Urban Fantasy produces haunting stories that can be appreciated on many levels.

Story Line

Fantasy is a genre of contrasts—good and bad, light and dark. In Horror a trace of the evil always survives to rise again, but in Fantasy there is the expectation of ultimate victory over evil forces, and that is very satisfying for fans. Fantasy is ultimately an optimistic genre, with the forces of good eventually conquering evil (although it may take several long books in a series to accomplish this). The pattern of the genre leads to a hopeful outcome, no matter how grievous the trials along the way.

In addition, Fantasy usually tells a continuous story, even if it is broken into sections and published in a series of separate books. (In contrast, Science Fiction is more likely to be episodic. Most Science Fiction novels in series relate a separate adventure, and these series are not as closely tied together as those in Fantasy.) Fantasy often tells a single story, but instead of being published as one unwieldy volume, it is broken into several, often leaving the reader hanging, waiting a year or more to take up the story again. (The end of the second volume of Tolkien's Lord of the Rings trilogy is a good example; the closing scene of *The Two Towers* is a literal cliffhanger, with Frodo hanging on for his life!) Other Fantasy series, such as Andre Norton's beloved Witch World or Weis and Hickman's Dragonlance saga, are composed of singletons, duets, trilogies, and more. All tell a single story and serve to form an all-encompassing history of the world the author has created.

Fantasy novels frequently involve a quest of some sort with a band of characters embarking on a dangerous mission and, after a series of adventures, succeeding in attaining their goal. Tolkien's Lord of the Rings is certainly the modern archetype of this story; however, although the quest appears in many forms, at the heart of the story the fate of the world (ours or that of the story) is always at stake, and the final confrontation involves a pitched battle against evil. Robin Hobb, a popular author of several quest trilogies, continues this tradition. Her characters come into their own powers and join the battle to save the world, as do Frodo, Gandalf, and their band in Tolkien's stories.

Another popular theme involves retellings of myths or fairy tales, as in the series edited by Terry Windling and featuring adaptations of fairy tales, some with modern settings. (In Jane Yolen's *Briar Rose,* the Sleeping Beauty story is reimagined in Nazi Germany.)[13] Another book of this type, John Connolly's *The Book of Lost Things,* incorporates several classic stories including familiar fairy tales, *The Wizard of Oz,* and *The Song of Roland.*[14] Arthurian legends are always popular, and although many of us catalog them in Fiction rather than with the Fantasy books, they certainly fit the criteria for Fantasy novels. How else would we classify Merlin, the ultimate magician; the treacherous sorceress Morgan le Fay; or the magical sword Excalibur? Many Arthurian stories also reflect the Fantasy genre's emphasis on coming-of-age stories, more generally showing youth coming into their own magical powers, and the retellings certainly exhibit a range in mood from Bernard Cornwell's dark Iron Age tales (beginning with *The Winter King*) to T. H. White's whimsical *The Once and Future King,* and much in between.[15] These reimaginings by Fantasy authors have rejuvenated other popular legends. Guy Gavriel Kay explores Norse, Anglo-Saxon, and Celtic legends in *The Last Light of the Sun,* while Jo Graham's *Black Ships* retells Aeneas's story after Troy.[16] Gregory Maguire may be the best known of the retellers, since *Wicked,* his version of *The Wizard of Oz,* told from the witch's point of view, became a hit Broadway musical![17]

Tone/Mood

Fantasy novels also provide various moods and tone. Although the genre is generally optimistic, an elegiac tone pervades many titles, as the victories are not accomplished without loss. Every Fantasy fan has mourned the death of a favorite character, one who has been sacrificed, albeit willingly and knowingly, to ensure victory. Still, the mood ranges from dark and bleak tales of Dark Fantasy and Urban Fantasy to uproariously humorous ones, with much in between.

At one end of the spectrum are Dark Fantasy novels that feature a bleak outlook. These are not Horror, but they are stories filtered through a dark worldview, where the stakes are seen as too high for much levity, and the price paid for victory is severe. Generally these are more atmospheric, more densely written, and directed toward weightier themes than their more humorous opposites. Stephen King's Dark Tower series is a good example (the first of these titles is *The Gunslinger*).[18] All elements combine to underline the mood of the book: short sentences, terse dialogue, desert landscape, and a haunted hero on an obscure mission (an anti-quest perhaps). As the hero explains, parodying Tolkien's words and theme, "There are quests and roads that lead ever onward, and all of them end in the same place—upon the killing ground."

Even Stephen R. Donaldson's leper antihero Thomas Covenant, whose story begins in *Lord Foul's Bane*, can hardly compete with King's hero for dark mood.[19] In contrast to King's sparse language, Donaldson employs more elegant, denser prose in describing Covenant's fate. In a story that harkens back to Samuel Taylor Coleridge's "The Rime of the Ancient Mariner" in tone and plot, Covenant, too, proves a reluctant hero. A man who does not understand his role and does not want to accept it, he is nevertheless sent on a mission to save the Land. Donaldson is now on his third series featuring Covenant, and the release of audio versions should increase his popularity.

In contrast, the Fantasy genre also features a number of popular series where humor is prominent, developed primarily through puns and other wordplay hijinks. Jasper Fforde's Thursday Next series offers this attitude, but his Nursery Crimes series takes it to another level. *The Big Over Easy* is the first to feature the pairing of Inspector Jack Spratt and Sergeant Mary Mary as they investigate the demise of Humpty Dumpty and encounter an endless supply of parodies of familiar tales and characters.[20]

Terry Pratchett is the classic author to remember for the humorous end of the Fantasy genre. His Discworld series, now more than thirty volumes, sets the standard for laugh-out-loud adventures, enjoyed on many levels by a wide range of readers, even those who also appreciate darker, more literary stories. Satirical, lampooning every available target, these novels set the stage with their titles and never let up. Some readers will insist on starting with the first, *The Colour of Magic*, but more adventurous readers should appreciate the layered satire of the recent *Going Postal*, as grifter Moist van Lipman tries his hand at revamping the post office.[21] Golem mailmen and vocal but undelivered letters add to the hilarity. Eccentric characters populate Pratchett's stories, and the wordplay, both in the text and in his special explanatory notes, verbal and visual gags, and over-the-top plots make them vastly entertaining reading. Also noteworthy for their puns and wordplay are Piers Anthony (Xanth) and Robert Asprin (Myth, as in *Myth Conceptions*), Orson Scott Card (Alvin Maker series), Fritz Leiber (Fafhrd and the Gray Mouser series), Patricia Wrede and Caroline Stevermer (*Sorcery and Cecelia; or, The Enchanted Chocolate Pot: Being the Correspondence of Two Young Ladies of Quality Regarding Various Magical Scandals in London and the Country*).[22]

Humor abounds in the Fantasy genre. Note, however, that just because titles include a strong vein of humor does not mean they are fluff. As in all genres, they can be read at many levels, and the humorous stories simply handle important issues differently. Watch too for dark humor in the Fantasy of authors such as Mike Carey and Jim Butcher. Their vampire-detective (Carey) and wizard-detective (Butcher) series generate contrasting noir backgrounds and humor, funny and frightening by turns.

Characterization

Just as the story lines focus on the battle between good and evil, so are the characters usually recognizable as one or the other. Clearly defined stereotypical characters are an appeal in many genres and Fantasy is no exception. They are not cardboard; within the confines of their type they are carefully and interestingly drawn, but they are types nonetheless. That is not to say that characters are branded as good or bad, but generally our protagonists know—they can feel the true nature of the characters—and even if they do not act on their impressions, they, and we readers, usually can tell the good guys from the bad. For example, in the second title of George R. R. Martin's series, *A Clash of Kings*, we meet Tyrion, a dwarf and scion of an evil family.[23] Yet we know his blood also contains vestiges of nobility that will win out in the end. Although unappealing physically and apparently of evil stock, Tyrion is recognizable by readers for his innate goodness.

Characters play a crucial role in the Fantasy genre, and the protagonist is particularly important. These often complex characters are frequently on journeys of discovery, whether actual physical journeys or less tangible mental or emotional journeys. They may have special gifts or powers, magical in their deepest nature, that they are just discovering in themselves and are seeking to master. These are books about discovering one's own potential, magical and otherwise, and thus have strong appeal as coming-of-age stories. Harry Potter in J. K. Rowling's enormously popular series beginning with *Harry Potter and the Sorcerer's Stone* must go to

Hogwarts School of Witchcraft and Wizardry to master his special powers.[24] In another variation, Sparrowhawk, hero of Le Guin's *A Wizard of Earthsea*, having accidentally unleashed an evil force into the world, must, as he matures, develop the power to subdue that evil.[25]

Characters in Fantasy novels are seldom what they seem. In Patrick Rothfuss's Kingkiller Chronicles, beginning with the award-winning *The Name of the Wind*, legendary hero Kvothe relates his adventures during his rise from magically gifted youth to formidable magician, now living incognito as a lowly innkeeper.[26] Sometimes the character does not realize that he is hiding his identity, as in Robert Silverberg's Majipoor series, in which Lord Valentine's own body has been taken over by the son of the king of the dreams (who now rules cruelly in Valentine's stead), and Valentine finds himself in a very different body. Once he discovers his true identity, he must work to resolve the political crisis that besets his land. *Sorcerers of Majipoor* is chronologically the first in this series.[27]

One last point about these characters: they are not always human. As in Science Fiction, where aliens may dominate a story, here nonhumans or partial humans are often protagonists. They have very human characteristics and are individuals we readily relate to and accept as human, although perhaps a little different. Beyond the wealth of dragons, fairies, and elves that have traditionally filled Fantasy tales, Tolkien's hobbits, Richard Adams's rabbits, and Brian Jacques's peace-loving creatures (mice, moles, shrews, and squirrels) pitted against the vicious rats, weasels, stoats, and foxes all speak to us with human voices and attributes. No matter what species of magical creatures they are, we readers relate to and care about them.

In this era of genre blending throughout fiction, wizards and mages may still promise Fantasy, but many Fantasy characters have found their way into other genres (such as Paranormal Romance in chapter 8) and staples of other genres have wandered into Fantasy. Readers should not be surprised to find vampires, werewolves, and other escapees from Horror, time-travelers from Science Fiction, Historical Fiction's royalty revealed as fairies, and more.

Pacing

Pacing in Fantasy is more closely related to that in Historical Fiction than other genres. Although the books almost always start slowly, setting the stage with the elaborately developed locales and multiple characters, the pace picks up later, when the forces of good engage those of evil in battle, and action and adventure elements play a more important role. Readers who are expecting stories that take off from page one may need to be warned! On the other hand, humorous Fantasy often moves more quickly from the first pages, or at least seems to do so, as it sucks readers in with the lavish wordplay. Fantasy written for teens and younger readers generally starts more quickly, although filling in the details may slow the pace midway (after the readers are hooked); it accelerates again toward the end as action builds.

Style/Language

The language of Fantasy ranges from more elegant and stylized in classic Fantasy to the more conversational prose and jargon of Urban Fantasy. Like the fairy tales and myths that form the backbone of the genre, Fantasy stories traditionally are meant to be read aloud. Cadence is important, as are the sounds of words. The colorful and dramatic language may also be elaborate, extravagant, and ornate for some stories and unusual and spare for others. Authors may also create unique languages, unusual names, or complex social and political structures to help reinforce the sense of "otherness." More than one fan has wryly commented that seeing a nice long glossary or list of characters is one way of knowing that you have a "real" fantasy in your hands!

While other genres experiment with interesting styles, Fantasy offers illustrations to enhance stories. Beyond the illustrated Fantasy of children's books and graphic novels, the genre increasingly provides maps, genealogical tracings, and illustrations to enhance the visual appeal of the stories and to help readers pinpoint where they are, literally and figuratively. Walter Moers's *The City of Dreaming Books* and Catherynne M. Valente's *In the Cities of Coin and Spice* exemplify the recent trend to add a visual element to their Fantasy tales.[28]

KEY AUTHORS

With its wealth of styles and moods, Fantasy requires familiarity with diverse authors. Many of us came to the Fantasy genre through J. R. R. Tolkien, popularly called the father of modern Fantasy. As such he has numerous imitators, but his writing has also set the standard of what is expected by fans of the genre. His are stories of epic quests, with unexpected heroes and their companions battling the forces of evil to save the world from ultimate darkness—and succeeding. Originally written for children in the 1950s, Tolkien's series found a mass audience in the 1970s when his popularity mushroomed, and again at the turn of the twenty-first century with the award-winning film versions. Newer (and often younger) Fantasy fans, however, remind us that there is much more to the genre than just Tolkien. They may read him, but many are interested in other stories and styles.

J. K. Rowling, Fantasy's most recent star, has captured an audience of children and adults with her Harry Potter series, in both book and film. Rowling's books are excellent examples of the ageless appeal of the genre. More than any other genre, Fantasy really knows no age limits. Younger readers appreciate some stories written for adults, and we adults can hardly resist much of what appears for children, from the classic authors (L. Frank Baum's Oz series, beginning with *The Wonderful Wizard of Oz*, and C. S. Lewis's Narnia series, starting with *The Lion, the Witch, and the Wardrobe*) to more recent series by Susan Cooper (The Dark Is Rising sequence, beginning with *Over Sea, Under Stone*) and Philip Pullman's trilogy, His Dark Materials, the first of which is *The Golden Compass*.[29] Film versions raise the profile of many titles. However, Rowling herself says that she is writing not simply for children, but rather the story she needs to tell. Those of us who promote reading for children should be grateful, but that the series is enjoyed by children should not detract from its universal appeal and the layers of meaning that characterize the best Fantasy—or the best in any genre.

Neil Gaiman established his reputation with his graphic novels—the epic Sandman Fantasy series—and continued with a range of character-centered, often humorous Fantasy novels that sometimes overlap with Horror and even Science Fiction. *Good Omens* (coauthored with Terry Pratchett), *American Gods,* and even his young adult novel *Coraline* blend humor with darker themes and make great suggestions for a range of readers.[30]

Jasper Fforde's pun-filled series featuring either literary detective Thursday Next or Jack Spratt and his Nursery Crimes division also appeal to a variety of readers, especially those who appreciate alternate universes and playful reinterpretations of literary and genre classics.

For fans of darker Fantasy, rich in political machinations and devious plans, George R. R. Martin makes a good choice. His Song of Ice and Fire saga, beginning with *A Game of Thrones,* creates a vast tapestry of power struggles and intrigue in a land where magic has almost disappeared, seasons last for decades, and the long winter has only brought infighting and a battle for the throne.[31] Politics and bloody political machinations drive these grim, layered stories.

Another author to be familiar with is Patricia Wrede. She writes humorous Fantasy, filled with Adventure and Romance, for a range of readers. From her classic Alternate World Regency Romance (beginning with *Sorcery and Cecelia*, coauthored with Caroline Stevermer) to her popular series for younger readers—and older—the Enchanted Forest Chronicles (beginning with the humorous *Dealing with Dragons*, which lampoons any number of Fantasy, fairy tale, and sexual conventions), Wrede continues to delight readers.[32]

Another classic author to remember is Orson Scott Card, whose novels may also be found in the Horror and Science Fiction genres. In Fantasy, he presents a carefully crafted alternate America in his Alvin Maker series, starring the seventh son of a seventh son (first is *Seventh Son*).[33] He has remarked that he has received letters praising this parallel American West; it is very like its historical antecedent, but it is also a place where very different events have occurred. The reader who wrote to thank Card for clarifying that George Washington had been hanged in this Alternate History of America was caught up in that other, but obviously very realistic, historical past.

WHAT WE KNOW ABOUT FANS

Those who particularly ask for Fantasy—and I have frequently had readers come to me to say they are interested in starting to read in this genre—are usually looking for stories with magical elements. They appreciate the fact that good triumphs over evil, and they expect a well-developed setting, populated by interesting characters. Beyond that there are any number of directions to pursue. From retellings of fairy tales and Arthurian legends, Celtic and Asian Fantasy, to stories of wizards, elves, and uncommon animals or other beasts, Fantasy celebrates the victory of good over evil, while exploring a variety of themes. A general understanding of the range of the genre, lists carefully crafted to reflect themes readers frequently request, and good reference sources are all invaluable to the readers' advisor.

Fans of Fantasy represent the widest age range of any genre. We need to be prepared to assist adults as well as much younger readers interested in exploring this genre. This is an excellent crossover genre for grade-school children who are good readers; in Fantasy and Science Fiction they often discover the treasures that await them throughout the adult collections of our libraries. We lure younger readers with Katherine Kurtz, Terry Brooks, Andre Norton, Anne McCaffrey, and Patricia A. McKillip and continue to enchant adults with Susan Cooper, Brian Jacques, and J. K. Rowling. Fantasy can be read and appreciated on many levels and reread for a new understanding of the deeper meaning of stories enjoyed in the past. One word of warning, however: Fantasy novels may also contain themes that parents are not keen on their children exploring. There may be sexual situations (sometimes homosexual) in some novels by authors who seem appropriate for teens and younger. I always encourage the parents to read the books first if they have any concerns.

Readers tend to be series-oriented, and, as do all series readers, they want to read the titles in order. Needless to say, they certainly expect the library to have copies of every title in a series they love. Because many Fantasy series start out as paperbacks, this can be a considerable problem. We need to be aggressive in ordering these series early on and then pursuing every avenue to fill in titles in popular series if books are out of print. Like fans of other genres, these readers never see interlibrary loan as a good alternative to actually having the desired titles in our collections. However, smaller libraries will earn the appreciation of genre fans by having at least the first few books in a series as well as the most current titles; somehow readers are more amenable to waiting for the magic of interlibrary loan to produce the middle volumes.

The Fantasy genre has also produced a large number of shared worlds, in which more than one writer places adventures in a world created by another author, as well as joint titles. For example, stories of Conan the Barbarian were first written by Robert E. Howard, but several popular authors have also tried their hand at these Sword and Sorcery stories, from L. Sprague de Camp to Robert Jordan. Other popular shared worlds include Thieves World and Bordertown (tales of Urban Fantasy). Another variation of the shared world is the series based on computer or role-playing games. The most popular examples are the myriad Dragonlance books, a spin-off of the Dungeons and Dragons role-playing game. Owned and published originally by TSR, Dragonlance features multiple, closely interconnected series that fans continually request and that remain difficult to sort out, not to mention purchase. Among the most requested are the Dragonlance series by Margaret Weis and Tracy Hickman (*Dragons of Autumn Twilight* is an early title), and the Forgotten Realms series by R. A. Salvatore (*The Crystal Shard* opens his Icewind Dale Trilogy).[34]

More recently, the Halo series follows the video game series. Two titles (*The Flood* and *First Strike*) are actual games, while others are simply set in that universe.[35] Fans appreciate being made aware of these series by multiple authors and consisting of shared worlds. These are often good suggestions for a fan of one of these authors currently at loose ends. At my library we catalog and shelve these titles under the series name, as that seems more useful and less frustrating for browsers or readers of the series than the names of the individual authors.

Fantasy offers big books and long series, and these readers are not daunted by size. Whether the story is complete in one large volume or several, readers seem to devour the series they enjoy and then demand the next volume before it is even written. Alternative suggestions of similar authors or series are always a good idea. We are not above quizzing fans for further reading suggestions and then sharing them with other interested readers.

Fantasy readers seem not quite so aloof as many Science Fiction fans. We have found them interested in discovering new authors that may have the same appeal as others they have enjoyed, and these readers may be willing to try our suggestions. That being the case, we need to be prepared for fans, and arm ourselves with possibilities to tide them over while they wait for the upcoming release in their favorite series—and since they may have to wait at least a year for the next volume, they are frequently receptive. It is important to identify the authors and series popular at our own libraries, talk with fans, and read the books and reviews to discover why they are so popular in order to discover authors that are similar. For example, readers of George R. R. Martin's *A Game of Thrones* might enjoy other series rich in political intrigue such as Robin Hobb's dark and complex trilogies (start with *Assassin's Apprentice*), Robert Jordan's Wheel of Time series (*The Eye of the World* is the first), or David Anthony Durham's Acacia series (*The War with the Mein*).[36] Fans of Jasper Fforde could be directed to Pratchett, Asprin, as well as Connie Willis's *To Say Nothing of the Dog*.[37]

One last issue to consider in working with Fantasy fans is a controversy among writers, a certain snobbishness it seems, about the superiority of one genre over another. There seems to be a feeling among some writers and readers that Science Fiction is the genre designation of choice, and that it is better to be considered a writer of Science Fiction than a writer of Fantasy. This affects a pair of very popular authors: Anne McCaffrey and Marion Zimmer Bradley. Both state emphatically that they write Science Fiction, but their books are beloved by Fantasy fans, and probably cherished more by them than by readers of Science Fiction. Yes, there may be a scientific basis for these stories set in other worlds, but the feel of the stories and characters appeals far more readily to Fantasy fans than to Science Fiction readers. Thus, we successfully offer McCaffrey's Dragonriders of Pern series and Bradley's tales of Darkover to Fantasy readers rather more frequently than to Science Fiction fans. It should also be noted that readers of Fantasy are more likely to delve into Science Fiction than vice versa. Figure 14.2 offers additional authors for fans of other genres to try to discover something similar in the Fantasy genre.

Figure 14.2 *An Introduction to the Fantasy Genre*

Fantasy Writers to Try, If You Enjoy . . .

Adrenaline:	Jacqueline Carey
	Scott Lynch
	George R. R. Martin
Biography/Memoir:	Margaret George (*Helen of Troy*)[38]
	Katherine Kurtz (*Two Crowns for America*)[39]
Gay/Lesbian:	Jim Grimsley
	Tanya Huff
Gentle Reads:	C. S. Lewis
	Walter Moers
	T. H. White
	Patricia Wrede
Historical Fiction:	Sara Douglass
	Naomi Novik
	Judith Tarr
	Jack Whyte
History:	Bernard Cornwell (Arthur Series)[40]
	Roberta Gellis and Mercedes Lackey
	Guy Gavriel Kay
Horror:	Alice Borchardt
	Mike Carey
	Laurell K. Hamilton
Humor:	Piers Anthony (Xanth series)
	Orson Scott Card (Alvin Maker series)
	Terry Pratchett
	Christopher Stasheff

(cont.)

Figure 14.2   An Introduction to the Fantasy Genre (cont.)

Inspirational:	Karen Hancock
	Stephen Lawhead
	C. S. Lewis (Narnia series)[41]
Literary:	Susanna Clarke
	Jasper Fforde
	Gregory Maguire
Multicultural:	Nalo Hopkinson
Mystery:	Jim Butcher
	Glen Cook (Garrett Files)[42]
	Jasper Fforde (Nursery Crimes series)
	Katherine Kurtz and Deborah Turner Harris (Adept series)[43]
Natural History:	Rachel Caine (Weather Warden series)[44]
Psychological Suspense:	Stephen R. Donaldson
Romance:	Catherine Asaro
	Anne Bishop
	Robin D. Owens (Summoning series)[45]
	Sharon Shinn
Saga:	Terry Brooks (various Shannara series)
	Terry Goodkind
	Juliet Marillier (Sevenwaters trilogy)[46]
Science Fiction:	Raymond E. Feist
	Eric Flint (Assiti Shards/Ring of Fire series)[47]
	David Gemmel
	Mary Gentle
	Judith Tarr
	Sean Stewart (*Galveston*)[48]
Travel:	Michael A. Stackpole (Age of Discovery series)[49]
True Crime:	Charles de Lint (Newford series)[50]
	China Miéville (*Perdido Street Station*)[51]
Western:	Emma Bull
	Stephen King (The Dark Tower series)[52]
Women's Lives:	Tamora Pierce
	Shanna Swendson
	Jane Yolen

THE READERS' ADVISORY INTERVIEW

Faced with a reader of a genre I am less comfortable discussing, I rely on what that reader says about what he enjoys in a genre or a particular type of story. Does he talk about a type of character? Or a story based on myth or legend? Or perhaps a setting that appeals? Or a story with a humorous or romantic or darker tone? Each of these should suggest directions to pursue.

With readers new to the genre who want to explore Fantasy, we prize all information about other authors or titles they have enjoyed, no matter what the genre. Are they in the mood for something similar or would they like to try something different? If they talk about characters, I might inquire further with questions about types of characters—human or animal or imaginary. How much overt magic would be interesting? Do they want a familiar story, a fairy tale, or Arthurian retelling? Or something completely new?

If readers ask for stories of parallel worlds, we turn to the reference books and databases, unless, of course, we really are knowledgeable fans of the genre. (Even then, we might appreciate the backup authority, and certainly readers enjoy discovering reference resources to explore on their own, especially those with many lists.) In fact, many of these requests can be answered in the reference tools available; types of characters and thematic groupings lend themselves to these tools.

On the other hand, readers who describe books by tone require us to probe further and sort by other factors, such as the amount of humor. Many humorous Fantasy novels are easily identified by the titles themselves. Puns in the title are likely to indicate a less serious bent. Time period may be another factor. Readers who want a medieval feel or a contemporary world can be helped by cover drawings or descriptions on book jackets.

I have also had readers seeking books with more Adventure elements. Here, as in Historical Fiction, maps may indicate Adventure elements, and I discover these as I flip through the pages with the reader. Reference books can help, too, as I know that Sword and Sorcery titles as well as quests are likely to contain adventure.

Short stories provide an excellent introduction to the genre for readers and librarians alike. In addition to the ongoing collections of award-winning Fantasy, *Legends* remains a popular collection, since it gathers short stories based on the series of some of the most popular Fantasy authors writing today: Stephen King, Pratchett, Card, Martin, Jordan, and more.[53] In addition, many Fantasy writers post short stories on their websites.

Short stories allow readers to experiment, to sample an author's style and subject matter before pursuing a title or series. In this case, especially, stories also provide readers with a taste of the series they might read.

Don't forget the classics. Fantasy ages well because it's based in story, not technology or mundane events. Since classic authors remain popular with readers young and old, also consider writers such as Richard Adams (*Watership Down*) and Lord Dunsany (*The King of Elfland's Daughter*).[54]

The Fantasy genre also boasts authors who have made their name and reputation in other genres. Stephen King comes immediately to mind. In addition to his reputation as a Horror writer, King has established himself in the Fantasy genre, with his classic *The Stand* and the Dark Tower series.[55] Science Fiction writers who also write popular Fantasy series include Piers Anthony, Roger Zelazny, Elizabeth Moon, Robin Hobb/Megan Lindholm, Raymond E. Feist, Catherine Asaro, and Orson Scott Card. Readers familiar with their Fantasy writing may also be interested in pursuing their work in other genres.

Since so much Fantasy appeals to a wide range of ages, don't be afraid to offer young adult and children's titles to adults and vice versa, if these seem good suggestions to match their interests. Walter Moers, Diana Wynne Jones, Robin McKinley, Christopher Paolini, Donna Jo Napoli, Cornelia Caroline Funke, and Garth Nix are among the many authors that make good crossover suggestions.

As in every genre, Fantasy has its share of authors who refuse to be confined to any single genre and its conventions. The Sure Bets below make good suggestions for a wide range of readers. Keep in mind too the authors whose writing overlaps with other genres. The Fantasy authors in figure 14.2 introduce readers of other genres to Fantasy, while those in figure 14.3 below lead readers from Fantasy to other genres they might find interesting. As genre boundaries merge and authors experiment in diverse genres, readers are often prompted to taste new genres and styles when they follow authors they enjoy. Among the many authors who write across genres, Neil Gaiman, Clive Barker, Roberta Gellis, and Jasper Fforde make good suggestions for Fantasy fans.

Sure Bets

Many of Neil Gaiman's titles qualify as Sure Bets. In *Neverwhere* contemporary London harbors another world, London Below, in the endless subway tunnels.[56] Here, a real earl holds court under Earl's Court tube station, and in this richly imagined world peopled by those who have fallen through the cracks of lives above, the doughty Door enlists the help of Londoner Richard Mayhew to discover the secret in her past that threatens her future. Suggest this for readers of gritty, coming-of-age stories who appreciate playful images and language, as well as the darker mood in this Urban Fantasy set in the near-future and in a near-realistic, recognizable locale.

Gregory Frost's *Shadowbridge* and its sequel *Lord Tophet* feature an imaginary world connected by bridge spans.[57] Here heroine Leodora, disguised as the shadow puppeteer Jax, travels the spans both collecting and telling stories. But her collection isn't random, and she understands her goal when she finally hears her own story and recognizes her fate as well as that of her parents. Frost creates beautiful and dangerous images, but it is the idea of stories and storytelling that resonates through these lyrical, layered novels.

Jonathan Strange and Mr Norrell, Susanna Clarke's award-winning Fantasy of the Napoleonic Wars fought in a similar but alternate universe in which magic and wizards play key roles, appeals to fans of Fantasy, as well as to readers who enjoy Alternate History, Literary Fiction, and Humor.[58] Grounded in historical research and detail, this imaginative novel even has lengthy footnotes worth reading for their humorous take on events. Despite its size—eight hundred pages—this is a tour de force that one can hand to a variety of readers.

EXPANDING READERS' HORIZONS WITH WHOLE COLLECTION READERS' ADVISORY

Fantasy readers discover much that appeals in other genres; if they find books of similar feel and tone, they seem not to mind the lack of magic too much. Consequently, since paranormal elements have infiltrated almost every genre, there are more and more genres and titles that attract Fantasy fans.

Historical Fiction has a wealth of material for Fantasy readers who appreciate the "historical" settings of much Fantasy. The Landscape emphasis, with the intricately detailed setting and the feel of an earlier time, connects the two genres (but bear in mind that these are not for fans of Urban Fantasy with its contemporary settings). Remember too that readers in both genres are not intimidated by long books. Fans of Naomi Novik's Temeraire Series might appreciate Historical novels and Historical Adventure with Napoleonic War settings, as well as popular histories of the times and biographies of the historical figures involved.

The Romance genre also offers a number of authors who are read and loved by Fantasy fans. Any of the authors of Paranormal Romances described in chapter 8, "Romance," might appeal to Fantasy readers, as these Romances offer elements borrowed from the Fantasy genre. Fairy tale figures as well as demon lovers abound in Paranormal Romance and make these good crossover stories for fans of both Horror and Fantasy. Patricia Rice's Magic series, for example, includes a historical setting, a family whose members all possess magical gifts, and passionate romantic entanglements. In addition, popular Romance authors such as Jo Beverley increasingly employ Fantasy elements in their Historical Romances, as do Jayne Ann Krentz (especially writing as Jayne Castle) and Nora Roberts in their Contemporary Romances and Romantic Suspense. Time Travel Romances by authors such as Lynn Kurland and Sandra Hill also make good suggestions for Fantasy readers who appreciate romantic elements.

Fantasy readers may also find satisfaction in the Horror genre and in the nonhuman creatures who dwell there, especially since many Horror prototypes have found their way into Fantasy. However, readers must be resigned to the fact that evil is not destroyed but is left to menace future generations. Dean R. Koontz's recent series of thoughtful Odd Thomas books, with their blend of Suspense, Horror, and Fantasy elements, certainly have much to offer readers of Fantasy. Because the links between Fantasy and Horror are so close, with many authors writing both Dark Fantasy and Horror, the popular Year's Best series groups the two into one volume, and these short stories make a particularly good introduction to new authors for readers.

Adventure pervades much Fantasy, and those Fantasy fans for whom the adventure element is important frequently find titles that appeal in that genre. As his work includes more and more fantastic elements, Clive Cussler makes a good suggestion for these readers as does James Rollins. Quest fans may also discover Adventure titles that they enjoy. Douglas Preston and Lincoln Child's Pendergast series overlaps with both Fantasy and Horror.[59] Earlier titles lean toward Horror, but later titles add more than a bit of Fantasy to drive the action.

Science Fiction attracts a significant number of Fantasy fans as well, in part because many authors write in both genres, and their fans read across the genre borders with abandon. Anne McCaffrey and Marion Zimmer Bradley, who claim to write Science Fiction, not Fantasy, are certainly reasonable choices. Science Fiction stories of alternate and parallel worlds, like Philip K. Dick's *The Man in the High Castle,* may also appeal.[60]

Among possibilities in the Mystery genre might be Eric Garcia's *Anonymous Rex*.[61] What fan of humorous Fantasy could resist this hard-boiled detective who just happens to be a dinosaur? In addition to Jim Butcher's wizard detective in the Dresden Files, there's also Kim Harrison's witch/bounty hunter series starring Rachel Morgan.[62] Don't forget the magical genie Diesel who appears in Janet Evanovich's Between the Numbers entries in her Stephanie Plum mysteries.[63]

Nonfiction links for Fantasy fans may be less straightforward. Certainly the Dewey 800s are filled with titles that expound on familiar characters and series. There are dozens of books related to Tolkien's and Rowling's series. Collections of fairy tales, myths, and legends make good suggestions for Fantasy fans who want to explore these archetypical stories across cultures. But by its nature, Fantasy defies rational explanations, and fans are not as likely to seek additional reading across the Dewey Divide—unless, of course, they are looking for "real books" about Atlantis, witchcraft, astral projection, magical herbs, and the like. Figure 14.3 offers non-Fantasy writers who might appeal to Fantasy fans.

TRENDS

Fantasy has invaded the world of genre fiction, adding elements of the paranormal to almost every genre, including Literary Fiction. While this trend certainly blurs the lines between genres, it makes suggesting titles to readers easier, as we can move from elements they enjoy to a much wider range of possible titles.

Successful Fantasy films—of novels and short stories as well as from original screenplays or expanded from video games—increase the genre's profile and popularity. Watch for links from media versions to books and market them together.

Series continue to dominate publishing. In books, graphic novels, and film, readers prolong their enjoyment as they follow series characters and their adventures over the years, often rereading previous volumes in preparation for new titles.

Alternate history is emerging as another popular trend and will likely continue, at least in the near future. The surprisingly wide appeal of epic works such as Novik's Temeraire series and Susanna Clarke's *Jonathan Strange and Mr Norrell* will no doubt lead to an explosion of new settings and scenarios; readers newly introduced to these may also be intrigued by the factual history behind them.[64]

Figure 14.3 *Expanding Readers' Horizons*

Authors to Take Readers beyond the Fantasy Genre

Adrenaline:	Clive Cussler
	James Rollins
Biography/Memoir:	Humphrey Carpenter (*The Inklings*)[65]
Historical Fiction:	Gillian Bradshaw
	Kathleen O'Neal Gear
	Morgan Llewelyn
	Lucia St. Clair Robson
Horror:	Raymond E. Feist
	Stephen King
	Dean R. Koontz
Literary:	Isabel Allende
	Haruki Marukami
	Steven Millhauser
Mystery:	Eric Garcia
Romance:	Susan Carroll
	Kristine Grayson
	Karen Hawkins (Talisman Ring series)[66]
	Patricia Rice
Romantic Suspense:	Kay Hooper
	Amanda Quick
	Nora Roberts
Science Fiction:	Marion Zimmer Bradley
	Anne McCaffrey
Westerns:	Don Coldsmith (Spanish Bit series)[67]
Women's Lives:	Sarah Addison Allen
	Barbara Samuel
	Deborah Smith

Urban Fantasy is another rich and diverse area that is just hitting its stride. The diversity of characters and settings, along with the darker tone of these stories, is expected to attract a growing share of the market for the foreseeable future.

Fantasy is a genre that inspires lifelong fans. They may read other genres at certain periods in their lives, but many come back to Fantasy, rereading their favorites and discovering new authors and new directions. Parents often bring their children to our desks, asking us to suggest titles that will introduce their offspring to the genre that saw them through their adolescence and beyond. When we read Fantasy authors to explore the genre, we get a taste of this long-lived appeal. These are often elegantly written stories with a haunting quality. We sense there is something just behind the story, something bigger than the story itself which hints at a larger meaning. These are the stories of legends come to life, and the popularity of the genre attests to the continuing importance of this kind of story in our lives.

Notes

1. Eva Ibbotson, *The Secret of Platform 13* (New York: Dutton Children's Books, 1998); Elizabeth Ann Scarborough, *The Healer's War* (New York: Doubleday, 1988).
2. Neil Gaiman, *Anansi Boys* (New York: Morrow, 2005).
3. Lloyd Alexander, *The Book of Three* (New York: Holt, 1964); Ursula K. Le Guin, *A Wizard of Earthsea* (Berkeley, CA: Parnassus, 1968); J. R. R. Tolkien, *The Fellowship of the Ring: Being the First Part of the Lord of the Rings* (Boston: Houghton Mifflin, 1965).
4. Patricia Wrede, *Raven Ring* (New York: Tor, 1994); David Anthony Durham, *Acacia, Book One: The War with the Mein* (New York: Doubleday, 2007).
5. Charles de Lint, Newford series, beginning with *The Dreaming Place* (New York: Atheneum, 1990).
6. Jasper Fforde, *The Eyre Affair* (New York: Viking, 2002).
7. Emma Bull, *Territory* (New York: Tor, 2007).
8. Katherine Kurtz, Chronicles of Deryni, beginning with *Deryni Rising* (New York: Ballantine, 1970).
9. Susanna Clarke, *Jonathan Strange and Mr Norrell* (New York: Bloomsbury, 2004); Naomi Novik, *His Majesty's Dragon* (New York: Ballantine, 2006).
10. de Lint, *Memory and Dream* (New York: Tor, 1994).
11. China Miéville, *Perdido Street Station* (New York: Ballantine, 2001); Bull, *War for the Oaks* (New York: Berkley, 1987).
12. Jim Butcher, *Storm Front* (New York: Roc, 2000).
13. Jane Yolen, *Briar Rose* (New York: Tom Doherty, 1992).
14. John Connolly, *The Book of Lost Things* (New York: Atria, 2006).
15. Bernard Cornwell, *The Winter King: A Novel of Arthur* (New York: St. Martin's, 1996); T. H. White, *The Once and Future King* (New York: Putnam, 1958).
16. Guy Gavriel Kay, *The Last Light of the Sun* (New York: Roc, 2004); Jo Graham, *Black Ships: A Novel* (New York: Orbit, 2008).
17. Gregory Maguire, *Wicked: The Life and Times of the Wicked Witch of the West* (New York: ReganBooks, 1995).
18. Stephen King, *The Gunslinger* (West Kingston, RI: Donald M. Grant, 1982).
19. Stephen Donaldson, *Lord Foul's Bane* (New York: Holt, 1977).

20. Fforde, *The Big Over Easy: A Nursery Crime* (New York: Viking, 2005).
21. Terry Pratchett, *The Colour of Magic: A Discworld Novel* (New York: St. Martin's, 1983); Pratchett, *Going Postal: A Novel of Discworld* (New York: HarperCollins, 2004).
22. Piers Anthony, Xanth series, beginning with *A Spell for Chameleon* (New York: Del Rey, 1977); Robert Asprin, *Myth Conceptions* (New York: Ace, 1985); Orson Scott Card, Tales of Alvin Maker series, beginning with *Seventh Son* (New York: Tom Doherty, 1987); Fritz Leiber, Fafhrd and the Gray Mouser series, beginning with *Swords and Deviltry* (New York: Ace, 1970); Patricia Wrede and Caroline Stevermer, *Sorcery and Cecelia; or, The Enchanted Chocolate Pot: Being the Correspondence of Two Young Ladies of Quality Regarding Various Magical Scandals in London and the Country* (Orlando, FL: Harcourt, 2003).
23. George R. R. Martin, *A Clash of Kings* (New York: Bantam, 2000).
24. J. K. Rowling, *Harry Potter and the Sorcerer's Stone* (New York: Arthur A. Levine, 1998).
25. Le Guin cited above.
26. Patrick Rothfuss, *The Name of the Wind: The Kingkiller Chronicle, Day One* (New York: DAW Books, 2007).
27. Robert Silverberg, *Sorcerers of Majipoor* (New York: HarperPrism, 1996).
28. Walter Moers, *The City of Dreaming Books: A Novel from Zamonia by Optimus Yarnspinner* (Woodstock, NY: Overlook Press, 2007); Catherynne M. Valente, *In the Cities of Coin and Spice* (New York: Bantam, 2007).
29. L. Frank Baum, *The Wonderful Wizard of Oz* (Chicago: G. M. Hill, 1900); C. S. Lewis, *The Lion, the Witch, and the Wardrobe* (New York: Macmillan, 1950); Susan Cooper, *Over Sea, Under Stone* (New York: Harcourt Brace, 1966); Philip Pullman, *The Golden Compass* (New York: Knopf, 1996).
30. Gaiman and Pratchett, *Good Omens: The Nice and Accurate Prophecies of Agnes Nutter, Witch* (New York: Workman, 1990); Gaiman, *American Gods: A Novel* (New York: Morrow, 2001); Gaiman, *Coraline* (New York: HarperCollins, 2002).
31. Martin, *A Game of Thrones* (New York: Bantam, 1996).
32. Wrede and Stevermer cited above; Wrede, *Dealing with Dragons* (San Diego: Harcourt Brace Jovanovich, 1990).
33. Card cited above.
34. Margaret Weis and Tracy Hickman, *Dragons of Autumn Twilight* (Renton, WA: TSR, 1984); R. A. Salvatore, *The Crystal Shard* (Lake Geneva, WI: TSR, 1988).
35. William C. Dietz, *Halo: The Flood* (New York: Del Rey, 2003); Eric S. Nylund, *Halo: First Strike* (New York: Ballantine, 2003).
36. Martin cited above; Robin Hobb, *Assassin's Apprentice* (New York: Bantam, 1995); Robert Jordan, *The Eye of the World* (New York: Tom Doherty, 1990); Durham cited above.
37. Connie Willis, *To Say Nothing of the Dog; or, How We Found the Bishop's Bird Stump at Last* (New York: Bantam, 1998).
38. Margaret George, *Helen of Troy* (New York: Viking, 2006).
39. Katherine Kurtz, *Two Crowns for America* (New York: Bantam, 1996).
40. Cornwell, Arthur series, beginning with *The Winter King* (cited above).
41. C. S. Lewis, Narnia series, beginning with *The Lion, the Witch, and the Wardrobe* (cited above).
42. Glen Cook, Garrett Files series, beginning with *Sweet Silver Blues* (New York: New American Library, 1987).
43. Kurtz and Deborah Turner Harris, Adept series, beginning with *The Adept* (New York: Berkley, 1991).
44. Rachel Caine, Weather Warden series, beginning with *Ill Wind* (New York: Roc, 2003).
45. Robin D. Owens, Summoning series, beginning with *Guardian of Honor* (New York: Luna, 2005).

46. Juliet Marillier, Sevenwaters Trilogy, beginning with *Daughter of the Forest* (New York: Tor, 2000).
47. Eric Flint, Assiti Shards/Ring of Fire series, beginning with *1632* (Riverdale, NY: Baen, 2000).
48. Sean Stewart, *Galveston* (New York: Ace, 2000).
49. Michael A. Stackpole, Age of Discovery series, beginning with *A Secret Atlas* (New York: Bantam, 2004).
50. de Lint cited above.
51. Miéville cited above.
52. King, Dark Tower series, beginning with *The Gunslinger* (cited above).
53. *Legends: Short Novels by the Masters of Modern Fantasy* (New York: Tor, 1998).
54. Richard Adams, *Watership Down* (New York: Macmillan, 1974); Edward John Moreton Drax Plunkett Dunsany, *The King of Elfland's Daughter* (New York: Del Rey, 1999, 1924).
55. King, *The Stand* (Garden City, NY: Doubleday, 1978).
56. Gaiman, *Neverwhere* (New York: Avon, 1997).
57. Gregory Frost, *Shadowbridge* (New York: Del Rey, 2008); Frost, *Lord Tophet: A Shadowbridge Novel* (New York: Del Rey, 2008).
58. Clarke cited above.
59. Douglas Preston and Lincoln Child, The Pendergast series, beginning with *Relic* (New York: Forge, 1995).
60. Philip K. Dick, *The Man in the High Castle: A Novel* (New York: G. P. Putnam's Sons, 1962).
61. Eric Garcia, *Anonymous Rex: A Detective Story* (New York: Villard, 2000).
62. Butcher cited above; Kim Harrison, Rachel Morgan series, beginning with *Dead Witch Walking* (New York: HarperTorch, 2004).
63. Janet Evanovich, *Visions of Sugar Plums* (New York: St. Martin's, 2002).
64. Clarke cited above.
65. Humphrey Carpenter, *The Inklings: C. S. Lewis, J. R. R. Tolkien, Charles Williams, and Their Friends* (Boston: Houghton Mifflin, 1979).
66. Karen Hawkins, Talisman Ring series, beginning with *An Affair to Remember* (New York: Avon, 2002).
67. Don Coldsmith, Spanish Bit series, beginning with *The Trail of the Spanish Bit* (Garden City, NY: Doubleday, 1980).

15

HISTORICAL FICTION

"I need to read a fiction book for my history class, and I need to be certain it's accurate. We're studying the Civil War."

"I just saw that movie about Marie Antoinette, and I'd love to learn more about her. Those biographies are just too dry. Is there anything else I can read?"

"We're going to France for our vacation. I'd like some Historical Fiction set there, especially in Lyon."

If these queries sound similar to ones asked in your library, you know how popular Historical Fiction can be, as well as the wide range of interests and reading tastes to which the genre appeals. Readers of Historical Fiction share a secret: they have discovered a painless method of learning history—through the fictionalized accounts of historical periods, people, and events presented by novels in this genre. When they read Historical Fiction that features real people, or stories that explore a particular time or event, they may have uncovered as much historical fact as many students of history. They have learned to explore history on the magic carpet of Historical Fiction.

Despite the genre's many pleasures, it can seem daunting even to the most avid fans. Historical novels are, for the most part, big books, which require a major investment of time to read. Nevertheless, it sometimes appears to harried readers' advisors that fans devote themselves to the genre, devouring Historical Fiction and always looking for more of the type they enjoy. It seems impossible to keep up with fans of this genre! However, understanding the characteristics of the genre and why readers love it helps us work with readers, no matter how little Historical Fiction we have read.

A DEFINITION

Formulating a definition that encompasses all aspects of a diverse genre is always difficult. And as we all know, each fan of Historical Fiction will have his own definition of the genre and books that are included. Of course, once we discover how this reader defines the genre and what he is looking for that day, we know how to proceed. A request for Historical Fiction similar to Julia Quinn's racy Historical Romances or Anne Perry's somber Historical Mysteries will likely lead us in different directions from a request for more novels like Charles Frazier's Pulitzer Prize–winning *Cold Mountain.*[1]

For purposes of this discussion, I define Historical Fiction as a novel set in the past, before the author's lifetime or experience. Thus, novels about World War II might be considered Historical Fiction if the author were born after 1945, but Jane Austen's comedies of manners are not Historical Fiction, as she writes about the times in which she lived. Through its serious respect for historical accuracy and detail, Historical Fiction enhances the reader's knowledge of past events, lives, and customs. The goal of authors of Historical Fiction is to bring history to life in novel form. Figure 15.1 lists characteristics of Historical Fiction based on this definition.

Although they may rely heavily on historical facts and details, Historical Romances, Mysteries, Thrillers, and Adventure are not considered in this chapter. Instead, they are covered in the respective genre chapters. This is a judgment call; Alan Furst fills his World War II novels with fascinating details of wartime and the Resistance, but the primary emphasis is on the intrigue rather than on the history of those times. While these books and others might have significant amounts of historical detail and background, the emphasis is not on the history but on Romance, Mystery, or Adventure. Readers may appreciate the historical details, but they aren't reading for the purpose of exploring a historical period. In the section "Expanding Readers' Horizons with Whole Collection Readers' Advisory," there are a number of suggestions of authors in other genres who are careful about their historical detail and are thus good suggestions for Historical Fiction fans. (See figure 15.3 below.)

Figure 15.1 *Characteristics of Historical Fiction*

---

1. There is a wealth of accurate historical detail relating to setting (geography, customs, beliefs, culture, society, habits) as well as to characters and events.

2. The mood of Historical novels runs the gamut from rollicking to somber, and this tone may be a major, if unacknowledged, factor in reading choices.

3. Story lines may focus on a particular historical event or time period, or they may follow the life of a character (real or fictional). Novels may raise difficult social or moral issues through the plot.

4. Characters may be real or fictional, but they are portrayed in such a way that they fit the times. Their lives and actions are shaped by the historical times and details, not vice versa.

5. Historical novels are usually big books, with stories that unfold at a leisurely pace. Even shorter Historical novels are usually so densely written that they must be read slowly.

6. Language and style may affect a reader's experience. Some readers appreciate an "authentic" style, while others find this distracting. Dialects and formats also affect reader reaction.

CHARACTERISTICS AND THE GENRE'S APPEAL

Frame/Setting

As with other genres that emphasize sense of place, "world-building" is crucial in Historical Fiction. However, unlike the magical worlds of Fantasy or the Western landscapes, which are sometimes realistic and sometimes mythical, worlds in Historical Fiction require accurate historical facts. In these books readers discover a wealth of details relating to the setting (geography, customs, beliefs, culture, society, habits, etc.) as well as to characters and events. Most readers would agree that the frame, constructed with these facts, is the first element they respond to as they read Historical Fiction. In fact, in many of the classic Historical novels of James A. Michener, this frame is almost a character in its own right. *Chesapeake,* for example, tells the story of an area of the Maryland shore and the generations of people that inhabit it.[2] The land itself is the dominant influence on human characters and events. Other novels present a combination of these frame components. Fans read to discover the details of life in a particular period or to follow a famous person's life. They expect a good story and interesting, believable characters, but readers want to be immersed in the times, to experience a particular period in history or to explore the life and times of a famous historical figure.

Some authors are more skilled at integrating historical information into the narrative than others. The best writers in this genre deftly blend history and story together, seamlessly melding the two without placing large sections of "history" in the midst of the plot. For example, Robert Harris illustrates the life and times of Cicero in *Imperium: A Novel of Ancient Rome* by presenting the politics, personalities, and power struggles in the last days of the Roman Republic.[3] He employs Cicero's amanuensis Tiro (also famous as the inventor of shorthand) to relate Cicero's rise from lawyer to senator, as well as the backroom dealings involving the famous men of the time: Pompey, Crassus, and Julius Caesar. As the reader follows Cicero and Tiro, Harris weaves the historical events and details of the period into the character's life experiences to make a wonderfully rich story.

It is not simply the wealth of details but also the accuracy that is so important to fans of the genre. Many readers, myself included, trace a great deal of our knowledge of history to Historical Fiction. We may not respond to the often dry style of straight history texts or biographies, with their interminable footnotes and caveats. We turn to Historical Fiction to understand history from the inside, from the perspectives of individuals caught up in events. Even though we know we are not consulting primary sources and understand that the authors have, by necessity, taken some liberties with characters and events in telling their stories, we trust the novelists—and their editors—to have the integrity to keep to the facts as they are generally known. Hence, fans and librarians look for presentations consistent with the times and known facts. To reassure readers, many writers (notably Bernard Cornwell) append historical notes to the end of their novels, thus establishing the accuracy of their interpretations and indicating areas in which liberties have been taken. Such notes provide fans a guarantee that details are accurate, and they also often point fans to further reading, enabling readers to explore areas of interest more deeply.

Tone/Mood

Second in importance to frame is the tone of the story and the mood it conveys. An integral aspect of this question is also the mood the reader is in—is she looking for an action-packed story or one that features more reflective characters? That question will be covered in the section "The Readers' Advisory Interview" below. Here, we'll simply consider the tone or mood conveyed by the book. There is a rich vocabulary to express this—and Historical Fiction reflects many moods.

What are we expected to feel when we read a book? It may be a sense of anticipation or foreboding. In Robert Harris's *Pompeii* we anxiously wait for the volcano to erupt, knowing already the devastation that will follow.[4] Or the tone may be exuberant. In *The Scandal of the Season* Sophie Gee playfully explores the characters and flirtation behind Alexander Pope's classic poem, "The Rape of the Lock."[5] A story may be heartwarming—Sandra Dallas's *Tallgrass* with its World War II home front setting and a Japanese internment camp in rural eastern Colorado—or softer, more romantic, as in Elizabeth Chadwick's medieval Historical novels (*Lords of the White Castle* et al.).[6]

Mood is everywhere in this genre, from the elegiac tone of E. L. Doctorow's *The March* to the thoughtful, introspective tone of Alison Weir's novel of Lady Jane Grey, *Innocent Traitor,* not to mention the relentlessly grim tone of *American by Blood,* Andrew Huebner's dark and violent follow-up to the Battle of the Little Big Horn.[7] Other titles may simply be atmospheric, moody, psychological, melancholy, edgy, upbeat, hopeful, or evocative. Since these tone and mood terms are so effective when we talk with readers—allowing us to offer a revealing glimpse of how the book might affect them—we need to be aware of mood as we read and include these adjectives in our oral and written descriptions.

Story Line

Story lines in Historical Fiction generally emphasize either a particular time or event or they follow the lives of characters in a time. Geraldine Brooks's *Year of Wonders: A Novel of the Plague* takes readers to a small English village in 1666.[8] When plague is found, the villagers decide to quarantine themselves to keep the disease from spreading. Thus we learn about village life and the ordinary people there, as well as about the devastating consequences of their decision as the outcome of their choice is revealed. Although this is an intimate first-person account, the narrator and the other characters are not famous historical figures but people of their time caught up in an event. Brooks captures the character of the community, and the emphasis is more on the details of everyday life than on individual stories. Ken Follett's *Pillars of the Earth,* which recounts the building of a medieval English cathedral, also focuses on the outcome, and the actions that lead to that outcome, more than on the characters themselves. (In contrast, Follett's sequel, *World without End*, falls into the character-centered camp, with more of a Family Saga feel.)[9]

In other Historical novels, characters take center stage, and the lives of the protagonists are more important than individual events. For example, Isabel Allende, perhaps better known as a writer of Literary Fiction than Historical, brings that literary emphasis on character to her historical novels *Daughter of Fortune, Inés of My Soul,* and even *Zorro.*[10] Although historical details frame these novels, the narrative emphasizes the characters and their stories within these times. In his numerous novels of American history and its shapers, Jeff Shaara offers a kind of warts-and-all Historical Fiction, presenting real people without idealizing them and exploring events in their lives without the constraints imposed by strict biography.

Family Sagas are another type of character-based Historical Fiction. These fall in and out of favor with the reading public, but they seem to be back again, and many Historical Fiction authors have contributed to this surge. Family Sagas, which overlap with many genres (Women's Lives and Relationships, Westerns, and even Fantasy and Science Fiction), generally provide extensive historical background in relating the adventures of the generations of a family. These tales may be complete in a single volume, or the author may follow the family's fortunes in several linked books. In these the family's story vies with history for prominence, but the best Family Sagas are well grounded in historical events and details. The benchmark Family Saga author is John Jakes. Although Jakes will never be one of the great stylists of the Historical Fiction genre, none of us in libraries can doubt his enormous popularity. From his initial success with the Kent Family Chronicles, detailing the story of the American Revolution (*The Bastard* is the first), he has maintained his reputation for providing popular accounts of events in American history, usually through generations of families, and he continues to attract readers as he mines a wealth of American historical backgrounds.[11] His recent *The Gods of Newport* continues his focus on family in this story of class struggle set against the backdrop of the summer houses of the very wealthy.[12]

Other popular contemporary writers of Family Sagas include Beverly Swerling with her generational Saga of the founding of New York City (*City of Dreams: A Novel of Nieuw Amsterdam and Early Manhattan* is the first), and Kevin Baker, whose darker, grittier look at New York City chronicles the place, rather than the characters, in the tradition of Michener and Edward Rutherfurd. *Paradise Alley*, which explores the draft riots during the Civil War, is the first chronologically.[13]

In some Historical novels, the distinction between event-centered and character- or family-centered is harder to make. These may combine characters and settings with particular events to create a vibrant story. In his novel *Gates of Fire* Steven Pressfield explores a historical event in considerable depth and with a great deal of emotion.[14] The Battle of Thermopylae in 480 BC is the ostensible topic, but in fact this novel, told through the eyes of a Spartan survivor, explores the nature of the Spartan warriors, their training as well as their psychological and emotional motivations, their families, and their philosophy toward war and the state. Descriptions of the battle take very little space by comparison, and the reader comes away with a more complete sense of the battle, those who fought, and the implications of their defeat. More recently, E. L. Doctorow has done the same in his novel of Sherman's march to the sea, *The March*.[15] In a style similar to Robert Altman's film technique, he presents a large cast of diverse characters whose stories are entwined against the backdrop of an important historical epoch. The details enhance and personalize our understanding of history. Readers may choose and appreciate these books for either the emphasis on character or on events—or for both.

Characterization

Readers expect accuracy in the presentation of characters as well as in other details. Even if they are not real historical personages, they must fit within the times. Glaring anachronisms of language, behavior, or straightforward fact distract and sometimes cause readers to distrust the author's research. For example, discovering twentieth-century colloquialisms in a novel set in the fourteenth century wreaks havoc in the context of a Historical novel and can, in fact, add unintentional humor.

Actual historical figures need to act in ways that are consistent with known facts, and fictional characters must act in a believable fashion for their time and place. All should fit within the story and act in ways that could have actually happened. Most important for readers is that they *feel* real. Conn Iggulden offers fascinating portraits of famous historical figures, first in his Emperor series—biographical novels about Julius Caesar—and then in his Conqueror series featuring Genghis Khan. Based on historical sources, these novels offer believable, complex, well-rounded character studies and take readers into those worlds. *Genghis: Birth of an Empire* is particularly interesting not only for the insights into the character of this man many readers know only as a byword for ruthless conquest, but also for the lyrical descriptions of the exotic and harsh landscapes of his early years on the Asian steppes.[16] Lisa See's fictional heroines in *Snow Flower and the Secret Fan* represent different classes and thus reflect the types of lives such characters would have led in nineteenth-century China.[17] See focuses on their friendship and the vagaries of fortune that affect each, all the while illuminating the times in which they lived, buoyed by their friendship and secret language.

Pacing

Historical novels are usually longer books (almost always more than three hundred pages), and they are not generally referred to as fast-paced, even if they include Adventure elements. A phrase such as "leisurely unfold-ing" or "unhurried" perhaps better describes the pacing of most novels in this genre. In many, however, there is an immediacy to the pacing that pulls the reader quickly into the story. This may occur because we usually know the outcome of the story and we are ensnared by the author's skill, as we read on to see how the author weaves his tale. Historical novels may be densely written, but the story envelops the reader, draws him in, and keeps him enthralled. In addition, the necessity of creating the detailed background often makes these books slow-starting, although the pacing may pick up midway. Even in Allende's *Zorro*, early details of the hero's life unfold slowly, but the mesmerizing (and often humorous) narrative voice draws readers quickly into this meandering story.[18] Intrigued by our colorful hero, we read on in expectation of the swashbuckling adventure that must eventually follow.

Style/Language

Language is particularly tricky in this genre. While some readers are put off by attempts to make the language authentic to the times, others relish that touch and look for it particularly when they seek new authors and titles. For example, Barbara Hambly's use of old-fashioned forms—thy, thine, thou—in *Patriot Heart* will be exactly what one reader wants and just the thing to put off another.[19] And frankly, most of us don't know enough to recognize when language is anachronistic and when it's used accurately for the time and place; many of us only notice the language if there are glaring errors, not necessarily when it actually suits. Some authors, such as Anne Easter Smith in *A Rose for the Crown*, simply employ a more formal

language which takes readers out of the present day.[20] Anachronisms—
phrases that don't fit the time or place—are often jarring, but only to those
who know they are incorrect. Dialect can intensify a reader's reaction—
positively or negatively, since readers often find nonstandard speech on
the page difficult to decipher. (Audiobooks may solve this problem, since
dialect heard is often much more easily understood.) We can't predict
what readers will like, and we don't always notice language ourselves, if
we're caught up in the story.

Other language issues are more straightforward. Some writers, such as
Stef Penney in *The Tenderness of Wolves,* write an elegant, lyrical prose that
adds another dimension to the novel. Others, such as Huebner's *American
by Blood,* are more Spartan.[21] Cadence is another factor to consider. While it
is more easily identified when it is heard (as in audiobooks), sometimes an
author's writing highlights a particular rhythm that sticks with the reader.
A good example is Frank Delaney, who writes lyrically about Ireland and
whose style reminds readers of what sitting and listening to a bard relate
a story might have been like. Alessandro Baricco's *Silk,* translated from
the Italian, reflects a storyteller's cadence and devices, such as the repeti-
tion of words and phrases. (It has also been dramatized to great effect as a
play by Mary Zimmerman and a screenplay by Francis Girard in the 2007
film.[22] Its structure and language would also lend themselves to opera.)

In some cases format or style drives the appeal. Novels written as dia-
ries or memoirs (Robin Maxwell's *The Secret Diary of Anne Boleyn,* Nancy
E. Turner's *These Is My Words: The Diary of Sarah Agnes Prine, 1881–1901,*
Allende's *Inés of My Soul*) remain popular, as do first-person narratives
(Sarah Dunant's *In the Company of the Courtesan,* fearlessly related by Fiam-
metta Bianchini's companion, the dwarf Bucino).[23]

KEY AUTHORS

To understand the popularity of the genre and work well with readers, it is
important to read popular authors who typify the genre's appeal. Several
contemporary authors make excellent introductions to the genre: Edward
Rutherfurd, Philippa Gregory, John Jakes, and Jeff Shaara.

Rutherfurd has assumed the mantle of James Michener, best-selling
author of numerous historical titles. As did Michener's, Rutherfurd's novels feature the history of a place even more than of an individual and are
applauded for their vast scope, immense size, and interesting details of
a place in time and the people who populated it. Novels such as *Sarum,*

Russka, and *London* offer layers of history and characters situated in a particular place through time.[24]

As mentioned earlier in the discussion of Family Sagas, John Jakes remains popular and prolific, and his writing certainly exemplifies this type of Historical Fiction. He typically tells an old-fashioned story with social themes that resonate with fiction readers and fans of social history alike. Interesting characters, historically detailed story lines, and just a touch of melodrama make his novels popular choices for a wide range of readers.

Even before the film version of her novel of Anne Boleyn's sister, *The Other Boleyn Girl,* Philippa Gregory was a good suggestion for many readers.[25] Her intriguing character-centered novels fascinate fans of Tudor England as well as Saga readers.

Jeff Shaara's compelling novels of American history also have broad appeal. His focus sweeps across the defining issues, characters, and battles of American history from the Revolution (*Rise to Rebellion*) to World War II (*The Rising Tide: A Novel of World War II*).[26] Characters and dialogue dominate his stories, which involve readers in key historical events.

Don't forget the classic authors who are still read and appreciated by fans of the genre, even though they are not as popular as they once were. It behooves us to keep and be aware of Mary Renault who brought ancient Rome and Greece to life for readers from the beginning of her career in the late 1950s. Try *The King Must Die* to sample her work.[27] This and its companion, *The Bull from the Sea,* retell the Theseus legend and offer insight into both ancient Greek custom and story, while *The Last of the Wine* explores the life and times of Alexander the Great.[28] Other authors who shouldn't be forgotten include Irving Stone (classic fictional biographies including Michelangelo's story in *The Agony and the Ecstasy*); Anya Seton with her timeless historical tales (*Katherine* and others); Jean Plaidy, whose chronicles of the English kings and queens remain unmatched (*The Bastard King* is the first); Howard Fast, known for single titles (*April Morning*) as well as Sagas (*The Immigrants*); and, of course, James Michener.[29]

WHAT WE KNOW ABOUT FANS

Fans read to learn about historical events, or characters, or the life and customs in another time. They are not just interested in dry facts and dates; they expect history to come alive through the stories these writers fashion. Historical Fiction allows them to explore characters and facts in story form, to place people and events in a larger perspective in ways that are more entertaining, involving, and expansive than straight history.

Having recognized that, we discover immediately that Historical Fiction offers a wide range of books that satisfy this interest—and meet readers' definitions of the genre. Some expect action-packed Historical novels that feature many of the elements of the Adventure genre. Other readers look for Historical novels that focus on characters and their lives. These character-centered novels provide glimpses into the lives of fictional and real people through the description of actual events and an interpretation of the characters' reactions to them. They often provide a very intimate portrayal of the protagonist, who is frequently a person from history.

Many fans prefer to read about a particular country and time, or they have particular countries and times they will not, by choice, read about. We have all met readers who will only read about the American West or nothing set in England. I even know one reader who will not read anything in which Oliver Cromwell appears! As in every other genre, readers may not be interested in exploring beyond these boundaries, no matter how similar another book may seem. We librarians should not be surprised by these restrictions.

On the other hand, if a reader is interested in a particular period or historical figure, he or she may tolerate a wide range of quality in the writing style and be willing to read across the genre and beyond to related genres—Mystery, Adventure, and Romance—to find books about that person or event.

While some fans read about particular characters or times, others look for a particular style of writing. These readers may read about a wide range of countries and historical periods, just to enjoy that style. For example, readers who love Literary Fiction may read a wide range of elegantly written or award-winning Historical Fiction, simply because they appreciate the quality of the writing. Others may prefer novels in diary form and read all, no matter the main character, country, or time period. We need to be open to these possibilities when we listen to readers talk about what they enjoy.

Finally, Historical Fiction readers like big books in which they can immerse themselves. Many appreciate a broad scope of history, a large cast of characters, and a wealth of historical, social, and cultural detail. Others may prefer a smaller scope, but they are no less adamant on the necessity of the detail. Unfortunately, writers can never write quickly enough to satisfy their fans, and in Historical Fiction, which requires extensive research, the pace of publishing lags far behind reader interest. Here especially, it behooves us to be on the lookout for additional authors that might appeal in order to satisfy fans while they wait for the next novel by their favorite authors.

In exploring an unfamiliar genre, it is often difficult to find a starting point. A good suggestion might be a book that appeals because it is similar to the type we already read and enjoy. Figure 15.2 lists Historical Fiction authors who provide a good introduction to this genre and whose writing also has similarities to another genre that the reader may already enjoy.

Figure 15.2 *An Introduction to the Historical Fiction Genre*

Historical Fiction Writers to Try, If You Enjoy . . .

Adrenaline:	C. C. Humphreys (Jack Absolute series)[30]
	Conn Iggulden
	Tim Willocks
Biography:	Anchee Min
Memoir:	David Kehlmann (*Measuring the World*)[31]
	Thomas Mallon
	Sena Jeter Naslund
	Alison Weir
Fantasy:	Judith Merkle Riley
Gentle:	Eugenia Price
	Jeanne Williams
Gay/Lesbian:	Sarah Waters
History:	Robert Alexander
	David Liss
	Steven Pressfield
	Alison Weir
Humor:	John Barth
	T. Coraghessan Boyle
Horror:	Barbara Hambly
Inspirational:	Orson Scott Card (Women of Genesis series)[32]
	Linda Chaikin
	Halter Marek
	Gilbert Morris
	Francine Rivers

(cont.)

Figure 15.2   *An Introduction to the Historical Fiction Genre (cont.)*

Literary:	Geraldine Brooks
	Tracy Chevalier
	Sena Jeter Naslund
	Iain Pears
Multicultural:	Alex Haley
	Lawrence Hill
	Amy Tan
Mystery:	Louis Bayard
Natural History:	James Michener
	Elizabeth Redfern
	Edward Rutherfurd
Romance:	Elizabeth Chadwick
	Sara Donati
	Ann Easter Smith
Romantic Suspense:	Judith Merkle Riley
Saga:	Frank Delaney
	Jennifer Donnelly
	John Jakes
	Beverly Swerling
Science Fiction:	Martin Cruz Smith (*December 6*)[33]
	Gore Vidal
Travel:	James Michener
	Edward Rutherfurd
	Paul Scott (The Raj Quartet)[34]
True Adventure:	Steven Pressfield
	Tim Willocks
Western:	Ivan Doig
Women's Lives:	Sandra Dallas
	Lisa See
	Susan Vreeland

THE READERS' ADVISORY INTERVIEW

In the readers' advisory interview, I have found it very useful to encourage readers to talk about Historical Fiction they have enjoyed, rather than asking first about a preference for country or time period. Even if they begin to describe an author or title I have read, I listen to what they tell me they liked about the book. (Too often I have found what they enjoy far different from what I liked about a book, so I am more careful now!)

- Do they talk about adventure or action, or do they mention evocative descriptions and interior, psychological views of characters?
- How do they describe the main characters? Are they real or fictional? Do real historical characters mingle with fictional ones?
- Does the story cover a long span of time or just a few days or weeks?
- Do they talk about the historical details, events, customs, or political and social issues? Or about how they got a sense of what life was like in a particular period?

All these elements give us clues as to the type of Historical Fiction they have enjoyed in the past and what they might be looking for today. For example, if a reader says she has just read Sena Naslund's *Abundance: A Novel of Marie Antoinette,* I listen to how she describes this lush biographical novel set in late eighteenth-century France.[35] If she talks about her pleasure in discovering intimate details of the queen's life, I might suggest another Historical novel that explores a royal life whether it is set in France or not. (For example, Michelle Moran's *Nefertiti* describes Egyptian court life and the renowned queen.[36] Margaret George's intimate historical novels might also be a good match.) If she talks about the historical details and life during the French Revolution, I might suggest James Tipton's *Annette Vallon: A Novel of the French Revolution,* which also includes famous figures—William Wordsworth among them—but focuses on life during those times through the eyes of a real but little-known woman.[37] A stronger interest in historical details might very well send me into nonfiction—biographies, histories, and accounts of the times.

The reader's mood is another important factor to consider. Readers may describe a title they've loved, but that may not really be what they want to read again right now. Are they in the mood for the same type of book or something different? We're introducing readers to possibilities, and asking about their mood is a useful technique. Readers who appreciate character-centered stories might enjoy something with action (Tim

Willocks's award-winning *The Religion* with its details of the 1565 siege of Malta and charismatic hero) or a book that moves more slowly with a reflective hero (Frazier's *Cold Mountain*).[38] Readers who want a particular time period may want more character or plot today and something very different on their next visit. As we train readers to be aware of the possibilities available, we too become more skilled in recognizing the range of titles we can offer.

When looking at books with readers, check for maps and genealogies. These are a bonus for fans, and they add to the authenticity of the novel. Sometimes the maps may be of an area, suggesting that the book covers a wider geographic region and includes more action and perhaps Adventure elements. Or they may be on a much smaller scale. Anchee Min provides a plan of the Forbidden City in *Empress Orchid*, as that area becomes the extent of Tzu Hsi's physical world. This smaller, more intimate scale suggests a more domestic emphasis, but her role as empress eventually moves her influence beyond these limited borders.[39] A genealogy or family tree, on the other hand, is a clear indication that Family Saga elements figure prominently in this novel.

Books that include historical notes at the end are particularly good suggestions for students who may be required to read Historical Fiction as a supplement to a history class or for any of us who expect to learn history through Historical Fiction. As mentioned earlier, most current writers of historical fiction now include such notes as a matter of course. Readers particularly concerned about historical accuracy prize this information.

As we offer titles to readers, we often develop descriptions that get to the heart of an author's appeal. We might talk about Jeff Shaara's warts-and-all characters, Adrenaline author Alan Furst's historical tales of world-weary spies, or Jim Harrison's evocative explorations of characters and landscape. Like Homeric epithets, these descriptions stick in our minds, and they alert readers to the kind of information they need to decide whether they're in the mood for that kind of book or not.

Appeal remains key in the readers' advisory interview as we share book possibilities with readers. These revealing adjectives allow us to forgo lengthy plot descriptions and focus on the information readers need to hear. While some readers may relate to extensive plot summaries, appeal-based descriptions are easier—we don't have to remember all the plot details—and even more effective. For example, we might describe Michael Shaara's *The Killer Angels* as an elegantly written, heartfelt, and melancholy story of the Battle of Gettysburg as seen through the eyes of the participants on both sides.[40] For another title, perhaps Anchee Min's novels of China's last empress (*Empress Orchid* and *The Last Empress*), we might mention the strong characterizations and political machinations that drive the story.[41]

Sure Bets

The variety of Historical Fiction means there are endless titles that work as Sure Bets. Lisa See's *Snow Flower and the Secret Fan* and *Peony in Love* have attracted many readers to the genre with her exquisitely detailed insights into women in seventeenth- and nineteenth-century China.[42] Books groups, too, have found here a wealth of material to explore and discuss.

Art-themed historical novels (and their authors) remain popular as Sure Bets. The Vermeer craze launched Tracy Chevalier (*Girl with a Pearl Earring*) and Susan Vreeland (*Girl in Hyacinth Blue*) and led to further popularity for their later novels.[43] (Chevalier's *The Lady and the Unicorn* presents a fine example of the melding of characters in their times with fascinating tales of the creation of an exquisite set of tapestries.[44] It makes a good reading suggestion for fans of Women's Lives and Relationships, Historical Fiction, the Middle Ages, and art history and technique.) Sarah Dunant, already an acclaimed Mystery writer, has also enjoyed success with her historical novels, which combine art, intrigue, and interesting bits of Italian history (suggest *The Birth of Venus*).[45]

Tim Willocks's *The Religion* documents the 1565 siege of Malta.[46] The action in this cinematic tale starts in the first chapters, as a French countess enlists Mattias Tannhauser, a sword-for-hire, to find her illegitimate son. The trail leads to Malta, and the ensuing action (and violence), not to mention intrigue and treachery, keep the pace unusually brisk for novels in this genre. In addition to the graphic details of the battle, there's also day-to-day coverage of the siege and what life was like for both combatants and those unfortunate enough to be caught in the violent religious war. There are also appealing and interesting characters and just enough humor and madcap antics to enliven the story.

EXPANDING READERS' HORIZONS WITH WHOLE COLLECTION READERS' ADVISORY

The very circumscribed definition of Historical Fiction considered in this chapter demands that we explore other genres when working with fans.

The crossover from Historical Fiction to the Mystery, Adventure, and Romance genres is extensive, and finding authors in related genres that satisfy Historical Fiction fans may be more straightforward than in any other genre. Basically, fans are seeking other fiction with that fully developed historical landscape they find in Historical Fiction.

Readers who appreciate adventure with their history will find a wealth of authors discussed in chapter 2, "Adventure," and chapter 5, "Thrillers." World War II stories continue to be very popular. Alan Furst's brooding Espionage Thrillers, set in countries occupied by the Nazis and filled with historical details and familiar figures, make good suggestions. Historical Naval Adventures remain popular—don't forget Patrick O'Brian and his series of Napoleonic War adventures. Bernard Cornwell, with multiple historical Military Adventures and his useful historical notes, also pleases a variety of readers.

Accurate historical settings, often including actual events and real people, figure in the work of some authors of Historical Romances, and these may appeal to Historical Fiction readers who appreciate this element. Any number of Regency Romances focus on figures and events in the Napoleonic Wars, and the novels of Jo Beverley and Lauren Willig make good suggestions. Rosalind Laker, who wrote in both the Historical Fiction and Romance genres, consistently explored specific time periods and the fictional and real characters who lived then. For example, *The Golden Tulip* features seventeenth-century Dutch painting and Vermeer.[47] Anya Seton's classic, *Katherine*, depicts the life of Katherine Swynford, mistress of John of Gaunt, in a compelling love story brimming with historical detail.[48]

Another popular technique involves mixing historical facts, often puzzles, with contemporary story lines, so that the author moves back and forth in time. Some Historical readers will find enough detail to satisfy. William Martin used this technique in his Adventure novel, *Back Bay*, relating the tale of a teapot crafted by Paul Revere for George Washington and following its fate through generations.[49] Martin has several titles in this vein. Paul Sussman employs a similar technique with his contemporary Adventure tales of archaeological excavations and ancient artifacts, often told across multiple time periods (*The Lost Army of Cambyses* is the first).[50] From the Romance genre, fans of this technique may want to try Lauren Willig, whose spinoffs of Baroness Orczy's *The Scarlet Pimpernel* have been very popular.[51] Her heroine is researching the Pimpernel and other spies in the era of the French Revolution, and the story lines in these romps move from past to present and back as she unearths material in her research. *The Secret History of the Pink Carnation* is the first.[52] Geraldine

Brooks's *People of the Book* uses the same technique with a more literary style and emphasis, as her heroine/book restorer examines a famous Jewish Haggadah.[53] Her research uncovers the provenance of the book in historical flashbacks that move backward in time to the book's creation.

The Mystery genre, too, offers much for Historical Fiction readers who may appreciate the puzzles of Mysteries with strong historical settings. Anne Perry writes three series, two set in Victorian England and the third during World War I. The longest-running features Inspector Pitt and his well-born wife, Charlotte, in a series of adventures that explore the serious social and class issues in Victorian England (*The Cater Street Hangman* is the first).[54] Humorous secondary characters give these a lighter feel than Perry's other Victorian series, which features William Monk, a policeman who has lost his memory in an accident. As he struggles to regain his memory and his career, he is assisted by, among others, Hester Latterly, a nurse who trained with Florence Nightingale in the Crimean War and who has her own forthright ideas of the role of nurses and women in general in Victorian society. This series, which opens with *The Face of a Stranger*, features bleak, evocative, atmospheric Mysteries that delve into the underside of Victorian society.[55] In the third series Cambridge professor Joseph Reavley is drawn into the war effort as a chaplain. The threat of a deadly conspiracy, led by the sinister Peacemaker, and espionage combine with horrendous details of life on the front lines in this compelling series. (*No Graves as Yet* opens the series.)[56]

Historical Mysteries provide an excellent, often shorter introduction to a particular historical period, and that may be one of the reasons for their popularity. Readers interested in ancient Rome, for example, might be more willing to pursue the Mystery series by either Steven Saylor (*Roman Blood*) or Lindsey Davis (*The Silver Pigs*) before embarking on Colleen McCullough's more daunting volumes that present Rome's history. (*The First Man in Rome* is the first.)[57] Readers intimidated by the heft of Sharon Kay Penman's historical novels may appreciate her Mystery series, also set in medieval England.

Fans of Historical Fiction are prime candidates for Whole Collection Readers' Advisory suggestions across the Dewey Divide in narrative nonfiction. Remember that readers of a particular period often appreciate seeing the accompanying nonfiction about the time, including materials about dress, customs, and culture. Those who are exploring a particular character in Historical Fiction also often value Biographies about that person or about others during that time. Don't forget Memoirs that explore the life and times of historical figures and provide that intimate first-person hook that so many readers appreciate. Since many Historical novels are set during particular wars, readers may also appreciate the nonfiction about the same momentous events.

Nonfiction readers can sometimes be enticed to explore the fiction collection if we identify the links between the history books they currently enjoy and fiction that is similar. As noted in figure 15.2, authors of Historical Fiction may also make excellent suggestions for readers of Biography and other nonfiction subjects. Authors such as Rutherfurd and Weir (who is famous for her biographies) expect their readers to have a certain basic knowledge of the period, or at least a historical perspective, and thus they move quickly into the specifics of a situation and characters, rather than providing extensive background information.

Many authors in sundry genres employ detailed historical settings, center their stories on real events, or feature characters from history. Figure 15.3 offers fans of the Historical Fiction genre a variety of directions to pursue in both fiction and nonfiction.

TRENDS

After years of focusing primarily on the histories of the United States and the United Kingdom, Historical Fiction has gone international. Europe certainly is now better represented than ever before, with Sarah Dunant's art and history tales *The Birth of Venus* and *In the Company of the Courtesan* set in Italy, Markus Zusak's *The Book Thief* in Nazi Germany, and Andromeda Romano-Lax's *The Spanish Bow* in early twentieth-century Spain.[58] Interest in East Asia is not particularly new, as China and Japan have been well covered for years, but other parts of Asia have been highlighted recently in Iggulden's *Genghis* and the numerous Historical novels set in India.[59] Chilean novelist Isabel Allende introduced many readers to her country's history in the nineteenth century with *Daughter of Fortune,* while *Inés of My Soul* explores history and the customs of both natives and conquerors in sixteenth-century South America.[60]

Historical Fiction has not escaped the craze to combine with other genres. Certainly there are the obvious overlaps with Adventure, Thrillers, Mystery, and Romance. Some authors are known for their playful approach to history—Gore Vidal with his provocative reinterpretations and E. L. Doctorow with his imaginative riffs on history and historical figures. Elizabeth Kostova's extraordinarily popular *The Historian* introduced Horror themes and the historical Dracula.[61] Time travel, a popular

Figure 15.3 *Expanding Readers' Horizons*

Authors to Take Readers beyond the Historical Fiction Genre

Adrenaline:	Dorothy Dunnett
	Alan Furst
	David Liss
	Patrick O'Brian
Biography/Memoir:	Doris Kearns Goodwin
	David McCullough
Fantasy:	Susanna Clarke
	Rosalind Miles (Tristan and Isolde Novels)[62]
	Naomi Novik
Gentle:	Van Reid
History:	Stephen Ambrose
	David McCullough
	Ross King
Horror:	Dan Simmons (*The Terror*)[63]
Literary:	Peter Carey
	Marilynne Robinson (*Gilead*)[64]
Mystery:	P. C. Doherty
	Anne Perry
	Jacqueline Winspear
Natural History:	John McPhee
Psychological Suspense:	Caleb Carr
Romance:	Jo Beverley
	Jane Feather
	Mary Jo Putney
Science Fiction:	Michael Flynn (*Eifelheim*)[65]
	Neal Stephenson (Baroque Cycle)[66]
Travel:	Bill Bryson
True Adventure:	Tony Horwitz
	Nathaniel Philbrick
True Crime:	Erik Larson
Western:	Don Coldsmith
	Will Henry
Women's Lives:	Jane Roberts Ward

device in several genres, is used to great effect in Historical Fiction. Diana Gabaldon's Outlander series was an early example.[67] Because of the way her novels flow, time travel is less obtrusive and less frequent than in some, and she also adds a tremendous amount of historical detail. Connie Willis's provocative *Doomsday Book,* with its parallel plagues in the fourteenth and twenty-first centuries, is another title that caught readers' imaginations with its wealth of historical details and thoughtful speculations.[68] Generally cataloged in Science Fiction, it pays heed to historical particulars sufficiently to appeal to historical fans.

This leads to one of the most remarkable trends in Historical Fiction today: the growing interest among many readers in Alternate History, which used to be anathema. Once the sole province of Science Fiction and Fantasy, Alternate History continues to grow in popularity with Historical readers. Naomi Novik's Temeraire series, beginning with *His Majesty's Dragon,* places readers firmly in the midst of the Napoleonic Wars but just as firmly in a Fantasy world where sentient Dragons wage battle on both sides.[69] (Think Anne McCaffrey writing with Patrick O'Brian.) Certainly Robert Harris's *Fatherland,* in which Germany won World War II, has long been popular among general readers as well as Historical Fiction fans.[70] Many of the authors discussed in the Alternative History section of chapter 13, "Science Fiction," may appeal to readers of Historical Fiction.

The Historical Fiction genre covers a wide range of novels, from the more serious and literary to Family Sagas and those with elements of Romance, Adventure, and Mystery. Some are intimate and psychological portraits of people of a particular time; others are more exterior and action-oriented. Setting or atmosphere—the frame—is the most important element.

Through fiction, much of a country's culture and story are preserved for future generations. Historical Fiction is part of a long tradition of retelling and preserving past events. Look at Homer and his stories of the Trojan War, sung for generations to keep the history and the story alive. The best Historical Fiction combines both those elements, story and history, in a way that helps readers understand and remember the past. Although readers appreciate a wide variety of Historical Fiction and fiction with historical settings in other genres, they share the same expectations: a well-researched and memorable story rooted in a time past, peopled with characters long dead and brought alive again through an author's imagination.

NOTES

1. Charles Frazier, *Cold Mountain* (New York: Atlantic Monthly Press, 1997).
2. James Michener, *Chesapeake* (New York: Random House, 1978).
3. Robert Harris, *Imperium: A Novel of Ancient Rome* (New York: Simon and Schuster, 2006).
4. Harris, *Pompeii: A Novel* (New York: Random House, 2003).
5. Sophie Gee, *The Scandal of the Season* (New York: Scribner, 2007).
6. Sandra Dallas, *Tallgrass* (New York: St. Martin's, 2007); Elizabeth Chadwick, *Lords of the White Castle* (New York: St. Martin's, 2002).
7. E. L. Doctorow, *The March: A Novel* (New York: Random House, 2005); Alison Weir, *Innocent Traitor: A Novel of Lady Jane Grey* (New York: Ballantine, 2007); Andrew Huebner, *American by Blood: A Novel* (New York: Simon and Schuster, 2000).
8. Geraldine Brooks, *Year of Wonders: A Novel of the Plague* (New York: Viking, 2001).
9. Ken Follett, *The Pillars of the Earth* (New York: Morrow, 1989); Follett, *World without End* (New York: Dutton, 2007).
10. Isabel Allende, *Daughter of Fortune,* trans. Margaret Sayers Peden (New York: HarperCollins, 1999); Allende, *Inés of My Soul,* trans. Margaret Sayers Peden (New York: HarperCollins, 2006); Allende, *Zorro: A Novel,* trans. Margaret Sayers Peden (New York: HarperCollins, 2005).
11. John Jakes, *The Bastard* (New York: Pyramid Books, 1974).
12. Jakes, *The Gods of Newport: A Novel* (New York: Dutton, 2006).
13. Beverly Swerling, *City of Dreams: A Novel of Nieuw Amsterdam and Early Manhattan* (New York: Simon and Schuster, 2001); Kevin Baker, *Paradise Alley* (New York: HarperCollins, 2002).
14. Steven Pressfield, *Gates of Fire* (New York: Doubleday, 1998).
15. Doctorow cited above.
16. Conn Iggulden, *Genghis: Birth of an Empire* (New York: Delacorte, 2007).
17. Lisa See, *Snow Flower and the Secret Fan: A Novel* (New York: Random House, 2005).
18. Allende cited above.
19. Barbara Hambly, *Patriot Heart: A Novel of the Founding Mothers* (New York: Bantam, 2007).
20. Anne Easter Smith, *A Rose for the Crown* (New York: Simon and Schuster, 2006).
21. Stef Penney, *The Tenderness of Wolves: A Novel* (New York: Simon and Schuster, 2007); Huebner cited above.
22. Alessandro Baricco, *Silk,* trans. Guido Waldman (New York: Vintage, 1998).
23. Robin Maxwell, *The Secret Diary of Anne Boleyn* (New York: Arcade, 1997); Nancy E. Turner, *These Is My Words: The Diary of Sarah Agnes Prine, 1881–1901; Arizona Territories* (New York: ReganBooks, 1998); Allende, cited above; Sarah Dunant, *In the Company of the Courtesan: A Novel* (New York: Random House, 2006).
24. Edward Rutherfurd, *Sarum: The Novel of England* (New York: Crown, 1987); Rutherfurd, *Russka: The Novel of Russia* (New York: Crown, 1991); Rutherfurd, *London* (New York: Crown, 1997).
25. Philippa Gregory, *The Other Boleyn Girl: A Novel* (New York: Simon and Schuster, 2004).
26. Jeff Shaara, *Rise to Rebellion* (New York: Ballantine, 2001); Shaara, *The Rising Tide: A Novel of World War II* (New York: Ballantine, 2006).
27. Mary Renault, *The King Must Die* (New York: Pantheon, 1958).
28. Renault, *The Bull from the Sea* (New York: Pantheon, 1962); Renault, *The Last of the Wine* (New York: Pantheon, 1956).
29. Irving Stone, *The Agony and the Ecstasy: A Novel of Michelangelo* (Garden City, NY: Doubleday, 1961); Anya Seton, *Katherine* (Boston: Houghton Mifflin, 1954); Jean Plaidy, *The Bastard King* (New York: Putnam, 1979); Howard Fast, *April Morning* (New York: Bantam, 1962); Fast, *The Immigrants* (New York: Bantam, 1962).

30. C. C. Humphreys, Jack Absolute series, beginning with *Jack Absolute* (New York: St. Martin's, 2006).
31. Daniel Kehlmann, *Measuring the World,* trans. Carol Brown Janeway (New York: Pantheon, 2006).
32. Orson Scott Card, Women of Genesis series, beginning with *Sarah: Women of Genesis* (Salt Lake City, UT: Shadow Mountain, 2000).
33. Martin Cruz Smith, *December 6* (New York: Simon and Schuster, 2002).
34. Paul Scott, The Raj Quartet, beginning with *The Jewel in the Crown* (New York: Morrow, 1966).
35. Sena Naslund, *Abundance: A Novel of Marie Antoinette* (New York: Morrow, 2006).
36. Michelle Moran, *Nefertiti: A Novel* (New York: Crown, 2007).
37. James Tipton, *Annette Vallon: A Novel of the French Revolution* (New York: HarperCollins, 2007).
38. Tim Willocks, *The Religion* (New York: Sarah Crichton Books, 2007); Frazier cited above.
39. Anchee Min, *Empress Orchid* (Boston: Houghton Mifflin, 2004).
40. Shaara, *The Killer Angels* (New York: McKay, 1974).
41. Min, *The Last Empress* (Boston: Houghton Mifflin, 2007).
42. See cited above; See, *Peony in Love: A Novel* (New York: Random House, 2007).
43. Tracy Chevalier, *Girl with a Pearl Earring* (New York: Dutton, 2000); Susan Vreeland, *Girl in Hyacinth Blue* (Denver, CO: MacMurray and Beck, 1999).
44. Chevalier, *The Lady and the Unicorn* (New York: Dutton, 2004).
45. Dunant, *The Birth of Venus* (New York: Random House, 2004).
46. Willock cited above.
47. Rosalind Laker, *The Golden Tulip* (New York: Doubleday, 1991).
48. Seton cited above.
49. William Martin, *Back Bay* (New York: Crown, 1979).
50. Paul Sussman, *The Lost Army of Cambyses* (New York: Thomas Dunne Books, 2003).
51. Emmuska Orczy, *The Scarlet Pimpernel* (New York: Grosset and Dunlap, [1935]).
52. Lauren Willig, *The Secret History of the Pink Carnation* (New York: Dutton, 2005).
53. Brooks, *People of the Book* (New York: Viking, 2008).
54. Anne Perry, *The Cater Street Hangman* (New York: St. Martin's, 1979).
55. Perry, *The Face of a Stranger* (New York: Fawcett Columbine, 1990).
56. Perry, *No Graves as Yet* (New York: Ballantine, 2003).
57. Steven Saylor, *Roman Blood* (New York: St. Martin's, 1991); Lindsey Davis, *The Silver Pigs* (New York: Crown, 1989); Colleen McCullough, *The First Man in Rome* (New York: Morrow, 1990).
58. Dunant cited above; Markus Zusak, *The Book Thief* (New York: Knopf, 2006); Andromeda Romano-Lax, *The Spanish Bow* (Orlando, FL: Harcourt, 2007).
59. Iggulden cited above.
60. Allende cited above.
61. Elizabeth Kostova, *The Historian: A Novel* (New York: Little, Brown, 2005).
62. Rosalind Miles, Tristan and Isolde Novels, beginning with *Isolde, Queen of the Western Isle* (New York: Crown, 2002).
63. Dan Simmons, *The Terror: A Novel* (New York: Little, Brown, 2007).
64. Marilynne Robinson, *Gilead* (New York: Farrar, Straus, and Giroux, 2004).
65. Michael Flynn, *Eifelheim* (New York: Tor, 2006).
66. Neal Stephenson, Baroque Cycle, beginning with *Quicksilver* (New York: Morrow, 2003).
67. Diana Gabaldon, Outlander series, beginning with *Outlander* (New York: Delacorte, 1991).
68. Connie Willis, *Doomsday Book* (New York: Bantam, 1992).
69. Naomi Novik, *His Majesty's Dragon* (New York: Ballantine, 2006).
70. Robert Harris, *Fatherland* (New York: Random House, 1992).

16

WESTERNS

Many librarians dismiss Westerns as a dying genre. It seems that publishers agree, since they currently reprint popular authors and titles from the past and publish fewer and fewer new titles. Still, the archetype of the lone man bringing justice has long been a dominant theme in American literature and one that still resonates with readers. Westerns were first popular as pulp fiction at the turn of the twentieth century, and their appeal was dramatized on radio and television shows and in the movies from the early years of that century through the 1960s. After languishing for several decades, Westerns are making a comeback on television and in the movies. Readers who appreciate the satisfying stories found in this genre can only hope that Western novels, such an integral part of our roots in legend and literature, will once again become a staple of our collections.

A DEFINITION

In traditional Westerns we expect cowboys, cattle drives, gunslingers, adventure, and gunplay. Fans do not necessarily require historical accuracy, although they do expect realistic detail in firearms and accoutrement. However, creating a strong a sense of time and place, the feel of the Old West, is essential. Westerns speak to basic, deep-seated feelings about the land and the men who brought justice to the wild, uninhabited country and thus helped make it safe for those who civilized it.

The West was viewed as a land of opportunity that offered the possibility of redemption for those who had escaped the confines of civilization. Westerns dramatize and romanticize the conflict between the civilizing influences of the East and the wild, untamed West, as they portray the dangers faced by the men who brought order to the new territory.

Westerns, as considered in this chapter, also encompass Historical novels set in the West during the same time period. These Novels of the West accurately depict the western expansion and emphasize historical details and events. These titles often feature explorers as well as the settlers who stayed on to civilize the West. In addition, they frequently include strong female characters, as it is usually the women who are responsible for bringing civilization. These novels explore the issues arising in the civilizing of the West; their focus is on the people who came and stayed. Traditional Westerns, in contrast, more frequently depict the lone man riding into a community and then leaving once his job is complete.

However, as those distinctions now increasingly blur in the novels read by fans of both Westerns and Historical Fiction, the differences between the two become harder to define and less important. Western readers, generally speaking, do not require the strong historical background vital to Historical Fiction fans, but they will enjoy many of these larger, historically accurate novels, because they are set against a familiar background, just as fans of Historical Fiction about the West will appreciate the sense of time and place they find in Westerns.

Westerns, then, are novels set in the western United States (with the Missouri and Mississippi Rivers as the eastern boundaries) primarily from the end of the Civil War to the beginning of the twentieth century. They feature the adventures of cowboys, scouts, Indians, settlers, and lawmen, and they explore the clash between civilization and anarchy in mythic stories of men and the land. While they may accurately depict the time and place in which they are set, the image and feel of the West and of those times, as well as the struggle to survive against myriad perils, take precedence over history. Figure 16.1 summarizes the characteristics of the Western.

CHARACTERISTICS AND THE GENRE'S APPEAL

Frame/Setting

Landscape dominates the Western, and it is often so carefully drawn that it is a character itself. Westerns take readers back to a time and place in which life is set against a dangerous but beautiful backdrop. Landscapes are carefully described, for it is the openness and the infinite possibilities this virgin landscape offers that set the tone for these stories. Nature is larger than life, and to survive in this kind of landscape, the men here

---

Figure 16.1 *Characteristics of Westerns*

---

1. The exterior descriptions of the landscape and terrain frame the books, which take place in the western United States in the decades between the Civil War and 1900. Since they may be set in unidentified places (simply *the West*) and in an unspecified past time, they often project a sense of timelessness.

2. The traditional hero is often a loner who arrives to right wrongs and then moves on. Heroes use strategy before guns to win arguments, although they are often forced to use violence in the end.

3. Plots may be complex or more straightforward. Common themes include the redemptive power of the West, the difficulties surviving in a harsh landscape, revenge, and the lack of law along with the necessity of creating just laws.

4. Nostalgia for times past creates an elegiac tone that permeates many Westerns.

5. Pacing may be breakneck in Westerns that feature action-packed stories or more measured in others.

6. Dialogue is generally spare, colorful, and rich in jargon, but many Westerns also feature lyrical descriptions of the landscape.

---

must also be larger than life, thus adding a heroic layer to the mythic dimension of the stories. The Western landscape is a paradox. While it is often lyrically and evocatively described, it may also be painted as barren, treacherous terrain, where survival may be difficult for both men and animals. This landscape is more rugged and merciless, yet more open to possibilities, than the confined landscapes of cities or civilized areas. For those who can survive in this landscape, the West offers limitless possibilities as well as transforming powers.

Another feature of Westerns is the imprecise time and place in which stories are often set. We know the time to be generally the twenty to thirty years after the Civil War, and the place is the West, but beyond that we are often at a loss. The point these writers make, of course, is that such precise details are not necessarily important for the story or for the reader. Dates and place-names add inflexibility and a forced reality that are at odds with the vague times and places found in some Westerns. Max Brand, for example, set his myriad adventures in the High Mountain Desert, which becomes a familiar but unidentifiable location to fans of his stories. Creating a place outside of specific geography and a time outside of time enhances the mythic dimension of these stories and their more universal message and appeal. The timelessness of the frame resonates with readers.

Characterization

Even though one might believe action to be more important, a large part of the appeal of Westerns for fans is the character of the hero, whose similarities to the medieval knight-errant as a champion of justice elevate these stories from tales of cowboys and lawmen to almost mythic proportions. The classic hero is a loner, a kind of paladin (as in the television hero, played by Richard Boone, on *Have Gun, Will Travel*, in the late 1950s), who rides throughout the land, righting wrongs and administering justice. Then, when his mission is completed, he moves on, rather than staying to settle down and start a family. This wanderer brings justice (surely one of the touchstones of civilization) but is unwilling to stay to become too civilized himself. *Shane*, Jack Schaefer's popular classic, exemplifies this kind of character.[1] Shane, the knight-errant, arrives mysteriously into a community torn apart by disputes between farmers and cattlemen. He is the strong, silent type, yet his presence creates fear only among those who have something to fear. The Starret family with whom he stays all come to love, not fear, this menacing gunfighter. And even when he is faced with violence, he tries reason first to achieve resolution before resorting to guns to solve the problem. He gains the respect of all and leaves his mark on the community when he rides away.

Another typical Western hero is a young man, a knight in training, and the Western provides an ideal setting for a bildungsroman, as the young cowboy learns the role he is to play. In these cases there is a mentor, an established knight, who teaches him the ropes, literally and figuratively. Elmer Kelton's *The Pumpkin Rollers* provides an example of this.[2] Young Trey McLean leaves home to make his own way as a cattleman. Along the way, he meets evil in the form of a man who steals his small herd, but Trey finds his mentor in drover Ivan Kerbow. He also discovers love with a rancher's daughter. Together the couple tries to create their future on Kerbow's isolated ranch, faced with dangers from ruthless ranchers and bad guys alike, not to mention the heartless landscape. There is even the good-guy-gone-wrong who finds redemption in the infinite healing landscape of the West. Trey and Sarah mature in this refining fire, facing their difficulties aided by their innate strength and the help of friends, and the book closes as civilization comes to west Texas. The cowboys are off again, rounding up herds to drive to the railroads in Kansas, but Trey and Sarah stay to make their own way, as this popular Western morphs seamlessly into a Novel of the West.

The character of the Western hero is reminiscent in many ways of the hard-boiled private investigator (chapter 11, "Mysteries"), another loner with few close companions. And if he does have comrades, they are likely unexpected—like the pairing of the Lone Ranger and his Indian partner, Tonto. Like the P.I., the Western hero may sometimes operate outside the law to administer "frontier justice" rather than the more traditional legal justice. Both operate under the aegis of a strict moral code, which supports their actions but does not always follow the letter of the law.

Recent representations of the Western hero have moved from the mythic to the more realistic. When he talks of the Western genre, Spur Award–winning author Don Coldsmith likes to joke that early heroes were six feet four inches and invincible; Kelton's heroes, on the other hand, are five feet eight inches and decidedly nervous in emergencies, as is clearly evident throughout *The Pumpkin Rollers*. Traditional Western heroes are men of iron; more recent writers, including Kelton and Larry McMurtry, have given them human frailties. Still, despite their weaknesses, they suggest the qualities of the idealized hero who brings justice to the uncivilized West.

Some authors introduce real historical figures, primarily lawmen or outlaws, into their novels. These stories run the gamut, presenting a range from the idealized to the more accurate versions of the lives of famous men. Loren D. Estleman often takes historical incidents—the trial of the killer of Wild Bill Hickok (*Aces and Eights*), the gunfight at the OK Corral (*Bloody Season*), the lives of Buffalo Bill Cody (*This Old Bill*) and Pat Garrett, who killed Billy the Kid (*Journey of the Dead*)—as the basis for his Westerns, an approach for which he has won three Spur Awards, the Western Writers of America's annual honor.[3] Other authors rely solely on fictional characters. The crucial point is that in most Westerns, except for the most literary, characters are generally stereotypes of good or bad men. Readers appreciate the clear distinctions.

Secondary characters also play a role in Westerns. Occasionally the hero has a sidekick, as in Terry C. Johnston's series beginning with *Carry the Wind*.[4] Mountain man and trapper Titus Bass takes on Josiah Paddock, fresh out of St. Louis, as his partner on adventures that lead them through the western mountains to New Mexico. Women and Indians often play important roles, and in much of the genre they are surprisingly well drawn. Racism and sexism, although present especially in titles from the first half of the twentieth century, do not run rampant in the genre. This is not to say that these portrayals are not stereotypical. Women are usually either fallen women who turn out to have hearts of gold, or very good women who stand by their men and work to make a home in the wilderness. Only occasionally do bad women appear in Westerns. Indians may be the force against whom the hero battles, but many novelists are nonjudgmental in their portrayal as well. In fact, many Western heroes have spent time with the Indians—sometimes raised or rescued by them, or simply as friends and fellow hunters. Recent writers, and many classic authors, know enough history to play fair with a group that has been lied to and cheated but who can also be disturbingly brutal in their encounters with those who try to take their game or their land. In fact, both women and Indians have become "heroes" in award-winning Westerns in the past years. Sandra Dallas won a Spur Award in 2003 for *The Chili Queen*, the New Mexico–set tale of a mail-order bride and a madam.[5] Two recent Spur winners, Tony Hillerman and Rick Steber, both won for more contemporary stories of Indians. Award-winner Don Coldsmith's Spanish Bit saga also attests to the positive role of Indians in the Western.[6]

Story Line

While the story line in some Westerns may follow a basic good-versus-evil arc with stereotypical characters righting wrongs, many titles in the genre are layered stories with depth in characters and serious issues considered in the story line. Westerns may involve interior struggles (Kelton's *The Smiling Country*, where old-time cowboy Hewey Calloway faces changes as the automobile arrives in the West and his own advancing age hampers his dreams) or focus on the exterior in action-adventure stories.[7]

In fact, morality frequently plays a role in the story lines. Westerns are stories in which justice restores order to a community. The character of the hero, as discussed above, demands that wrongs be righted and order restored. His moral code pervades the story and directs the story line.

Survival in this harsh landscape is another common theme in Westerns. This is a dangerous world, and the perils come from the terrain and animals as well as from other people. Westerns are frequently stories of lives lived at the edge of death. Death permeates these books; small wonder since adversaries range from dangerous predators—human and animal—to the landscape itself, the latter sometimes so rugged that nothing can survive there. Only the strong can pass through the life-and-death confrontations between good and evil that characterize the stories. Although gunfights may not be as frequent and graphic as one might expect, the image of the gunfight, that ultimate showdown, pervades the novels and defines this sense of ritual: the good man facing death at the hands of his opponent, whether man or nature. Westerns are, in many ways, the ultimate adventure/survival novel.

Damaged characters come to the West both to escape and to find healing or redemption there. It is a place where one might start over, begin anew with a clean slate. Something about the landscape and the perils in which characters are placed initiates healing, as well as a sense of purpose and of well-being in the hero. That is one of the primary themes; even "bad guys" occasionally find redemption here. In Owen Wister's classic, *The Virginian,* our hero brings justice and peace to a Wyoming community and offers the possibility of redemption to bad-boy Trampas, only to have to fight him in a gun duel at the end.[8] Other characters, such as Chris in Schaefer's *Shane,* accept the proffered olive branch and reform.

Revenge, a common theme in genre fiction, finds a place in the Western genre as well. Betrayal and the consequent revenge are themes that fit easily into the mythic nature of the West and are often played out against this background. Brand's *Destry Rides Again* is a classic example.[9] Destry, a favorite in town until he is convicted of robbing the stage, serves his term in jail and returns, supposedly a broken man but actually to exact revenge against the real thief. Charles Hackenberry updates this theme in his more recent Western, *Friends.*[10] Here, Willie Goodwin, deputy sheriff in the Dakota Territory in the 1870s, seeks the man who shot his friend the sheriff and killed two other friends by burning their cabin. Is it revenge or justice when he takes the law into his own hands? Who better to do this than a sworn lawman? This questioning of the rectitude of frontier justice would never have arisen in the earlier title, and it reflects a change in tone from classic to newer titles in the genre.

Resolution is key to the end of the Western story. This closure may not parallel that of other genres, but it is a resolution nonetheless. The hero may ride off into the sunset, but not until his mission is accomplished. In fact, the hero may even die at the end of the story. This seldom happens in other genres, but here it serves another purpose and is the natural result of the action. The point of the conclusion is that justice is brought to the Wild West, whether conventional legal justice or frontier justice, and lives are sometimes lost in the process. Elmore Leonard's *Hombre* features a man who has outlived his time.[11] In a story narrated by an anonymous friend to set Jack Russell's story straight, we learn that Russell, the Hombre, was on a stagecoach with a government employee who was escaping with embezzled funds. The stage was held up and all aboard escaped to a mining shack from which there seemed no rescue. Russell must then decide whether to help this motley group, who had scorned him earlier on their journey. There are, of course, no good choices: Either they die in the shack from lack of food or water or Russell must sacrifice his own life to allow the others freedom. We know which choice he has made from the beginning of the novel, and an evocative, elegiac tone pervades this story of a man who no longer fits in his world. Now, death seems his only future. This is a fast-paced story of survival that highlights the most enduring themes in the genre.

Tone/Mood

From the action-packed adventure tales of cowboys and Indians or lawmen and desperados in the dime novels of the nineteenth century to the nuanced treatment of serious issues involving the West, past and present, Westerns offer a wide range of mood and tone, sometimes within the same novel. In all, however, there is a sense of longing for times past and a knowledge that these days will not come again. Westerns are imbued with a nostalgic tone, full of memories of and longing for another time.

To get a good sense of the tone of most Westerns, listen to a few mournful cowboy songs ("Red River Valley," "Streets of Laredo," and "Old Paint," to name a few). The melancholy melodies, along with lyrics that speak to past hard times and an uncertain future, have shaped our sense of this genre—in the pages of books as well as through radio, television, and the movies. These songs and stories form an integral part of our popular culture and consciousness and celebrate the past. Hard times are the norm, but they are also the best hard times.

Tone underlies and enhances these stories. Often nostalgic and even elegiac, with the author forcing the reader to look back on a time when this kind of story was possible, the tone permeates these novels. Like the knights of old, heroes of Westerns cannot easily exist in today's world. Westerns take us back to a time when, in fiction at least, it was possible for a moral man to make a big difference in the world. This elegiac tone is especially easy to recognize in a book such as *I, Tom Horn*, by Will Henry, in which the protagonist and the reader look back longingly to that time when the West was a more open territory.[12] This story takes place after the turn of the twentieth century, when civilization has all but wiped out the last of the true West, and poor Tom Horn, having lived too long, finds the modern West no place for someone seeking the personal freedom, honor, and dignity he once found there. Henry creates a nostalgic, introspective account of a cowboy who has outlived his time.

Other Westerns, particularly those written more recently, may feature a dark tone or mood, with gritty details of gunfights and violence underpinning the action of the story. Matt Braun's *Tombstone,* an exposé that offers a negative appraisal of the Earp family, fits this category, as do novels by Ralph Cotton, such as *Guns of Wolf Valley,* with its building sense of menace, scenes of torture, and ambiguity.[13]

Still other Westerns add more than an undertone of humor. Win Blevins's *Misadventures of Silk and Shakespeare,* a picaresque coming-of-age tale, follows a young man in search of his father.[14] In the tradition of Mark Twain and the tall tales about Davy Crockett, it is also a send-up of mountain men and a romp through the West in the first part of the nineteenth century. Larry McMurtry often adds touches of humor to his novels, and some, like *Telegraph Days,* the story of sassy telegraph operator Nellie Courtright and her escapades, offer broad humor in the characters and events in the changing West.[15]

Pacing

Although traditional Westerns are smaller books, they are not necessarily fast-paced. The creation of mythic elements in character, description, and plot may slow the pacing, while action certainly increases the speed at which we read the novels. For example, while almost nonstop action drives the pacing of Louis L'Amour's Westerns, novels such as Wister's *The Virginian* and Schaefer's *Shane* move at a more leisurely pace, as details and atmosphere slow the action. Still, in many traditional Westerns action and adventure dominate, and the spare language is another factor in increasing the pace at which we read these novels.

Style/Language

Western characters are known for their monosyllabic dialogue, and that spare language is essential. Jargon also features prominently, especially related to weapons and horses, and colorful language is the norm. But Westerns also offer lyrical descriptions of the country—the rugged mountains and endless plains or desert. In fact, nature generally receives more descriptive attention than do the characters! Westerns generally do not experiment with format, and stories are told in a straightforward fashion, rather than through diaries or letters. (Nancy E. Turner's *These Is My Words: The Diary of Sarah Agnes Prine, 1881–1901* is a notable exception.)[16] However, Western graphic novels are beginning to appear and may attract a wider audience to the genre. Short stories are popular, and they offer a good introduction to readers unfamiliar with the genre.

KEY AUTHORS

If you are new to the Western genre, it is useful to know that the classic authors are almost as popular now as they were when they were originally published. In fact, titles of many popular Western authors are being reprinted for a new audience, and we can go a long way with Western fans if we are familiar with a few classic authors. Even though he died in 1988, Louis L'Amour remains one of the most popular Western writers, with good reason: his adventure-filled Westerns still thrill readers. Action plays a role in every chapter, and he pulls readers into the stories with his inviting characters and detailed descriptions of the terrain. Although the early entries in his saga of the Sacketts include more historical details, later additions attest to his place as the most popular writer in the genre, with stories set in the Wild West, featuring action and adventure as the progeny of the original Sackett travel across the United States. *Sackett's Land* starts the series.[17] Another good choice is *Hondo*, which, although not one of the Sackett series, boasts all the trademark elements of the traditional Western: the murderous landscape, an Apache uprising, the lone hero, and a woman in distress.[18] (Many titles are also available in audio, and those narrated by actor David Strathairn are particularly fine.)

Additional prominent, classic, prolific, and still popular authors include Zane Grey (*Rangers of the Lone Star*), Max Brand (*Destry Rides Again*), and Will Henry (*Chiricahua*).[19] Others, like Jack Schaefer and Owen Wister, are primarily known for only one title each, but Schaefer's *Shane* and Wister's *The Virginian* helped form the genre and establish its popularity.

Among those still writing, Don Coldsmith follows the cultural development of the Plains Indians from the arrival of the Spanish conquistadors in the sixteenth century to the early eighteenth century in his Spanish Bit series. In the first, *The Trail of the Spanish Bit*, a young Spanish soldier falls injured on a scouting foray, and he is nursed back to health by the Indians.[20] Eventually he becomes part of the tribe and helps initiate the change in Indian culture from the more peaceful nomadic existence, concerned primarily with hunting, to the warrior life, aided by horses in battle as well as in day-to-day existence. Coldsmith's treatment of the Plains Indians as protagonists sets the standard for the genre. Like his Great Plains series, these books also appeal to readers of Historical novels, but this Spur Award–winning author captures the spirit of the West and the Western with his evocative settings, characters, and themes, and the primary appeal of his books is to the fans of Westerns. Matt Braun and Elmer Kelton, mentioned earlier in this chapter, are additional established authors worth exploring.

Steven Overholser, a popular newer voice, writes critically acclaimed, character-centered Westerns, rich in action and in story. They also project a darker, almost noir tone. Try *Night Hawk: A Western Story,* a nineteenth-century coming-of-age story set on a Colorado ranch.[21]

The Western genre boasts some unexpected practitioners. Not only do writers such as Larry McMurtry qualify as writers of Literary Fiction as much as of Westerns, others have made a name and reputation in another genre, sometimes while still writing Westerns. Loren D. Estleman, although better known for his Mysteries, continues to write provocative, rather melancholy Westerns, sometimes featuring real characters from the past, and in which it is often difficult to make a clear distinction between the good guys and the bad. Robert B. Parker, best known for his contemporary Boston Mystery series featuring private investigator Spenser, occasionally writes popular and critically acclaimed Westerns, such as *Appaloosa,* recently made into a motion picture.[22] Elmore Leonard wrote Westerns before he turned to Crime Thrillers, and his *Hombre,* in both book and film versions, remains a classic in the genre.[23]

As Traditional Westerns became less profitable in the late 1960s and 1970s, another type of Western emerged from publishing houses—the "Adult" Western, featuring explicit sexual situations and descriptions. Jake Logan's Sheriff John Slocum series, Tabor Evans's Marshall Longarm stories, and Jon Sharpe's Skye Fargo series (with more than two hundred titles in print!) are examples of these publishers' series, often written by several writers to a particular formula. Although they may appeal to some Western readers and others, these are often not what fans of classic Westerns are seeking.

WHAT WE KNOW ABOUT FANS

Western fans appreciate a good, action-filled story, set in the West during the nineteenth century and featuring the knight-errant hero who searches out injustice and brings his own form of justice to the wilderness. Readers have had to make adjustments over the years, as fewer Westerns have been published and many reflect different mores than they might expect. (Even Charles Hackenberry's *Friends,* described above, contains more sex than the traditional Western, and the Adult Westerns are another matter altogether.) Because story, character, action, and sense of place are the primary attractions for them, they enjoy a range of books set in that specific geographic location.

Patrons asking for a Western are likely seeking a shorter book about cowboys and the Wild West, and many prefer books without graphic or excessive violence (or sex and strong language). Western readers want adventure in their stories; they seek escapism, but not stories full of technological details, as in Techno-Thrillers or Clive Cussler's Adventures. They may or may not appreciate the ambiguity of character by writers such as Estleman and Leonard. Many read for the black-and-white characters, the clear-cut distinctions between good and evil. They like to know where they stand.

Although we often use the masculine pronoun in discussing these readers, I would be remiss not to point out that the genre has many female fans, myself included. I came late to appreciate the pleasures of this genre, but I confess to finding these stories extraordinarily satisfying and affirming.

Fans of the Western might also appreciate Jane Tompkins's *West of Everything: The Inner Life of Westerns.*[24] This is a classic study of major authors, books, and films, as well as an accessible look at the genre for fans and students alike, from an author who writes lovingly and evocatively about the Western genre. See figure 16.2 for authors whose Western novels share elements with other genres and thus might provide a good introduction to the Western genre for readers and librarians alike.

THE READERS' ADVISORY INTERVIEW

When a reader asks for a Western in a readers' advisory interview, he is likely not looking for classic stories of the Old West by authors such as Bret Harte, Mark Twain, or Jack London. Readers seeking Westerns want the traditional stories of Louis L'Amour and Zane Grey or their more modern

Figure 16.2 *An Introduction to the Western Genre*

Western Writers to Try, If You Enjoy . . .

Adrenaline:	Louis L'Amour
	Max Brand
Biography/Memoir:	Loren D. Estleman
Fantasy:	Louis L'Amour (*The Haunted Mesa*)[25]
Gay/Lesbian:	E. Annie Proulx
	Tom Spanbauer
Gentle:	Judy Alter
Historical Fiction:	Don Coldsmith
	Will Henry
History:	Stephen Harrigan (*The Gates of the Alamo*)[26]
	Richard S. Wheeler
Humor:	Baxter Black
Inspirational:	Stephen Bly
	Jane Kirkpatrick
	Lauraine Snelling
Literary:	Larry McMurtry
Multicultural:	Don Coldsmith
	Loren D. Estleman (*Black Powder White Smoke*)[27]
	Judith McCoy-Miller (Freedom's Path series)[28]
Mystery:	Loren D. Estleman (Page Murdock series)[29]
	A. B. Guthrie Jr. (Chick Charleston and Jason Beard series)[30]
	Elmer Kelton (Texas Rangers series)[31]
Romance:	Cindy Bonner (*Lily*)[32]
Saga:	Louis L'Amour (Sackett series)[33]
	Larry McMurtry (Berrybender Narratives)[34]
Science Fiction:	Patrick Culhane (*Black Hats: A Novel of Wyatt Earp and Al Capone*)[35]
	Kurt R. A. Giambastiani (Fallen Cloud saga)[36]
Women's Lives:	Jane Candia Coleman
	Molly Gloss
	Tracie Peterson
	Nancy E. Turner

and perhaps bleaker versions by authors such as Larry McMurtry and Loren D. Estleman. Traditional Westerns by classic authors of the genre remain in print and make good choices for fans.

Some readers ask for novels that deal with historical figures—the lives of gunfighters and lawmen, for example. Many of the reference sources will help with this, but it is also useful to know that there are authors who write primarily about real characters from the Wild West. For example, any number of writers have delved into the life of Wyatt Earp, from Matthew Braun (*Tombstone* and *Wyatt Earp*) and Estleman (*Bloody Season*) to Richard Parry, with his series featuring Wyatt Earp at the end of his life, living in Alaska, and hunted by his son (*The Winter Wolf* is the first).[37]

Traditional themes with wider implications make a good bridge from the traditional Western to the larger Novel of the West. Ivan Doig might be a good choice. His series, set in Montana from the late nineteenth through the twentieth centuries, features the problems and uncertainties of the Old West as well as the New. *Dancing at the Rascal Fair* is the first chronologically.[38] Richard S. Wheeler, with his multiple series and award-winning stand-alone Western historical titles, makes another good suggestion, as does Molly Gloss with titles such as *The Jump-Off Creek* and *The Hearts of Horses*.[39]

Other readers may also enjoy contemporary Westerns, a phrase that seems almost an oxymoron, because we are so accustomed to thinking of Westerns and Novels of the West as set in the nineteenth century. Novels set on twentieth-century Texas or Montana ranches (McMurtry's *Horseman Pass By* or Ivan Doig's *Ride with Me, Mariah Montana*) and featuring the loner-hero may work for these readers.[40] It is sometimes more difficult in these Westerns set in modern day to find the same kind of hero, who lives only on the edge of civilization, but usually fans are prepared to be generous in the interpretation of the Western appeal characteristics. Leif Enger's *Peace like a River* is an excellent recent example with many of the traditional themes.[41]

Looking at the books themselves, as in every genre, provides clues about the nature of the Western in hand. Maps imply an adventurous journey over an area, and they certainly suggest more adherence to a specific place and perhaps time. The size of the book may be indicative, as Westerns—traditionally at least—are smaller books. Flipping through the pages, we might notice more white space, implying more dialogue and a faster pace. Denser writing, less white space, likely means the book is more descriptive, with more emphasis placed on creating the evocative mood that characterizes many titles in the genre.

Sure Bets

As I mentioned above, L'Amour is an author who still has enormous appeal for readers. Anyone who enjoys action finds great satisfaction in his fast-paced novels of strong heroes fighting for justice in a Western landscape. These are books that I hand sell. (Although Westerns remain popular in some areas of the country, they do not necessarily fly off our displays.) Readers return to tell me of the pleasure they found in L'Amour's books.

Elmer Kelton also writes the kind of Westerns that make him a Sure Bet. In contrast to L'Amour's books, Kelton's tend to be more character-centered, often featuring young men in difficult situations. Kelton has won multiple Spur Awards for these historically accurate novels set in his native Texas, which rely less on action and more on characters placed in realistic, believable situations. *6 Bits a Day* blends traditional themes—cowboys and a cattle drive—with a cowboy's unexpected desire to settle down.[42]

Two popular Mystery writers, Elmore Leonard and Robert B. Parker, are also guaranteed reads for many fans of Westerns as well as others who appreciate independent heroes and a darker mood. Display and suggest Leonard's classic Western, *Hombre,* described above, and Parker's *Gunman's Rhapsody,* the story of the Earp family leading up to the famous gunfight at the OK Corral.[43] *Booklist's* Wes Lukowsky describes Parker's Earp as "Spenser in spurs," an epithet which may also attract fans of Parker's Mysteries to his Westerns.[44]

Another Mystery writer, James Lee Burke, writes a Western series that also resonates with readers. Titles in his Billy Bob Holland series, beginning with *Cimarron Rose,* explore the modern West with Texas Ranger Holland.[45] The perils Holland faces may differ slightly from those faced by his nineteenth-century predecessors, but the satisfactions remain the same.

Sure Bets are often books that transcend genre boundaries with their broad appeal. Molly Gloss writes realistically of pioneers' lives in novels that explore the role of women as well as the landscape of the frontier, which in more isolated areas remained rugged until after World War II. *The Hearts of Horses* reveals much about life on the home front on Oregon farms as the men leave to fight in World War I, about gentling horses, about coping in a hardscrabble life and making one's place.[46] This is rustic country but the lyrical prose transforms this heartwarming, homespun tale into an elegant, layered novel that transcends the genre. This is a title for fans of Women's Lives and Relationships, Historical Fiction, Westerns, and Literary Fiction.

EXPANDING READERS' HORIZONS WITH WHOLE COLLECTION READERS' ADVISORY

Books that appeal to fans of Westerns run the gamut from the traditional Western to the more historical, broadly interpreted Novel of the West, and even to more contemporary novels with classic Western themes. Unfortunately, Westerns are not currently in vogue, so readers' advisors need to keep an eye out for new titles, as well as authors and titles in other genres that provide the reader with the same satisfying experience. Discovering and sharing these non-Westerns that may please Western fans help us draw readers out from the confines of the genre (and may also allow us to introduce other readers to the pleasures of Westerns).

Fans of Westerns are often pleased with books in other genres that include the familiar elements. For example, readers who talk about the character of the hero may be interested in other genres with that loner-as-hero character. Mysteries featuring private investigators, for example, may be a good choice, especially those by authors who also write Westerns (Estleman, Leonard, Parker), since their characters often have a great deal in common with their Western hero counterparts. Tony Hillerman's Mysteries, set in the modern Southwest and featuring Native American detectives, offer the landscape, tone, and spare dialogue of the Western, but set in a different time period. Michael McGarrity's contemporary Western setting and introspective, loner detective might also appeal to these readers. C. J. Box, whose game warden hero prefers a horse to a truck, would also be a good choice.

Other readers may enjoy Historical Fiction featuring an adventurer-hero. Dorothy Dunnett's series featuring Francis Crawford of Lymond, whose swashbuckling adventures lead him across seventeenth-century Europe and Asia might be a good suggestion, as well as L'Amour's historical Adventure novel, *The Walking Drum*, with its medieval setting and young hero, and Bernard Cornwell's series featuring the exploits of Sharpe, as he moves up through the ranks of Wellington's army (*Sharpe's Tiger* is the first chronologically).[47] In addition, many historians of the West offer true tales which may please these readers and provide a counterpoint to fictional representations of historical characters. Dee Brown, best known for *Bury My Heart at Wounded Knee*, would be a good suggestion.[48]

Fans of the independent, skilled hero might also enjoy Thrillers that feature action and adventure, although the addition of too much modern technology may be a drawback. Still, these are areas worth exploring, and even L'Amour wrote an Espionage Thriller (*Last of the Breed*), which might provide an entrée into that genre.[49] Mystery writer C. J. Box also has a stand-alone Suspense title, *Blue Heaven,* which clearly exposes its Western roots.[50]

Readers who read for the mythic landscape may even appreciate stories with similarly timeless settings and characters, such as quest Fantasies and the Dune and Star Wars series from Science Fiction. These are not suggestions for every Western fan, as outer space and the addition of magic, not to mention the nature of the nonhuman characters in these genres, put some of these stories well outside the interest of Western readers. More adventurous readers, however, might be interested in trying them.

Don't forget that women read Westerns too, and they may value titles that focus on heroines as well as the traditional hero. Several writers of Historical Romances set in the West may appeal to these readers. Linda Lael Miller's Western Romances provide the proper setting as well as action and adventure for those readers who do not mind the added element of a strong romantic interest. (Try her McKettrick Cowboys series, beginning with *High Country Bride.*)[51] Janet Dailey's Calder series (*This Calder Sky* is the first) follows the lives of the Calder family and their Montana ranch.[52] Jeanne Williams's novels have strong Western settings and less Romance, which make them a good suggestion for fans of Historical Fiction as well. (*No Roof but Heaven* is set on the Kansas frontier just after the Civil War.)[53] Kathleen Eagle writes sensitively about Native Americans in many of her Contemporary Romances, and a good suggestion for Western fans might be *The Last True Cowboy,* which features city girl Julia Weslin, who enlists the help of cowboy K. C. Houston to help her save her family's ranch from the grasp of developers.[54] Modern ranching issues, the traditional Western mythos, and a strong love story propel this novel. Jo-Ann Mapson's contemporary novels feature strongly realized western settings and women who are true descendants of their plucky ancestresses. Mystery writer Nevada Barr, who sets her Anna Pigeon series in National Parks, might also appeal, as Anna relies on many of the outdoor skills at which Western heroes also excel, and Barr lovingly details the landscapes in which she sets her stories.

Mainstream novels also consider themes and characters borrowed from the Western. For example, who could miss the parallels to the Western hero in Nicholas Evans's popular *The Horse Whisperer*?[55] Cowboy Tom Booker may be able to heal and communicate with horses, but this loner's foray into love and a relationship leads only to tragedy. Many of Cormac McCarthy's novels of Literary Fiction also make interesting suggestions, from *All the Pretty Horses* to *No Country for Old Men.*[56] Leif Enger's *Peace like a River* is another that demonstrates the lure of the West and its power to offer a second chance.[57]

As we cross the Dewey Divide there is a wealth of topics and titles that might attract Western readers. Obvious suggestions include biographies of historical figures associated with the West, histories of the West, and travel books, both historical and contemporary, that offer details of the land, not to mention Memoirs of writers, such as Elmer Kelton's *Sandhills Boy: The Winding Trail of a Texas Writer.*[58] Books about guns, cattle drives, lawmen, wagon trains, and homesteading should be included in any displays to attract Western readers, as well as titles about the Indian experience, Indian Wars, and other aspects of the Western expansion. However, for those readers who extol the evocation of landscape in Westerns, geologist John McPhee is not to be missed. His lovingly described landscapes in titles such as *Annals of the Former World* will provide readers with similar satisfaction in terms of tone with the added benefit of geologic background.[59]

Figure 16.3 lists other authors outside the genre that Western fans might enjoy.

TRENDS

As Western elements bleed into other genres and Western writers continue to incorporate characteristics from fiction genres into their own books, genre blending stands out as the most noticeable trend. Overlap with Historical Fiction continues to dominate the genre, but more recently Western-set Mysteries and Romances are particularly popular, with both historical and contemporary settings.

The bleak, almost noir mood that has infiltrated so many genres has even found a home in Westerns. Dark and gritty Westerns by authors such as Loren D. Estleman in his Page Murdock series have found an audience with readers who appreciate this edgy tone.[60]

Christian Fiction with Western settings and characters continues to thrive. Fewer follow the pattern of pure Westerns, with cowboy casts; more frequently these novels blend with Historical Fiction elements as Novels of the West. Popular authors include Stephen Bly, Tracie Peterson, Lori Wick, and Al Lacy.

Westerns related from the viewpoint of Indians have also remained popular, but in response to the increased interest in Multicultural fiction, there are also books that emphasize African American, Hispanic, and

Figure 16.3 *Expanding Readers' Horizons*

Authors to Take Readers beyond the Western Genre

Adrenaline:	Dorothy Dunnett
	Louis L'Amour
Biography/Memoir:	Evan S. Connell (*Son of the Morning Star*)[61]
	Elmer Kelton
	Robert Morgan (*Boone*)[62]
Fantasy:	Emma Bull (*Territory*)[63]
	Stephen King (Dark Tower series)[64]
Gentle Reads:	Jeanette Oke
Historical Fiction:	Douglas C. Jones
	David Nevin
	Glendon Swarthout
History:	Dee Brown
	David Dary (*True Tales of the Old Time Plains*)[65]
	Jonathan Raban (*Bad Land: An American Romance*)[66]
	Geoffrey C. Ward
Literary:	Kent Haruf
	Cormac McCarthy
	Wallace Stegner
Mystery:	C. J. Box
	Tony Hillerman
	Michael McGarrity
Natural History:	Edward Abbey
	William Least Heat Moon
	John McPhee
	Terry Tempest Williams
Romance:	Rosanne Bittner
	Janet Dailey
	Linda Lael Miller
Science Fiction:	Star Wars series
Travel:	Isabella Bird (*A Lady's Life in the Rocky Mountains*)[67]
	Ian Frazier

(cont.)

Figure 16.3 *Expanding Readers' Horizons (cont.)*

True Adventure:	Dee Brown
	David Laskin (*The Children's Blizzard*)[68]
	George R. Stewart (*Ordeal by Hunger:*
	The Story of the Donner Party)[69]
True Crime:	T. J. Stiles (*Jesse James: Last Rebel*
	of the Civil War)[70]
Women's Lives:	Elizabeth Crook
	Sandra Dallas
	Jo-Ann Mapson

Chinese American stories, among others, in relation to the Western genre. From Isabel Allende's *Daughter of Fortune* to Lisa See's *On Gold Mountain,* a nonfiction exploration of the impact of Chinese immigrants on California's history, these titles delve into the impact of both native and nonnative Americans on the settling of the West.[71]

Although readers accept and expect that Westerns are genre titles fraught with stereotypes and clichés, some read them for reasons beyond the logical. In the interviews with readers that form the backbone of his readers' advisory training, Duncan Smith talked with one reader, a North Carolina native, who reads Westerns for the pleasure they bring as they take him to a place he has never been.[72] They take him outside the context of his everyday life; they carry him away. Jane Tompkins, in *West of Everything,* writes of another reader who chooses them for the way they take him back to his roots, to an area and landscape he has known and is now distant from.[73] They take him back, and the stories allow him to relive his memories. We read for the basic pleasure these stories bring, whatever the reason they affect us.

Notes

1. Jack Schaefer, *Shane* (Boston: Houghton Mifflin, 1949).
2. Elmer Kelton, *The Pumpkin Rollers* (New York: Forge, 1996).
3. Loren D. Estleman, *Aces and Eights* (Garden City, NY: Doubleday, 1981); Estleman, *Bloody Season* (New York: Bantam, 1987); Estleman, *This Old Bill* (Garden City, NY: Doubleday, 1984); Estleman, *Journey of the Dead* (New York: Forge, 1998).
4. Terry C. Johnston, *Carry the Wind* (Aurora, IL: Green Hill; Caroline House, 1982).

5. Sandra Dallas, *The Chili Queen* (New York: St. Martin's, 2002).
6. Don Coldsmith, Spanish Bit saga, beginning with *The Trail of the Spanish Bit* (Garden City, NY: Doubleday, 1980).
7. Kelton, *The Smiling Country* (New York: Forge, 1998).
8. Owen Wister, *The Virginian* (New York: Macmillan, 1902).
9. Max Brand, *Destry Rides Again* (New York: Mead, 1930).
10. Charles Hackenberry, *Friends* (New York: M. Evans, 1993).
11. Elmore Leonard, *Hombre* (New York: Ballantine, 1961).
12. Will Henry, *I, Tom Horn* (New York: Bantam, 1975).
13. Matt Braun, *Tombstone* (New York: Pocket Books, 1981); Ralph Cotton, *Guns of Wolf Valley* (New York: Signet, 2004).
14. Winfred Blevins, *The Misadventures of Silk and Shakespeare* (Ottawa, IL: Jameson Books, 1985).
15. Larry McMurtry, *Telegraph Days* (New York: Simon and Schuster, 2006).
16. Nancy E. Turner, *These Is My Words: The Diary of Sarah Agnes Prine, 1881–1901; Arizona Territories* (New York: ReganBooks, 1999).
17. Louis L'Amour, *Sackett's Land* (New York: Bantam, 1975).
18. L'Amour, *Hondo* (New York: Fawcett, 1953).
19. Zane Grey, *Rangers of the Lone Star* (Unity, ME: Five Star, 1999); Brand cited above; Henry, *Chiricahua* (Philadelphia: Lippincott, 1972).
20. Coldsmith cited above.
21. Steven Overholser, *Night Hawk: A Western Story* (Waterville, ME: Five Star, 2006).
22. Robert B. Parker, *Appaloosa* (New York: G. P. Putnam's Sons, 2005).
23. Leonard cited above.
24. Jane Tompkins, *West of Everything: The Inner Life of Westerns* (New York: Oxford University Press, 1992).
25. L'Amour, *The Haunted Mesa* (New York: Bantam, 1987).
26. Stephen Harrigan, *The Gates of the Alamo* (New York: Knopf, 2000).
27. Estleman, *Black Powder White Smoke* (New York: Forge, 2002).
28. Judith McCoy-Miller, Freedom's Path series, beginning with *First Dawn* (Minneapolis: Bethany House, 2005).
29. Estleman, Page Murdock series, beginning with *The High Rocks* (Garden City, NY: Doubleday, 1979).
30. A. B. Guthrie Jr., Chick Charleston and Jason Beard series, beginning with *Wild Pitch* (Boston: Houghton Mifflin, 1973).
31. Kelton, Texas Rangers series, beginning with *Buckskin Line* (New York: Tom Doherty, 1999).
32. Cindy Bonner, *Lily* (Chapel Hill, NC: Algonquin, 1992).
33. L'Amour, Sackett series, beginning with *Sackett's Land* (cited above).
34. McMurtry, Berrybender Narratives, beginning with *Sin Killer* (New York: Simon and Schuster, 2002).
35. Patrick Culhane, *Black Hats: A Novel of Wyatt Earp and Al Capone* (New York: Morrow, 2007).
36. Kurt R. A. Giambastiani, Fallen Cloud saga, beginning with *The Year the Cloud Fell* (New York: New American Library, 2001).
37. Braun, *Tombstone* (New York: Pocket Books, 1981); Braun, *Wyatt Earp* (New York: St. Martin's, 1994); Estleman cited above; Richard Parry, *The Winter Wolf: Wyatt Earp in Alaska* (New York: Forge, 1996).
38. Ivan Doig, *Dancing at the Rascal Fair* (New York: Atheneum, 1987).
39. Molly Gloss, *The Jump-Off Creek* (Boston: Houghton Mifflin, 1989); Gloss, *The Hearts of Horses* (Boston: Houghton Mifflin, 2007).
40. McMurtry, *Horseman Pass By* (New York: Harper, 1961); Doig, *Ride with Me, Mariah Montana* (New York: Atheneum, 1990).

41. Leif Enger, *Peace like a River* (New York: Atlantic Monthly Press, 2001).
42. Kelton, *6 Bits a Day* (New York: Forge, 2005).
43. Parker, *Gunman's Rhapsody* (New York: Putnam, 2001).
44. *Booklist*, March 15, 2001.
45. James Lee Burke, *Cimarron Rose* (New York: Hyperion, 1997).
46. Gloss cited above.
47. L'Amour, *The Walking Drum* (New York: Bantam, 1984); Bernard Cornwell, *Sharpe's Tiger* (New York: HarperPaperbacks, 1997).
48. Dee Brown, *Bury My Heart at Wounded Knee: An Indian History of the American West* (New York: Holt, 1971).
49. L'Amour, *Last of the Breed* (New York: Bantam, 1987).
50. C. J. Box, *Blue Heaven* (New York: St. Martin's Minotaur, 2008).
51. Linda Lael Miller, *High Country Bride* (New York: Pocket Books, 2002).
52. Janet Dailey, *This Calder Sky* (New York: Pocket Books, 1981).
53. Jeanne Williams, *No Roof but Heaven* (New York: St. Martin's, 1990).
54. Kathleen Eagle, *The Last True Cowboy* (New York: Avon, 1998).
55. Nicholas Evans, *The Horse Whisperer* (New York: Delacorte, 1995).
56. Cormac McCarthy, *All the Pretty Horses* (New York: Knopf, 1992); McCarthy, *No Country for Old Men* (New York: Knopf, 2005).
57. Enger cited above.
58. Kelton, *Sandhills Boy: The Winding Trail of a Texas Writer* (New York: Forge, 2007).
59. John McPhee, *Annals of the Former World* (New York: Farrar, Straus, and Giroux, 1998).
60. Estleman cited above.
61. Evan S. Connell, *Son of the Morning Star* (San Francisco: North Point Press, 1984).
62. Robert Morgan, *Boone: A Biography* (Chapel Hill, NC: Algonquin, 2007).
63. Emma Bull, *Territory* (New York: Tor, 2007).
64. Stephen King, Dark Tower series, beginning with *The Gunslinger* (West Kingston, RI: Donald M. Grant, 1982).
65. David Dary, *True Tales of the Old Time Plains* (New York: Crown, 1979).
66. Jonathan Raban, *Bad Land: An American Romance* (New York: Pantheon, 1996).
67. Isabella Bird, *A Lady's Life in the Rocky Mountains* (Mineola, NY: Dover, 2003).
68. David Laskin, *The Children's Blizzard* (New York: HarperCollins, 2004).
69. George Rippey Stewart, *Ordeal by Hunger: The Story of the Donner Party* (New York: Holt, 1936).
70. T. J. Stiles, *Jesse James: Last Rebel of the Civil War* (New York: Knopf, 2002).
71. Isabel Allende, *Daughter of Fortune*, trans. Margaret Sayers Peden (New York: HarperCollins, 1999); Lisa See, *On Gold Mountain: The 100-Year Odyssey of a Chinese-American Family* (New York: St. Martin's, 1995).
72. Duncan Smith, Readers' Advisory Workshop, Joliet, IL, November 1999.
73. Tompkins cited above, 221–23.

APPENDIX

THE FIVE-BOOK CHALLENGE

In her excellent introduction to the Romance genre, *The Romance Readers' Advisor: The Librarian's Guide to Love in the Stacks*, author Ann Bouricius issued her "Five-Book Challenge": read five books in a new genre every year to gain an understanding of that genre.[1] In the spirit of that challenge, I offer five authors and titles in each of the fifteen genres covered in this guide. These are suggestions, culled from the titles mentioned in each chapter. However, I have made an attempt to acknowledge the range of each genre's appeal, to name popular authors and titles that will stand you in good stead with fans if you read them. I hope these will provide a starting place for your exploration of a genre and its appeal, and, more important, that you will enjoy what you discover.

ADRENALINE GENRES

Adventure

Steve Berry. Adventure readers who enjoy treasure hunts and tales featuring storied artifacts will find much to please them in Berry's novels. Fascinating missions, exotic locales, dangerous villains, and plot twists galore characterize Berry's popular Adventure novels. *The Amber Room* leads Judge Rachel Cutter on a quest to discover the fabled room, missing since World War II.[2]

Bernard Cornwell. With multiple series set in distinct historical periods, Cornwell sets the standard for detail-rich Historical Military Adventure. These dark tales are often centered on particular battles, and historical notes add to the authenticity of the novels. Readers can start with the first of any of his series, set before and during the Napoleonic Wars (*Sharpe's Tiger: Richard Sharpe and the Siege of Seringapatam, 1799*), in the U.S. Civil War (*Rebel*), in Saxon Britain (*The Last Kingdom*), during the Hundred Years' War (*The Archer's Tale*), or in Arthurian Britain (*The Winter King: A Novel of Arthur*).[3]

Arturo Pérez-Reverte. His ongoing Captain Alatriste series (beginning with *Captain Alatriste*) introduces the antic adventures of a seventeenth-century swordsman-for-hire.[4] Harkening back to swashbuckling Adventure novels of previous centuries, these romps feature a hero who battles with both weapons and wits. Pérez-Reverte is also known for his intricately plotted, more literary treasure hunts, as in *The Nautical Chart*, a modern-day quest with a sunken ship and an ancient map.[5]

Matthew Reilly. Carrying on the tradition established by H. Rider Haggard—exotic locales, dangerous missions, deadly terrain, and vicious villains—Reilly offers elaborate background details and outlandish adventure. His Shane Schofield series (*Ice Station* is the first) will satisfy fans of Military Adventure, while his more recent novels (beginning with *7 Deadly Wonders*) create a team on missions with the fate of the world at stake.[6]

James Rollins. In *Map of Bones* Rollins introduces Sigma Force, a secret U.S. military team, which battles nefarious villains in exotic locales.[7] There's a secret society, nonstop action, and, of course, a threat to world order. The team continues their adventures against a host of foes in subsequent installments.

Romantic Suspense

Suzanne Brockmann. Romance, Adventure, and Suspense fill Brockmann's popular Team Sixteen series, stories centered on a group of Navy SEALs. Danger always threatens but Romantic relationships, including a credible gay romance, share equal billing. *The Unsung Hero* is the first in the series.[8]

Dee Henderson. Tough social issues frame Henderson's Christian Romantic Suspense novels, and she never fails to put her heroines in dangerous situations, sometimes in their jobs (detectives or firefighters), sometimes because of what they know. Intriguing characters, building suspense, and fast pacing, along with an inspirational slant, make her popular with fans of Christian Fiction as well as others. *Before I Wake* is a recent example of her style.[9]

Lisa Jackson. Lush but sinister settings in the contemporary South add to the impact of Jackson's novels of Romantic Suspense, especially her New Orleans series. Brutal crimes and diabolical villains lead the protagonists—usually including a member of law enforcement—into dangerous investigations, and, eventually, love. *Absolute Fear* provides a good introduction.[10]

Iris Johansen. Paranormal elements sometimes enhance the dangers in Johansen's popular titles. Although best known for her series featuring forensic sculptor Eve Duncan (*The Face of Deception* is the first), her stand-alones also display her distinctive suspense, with characters on the run from the very beginning, and satisfying romantic entanglements.[11] Try *On the Run.*[12]

Nora Roberts/J. D. Robb. Under both names, Roberts now writes Romantic Suspense and Paranormal Romantic Suspense almost exclusively. Whether one reads her long-running Eve Dallas series (beginning with *Naked in Death*) written under the Robb pseudonym, one of her paperback paranormal Romantic Suspense trilogies (in the recent Sign of Seven three brothers and the women they love battle evil), or her stand-alone hardcover titles (*High Noon* is a recent title), readers can expect capable, independent heroines; men who respect their abilities; steamy romance; and dangerous situations.[13]

Suspense

Lee Child. In his series starring Vietnam veteran and freelance investigator Jack Reacher, both suspense and pacing build as Reacher uncovers danger in each episode. Intricately layered plots, a fascinating hero, and a dark tone characterize this series. Start with *Tripwire.*[14]

Mary Higgins Clark. A romantic tone; roller-coaster pacing; appealing, classy heroines placed in dangerous situations from which they try to extricate themselves; stalking rather than overt violence; plots that center around timely topics; and old-fashioned storytelling characterize Clark's popular, softer-edged Suspense. *No Place like Home* is a recent title.[15]

Harlan Coben. Complex and terrifying plots; a brooding, atmospheric tone; and sympathetic characters caught up in frightening situations, as evil has suddenly intruded into their ordinary lives—these characterize Coben's page-turning Suspense novels. Start with *Tell No One*.[16]

Jeffery Deaver. Whether in his series titles or stand-alones, Deaver demonstrates the genre's frantic pacing as his sympathetic protagonists battle against time and terrifying villains. *The Sleeping Doll* includes time/place/date stamps, cliff-hanger chapter endings that reverse expectations, and cat-and-mouse chases.[17]

Lisa Gardner. With appealing characters, twisting plots, forensic details, powerful descriptions, and natural dialogue, Gardner writes contemporary tales of fast-paced Suspense with strong romantic undercurrents. In the recent *Hide,* a young woman reads in the newspaper that hers was one of six bodies discovered in an underground bunker near a mental institution.[18]

Thrillers

David Baldacci. Although his books are basically Political Thrillers, Baldacci's intricately plotted, fast-paced tales of conspiracy and corruption appeal to a wide range of readers. His sympathetic characters are especially evident in his new Camel Club series; *The Camel Club* is the first.[19]

Barry Eisler. In these edgy, claustrophobic Crime Thrillers, Japanese American hitman hero John Rain thinks too much to be a gun-for-hire. Step-by-step details set up the crimes. *Rain Fall* starts the series.[20]

Linda A. Fairstein. These dangerous, intriguing puzzles filled with gritty forensic and fascinating legal and historical details feature Alexandra (Alex) Cooper, head of the District Attorney's Sex Crimes division. Each highlights the history of a New York institution or landmark. *Final Jeopardy* is first.[21]

Alan Furst. For those who believe the Espionage Thriller is dead, Furst has invigorated the historical spy drama with his tales of Europe before and during World War II. There's a melancholy feel to his brooding, cynical, and atmospheric tales that may remind readers of John le Carré. Try *Red Gold*.[22]

Lisa Scottoline. Combining legal expertise with investigative details and suspenseful woman-in-jeopardy tales, leavened with witty dialogue and a touch of humor, Scottoline creates compelling stories of female lawyers fighting for justice. Both series and stand-alone titles provide the requisite thrills. *Everywhere That Mary Went* starts the series featuring the law firm of Rosato and Associates.[23]

EMOTIONS GENRES

Gentle Reads

Jennifer Chiaverini. The Elm Creek Quilters series, beginning with *The Quilter's Apprentice,* are nostalgic, heartwarming tales that center on the art of quilting.[24] Friendship and family are key elements in these novels, and home truths and conversations direct these inspirational stories. In the first, a young woman new to the community takes quilting lessons from a reclusive older woman and slowly uncovers the secrets that have isolated her mentor.

Debbie Macomber. Although she began her career as a Romance writer, Macomber established her reputation with her gentle stories of women and their lives. These old-fashioned, often romantic and inspirational stories focus on ordinary women and the communities they create. In her Knitting series, beginning with *The Shop on Blossom Street,* she explores the lives of generations of women engaged in the pleasures of knitting.[25]

Alexander McCall Smith. Although they may technically be Mysteries, McCall Smith's *No. 1 Ladies' Detective Agency* and its sequels are quintessential Gentle Reads.[26] Proprietor Mma Precious Ramotswe employs her knowledge of human nature more than traditional detecting skills, and the carefully drawn Bostwana setting, cast of interesting characters, and fascinating cultural and social details underline the universal appeal of the genre.

Sharon Owens. Relative newcomer Owens sets her novels in Belfast, Northern Ireland, and the setting and characters will surely remind readers of Maeve Binchy. These character-centered novels reveal the lives of the denizens of a cluster of Belfast streets and gathering places. *The Tea House on Mulberry Street* is the first of these timeless, nostalgic tales.[27]

Adriana Trigiani. Although her books may push the "gentleness" boundaries of the genre, Trigiani's family-centered novels appeal to a wide range of readers. Humor (sometimes a bit bawdy), charming and often quirky characters, and hopeful outcomes in the face of difficult situations characterize her novels. Start with *Big Stone Gap*, the first in her popular series.[28]

Horror

Ramsey Campbell. Representing psychological Horror, Campbell writes distinctly disturbing novels that feature supernatural events and deranged characters. Situations start out normally but quickly go awry and build to shocking climaxes in his classic English tales. *The Grin of the Dark*, a recent title, is a good example of his lyrical writing and unsettling stories.[29]

Joe Hill. Following in his famous father's footsteps, Hill (Stephen King's son) creates atmospheric tales of vulnerable characters. Colorful language, a menacing mood, and graphic violence combine with horrific situations that arise from the everyday. Try his award-winning *Heart-Shaped Box* about an aging rock star who buys a ghost online with terrifying results.[30]

Stephen King. The King of Horror remains at the top of his form. His books are generally characterized by sympathetic, although certainly haunted, protagonists and nightmare situations that emerge from the everyday. In his recent *Duma Key*, dreams come to life.[31]

Sarah Langan. Like Stephen King, Langan sets her stories in Maine. In *The Missing*, which won the Bram Stoker Award for Best Novel in 2007, she creates a community invaded by something very bad—a possession which spreads like a contagion and ravishes the town, turning the citizens into monsters. Meg, who narrates the prologue and epilogue, survives, but we all know that the Horror lives on as well.[32]

Peter Straub. Known for his creepily atmospheric tales, Straub has a fondness for hauntings and haunted houses. In his recent *In the Night Room*, ghosts and spirits come to life and the borders between fantasy and reality blur.[33] This moody, suspenseful tale, a story within a story, is leavened by occasional humor and remains noteworthy for the complex plot and characters.

Romance

Katie Fforde. These chatty, contemporary English Romances will likely attract fans of Gentle Reads and Women's Lives and Relationships with their tales of women, young and old, and their discovery of romance in their lives. Her heroines may be widows with families or young professional women or women discovering the direction of their lives, but all find satisfying romantic relationships with men who love them. In *Restoring Grace* two plucky, independent women, one younger and one older, allow love into their lives.[34]

Sherrilyn Kenyon. Representing the hottest Romance subgenre, the Paranormal, Kenyon draws on her doctorate in history and her knowledge of ancient Greece for characters and story lines in her brooding Dark Hunter series, set in a universe where werebeasts flourish and humor vies with darker emotions. *Fantasy Lover* is the first.[35]

Linda Lael Miller. Best known for her Historical Romances set in the American West, Miller now writes Contemporary Romances, Paranormal Romance, and Romantic Suspense as well. Her series about the McKettrick family offers titles in both the past and present day. A strong sense of the West and the western landscape add to their popularity. *McKettrick's Choice,* set in nineteenth-century Texas, displays the independent and quirky heroes and heroines that fill Miller's novels.[36]

Susan Elizabeth Phillips. The reigning queen of contemporary romantic comedy writes charming stories featuring engaging characters, frequently involved in a battle of wits. Families and recurring characters fill her novels, which have interesting settings—many involving Chicago's fictional Stars football team. Provocative issues coupled with the heartwarming tone give these broad appeal. Try her recent, award-winning *Natural Born Charmer.*[37]

Julia Quinn. Set among the members of Regency England's elite, Quinn's historical romps offer sparkling wit and humor along with appealing, intelligent characters and satisfying romantic entanglements. Although not the first in her series starring the eight Bridgerton siblings, *The Viscount Who Loved Me* provides Quinn's trademark style plus a wicked game of croquet.[38]

Women's Lives and Relationships

Sarah Addison Allen. Written in lyrical, evocative prose, Allen's charming novels follow women's lives and add just enough believable magic to enchant a wide range of readers, especially fans of Romance and Gentle

Reads. In *Garden Spells* the story unfolds one secret at a time, lazily flowing to its satisfying conclusion.[39]

Elizabeth Berg. Still a mainstay of the genre's fans—and a good introduction to the genre for other readers—Berg captures emotional depths in her novels and sets feelings and issues in lyrical prose. *Open House,* an Oprah Book Club pick, remains a favorite.[40]

Sophie Kinsella. Best known for her series of Shopaholic novels, Kinsella also writes stand-alones that focus on young women and the issues they face. In all she provides a humorous, often madcap, but heartwarming tone, sympathetic and interesting characters who are vividly drawn and more down-to-earth than one might expect, and story lines that address relationships and issues. In addition to her series, try a stand-alone title like *The Undomestic Goddess.*[41]

Elinor Lipman. Filled with wit, charm, and a heavy dose of humor, Lipman's observations of contemporary society appeal to a wide range of readers. Intriguing and often quirky characters whose lives are filled with unexpected twists, amusing dialogue, and optimistic story lines that probe women's lives characterize her novels, which often delve deeper into issues than one at first expects. As *The Pursuit of Alice Thrift* demonstrates, her stories and her heroines are all heart.[42]

Jennifer Weiner. Her thoughtful but humorous take on her carefully drawn women characters and their relationships has made Weiner a best seller since her first novel, *Good in Bed.* Snappy dialogue, feisty heroines, and imaginative story lines with realistic characters and their dilemmas make these compelling stories.[43]

INTELLECT GENRES

Literary Fiction

Michael Chabon. An award-winning Literary Fiction writer known for his wit and innovative style, Chabon excels at playing with genre conventions in his layered stories filled with intriguing characters. His provocative, Pulitzer Prize–winning *The Amazing Adventures of Kavalier and Clay* incorporates history and the history of comic books into a powerful story, both amusing and profound, of the golden age of comic books, Jewish mysticism, and the importance of family.[44]

Ian McEwan. This winner of the Booker Prize and the National Book Critic's Circle Award writes exquisitely crafted, distinctly unsettling novels that make excellent book discussion choices. McEwan deals with issues large and small, and his realistic studies of characters in crisis have brought him critical and popular acclaim. *Saturday,* which relates a neurosurgeon's brush with outside violence, is a good place to start.[45]

Toni Morrison. Nobel Prize–winner Morrison writes about serious issues and difficult dilemmas in lyrical, seductive prose. While her novels focus on the African American experience, they tell universal stories that resonate with readers. *Sula,* an Oprah Book Club choice, makes a good starting point.[46]

Haruki Murakami. Often using first-person narration to explore his solitary, alienated protagonists, Murakami employs spare, haunting, lyrical prose to create a dreamy mood and haunting atmosphere. Jazz motifs frequently play prominent roles as in his recent *After Dark.*[47]

Joyce Carol Oates. Prolific, provocative, often political, Oates writes novels that address significant social issues—race, incest, the environment— seamlessly woven into arresting stories with fully developed characters. She often writes novels of relationships: of families, of man and the environment, of men and women responding to power and violence, and these layered stories afford a sometimes-disturbing perspective on American life. *The Falls* is family tale set at Niagara Falls and later, Love Canal.[48]

Mysteries

Michael Connelly. Harry Bosch, star of Connelly's perennially best-selling series, is a Vietnam veteran and Los Angeles police detective who really prefers to work alone. Intriguing characters, detailed investigations, violent scenes from the gritty underside of Los Angeles, damaged heroes, and suspenseful story lines distinguish his Mysteries. *Black Echo* is the first Bosch book.[49]

Diane Mott Davidson. Fans of Cozy Mysteries flock to Davidson's best-selling cooking mysteries starring Colorado caterer Goldy Schulz. Set in a small town with the colorful Rockies as a backdrop, these family-centered stories generally place the body well off-stage and focus on the resourceful, intelligent, and amusing heroine and her recipes, always included in the book. Start with *Dying for Chocolate.*[50]

Donna Leon. Leon's long-running series features Commissario Guido Brunetti of the Venetian Questura and his family in Mysteries that explore provocative political and social issues, including government and departmental corruption. Although these puzzles are satisfyingly complex, they sometimes take second place to the fascinating characters and their relationships. Start the series early—*Death at La Fenice* is the first—to get a sense of the family feeling that underlines these Mysteries.[51]

Henning Mankell. Probably the best-known of the recent invasion of Scandinavian Mystery authors, Mankell won fans with his Police Procedural Mysteries starring Kurt Wallander. Titles in the series are rich in landscape descriptions and present a dark, moody tone as the very human middle-aged detective with family issues solves his cases. Try *Faceless Killers.*[52]

Jacqueline Winspear. In her historical series set in London just after World War I, Winspear highlights social and cultural details—especially the fate of veterans—as well as provocative puzzles. Maisie Dobbs, a nurse in the war, now runs a detective agency and relies as much on standard investigative techniques as on intuition. *Maisie Dobbs* is the first in this series.[53]

Psychological Suspense

Keith R. Ablow. Although psychologists are generally not the protagonists of novels of Psychological Suspense, Ablow's Frank Clevenger is the exception. Disturbing, often grisly, murders fill these tales of a doctor who is almost as unbalanced as his clients. *Denial* is the first.[54]

Peter Abrahams. *Twists* is the key word to remember with Abrahams; plot twists and twisted characters distinguish these books. Abrahams writes nightmare tales of crimes that are interior and chilling, too disturbing to be Mysteries or Thrillers. Try *End of Story.*[55]

Carol Goodman. Goodman's image-rich prose is filled with mythical and magical allusions. Stories within stories often add to the escalating tension and sinister atmosphere in these haunting, layered novels, which involve secrets from the past and sometimes interweave myth with contemporary stories. Try *The Seduction of Water.*[56]

Jeffry P. Lindsay. Lindsay plays with our minds and our perceptions in his darkly comedic series starring Dexter Morgan, splatter analyst for the Miami police. Born without any moral sense, he has become a serial murderer of serial murderers. Graphic violence and a very twisted mind dominate this series, beginning with *Darkly Dreaming Dexter*.[57]

Ruth Rendell/Barbara Vine. The grande dame of the genre, Rendell continues to chill her readers with her elegant and haunting tales of disturbed minds. *13 Steps Down* is a recent title.[58]

Science Fiction

C. J. Cherryh. In her Science Fiction universe of postapocalyptic, alien, and parallel worlds, Cherryh sets her Foreigner series with thought-provoking stories of cultures in collision. Her novels examine the ramifications of technology as well as the question of what it means to be human. *Foreigner: A Novel of First Contact* is first.[59]

Kathleen Ann Goonan. Provocative and stylish Science Fiction author Goonan made her reputation with her nanotechnology series, but her award-winning *In War Times* raises additional philosophical questions (for example, can technology save humanity from destruction?) and presents lyrical jazz riffs, time travel, and historical details from World War II to supplement the complex plot and intriguing characters.[60] An excellent introduction to the genre for a wide range of readers.

Kim Stanley Robinson. Before global warming became a byword, Robinson wrote provocative tales of science and the environment. His issue-oriented novels provide copious scientific detail and technology, interesting characters, and a distinctive literary style. The near-future *Antarctica* provides an excellent introduction to his writing.[61]

Neal Stephenson. Wit and language dominate Stephenson's varied oeuvre, from his early Cyberpunk novels to his latest playful Alternate Histories. *Cryptonomicon* may be his masterpiece, but *The Diamond Age; or, A Young Lady's Illustrated Primer* is a more accessible introduction to his exuberant, flamboyant style; fast-paced and complex story lines; detailed and innovative science; and surprising, well-drawn characters.[62]

Harry Turtledove. Popularizer of the ultimate "what if?" aspect of Science Fiction, the Alternate History, Turtledove crafts an alternate Earth filled with recognizable names and events that are just a bit askew—and then explores the consequences of the alterations. *Days of Infamy* makes a good starting point.[63]

LANDSCAPE GENRES

Fantasy

Jim Butcher. Professional wizard and supernatural investigator Harry Dresden haunts an alternate Chicago in this long-running series that begins with *Storm Front* and blends Horror, Fantasy, and Mystery.[64] Dresden is a complicated, dangerous hero, and his adventures are related with elements of noir detective novels leavened by lighthearted humor and wit, magic, and an intriguing community of offbeat, supernatural characters.

Jasper Fforde. Either of his two fantasy series provides an excellent introduction to the humorous side of the genre. In the Nursery Crimes series, investigator Jack Spratt, ably assisted by Mary Mary, solves crimes involving familiar childhood characters. (*The Big Over Easy* starring Humpty Dumpty is the first.)[65] The adventures of literary detective Thursday Next enliven the second series, set in an alternate-world England. *The Eyre Affair* is the first of these pun-rich, playful novels featuring classic literature and fictional characters who come to life.[66]

Neal Gaiman. Although he writes beyond the Fantasy genre, readers—and certainly librarians—should know Gaiman, whose stories of the fantastic resonate with intriguing characters, complex story lines, detailed settings, and lyrical, image-rich language. There's usually humor too. (He did, after all, collaborate with Fantasy author/humorist Terry Pratchett on *Good Omens: The Nice and Accurate Prophecies of Agnes Nutter, Witch.*)[67] *Anansi Boys,* a brilliant reimagining of the Anansi (spider) tale from West Africa provides a relatively short introduction to his style. The audio version is especially fine.[68]

George R. R. Martin. The quintessential dark, political fantasy series Song of Ice and Fire begins with *A Game of Thrones* and tracks political machinations involving the Stark and Lannister families and their quest for power.[69] Layered stories, complex characters, a dark tone, and fierce battles characterize this saga.

Naomi Novik. Imagine the Napoleonic Wars fought with the aid of dragon forces. Historical personages and fictional characters join sentient, verbal dragons, lead by the inimitable Temeraire, in fast-paced adventures filled with historical details and dragon lore. *His Majesty's Dragon* is the first in the series.[70]

Historical Fiction

Phillipa Gregory. Before she turned to her explorations of Tudor personalities (*The Other Boleyn Girl*, made into a movie, is probably the best known), Gregory wrote eighteenth-century sagas set in rural England.[71] She skillfully blends fact and fiction to tell mesmerizing stories of characters in another time.

John Jakes. With Family Sagas becoming more popular, Jakes remains the name to know. He established his reputation with his Revolutionary War series (*The Bastard* is the first of his Kent Family Chronicles), and he continues to document the history of a time through the lives of real and fictional families.[72]

Edward Rutherfurd. With his detail-filled historical novels that focus as much on a place as on characters or events, Rutherfurd has assumed the mantle of the late James Michener, who established a readership for this type of historical fiction. *Sarum: The Novel of England* follows the lives of five families in Salisbury from the Ice Age to the present.[73]

Jeff Shaara. Shaara has followed the wartime history of the United States from the Revolutionary War onward. He explores the people and events that shaped American history, without romanticizing either. *The Steel Wave: A Novel of World War II* tells the story of D-day and the Allied invasion of Europe, focusing on those involved, from common soldiers to General Eisenhower.[74]

Susan Vreeland. Her first Historical novel was part of the Vermeer craze in the late 1990s, and she has continued to write compelling tales of artists in history. In *Girl in Hyacinth Blue* she traces the provenance of a Vermeer painting from the modern day back in time to its creation, and in so doing, she paints a full picture of Dutch social life and customs from the seventeenth century on.[75]

Westerns

Don Coldsmith. Focusing mostly on Indian life during the expansion of the West, Coldsmith's stories capture the spirit of the West with evocative settings, characters, and themes. In the Spanish Bit series (*The Trail of the Spanish Bit* is the first), his conquistador hero becomes lost and is then rescued by the native Indians.[76]

Ivan Doig. Set primarily in the contemporary West with a few forays into historical times, Doig's novels, featuring homesteaders rather than cowboys, offer a more realistic look at the West. Lyrical writing, a strong sense of place, and love of the land tie him firmly to the traditional Western. Try his nostalgic *The Whistling Season,* which explores Montana's storied past.[77]

Loren D. Estleman. That he is known as much for his Mysteries (the Amos Walker series set in Detroit) as for his Westerns demonstrates the close link between the Western hero and private investigator—each with code of ethics that drives actions, each working for justice independently of law, each a loner. Solid research and writing a cut above the expected make his gritty novels, with their details of the western landscape, good bets for many readers. *The High Rocks* is the first of his Page Murdock series.[78]

Stephen Overholser. Master of the character-driven Western, Overholser writes gritty, dark novels that are realistic and rich in action. *Night Hawk: A Western Story* offers a familiar theme: a coming-of-age story set on a nineteenth-century Colorado ranch.[79]

Richard S. Wheeler. With several series set in the West, Wheeler provides a good introduction to a range of themes and characters. As his mountain-man hero Barnaby Skye explores the West (beginning with *Sun River*), Wheeler addresses issues of racism and frontier life and depicts the rugged landscape and hardships his characters must confront.[80]

NOTES

1. Ann Bouricius, *The Romance Readers' Advisory: The Librarian's Guide to Love in the Stacks* (Chicago: American Library Association, 2000), 67.
2. Steve Berry, *The Amber Room* (New York: Ballantine, 2003).
3. Bernard Cornwell, *Sharpe's Tiger* (New York: HarperPaperbacks, 1997); Cornwell, *Rebel* (New York: HarperCollins, 1993); Cornwell, *The Last Kingdom* (New York: HarperCollins, 2005); Cornwell, *The Archer's Tale* (New York: HarperCollins, 2001); Cornwell, *The Winter King: A Novel of Arthur* (New York: St. Martin's, 1996).
4. Arturo Pérez-Reverte, *Captain Alatriste,* trans. Margaret Sayers Peden (New York: G. P. Putnam's Sons, 2005).
5. Pérez-Reverte, *The Nautical Chart,* trans. Margaret Sayers Peden (New York: Harcourt, 2001).
6. Matthew J. Reilly, *Ice Station* (New York: St. Martin's, 1999); Reilly, *7 Deadly Wonders: A Novel* (New York: Simon and Schuster, 2006).
7. James Rollins, *Map of Bones* (New York: Morrow, 2005).
8. Suzanne Brockmann, *The Unsung Hero* (New York: Ivy, 2000).
9. Dee Henderson, *Before I Wake* (Carol Stream, IL: Tyndale House, 2006).
10. Lisa Jackson, *Absolute Fear* (New York: Kensington, 2007).
11. Iris Johansen, *The Face of Deception* (New York: Bantam, 1998).
12. Johansen, *On the Run* (New York: Bantam, 2006).

13. J. D. Robb, *Naked in Death* (New York: Berkley, 1995); Nora Roberts, Sign of Seven series, beginning with *Blood Brothers* (New York: Jove, 2007); Roberts, *High Noon* (New York: G. P. Putnam's Sons, 2007).
14. Lee Child, *Tripwire* (New York: Jove, 2000).
15. Mary Higgins Clark, *No Place like Home* (New York: Simon and Schuster, 2005).
16. Harlan Coben, *Tell No One* (New York: Delacorte, 2001).
17. Jeffery Deaver, *The Sleeping Doll* (New York: Simon and Schuster, 2007).
18. Lisa Gardner, *Hide* (New York: Bantam, 2007).
19. David Baldacci, *The Camel Club* (New York: Warner, 2005).
20. Barry Eisler, *Rain Fall* (New York: G. P. Putnam's Sons, 2002).
21. Linda Fairstein, *Final Jeopardy* (New York: Scribner, 1996).
22. Alan Furst, *Red Gold* (New York: Random House, 1999).
23. Lisa Scottoline, *Everywhere That Mary Went* (New York: HarperPaperbacks, 1993).
24. Jennifer Chiaverini, *The Quilter's Apprentice: A Novel* (New York: Simon and Schuster, 1999).
25. Debbie Macomber, *The Shop on Blossom Street* (Don Mills, ON: Mira, 2004).
26. Alexander McCall Smith, *The No. 1 Ladies' Detective Agency* (New York: Anchor, 2002).
27. Sharon Owens, *The Tea House on Mulberry Street* (New York: G. P. Putnam's Sons, 2004).
28. Adriana Trigiani, *Big Stone Gap: A Novel* (New York: Random House, 2000).
29. Ramsey Campbell, *The Grin of the Dark* (New York: Tor, 2008).
30. Joe Hill, *Heart-Shaped Box* (New York: Morrow, 2007).
31. Stephen King, *Duma Key* (New York: Scribner, 2008).
32. Sarah Langan, *The Missing* (New York: Harper, 2007).
33. Peter Straub, *In the Night Room* (New York: Random House, 2004).
34. Katie Fforde, *Restoring Grace* (New York: St. Martin's, 2006).
35. Sherrilyn Kenyon, *Fantasy Lover* (New York: St. Martin's Paperbacks, 2002).
36. Linda Lael Miller, *McKettrick's Choice* (Don Mills, ON: HQN, 2005).
37. Susan Elizabeth Phillips, *Natural Born Charmer* (New York: Morrow, 2007).
38. Julia Quinn, *The Viscount Who Loved Me* (New York: Avon, 2000).
39. Sarah Addison Allen, *Garden Spells* (New York: Bantam, 2007).
40. Elizabeth Berg, *Open House* (New York: Random House, 2000).
41. Sophie Kinsella, *The Undomestic Goddess* (New York: Dial, 2005).
42. Elinor Lipman, *The Pursuit of Alice Thrift: A Novel* (New York: Vintage, 2004).
43. Jennifer Weiner, *Good in Bed* (New York: Pocket Books, 2001).
44. Michael Chabon, *The Amazing Adventures of Kavalier and Clay* (New York: Random House, 2000).
45. Ian McEwan, *Saturday* (New York: Nan A. Talese/Doubleday, 2005).
46. Toni Morrison, *Sula* (New York: New American Library, 1982).
47. Haruki Murakami, *After Dark*, trans. Jay Rubin (New York: Knopf, 2007).
48. Joyce Carol Oates, *The Falls: A Novel* (New York: Ecco, 2004).
49. Michael Connelly, *Black Echo* (Boston: Little, Brown, 1992).
50. Diane Mott Davidson, *Dying for Chocolate* (New York: Bantam, 1992).
51. Donna Leon, *Death at La Fenice: A Novel of Suspense* (New York: HarperCollins, 1992).
52. Henning Mankell, *Faceless Killers: A Mystery*, trans. Steven T. Murray (New York: New Press, 1997).
53. Jacqueline Winspear, *Maisie Dobbs: A Novel* (New York: Soho Press, 2003).
54. Keith R. Ablow, *Denial* (New York: Pantheon, 1997).
55. Peter Abrahams, *End of Story: A Novel of Suspense* (New York: Morrow, 2006).
56. Carol Goodman, *The Seduction of Water* (New York: Ballantine, 2003).
57. Jeffry P. Lindsay, *Darkly Dreaming Dexter* (New York: Doubleday, 2004).
58. Ruth Rendell, *13 Steps Down* (New York: Crown, 2004).

59. C. J. Cherryh, *Foreigner: A Novel of First Contact* (New York: DAW Books, 1994).
60. Kathleen Ann Goonan, *In War Times* (New York: Tor, 2007).
61. Kim Stanley Robinson, *Antarctica* (New York: Bantam, 1998).
62. Neal Stephenson, *Cryptonomicon* (New York: Avon, 1999); Stephenson, *The Diamond Age; or, Young Lady's Illustrated Primer* (New York: Bantam, 1995).
63. Harry Turtledove, *Days of Infamy* (New York: New American Library, 2004).
64. Jim Butcher, *Storm Front* (New York: Roc, 2000).
65. Jasper Fforde, *The Big Over Easy: A Nursery Crime* (New York: Viking, 2005).
66. Fforde, *The Eyre Affair* (New York: Viking, 2002).
67. Neil Gaiman and Terry Pratchett, *Good Omens: The Nice and Accurate Prophecies of Agnes Nutter, Witch* (New York: Workman, 1990).
68. Gaiman, *Anansi Boys* (New York: Morrow, 2005).
69. George R. R. Martin, *A Game of Thrones* (New York: Bantam, 1996).
70. Naomi Novik, *His Majesty's Dragon* (New York: Ballantine, 2006).
71. Philippa Gregory, *The Other Boleyn Girl: A Novel* (New York: Simon and Schuster, 2004).
72. John Jakes, *The Bastard* (New York: Pyramid Books, 1974).
73. Edward Rutherfurd, *Sarum: The Novel of England* (New York: Crown, 1987).
74. Jeff Shaara, *The Steel Wave: A Novel of World War II* (New York: Ballantine, 2008).
75. Susan Vreeland, *Girl in Hyacinth Blue* (Denver, CO: MacMurray and Beck, 1999).
76. Don Coldsmith, *The Trail of the Spanish Bit* (Garden City, NY: Doubleday, 1980).
77. Ivan Doig, *The Whistling Season* (Orlando, FL: Harcourt, 2006).
78. Loren D. Estleman, *The High Rocks* (Garden City, NY: Doubleday, 1979).
79. Steven Overholser, *Night Hawk: A Western Story* (Waterville, ME: Five Star, 2006).
80. Richard S. Wheeler, *Sun River* (New York: Tom Doherty, 1989).

INDEX

Authors, titles, subjects, and series are interfiled in one alphabet. Authors and series are printed in roman, titles in italics, and subjects in boldface. Titles and series which appear only in the notes are indicated by *n* in the page number (e.g., 227n42). Entries followed by *f* indicate figures.

You may also be interested in

Serving Teens through Readers' Advisory: Getting teens to read for fun is the ultimate challenge, yet research shows that it improves skills in grammar and spelling while expanding vocabularies. Readers' advisors who serve teens (or want to) now have a ready-to-use resource from an expert in teen readers' advisory. Accessible and encouraging for beginners and an informative refresher for those more experienced, this hands-on guide addresses teens' unique needs with practical tools.

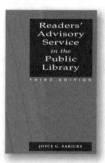

Readers' Advisory Service in the Public Library, 3rd edition: In public libraries, reference librarians are often called on to make recommendations to readers, sometimes in genres that they don't personally read. Learning how to frame a discussion and articulate the appeal of a book, author, or genre marks the essence of a successful readers' advisor. This third edition has been expanded and improved with practical guidelines for conducting the advisory interview so it's a comfortable exchange, confidence-boosting tactics for drawing on reviews to make recommendations, additional resources and online tools, and much more.

The Readers' Advisory Guide to Nonfiction: Navigating what she calls the "extravagantly rich world of nonfiction," renowned readers' advisor Neal Wyatt builds readers' advisory bridges from fiction to compelling and increasingly popular nonfiction to encompass the library's entire collection. She focuses on eight popular categories: history, true crime, true adventure, science, memoir, food/cooking, travel, and sports. Within each, she explains scope, popularity, style, major authors and works, and the subject's position in readers' advisory interviews.

Research-Based Readers' Advisory: In recent years, many excellent research projects on topics related to readers' advisory services have been published. Yet keeping up with the latest research findings is a challenge for many readers' advisors. Written by readers' advisor Jessica Moyer with contributions from leading RA luminaries, *Research-Based Readers' Advisory* approaches research from two vantage points: the Research Review provides an expert overview of new research, and the Librarian's View, written by RA experts, discusses practical issues.

Check out these and other great titles at www.alastore.ala.org!